Practically Speaking

A Sourcebook for Instructional Consultants in Higher Education

edited by

Kathleen T. Brinko

Appalachian State University

Robert J. Menges

Northwestern University and National Center
on Postsecondary Teaching, Learning, and Assessment

Preparation of this book was supported by the National Center on
Postsecondary Teaching, Learning, and Assessment

NEW FORUMS PRESS INC.
Stillwater, Oklahoma U.S.A.

Table of Contents

Foreword and Acknowledgments

Robert J. Menges

While planning the Research Program on Faculty and Instruction for the National Center on Postsecondary Teaching, Learning, and Assessment, I realized that the topic of instructional consultation warranted examination. Consultation services are being offered at an increasing number of colleges, universities, and professional schools, and consultation is widely regarded as a powerful intervention for improving teaching and learning. My own assessment of instructional consultation is very positive. I believe that no service provided by teaching centers has greater potential for producing deep and enduring effects on teachers and teaching.

In consultation with Maryellen Weimer, the project on instructional consultation was conceived. I asked Kate Brinko to head the project and to convene a "think tank," whose members were charged with identifying the knowledge base underlying instructional consultation, examining current practices, and recommending how best practices might be effectively disseminated. This impressive book is the ultimate result of that group's efforts.

This sourcebook is notable for several reasons:

- Scope. These 37 chapters constitute a uniquely comprehensive resource about instructional consultation in higher education. Chapters deal with program planning and organization, with consultant training, and with assessment of both consultants and programs.
- Originality. All but one of the chapters was prepared expressly for this book.
- Representativeness. The activities described in these chapters and the people who write about them reflect the institutional diversity of postsecondary education in the United States and Canada, including community colleges, four-year colleges and universities, and professional schools.
- Credibility and utility. The book offers a thoughtful blend of research-based principles and practical advice. It "speaks practically" to the practioner.

My thanks go to members of the think tank, all of whom also contributed chapters: Kathleen T. Brinko, Head, Michael Kerwin, Lisa Firing Lenze, Diane Morrison, and Richard G. Tiberius. I also thank those who reviewed early drafts of the chapters: Joanne Gainen, Chuck Spuches, Lee Warren, and Dina Wills. The list of contributors at the end of the book includes titles and affiliations of chapter authors and reviewers. Finally, thanks to Arlene DeLong for managing many details of manuscript preparation.

The work of the instructional consultation think tank was supported by the National Center through funding from the Office of Educational Research and Improvement, US Department of Education. The only federally-funded national research and development center devoted specifically to postsecondary education, the National Center on Postsecondary Teaching, Learning, and Assessment is a consortium housed at The Pennsylvania State University and includes the University of Illinois at Chicago, Arizona State University, Syracuse University, Northwestern University, and the University of Southern California. The findings and opinions expressed in these chapters are those of the authors.

Readers will be pleased to know that one of the core resources in the field of faculty development has recently been revised and re-published. Several chapters in the present volume cite the multi-volume *Handbook for Faculty Development* authored by William H. Bergquist and Stven R. Phillips and published more than twenty years ago by the Council for the Advancement of Small Colleges. The revision, *Developing Human and Organizational Resources: A Comprehensive Manual*, is now available in a single loose-leaf volume from the Peter Magnusson Press, P.O. Box 182, Point Arena, CA 95468.

Robert J. Menges

Professor, Northwestern University, and Director, Research Program on Faculty and Instruction, National Center for Postsecondary Teaching, Learning, and Assessment

Introduction

Kathleen T. Brinko

*A*lthough the majority of colleges and universities claim teaching as their primary mission, recent studies have expressed disappointment with American higher education. Over the past decade, a number of individuals and organizations have found undergraduates to be inadequately prepared and have pressed for substantive change in higher education (Alexander, Clinton, & Kean, 1986; American Council on Education, 1983); Association of American Colleges, 1985; Bennett, 1984; Boyer, 1987; National Commission on Excellence in Education, 1983; National Institute on Education, 1984; Wingspread Group on Higher Education, 1993). Consistently these reports have criticized the quality of postsecondary instruction and have clamored for the improvement of teaching.

We believe that it is faculty who hold the key to instructional effectiveness, since it is faculty who design and deliver courses and curricula. Further, we believe that among all faculty development efforts, the most promising way of fundamentally changing postsecondary teaching is to provide faculty with instructional consultation. In the consultation process, information about an instructor's teaching is collected, summarized, and fed back to the faculty member.

Frequently Asked Questions About Instructional Consultation

Currently we can claim no "correct" way to provide instructional consultation. Instructional consultation is a complex process practiced in a myriad of ways by individuals with a range of training and styles. Thus the field is characterized by great variation in both the approach and the practice. However, we will attempt to provide an overview of the field by giving some basic answers to frequently asked questions. The reader should keep in mind that these answers are greatly simplified; more complete answers can be found throughout this sourcebook.

What Is Instructional Consultation?

Instructional consultation is a process by which teaching is assessed for formative purposes, that is, for improvement. A consultant visits the classroom of an instructor, collects information about the teaching, then feeds back to the instructor the information that he or she gathered from the visit.

Why Offer Instructional Consultation?

Instructional consultation has been found to dramatically improve teaching as evidenced by scores on student ratings. Two meta-analyses of studies on student ratings (Cohen, 1980; Menges & Brinko, 1986) found that feedback from student ratings plus consultation was on the average four times more effective than feedback from student ratings alone. Teachers who participate in the instructional consultation process report that the experience is helpful, meaningful, worth their time, and continues to have an effect on their teaching long after they cease contact with the consultant.

Is Instructional Consultation a Common Practice in Faculty Development?

Instructional consultation is a fairly common component of faculty development programs. Instructional consultation is offered by approximately half of the faculty development programs in North America (Erickson, 1986).

What Are the Components of Instructional Consultation?

In general, there are four phases in the process of instructional consultation: initial contact, pre-visit conference, information collection, and the feedback session.

The initial contact is the first encounter between the consultant and teacher. It may be either face-to-face or over the telephone, but usually is quite brief. It may be used to broach a problem, to explore availability of appropriate assistance, and/or to set an appointment for the pre-visit conference. The second phase, the pre-visit conference, is a discussion between the consultant and the instructor. The content of this discussion varies, but usually the consultant attempts to understand the context of the instructor's teaching situation including the goals of the course, the types of students in the course, the syllabus, instructional aids, problems encountered, and the like.

In the third phase, the consultant gathers information about the teaching process during a visit to the classroom. Most commonly, consultants collect information by observing the class, videotaping the class, or talking with students about the class. The kind of information that the consultant collects is influenced by the questions that the teacher has. For example, questions about presentation style are best answered by an trained observer who systematically evaluates the teacher's presentation; questions about the effectiveness of explanations are best answered by students.

In the fourth phase, the feedback session, the consultant shares the gathered information with the instructor. In addition to the problems discussed in the conference, other problems may be identified as the consultant and teacher review the data. These problems are then diagnosed and specific solutions are explored. Because instructional consultation is so labor-intensive, some instructional consultation programs—to save time—omit the pre-visit conference and ask about the instructor's course, students, and goals at the beginning of the feedback session.

The instructor may choose to end the instructional consultation process at this point or may ask the consultant to collect additional information, either immediately to answer a pressing question or at some future time to assess change and improvement.

Who Initiates Instructional Consultation?

Generally, most faculty development activities including instructional consultation are opportunities offered to faculty and teaching assistants, and thus are voluntary. However, a few instructional consultation programs are mandatory and are part of the requirements of the position, especially for teaching assistants.

What Approach Works Best?

Currently, we do not know that any one approach works better than another. The two most common approaches, or models, of instructional consultation are the prescription model and collaborative/process model. In the prescription model the consultant's role is "identifier,

diagnoser, and solver of problems" and the client's role as "receiver thereof." Thus, the instructor may describe his or her concerns about teaching, but the consultant assumes authority and responsibility for identifying, diagnosing, and solving problems. In the collaborative model the consultant's role is "facilitator of change" and the instructor's role is "content expert." Both the consultant and instructor may identify, diagnose, and suggest solutions to problems; however, the instructor may accept or reject the consultant's contributions. Unlike the prescription model, the instructor retains authority and responsibility for the process and its results.

These two approaches represent the ends on a continuum in which consultants may be more or less prescriptive and more or less collaborative. Consultants report that they prefer to use one approach but may change their approach if they think that another would be more effective with a particular client.

What Practices Work Best?

The remainder of this sourcebook attempts to describe the skills and knowledge needed to conduct instructional consultation effectively. This sourcebook addresses the instructional consultation practices that work best, the context of higher education for the instructional consultation process, the evaluation of instructional consultation programs, and instructional consultation training programs. The following chapters are authored by instructional consultants nationally recognized for their interest, experience, and expertise in instructional consultation. These chapters represent state-of-the-art thinking about the practice of instructional consultation.

History of the Sourcebook

Although instructional consultation has been found to be extremely powerful, it has not been consistently successful (Cohen, 1980; Menges & Brinko, 1986), possibly because many who feed back the information to the teacher are not trained (Brinko, 1988). There is a dearth of specific information about instructional consultation, and most faculty developers report that they practice instructional consultation "by the seat of their pants."

In response to this need, the National Center on Postsecondary Teaching, Learning, and Assessment initiated the Project on Instructional Consultation with the goal to develop systematic materials for training and evaluating consultation. Over a three-year period, we: 1) reviewed the literature to determine skills and attributes needed by an instructional consultant; 2) gathered information from practicing consultants through structured telephone interviews and a written survey; and 3) assembled a think tank of experts in instructional consultation to analyze the data and give direction to the project. Designed to represent a diversity of constituents, this think tank contained instructional consultants from the United States and Canada who represented a community college system, a research university, a comprehensive university, a professional school, and a cross-institution consultation program.

Over this three-year period we identified a pressing need for three types of practical materials for instructional consultants: 1) training materials for novices, 2) professional development materials for experienced consultants, and 3) evaluation materials. These three kinds of materials form the basis of the content of this sourcebook.

Features of the Sourcebook

The purpose of this sourcebook is to disseminate state-of-the-art thinking about the content and practice of instructional consultation to practicing instructional consultants, prospective consultants, and those who wish to train others to provide consultation. Because there is a dearth of information available on consultation, each chapter was written in the spirit of "speaking practically"—colleagues helping colleagues, giving their best advice and sharing the print materials that they have developed in their own practice. Toward this end, the sourcebook includes several features worth noting:

- Practitioner-designed materials (including intake forms, ratings instruments, checksheets, case studies) are camera-ready for duplication and adaptation into local consultation programs.
- A variety of approaches to consultation are described—consultation by experts, consultation by peers, consultation in single institutions, and consultation in multiple institutional consortia.
- Examples and materials are drawn from different post-secondary institutions—two-and four-year colleges, universities, and professional schools.
- Materials can be adapted for self-instruction as well as for training others.
- The sourcebook approaches instructional consultation developmentally; materials range in appropriateness for consultants at all levels of experience.

Readers will note a diversity of scope, writing styles, and terminology. Some chapters take a broad historical view; others focus on the practice of one part of the consultation process. Some chapters are formal; others are informal. Some are written in the first person; others are written in the second or third person. Some use the term "instructional consultant"; others use the term "teaching consultant" or "instructional developer" or "educational consultant." No attempt has been made by the editors to standardize; we believe that this is appropriate. It reflects the diversity of kinds of institutions, approaches, and practice contained within this volume.

Organization of the Sourcebook

The sourcebook is divided into five parts. Parts One and Two are especially helpful to novices as they begin their work as consultants. Part One surveys the basic practice of instructional consultation. It examines the interaction between the instructional consultant and the faculty client during the pre-visit conference with the client, the information collection, and the feedback session. Part Two describes a variety of instructional consultation programs. They vary in philosophy, in the roles that consultants play, in methods for data collection, and in length of involvement between the consultant and client.

Parts Three, Four, and Five are especially helpful to experienced consultants wishing to improve their practice and to those who design training programs for novice consultants. Part Three describes the larger issues surrounding and affecting consultation: the context of higher education in North America, the institutional context, and the variability in instructors, students, learning environments, and individual consultants. Part Four examines issues in evaluating an instructional consultation program, and provides two case studies of program evaluation. Part Five contains training programs for novice consultants and skill-building programs for experienced consultants.

Each part is preceeded by an overview that briefly describes the contribution of each chapter and clarifies the organization of the chapters within that part. The book concludes with a list of contributors and a list of professional organizations that are concerned with instructional consultation.

Using This Book

This sourcebook represents the effort of many practicing instructional consultants who needed a hands-on resource for novice consultants and for themselves. Unique in its scope, currency, and usefulness, this sourcebook is probably best utilized by referring as the need arises.

On behalf of everyone who worked to make this sourcebook a reality, we sincerely hope and expect that this sourcebook will be a valuable resource. We look forward to your response.

References

Alexander, L., Clinton, B., and Kean, T. (1986). *Time for results: The governors' 1991 report on education.* Washington, DC: National Governors' Association, Center for Policy Research and Analysis.

American Council on Education. (1983). *America's competitive challenge: The need for a national response.* Washington, DC: American Council on Education, Business-Higher Education Forum.

Association of American Colleges. (1985). *Integrity in the college curriculum: A report to the academic community.* Washington, DC: Association of American Colleges, Project on Redefining the Meaning and Purpose of Baccalaureate Degrees.

Bennett, W. J. (1984). *To reclaim a legacy: A report on the humanities in higher education.* Washington, DC: National Endowment for the Humanities.

Boyer, E. L. (1987). *The undergraduate experience in America.* New York: Harper and Row.

Brinko, K. T. (1988). Instructional consultation with feedback in higher education: A qualitative and quantitative analysis. *Dissertation Abstracts International, 49*(8), 2120A-2121A. (University Microfilms No. 8822955)

Cohen, P. A. (1980). Effectiveness of student-rating feedback for improving college instruction: A meta-analysis of findings. *Research in Higher Education, 13,* 321-341.

Erickson, G. R. (1986). A survey of faculty development practices. *To Improve the Academy, 5,* 182-196.

Menges, R. J., & Brinko, K. T. Effects of student evaluation feedback: A meta-analysis of higher education research. Paper presented at the 70th annual meeting of the American Educational Research Association, San Francisco, April 16-20, 1986. (ED 270 408)

National Commission on Excellence in Education. (1983). *A nation at risk: The imperative for educational reform.* Washington, DC: Department of Education.

National Institute on Education. (1984). *Involvement in learning: Realizing the potential of American higher education.* Washington, DC: Department of Education.

Wingspread Group on Higher Education. (1993). *An American imperative: Higher expectations for higher education.* Racine, WI: The Johnson Foundation.

Part One:

Skills and Techniques of Instructional Consultation

_I_n organizing information about instructional consultation with feedback, it seemed logical to approach the material in the same way that a consultant approaches consultation: to begin by defining the parameters of the practice, to identify the knowledge and skills needed for successful consultation, and to examine each phase of the consultation process. Thus Part One focuses on these fundamentals of instructional consultation practice. It should be helpful to novices beginning their work as consultants and to experienced consultants wishing to hone their consulting skills.

In Chapter 1, Brinko provides an overview of the consultation process as it is usually practiced in higher education. She describes four phases of the process—initial contact, conference, information collection, and the information review and planning session—and she presents the four models of interaction most commonly used by instructional consultants—product, prescription, collaborative/process, and affiliative. In Chapter 2, Fink proposes a model of four dimensions of teaching: skills, decisions, philosophies, and attitudes. He posits that this model provides instructional consultants with a framework about teaching. The framework has two uses: to help analyze clients' teaching problems and to help guide consultants in their own development as professionals. Border, in Chapter 3, presents the knowledges and skills in pedagogy, psychology, counseling, ethics, and higher education that consultants need for successful consultation. She asserts that the cornerstones of consultation are establishing trust and clarifying goals.

Chapters 4 through 9 provide an in-depth examination of the phases of the consultation process-the initial conversation with the client, the data collection, and the feedback session. In Chapter 4, Erickson and Sorcinelli discuss the initial conversation with the client—a process that occurs regardless of how data are collected. They explore the kinds of questions that assess the instructor's

motive for seeking consultation and the kinds of questions that uncover pertinent background information about the course, about the students, and about the instructor.

Chapters 5 though 8 focus on methods by which instructional consultants can collect information about teaching and learning—classroom observation, discussion with students, videotape, and student rating questionnaires. In Chapter 5, Lewis examines the type of information that can be obtained through classroom observation—information about use of media, speaking style, teaching technique, nonverbal gestures and mannerisms, teacher-student rapport, organization of content, student attentiveness, student participation, and instructor utilization of space. She then describes five categories of classroom observation protocols—narrative, descriptive, category, technological, and visual systems—and appends ten examples of classroom observation data collection instruments. In Chapter 6, Tiberius presents seven methodologies for collecting information about the teaching-learning process, each utilizing discussions with small groups of students—brainstorming, focus group interviews, advisory groups, face-to-face focus groups, small group instructional diagnosis, nominal group technique, and the Delphi technique. He describes procedures for each methodology and provides recommendations for the use of each. Kristensen (Chapter 7) discusses collecting information about the classroom via videotape. After presenting the strengths and limitations of videotape data, Kristensen addresses the technical aspects of making a videotape appropriate for consultation as well as considerations and recommendations in using a videotape in consultation. In Chapter 8, Theall and Franklin examine the issues around collecting information via student ratings. First Theall and Franklin discuss what we know about student ratings and what consultants need to know about evaluation; later they outline policies and procedures that support the collection of valid and reliable data.

Finally, Erickson and Sorcinelli (Chapter 9) outline the process they use when feeding back information to the instructor, regardless of type of data collected. Erickson and Sorcinelli describe several aspects of the feedback session—preparing for the feedback session, opening conversation, broaching strengths and weaknesses, selecting a plan for action-and present several ways that they follow up on the consultation using experimental cycles, colleagues, students, and/or print materials.

In Chapters 10 and 11 we consider two special cases of instructional consultation—consulting with international faculty and consulting with small groups of faculty. In Chapter 10, Porter and Kozuh present the collaborative consultation model that they use to meet the language proficiency, cultural, and teaching needs of international clients. Porter and Kozuh describe the five stages of the model—data collection, data analysis, program design, implementation, and evaluation—and their clients' reaction to the model. In Chapter 11, Rando discusses how he consults with faculty in small groups. He offers four princples that facilitate faculty learning in group consultation—faculty interaction, faculty interdependence, process awareness, and group independence—and he provides a model for developing four different types of small groups.

From reading these chapters, novice consultants will have grasped the fundamental issues about instructional consultation, and experienced consultants will have gained a broader and deeper perspective about the practice of instructional consultation. It is our intention to illustrate for both novice and experienced consultants the variety and complexity of the process of instructional consultation as it is currently practiced in North America.

1. *The Interactions of Teaching Improvement**

Kathleen T. Brinko

*W*hen trying to improve their instruction, many faculty seek feedback (Ashford & Cummings, 1983) about their teaching from a peer, colleague, or instructional consultant. In fact, instructional consultation is a vital part of approximately half of faculty development programs (Erickson, 1986).

Several reviews of the literature have advocated consultation as an important part of teaching improvement (Levinson-Rose & Menges, 1981; O'Hanlon & Mortensen, 1980), and empirical studies have found evidence concerning the efficacy of consultation. Cohen (1980) conducted a meta-analysis on the effectiveness of student ratings as a feedback mechanism and found that feedback from student ratings coupled with consultation was more effective than feedback from student ratings alone. When they replicated and updated Cohen's work, Menges and Brinko (1986) found that consultation quadrupled the effect of student ratings feedback. However, among individual studies there was great variation in the effectiveness of the consultation, and unfortunately the studies do not contain detailed descriptions of the interactions between the consultants and faculty members in sufficient detail to permit determination of the factors that contributed to the variability.

In the past decade there have been several efforts made to analyze the interactions within the consultation process (Brinko, 1988, 1990; Orban, 1981; Price, 1976; Rutt, 1979). What these studies have showed us is that there is no one way in which university people "consult" with each other, and that no one kind of instructional consultation is more effective than others. However, within this tapestry of consultation are several patterns of behavior that are commonly recognized and shared by instructional consultants.

Phases of Interaction

When a faculty member requests assistance with his or her teaching, the interaction between the instructional consultant and the faculty member generally cycles through four phases: *initial contact, conference, information collection*, and the *information review and planning session* (Figure 1). Whether they flow together or whether

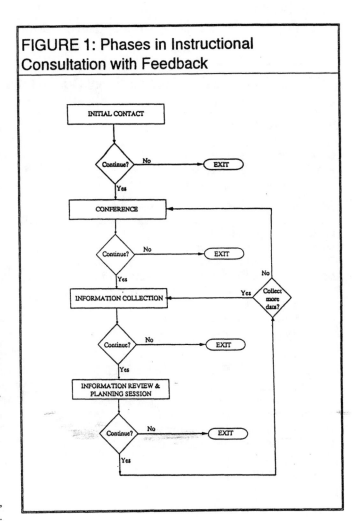

FIGURE 1: Phases in Instructional Consultation with Feedback

they occur discretely in time, each phase has a distinct purpose and contributes to the success of the endeavor.

The initial contact is the first encounter between the consultant and client. It may be either face to face or over the telephone, but usually is quite brief. It may be used to broach a problem, to explore availability of appropriate assistance, or to set an appointment to meet for the next phase. If both parties are amenable, it may flow into the next phase without any lapse in time.

The second phase, the conference, is an extensive discussion between the consultant and the client. The content of this discussion varies, but usually the consultant attempts to understand the context of the faculty member's teaching situation, including the goals of the course, the types of students in the course, the syllabus, the instructional aids, the problems encountered, and the like. If the faculty member seeks advice based on this conversation, the process may be terminated at this point (for insightful analyses of consultation without feedback, see Price, 1976; Rutt, 1979). If the faculty member has questions that can be answered only by the collection of additional information, the process may continue (see Orban, 1981; Brinko, 1988, 1990).

In the information collection phase, the consultant gathers data that are to be fed back to the client. The kinds of information that the consultant collects are dictated by the questions that the faculty member brings to the conference. For example, questions about presentation style are best answered by an trained observer who systematically evaluates the faculty member's presentation in one or more classes. Questions about the effectiveness of explanations are best answered by students—whether in small group interviews, in written comments, or in achievement tests. On the other hand, questions about congruity between theory and practice are best answered by examining course materials or videotaping teacher-student interaction.

In the fourth phase, the information review and planning session, the consultant shares the collected information with the faculty member. In addition to the problems discussed in the conference, other problems may be identified as the consultant and client review the data. These problems are then diagnosed, and specific solutions are explored.

Because instructional consultation is so labor-intensive, many instructional consultation programs combine an abbreviated version of the conference with the information review and planning session. It is sensible to

Table 1: Four Phases of Instructional Consultation with Feedback and their Opportunities for Consultant and Client

Consultant Opportunities	*Client Opportunities*
Initial Contact	
Get a first impression of client	Get a first impression of consultant
Establish the reason for consultation	Convey the reason for contact
Set an appointment for a conference	Determine the desirability of consultation
	Reduce feelings of isolation in teaching
Conference	
Establish rapport with the client	Establish rapport with consultant
Analyze the client's teaching situation	Receive another perspective
Determine the client's philosophical and professional orientations	Determine consultant's philosophical and professional orientations
Make a written or verbal contract with client regarding timetable, type of information to be collected, preliminary goals, problems in the client's teaching	Make a written or verbal contract with consultant regarding timetable, type of information to be collected, preliminary goals, problems in client's teaching
Make a verbal or psychological contract with the client regarding expectations, assumptions	Make a verbal or psychological contract with consultant regarding expectations, assumptions
Information Collection	
Systematically gather information about teaching performance	
Information Review & Planning Session	
Convey information gathered about teaching performance	Receive systematically collected information about teaching performance
Offer interpretations of the information collected	Offer interpretations of the information collected
Suggest alternative behaviors or strategies for change	Choose alternative behaviors or strategies for change
Assist in decision making	Receive support for decisions made
Provide support for decisions made	Decide whether further assistance is desirable
Offer further assistance	Determine the effectiveness of the process

assume that a condensing of the process will have little impact on consultation effectiveness in some cases, such as when a consultant works with a group of teaching assistants in the same course. However, at this time we have no empirical evidence to support this assumption.

The information review and planning session may be the final phase of the interaction, or it may trigger more interaction between the consultant and client (for several examples of information collection and review techniques, see Cooper, 1982; Lewis, 1988). Figure 1 illustrates the four phases of interaction and highlights critical decision points in the instructional consultation process.

The effectiveness of the consultation process is determined by how well the client and consultant utilize the opportunities of each of the four phases. Each phase presents consultants and clients with occasions to obtain important information about the process and each other, and to make informed decisions based on this knowledge. In each of these phases, consultants and clients assess their compatibility with each other, learn new perspectives about the teaching-learning process, and determine whether instructional consultation will answer the questions at hand. Table 1 summarizes the opportunities of each of the four phases.

Models of Interaction

In the education, psychology, and organizational behavior literature, several researchers (Blake & Mouton, 1983; Cash & Minter, 1979; Dalgaard, Simpson, & Car-rier, 1982; Davies, 1975; Gallessich, 1974, 1982; Rutt, 1979; Schein, 1969; Tilles, 1961) have proposed models of consultative interaction. Although the names vary, the descriptions of these models are remarkably similar and can be distilled into eight different models of consultative interaction. Using Gallessich's (1974) terminology, these eight are (1) information transmission, (2) medical, (3) mental health, (4) program consultation and implementation, (5) process consultation, (6) advocacy consultation, and, using Blake and Mouton's (1983) terminology, (7) acceptant and (8) confrontation. These models are compared in Table 2.

When considering the special case of instructional consultation, four of these models appear to be the most useful. Using Rutt's (1979) terminology, these four models are product, prescription, collaborative/process, and affiliative. Each model typifies a different philosophy and set of expectations that influence the interactions between consultant and client.

Product model. Consultants and clients working in the product model view the consultant's role as "expert" and the client's role as "seeker of expertise." Before even approaching the consultant, the client identifies and diagnoses the problem and chooses a solution. The client then engages the expertise of the consultant to produce the solution. Sometimes the solution is expertise about "how to" or "the best way to," but often the solution is expertise to produce a test, slide show, video, lab manual, or other "product" that can remediate the problem. In effect, the

Table 2: Comparison of Models of Consultation, by Discipline

Discipline			
School Psychology	**Organizational Behavior**		
Gallessich, 1974	*Blake & Mouton, 1983*	*Tilles, 1961*	*Schein, 1969*
1. Information transmission	Theory principles	Purchase-Sale	Purchase
2. Medical	Prescriptive	Doctor-Patient	Doctor-Patient
3. Mental health			
4. Program consultation and implementation			
5. Process consultation	Catalytic	Constructive	Process
6. Advocacy consultation			
7.	Acceptant		
8.	Confrontation		

client "purchases" what the consultant has "for sale" (Schein, 1969; Tilles, 1961).

Prescription model. Consultants and clients working in the prescription model view the consultant's role as "identifier, diagnoser, and solver of problems" and the client's role as "receiver thereof." Also known as the medical model, the relationship between consultant and client is much like the 1950's relationship between doctor and patient (Gallessich, 1974; Schein, 1969; Tilles, 1961). Only the consultant possesses valid opinions or knowledge about instructional matters; the client accepts those opinions or knowledge without question. Thus, the prescription client may describe his or her concerns about teaching, but the consultant assumes authority and responsibility for identifying, diagnosing, and solving problems—which may or may not be related to the concerns expressed by the client.

Collaborative/process model. Consultants and clients working in the collaborative/process model view the consultant's role as "catalyst" or "facilitator of change" and the client's role as "content expert" (Blake & Mouton, 1983; Dalgaard, Simpson, & Carrier, 1982). Collaborative consultants and clients are partners, each having some unique expertise to contribute to the teaching improvement process. Proponents of collaborative consultation believe that such a synergistic relationship produces a result that is far better than what each person working alone may be able to produce. Both the consultant and client may identify, diagnose, and suggest solutions to problems; however, it is the client's prerogative to accept or reject the consultant's contributions. Unlike the pre-scription model, the client retains authority and responsibility for the process and its results.

Affiliative model. Consultants and clients working in the affiliative model view the consultant's role as a combination of instructional consultant and psychological counselor and the client's role as seeker of personal as well as professional growth (Andrews, 1978; Dalgaard, Simpson, & Carrier, 1982). Affiliative consultants focus on empowering the client and solving personal problems that may cause or exacerbate the client's instructional problems. The client identifies and diagnoses problems, and the consultant accepts these perceptions (Blake & Mouton, 1983). Like the collaborative model, both the consultant and client may suggest solutions, but it is the client who retains control of the process. Although it is not a common approach to instructional consultation (Brinko, 1988), the affiliative model has been used successfully to improve teaching (Andrews, 1978).

Confrontational model. A fifth model that has not been suggested previously as a viable alternative in instructional consultation is the confrontational model (Blake & Mouton, 1983). In this model, the consultant takes the role of "challenger" or "devil's advocate" which coerces the client into the role of either defender or accepter. The consultant and client may begin the consultation process using either the collaborative or the affiliative model, but at some point the consultant recognizes that the problem is different from that identified by the client. Perhaps the client is denying the problem or is personally or professionally threatened by it. Thus, to bring about any meaningful change, the consultant feels a need to confront the client as a first step in solving the problem.

Table 2 (Cont'd)			
Discipline			
Education			
Davies, 1975	*Rutt, 1979*	*Dalgoard, et. al. 1982*	
1. Product oriented	Product	Consultant as expert	
2. Prescritpion oriented	Prescription	Consultant as problem solver	
3.			
4.			
5. Product-Process	Collaborative/Process	Consultant as collaborator	
6. Advocacy consultation			
7.	Affiliative	Consultant as counselor	
8.			

While the confrontational model is not currently recognized in the instructional consultation literature, it has potential for facilitating change with some faculty. For example, I wonder whether the result achieved would have been different had the confrontational model been used with one of the faculty clients in a previous study (Brinko, 1988). In the beginning of the information review and planning session, the consultant working with this faculty member used a very prescriptive style, authoritatively yet kindly setting the agenda and reviewing the gathered information. But after five minutes of this style of interaction, the client seized control and continued to control the conversation for the remainder of the meeting. For the next forty-five minutes, this instructor quickly and repeatedly interrupted and rebuffed the consultant when he offered his observations and opinions. This faculty member assumed no responsibility for any of his instructional problems and insisted that they resulted from his students' unwillingness to learn, laziness, and irresponsibility. It became clear to this consultant (and to me as the researcher) that this faculty member had no desire to change any of his teaching attitudes or practices. Toward the middle of the session, the consultant abandoned his prescriptive model and adopted the collaborative model, accepting the client's interpretation of events. Undoubtedly the client left with what he had come for: a validated perspective about his teaching and a certificate of participation for purposes of promotion, tenure, and merit. But it would be difficult by any standards to call this consultation a success. Had the consultant challenged, rather than accepted, the client's negative attitudes and assumptions about his students, some positive change may have been effected in this instructor's behavior. In this case, the confrontational model may have proved to be a useful tool had the consultant been able or willing to use it.

Dynamics of Consultative Interaction

Many researchers maintain that consultative interaction must be client-centered and collaborative if it is to be useful to the client and if it is to be effective in producing behavior change (Carroll & Goldberg, 1989; Cooper, 1982; Dalgaard, Simpson & Carrier, 1982; Orban, 1981; Sweeney & Grasha, 1979). However, as the above example illustrates, an accepting and collaborative consultant may not be effective for all clients all of the time.

Many practicing consultants recognize the need for more than one type of consultative interaction (Blake & Mouton, 1983; Gallessich, 1974; Schein, 1969; Tilles, 1961). In their experience as instructional consultants,

Wergin, Mason, and Munson (1976) reported that their roles shifted from "experts" to "collaborators" as their relationship matured with the client and as the client developed more teaching expertise. When consulting with novice teachers, these consultants felt the need to be more directive and didactic until the client's knowledge base about teaching was expanded; thus their interactions with novice teachers focused on expert and professional information. Also, early in their relationships with clients, these consultants felt the need to establish trust and credibility; thus consultative interactions with new clients focused on expert and professional information. However, when the faculty member became better acquainted either with pedagogy or the consultant, consultative interactions reportedly became more personal and collaborative.

Like Wergin, Mason, and Munson (1976), consultants in another study (Brinko, 1988) reported they were more likely to be prescriptive with new clients and more likely to be collaborative with returning clients. However, their reported behavior differed greatly from their observed behavior. The consultative style of these consultants ranged from very prescriptive to very collaborative, with both new and returning clients. In addition, neither gender, training, nor experience as a consultant correlated with consultative style.

These mixed results indicate that consultative interaction can not be predicted simply by demographics; any model of consultative interaction may emerge depending on the dynamics between consultant and client. Consultant behavior is greatly influenced by client behavior, and in turn, client behavior is greatly influenced by consultant behavior. In my earlier example, the overbearing and controlling client's behavior greatly influenced—if not caused—the consultant to change his approach to the consultation. Another consultant in the same study effectively used a collaborative style, accepting his client's problem identifications, diagnoses, and solutions; but this consultation apparently succeeded because this client seemed very willing to examine his teaching honestly, to admit error and problem areas, and to be receptive to change. A third consultant in this study, who was collaborative almost to the point of being passive, well complemented an assertive, self-analyzing client. However, had this same self-knowledgeable client encountered a highly prescriptive consultant, the mismatch of styles could have seriously impeded the success of the consultation.

Future Directions

The above examples point to the need to consider the interactive style of the consultant-client dyad as a whole.

Rather than the consultant's style of interaction, instructional consultation practitioners and researchers need to consider the consultative style that emerges from the interaction between the consultant and the client.

Practitioners who use only one style of consultation focus on their own needs (for example, a need for control or approval) and neglect the needs and expectations of their clients. Thus, the use of only one style of instructional consultation with all clients can affect the success of the consultation and can diminish the satisfaction of clients who have different styles of interaction. Practitioners can meet the needs of a greater number of clients with one of two strategies. In the first strategy, the consultant discusses client's expectations, is responsive to the client's wishes and cues, and is flexible in his interactional style. This method may be effective for the consultant who possesses a repertoire of consultation models and is comfortable switching back and forth among them. In the second strategy, the consultant discusses her own consultative style and expectations and presents the client with the option of consulting with her. This method may be effective for the instructional consultant who has one particular model in which she has expertise. Both methods are proactive, turning the psychological contract into a verbal contract. Each strategy helps consultants to minimize their assumptions and inferences about clients and to make consistent their espoused theories and theories-in-use (Smith & Schwartz, 1985).

Although there is some agreement in the literature about consultant attitudes and behaviors in general that contribute to effective consultation, we still have no empirical evidence to differentiate between strategies and practices that make consultation successful and those that do not. Researchers need to compare successful and unsuccessful consultation, as defined by the consultant and client, to determine which practices are effective, with whom they are effective, and under what conditions they are effective.

References

Andrews, J. D. W. (1978). Growth of a teacher. *Journal of Higher Education, 49*, 136-150.

Ashford, S. J., & Cummings, L. L. (1983). Feedback as an individual resource: Personal strategies of creating information. *Organizational Behavior and Human Performance, 32*, 370–398.

Blake, R. R., & Mouton, J. S. (1983) *Consultation: A handbook for individual and organization development.* Reading, Mass.: Addison-Wesley.

Brinko, K. T. (1988). Instructional consultation with feedback in higher education: A quantitative and qualitative analysis. *Dissertation Abstracts International, 49* (8), 2120A–2121A. (University Microfilms No. 8822955)

Brinko, K. T. (1990). Instructional consultation with feedback in higher education. *Journal of Higher Education, 61*, 65–83.

Carroll, J. G., & Goldberg, S. R. (1989). Teaching consultants: A collegial approach to better teaching. *College Teaching, 37*, 143–146.

Cash, W. B., & Minter, R. L. (1979). Consulting approaches: Two basic styles. *Training and Development Journal, 33*, 26–28.

Cohen, P. A. (1980). Effectiveness of student-rating feedback for improving college instruction: A meta-analysis of findings. *Research in Higher Education, 13*(4), 321–341.

Cooper, C. R. (1982). Getting inside the instructional process: A collaborative diagnostic process for improving college teaching. *Journal of Instructional Development, 5*(3), 2–10.

Dalgaard, K. A., Simpson, D. E., & Carrier, C. A. (1982). Coordinate status consultation: A strategy for instructional improvement. *Journal of Instructional Development, 5*(4), 7–14.

Davies, I. K. (1975). Some aspects of a theory of advice: The management of an instructional developer-client, evaluator-client relationship. *Instructional Science, 3*, 351–373.

Erickson, G. R. (1986). A survey of faculty development practices. *To Improve the Academy, 5*, 182-196.

Gallessich, J. (1974). Training the school psychologist for consultation. *Journal of School Psychology, 12*, 138–149.

Gallessich, J. (1982). *The profession and practice of consultation: A handbook for consultants, trainers of consultants, and consumers of consultation services.* San Francisco: Jossey-Bass.

Levinson-Rose, J., & Menges, R. J. (1981). Improving college teaching: A critical review of research. *Review of Educational Research, 51*, 403–434.

Lewis, K. G., & Povlacs, J. T. (Eds.) (1988). *Face to face: A sourcebook of individual consultation techniques for faculty/instructional developers.* Stillwater, OK: New Forums Press.

Menges, R. J., & Brinko, K. T. (1986). Effects of student evaluation feedback: A meta-analysis of higher education research. Paper presented at the 70th annual meeting of the American Educational Research Association, San Francisco. (ED 270 408)

O'Hanlon, J., & Mortensen L. (1980). Making teacher evaluation work. *Journal of Higher Education, 51*, 664–672.

Orban, D. A. (1981). An ethnographic study of consultation to improve college instruction. *Dissertation Abstracts International, 42*, 5040A. (University Microfilms No. DA8212435)

Price, R. D. (1976). A description of the verbal behavior of selected instructional developers in their initial conference with new clients: An exploratory study. *Dissertation Abstracts International, 37* (9), 5576A.

Rutt, D. P. (1979). An investigation of the consultation styles of instructional developers. *Dissertation Abstracts International, 40* (2), 624A.

Schein, E. H. (1969). *Process consultation: Its role in organization development.* Reading, MA: Addison-Wesley.

Smith, R. A., & Schwartz, F. S. (1985). A theory of effectiveness. *To Improve the Academy, 4*, 63-74.

Sweeney, J. M., & Grasha, A. F. (1979). Improving teaching through faculty development triads. *Educational Technology, 12*(2), 54–57.

Tilles, S. (1961). Understanding the consultant's role. *Harvard Business Review, 39*, 87–89.

Wergin, J. F., Mason, E. J., & Munson, P. J. (1976). The practice of faculty development: An experience-derived model. *Journal of Higher Education, 47*, 289–308.

2. Instructional Consulting: A Guide for Developing Professional Knowledge

L. Dee Fink

*C*onsultants, by definition, are those whose prior knowledge about a subject allows them to be of help to someone else. In this sense, instructional consultants are similar to lawyers, doctors, car mechanics, tax consultants, farm extension agents, and so on. Like these counterparts, the "prior knowledge" needed by an instructional consultant may take two forms. The first form, useful in simpler problems, is specific knowledge that allows the consultant to give a direct answer to the client's question. For example, a teacher may contact a consultant and ask: "What are the advantages and disadvantages of essay tests versus multiple choice tests?" In this case, a well-informed consultant should be able to identify two or three advantages and disadvantages of each form of testing (or be able to pull a book or article from their collection that would do the same thing with somewhat more detail).

A second and very different form of knowledge is needed to deal with more complex problems. This is conceptual knowledge, that is, the analytical framework that allow the consultant to (a) identify the source of the client's problem or question, and (b) identify what needs to be learned in order to solve the problem or answer the question.

For example, when a teacher comes in and says: "My students don't like my teaching" (that is, they give me low teacher evaluations), or "My students don't seem to be learning what they should," their questions really are: "What is causing this?" and "What can I do about it?" In order to answer such questions of "cause" and "response," the consultant needs (a) a model of the act of teaching that will guide their efforts to collect the information necessary to identify the cause of the problem, and (b) a knowledge of alternative responses in the act of teaching that will enable the client to make some changes.

In this chapter, I present two models: one of the teaching/learning situation and one of the act of teaching,

each of which can be useful as a conceptual or analytical framework for analyzing the problems of teachers. I then present some ideas and resources for identifying alternative responses in the act of teaching.

The Teaching/ Learning Situation

Whenever a teacher intends to teach, he or she must recognize that this situation involves three key factors: the teacher, the learner and a subject. The relationships between these three factors can be illustrated in the following diagram:

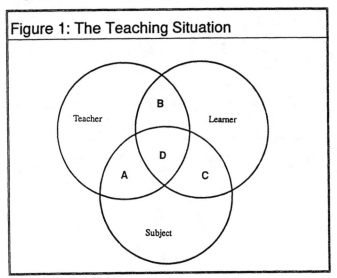

Figure 1: The Teaching Situation

This diagram reminds us of the importance of the four overlapping areas: A, B, C, and D. Area A represents the knowledge the teacher has about the subject. The diagram highlights the reality that the teacher cannot convey all of his own knowledge to the students. This "fact" implies a basic principle of course planning: the teacher must exercise restraint when selecting the goals and scope of the course.

Area B refers to the knowledge or relationship the teacher has or can have with the learner. Sometimes this knowledge or information about the learners as students or as individuals can be helpful in building motivation to learn. It can also be helpful in finding analogies to explain the subject matter of the course.

Area C represents the prior knowledge or beliefs the learner may have about the subject before the course even begins. The extent and validity of this knowledge varies from almost nothing to a considerable amount, depending on the subject and the student. Either way, it is important for the teacher to take into account what learners know or what they believe they know about a subject, before undertaking to expand that knowledge.

Area D, however, is the most critical. This is where the teacher, the learner, and the subject all come together and interact for a period of time. The intended beneficiary of this interaction is the learner; the primary goal is to enlarge the learner's knowledge or understanding of the subject; but the primary initiator of action is the teacher.

How then can the teacher understand his or her own responsibilities in this critical center of interaction? The following model of the four dimensions of teaching can help explain what all teachers do when they teach.

The Four Dimensions of Teaching

The basic idea of this model is that everyone who teaches, regardless of the subject and regardless of how good or poor they are as teachers, engages four dimensions of teaching: skills, decisions, philosophies, and attitudes.

Figure 2: The Four Dimensions of Teaching

Skills

Decisions

Philosophies

Attitudes

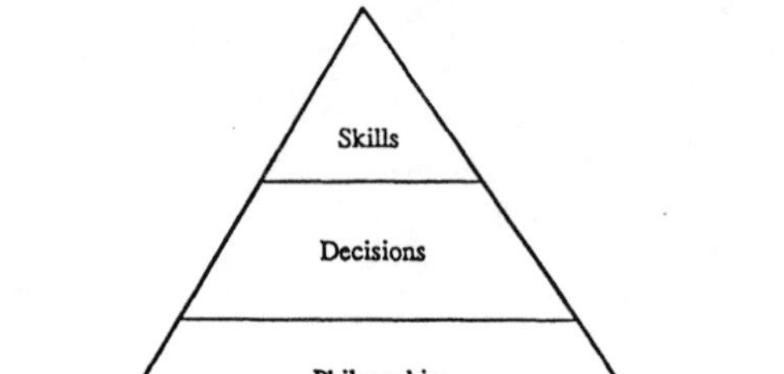

The model also implies that the four dimensions have a hierarchical relationship to each other, that is, the higher dimensions are dependent in an important way on the lower or more fundamental dimensions.

In the next portion of this chapter, I comment in more detail on each of the four dimensions.

Skills in Teaching

The first dimension refers to the many skills that a teacher needs when interacting with students. Many of these are communication skills that take place in the classroom. The two most common are undoubtedly lecturing and leading discussions. These are clearly important skills and are used to some degree or other in nearly all courses, regardless of which general teaching strategy is used.

Sub-components of these more general skills usually include such things as: explaining a concept, providing a metaphor or analogy for a relationship, asking thought-provoking questions, generating humor, revealing one's own experiences and/or shortcomings, giving students critical feedback on their responses without being condescending or making the student feel inept, developing rapport with students, providing closure for a given session, linking one session's topic to the subject of other sessions, and so on.

In addition, there are a number of important teaching skills that occur outside the classroom. These include writing tests, designing in-class activities for individuals and/or groups, and critiquing written material.

One important point to remember about skills is that they are, by definition, learnable and hence can be improved.

A second important point is that not all courses require the same skills. A course that is essentially a lecture course does not require discussion leading skills; a discussion course does not require as much in the way of presentational skills; a course built around "team learning" depends more on skills in designing effective group activities for in-class use. Instructional consultants need to be familiar with published material that can help professors learn and develop the skills they need. Much of the literature on college teaching is focused on the skill dimension of teaching. Selected items are provided in the references at the end of this chapter.

Decisions about Course Design

The second dimension, "Decisions," refers to the decisions all teachers need to make, primarily before a course starts, about the design of a course. Any course, if it is to be a good course, must have a good design. And designing a good course calls for the same balance of technical knowledge and creative imagination as the task of designing a building or designing a picture.

This particular dimension is one where consultants can have a big impact on the teaching done by faculty in a relatively short amount of time. Therefore I am going to make some extended comments on two different tools that have been helpful in working with many faculty members on course design: five principles of good course design (described below) and an 11-step "Decision Guide" contained in Appendix A.

The basic idea behind what I have whimsically come to call "Fink's Five Principles of Fine Course Design" is that any course, to be a good course, must:

1. Challenge students to higher level learning.
2. Use active learning.
3. Give students frequent and immediate feedback on the quality of their learning.
4. Use varied forms of learning.
5. Have a fair system of testing and grading.

My proposition is that, if a course does these five things well, the results will be good, no matter what else is bad about the course. What do these principles mean and how do they affect decisions about course design?

Challenge students to higher level learning. The proposition here is that there are two levels of learning: higher and lower. Both are important. Lower level learning refers to simply understanding and remembering basic information and ideas. All significant learning requires a certain amount of this. But higher level learning refers to such things as critical thinking, creative thinking, problem solving, decision making, and so on. My argument is that, unless students achieve a significant amount of higher level learning, the course simply will not make a major contribution to the students' "higher education."

When designing a course, a teacher must find a way to incorporate both types of learning in the course. This is the main task of Step Two in the "Decision Guide" shown in the Appendix. One response is to design the course so that students spend the first half of the course learning the basic material, and the second half working on higher level learning. A more creative approach might be to have them learn the basic concepts about just one topic and then learn how to use these concepts (by thinking critically about them, solving problems with them, making decisions, or whatever), before moving on to the next topic.

Use active forms of learning. The idea here is that there are two basic kinds of learning: passive and active. I define passive learning as receiving information or ideas, that is, as what typically happens when someone reads a book or listens to a lecture. Active learning, on the other hand, occurs when a person uses information or ideas to engage in a complex intellectual activity such as decision making or critical thinking.

As an analogy, try to imagine teaching someone to do push-ups who does not know how to do push-ups. Lecturing to them about the muscle groups involved and the movements needed can be helpful. Even modeling some push-ups can be helpful. But eventually, if the person is going to learn to do push-ups, they are going to have to do push-ups themselves—repeatedly, and preferably with immediate and frequent feedback.

The same thing is true with anyone trying to learn how to do "intellectual push-ups" (that is, critical thinking, problem solving, and so on). Providing relevant information and modeling can be helpful, but eventually the learner has to DO the "intellectual push-ups" him/herself—repeatedly, preferably with immediate and frequent feedback. The basic argument here is that a student CANNOT acquire higher levels of learning with passive learning; higher levels require active learning.

When designing the course, the teacher must decide when, where and how the passive and active learning will occur. These are the questions involved in Steps Five and Six of the "Decision Guide." Whereas teachers often use class time for lectures (usually a passive form of learning), a better strategy might be to motivate students to spend more time reading before coming to class, and then use class time to have students actively engage in decision making, problem solving, or other forms of active learning—with periodic feedback from the professor.

Give students frequent and immediate feedback on the quality of their learning. One of the main findings in a study of quality teaching at Harvard (R. J. Light, 1990, *The Harvard Assessment Seminars, First Report.* Cambridge, MA: Harvard University) was that students thought "immediate and detailed feedback on both written and oral work" was critically important (p. 8). To extend the "push-up" analogy given above, the professor may need to give the student periodic feedback on where to place the hands, how to hold the back, and so on. It is also likely that the feedback will be more important in the early phase of learning than in the later phases of practice and strengthening.

When planning a course, then, a teacher needs to find ways of giving students weekly or even daily feedback of some kind. This might take the form of frequent short quizzes, responses to short written work, oral comments, as well as more substantial graded work. If one accepts the importance of "frequent feedback," then the widespread practice of using "two mid-terms and a final" simply does not suffice as sufficient feedback.

Vary the forms of learning used. This has value for two reasons. The first is simply that variety adds interest. No matter how good a teaching technique is, it can become repetitious and boring if it is used over and over.

The second reason, relates to the fact that different students learn differently. Some are inductively inclined, others prefer deductive reasoning; some work best in verbal forms, others in visual forms; some like to work individually, others in groups; and so on. If a course offers different kinds of learning opportunities, a greater number of students will probably find one or more modes of learning that work well for them.

When designing a course, the teacher needs to identify different kinds of in-class and out-of-class learning activities, and then fit these together in a dynamic way.

Have a fair system for grading. Nothing leaves a sour taste in students' mouth more than working hard in a class, feeling like they have learned something significant, and then having the professor give grades that are significantly lower than they think they deserved.

Fairness in **tests** can be enhanced by: formulating questions that focus on stated learning objectives and that also stay within the confines of what the class actually did; using several different kinds of questions (for example, multiple choice, essay); and using grading standards that are appropriate for the institution, level of students, and so on.

Fairness in the **grading system** can be enhanced by such things as using several kinds (at least four) of graded activities (for example, tests on recall information, application exercises, formal essays, small group tests), providing flexibility (for example, drop one of seven quizzes), and having the grading system communicated clearly in writing (see Step 10 of the "Decision Guide").

Longer-Term Changes: Philosophy and Attitudes

The third dimension of the act of teaching, "Philosophy," refers to the many values and beliefs that a teacher has—values and beliefs about knowledge, teaching and learning. Teaching is a goal-seeking behavior and, as such, it forces us to make choices about which goals are preferable (values) and how best to attain them (beliefs). What is knowledge? Teaching? Learning? What is *good* knowledge? Good teaching? Good learning?

Most professors have difficulty articulating their philosophy of teaching because they have not thought extensively about it. A good way to coax these philosophies out for more careful examination is to ask them to draw a picture of the teaching and learning process or to identify a metaphor. Most metaphors will fall into one of four categories:

Transferring - The teacher knows a lot and his/her task is to transfer as much as possible to the students. The teacher is a "pitcher" and the student is a "vessel."

Shaping - The teacher is a coach or trainer or pottery maker. The teacher's task is to shape the student into a desirable form.

Traveling - The teacher is a guide or leader, someone who points the way. The task is to lead the students on an exploration of new places and vistas.

Growing - The teacher is a gardener who develops, cultivates or nurtures students. The task is to provide proper support, but the growing comes from something innate in the student.

The fourth and final dimension, "Attitudes," refers to the feelings and images we have—about the subject, about the students and about ourselves. Do we have a love for the subject, or is it just something we learned along the way and can tell others about if necessary? How do we feel about the students? Can we see that which is attractive in them as learners, or only that which is negative (for example, their ignorance of the subject, their lack of motivation, and so on.)? How do we feel about ourselves? Do we like ourselves and feel good about how we act and what we know? Or do we feel inept and incomplete in our knowledge? What images do we have of the subject, of the students, and of ourselves that give rise to these feelings? If we were asked to draw pictures of the subject, the students, and ourselves, what would the pictures look like?

Once an instructional consultant recognizes the importance of professors' philosophies and attitudes, the action question becomes: What can the consultant do to help professors examine and modify their philosophies and attitudes?

First, a consultant needs to become familiar with the different beliefs and values (that is, philosophies) related to teaching. Some of this familiarity comes from hearing people talk about why they do what they do as teachers. But, with a few exceptions, most professors' philosophies of teaching are not very sophisticated because they haven't read or thought that deeply about the issues involved.

Second, a consultant needs to become familiar with alternative and more carefully developed philosophies. Usually this comes from reading and sometimes from conversations with people who have developed their philosophies with some care.

Three authors who have articulated different philosophies of teaching are Joseph Axelrod, Kenneth Eble and Joseph Lowman. Axelrod described four "teaching prototypes" held by different teachers in his study, *The University Teacher as Artist* (1973). These can be summarized as: "I teach what I know," "I teach what I am," "I train inquiring minds," and "I work with students as people." Eble was a thoughtful, witty, and prolific writer. In his book on *The Aims of College Teaching*, he laid out what he considered to be the appropriate aims of higher education, where instructors have strayed from them, and what should be done to return to them. Lowman, in his book on *Mastering the Techniques of Teaching*, presents the view that "masterful" teaching requires effectiveness in each of two aspects of teaching: intellectual excitement and interpersonal relationships.

These first two steps, becoming familiar both with professors' actual philosophies and attitudes and with alternative views, are necessary to prepare a consultant for addressing questions related to these two dimensions of teaching. But what can the consultant do to help professors make needed changes in this realm? The first part of the answer is "be patient." It takes time to engage a person at this level, and it takes time for changes to evolve. But I can report from personal experience as a consultant that it is possible to promote and see significant change at this level. And it is exciting and powerful when it happens.

One way to promote such change is to have sustained and recurring contact with a professor in a one-on-one situation, usually in discussions about a given course or set of courses. By keeping notes on discussions with clients, the consultant can begin to see patterns and make connections, see what the values, beliefs, and feelings are behind the decisions and choices a professor has been making as a teacher. Then, after making the professor conscious of these patterns, one can start the process of evaluating their philosophy and attitudes, and examining alternatives.

A second way of addressing these two dimensions of teaching is through group discussions. At the University of Oklahoma we have had an activity called "Faculty Luncheon Discussion Groups" for many years. In these, fifteen or so faculty members meet every two weeks all year long for a half-hour lunch and a one-hour discussion on some aspect of teaching. A feeling of group rapport and trust develops that allows the participants not only to present their deepest concerns about teaching, but also to challenge and be challenged on their beliefs, values, and feelings about teaching. Again, because of the long-term nature of this contact and the degree to which it engages people at fundamental levels, many professors have made significant changes in their philosophies and attitudes.

Conclusions

This model of the four dimensions of teaching has two important values for instructional consultants: it provides a framework for analyzing the more complex problems that teachers bring us, and it offers guidance for our own professional development.

When faculty members come to us for assistance with a major teaching problem, we may conclude that the source of the problem is located in one of the individual dimensions. For example, they may need to improve a particular skill, or make different decisions in their course design. On the other hand, their problem may be the result of dissonance between two or more of the dimensions. For example, they may have chosen a course design that requires classroom skills they don't have. Such teachers could then either develop the needed skills or change their course design. A second example may be someone who has selected a teaching strategy that does not reflect their real philosophy or attitude. In this case, they need to think about whether this is their real philosophy and/or attitude; if not, they need to modify their philosophy or attitude, or select a different teaching strategy.

The second value of this model of teaching concerns the professional development of instructional consultants themselves. We need to learn about the various skills involved in teaching, about traditional and alternative course designs, and about the variety of philosophies and attitudes that people have towards teaching. We need to know what options and possibilities exist in each of the dimensions, what their relative advantages and disadvantages are, and what relationships exist between a given dimension and the other dimensions.

Learning about all this is a large agenda. But it is large because the act of teaching is complex. On the one hand this makes learning enough about teaching to be an effective consultant a demanding task. On the other hand, this same complexity also makes the study of teaching a source of enduring richness.

Additional Readings

Skills

McKeachie, W. (1994). *Teaching tips: Strategies, research, and theory for college and university teachers* (9th ed.). Lexington, MA: D. C. Heath.

Bligh, D. A. (1972). *What's the use of lectures?* Harmondworth, United Kingdom: Penguin.

Eble, K. E. (1976). *The craft of teaching.* San Francisco: Jossey-Bass.

Jacobs, L. C., & Chase, C. I. (1992). *Developing and using tests effectively.* San Francisco: Jossey-Bass.

Civikly, J. M. (Ed.) (1986). Communicating in college classrooms. *New Directions for Teaching and Learning, no. 26.* San Francisco: Jossey-Bass.

Decisions

Diamond, R. M. (1989). *Designing and improving courses and curricula in higher education.* San Francisco: Jossey-Bass.

Svinicki, M. D., & Dixon, N. M. (1987). The Kolb model modified for classroom activities. *College Teaching, 35*(4), 141-146.

Bonwell, C. C., & Eison, J. A. (1991). *Active learning: Creating excitement in the classroom.* (ASHE-ERIC Higher Education Reports, No. 1.) Washington, DC: George Washington University.

Kurfiss, J. G. (1988). *Critical thinking: Theory, research, practice, and possibilities.* (ASHE-ERIC Higher Education Reports, No. 2.) Washington, DC: Association for the Study of Higher Education.

Brookfield, S. D. (1991). *Developing critical thinkers.* San Francisco: Jossey-Bass.

Fuhrmann, B. S., & Grasha, A. F. (1983). *A practical handbook for college teachers.* Boston: Little, Brown and Co.

Svinicki, M. (Ed.). (1990). The changing face of college teaching. *New Directions for Teaching and Learning, no. 42.* San Francisco: Jossey-Bass.

Philosophy and Attitudes

Eble, K. E. (1983). *The aims of college teaching.* San Francisco: Jossey-Bass.

Fuhrmann, B. S., & Grasha, A. F. (1983). *A practical handbook for college teachers.* Boston: Little, Brown and Co.

Palmer, P. J. (1983). *To know as we are known: A spirituality of education.* New York: Harper & Row.

Lowman, J. (1991). *Mastering the techniques of teaching.* San Francisco: Jossey-Bass.

Svinicki, M. (Ed.). (1990). The changing face of college teaching. *New Directions for Teaching and Learning, no. 42.* San Francisco: Jossey-Bass.

Axelrod, J. (1973). *The university teacher as artist.* San Francisco: Jossey-Bass.

Appendix A
Planning Your Course: A Decision Guide

1. **Where are you?** Size up the situation.
    - Kind of students: number, prior knowledge, motivation, etc.?
    - Kind of learning spaces: classroom, lab, fixed desks/chairs? In what kind of curriculum is this course embedded?
    - Are there external professional standards that need to be met? What are your own beliefs, values, attitudes, skills as a teacher?

2. **Where do you want to go?** What are your goals? Ideally, what would you like students to get out of this course? This works well by asking the following sub-questions:
    - What do you want students to be able to DO, once the course is over? (Identify 3-5 general goals.)
    - What would students have to KNOW in order to do each of the items listed above?
    - What would students have to DO in order to learn each of the items listed above?

3. **How would you know if you/they got there?** (In other words, how would you know if the students achieved these goals? How can you assess student learning/achievement?)
    - For each general goal specified above, what information can you gather that would tell how well the goal was achieved for each student individually? For the class as a whole?
    - For which are multiple-choice exams sufficient? Essay exams? Project assignments? Writing assignments? Other "products"?

4. **How are you going to get there?** Select a general strategy. What general structure of learning activities do you want to use?
    A. Continuous series of lectures and reading assignments, periodically interrupted by 1 or 2 mid-terms.
    (hear - read - test)
    B. Sequence of reading, reflective writing, and whole class discussion (sequence repeated for each topic).
    (read - write - talk)
    (A variation is read - talk - write.)
    C. Start with some field or lab work observations, followed by readings and whole class discussions.
    (do/look - read -talk)
    (Write-ups of lab/field work is sometimes included.)
    D. Present lectures, followed by field work or lab observations.
    (hear—see/do)
    E. Have students do assigned readings, followed by mini-tests done individually and in small groups; then move on to group-based application projects.
    (read - individual/groups tests - DO)
    F. Work through a series of developmental stages: build some knowledge and/or skills (4-6 wks),
    work on small application projects (4-6 wks), and then on larger, more complex projects (4-6 wks).
    (know/knowhow - do - DO)
    G. Contract for a grade: (for example: read text and pass exams = C; in addition, do research paper = B;
    in addition do extended project = A).
    H. Other?????

5. **What are the students going to do?** What are your specific learning activities?
    In the final step of No. 2 above, you identified several kinds of learning activities. Now examine these activities to see if they are sufficient to generate the kind of learning you desire. Is "hearing" sufficient? Or "reading"? Or

"doing"? Or does the learning goal require some combination of activities? How much hearing, reading, doing, etc., are needed?

6. **When are you going to do what?** Develop a sequence of activities.

Develop a week-by-week schedule for the whole term.
- What activities need to come first?
- What activities do you want to conclude with?
- What sequence do you need in the middle?

7. **Who/what can help?** Find resources.

What resources do you need (and can you get) to support each of the goals listed in No. 2 above? (People, places, and things, including media.)

8. **How are you going to grade?** Develop your grading system.
- It should reflect the full range of learning goals and activities. (Remember, NOT everything has to be graded.)
- The relative weight of each item on the course grade should reflect the relative importance of that activity.

9. **What could go wrong?** "De-bugging" the design.

Analyze and assess this "first draft" of the course. What kinds of undesirable situations might it generate? Will students be motivated to do the work? Does the design encourage student involvement? Are the students getting sufficient feedback on their performance? What could you do to prevent (or at least minimize) these problems? Make the necessary modifications in the design.

10. **Let them know what you're planning.** Now write the syllabus.

This should include, among other things:
- General management information—instructor, office hours, phone, etc.
- Goals for the course
- Structure and sequence of class activities, including due dates for major assignments/tests/projects
- Text and other required reading material
- Grading procedures
- Course policies: attendance, work turned in late, make-up assignments/exams, etc.

11. **How will you know how the course is going? How it went?**

Plan an evaluation of the course itself and your teaching performance.
- What kinds of mid-term and end-of-term feedback will you need?
- What specific questions do you have: About the degree to which your goals for the course were achieved? About the effectiveness of particular learning activities? About your classroom performance?
- What sources of information can help you answer these questions: video/audio-tape, student interviews, questionnaires, outside observers, test results?

3. *The Creative Art of Effective Consultation*

Laura L. B. Border

*P*ersonally, I find expertise in consultation to be very much like expertise in cooking. It isn't enough for a cook to predict or to gather and present information. A cook has to pick a recipe, select ingredients, know how to put them together, mix and match, watch her/his timing, choose to sauté, bake, fry, broil, or boil, and have a pretty clear idea of what the result of each might be. And, while educators are often uncomfortable with evaluation, both cook and consumer find evaluation completely natural—once the dish is served, they immediately compare and contrast the success of various tastes, textures, and colors; pronounce the result good or bad; and make suggestions and plans for improvement. (Or they simply choose a new recipe).

Both teaching consultants (TCs) and cooks recognize the importance of knowledge and creativity, coupled with concern and consideration for the consumer. Expert consultation, like cooking, takes place in a comfortable and inviting environment and is meant to nurture. Although the same kind of feeling is essential in an effective consultation process, it is often assumed that it just happens because the TC is "nice." Consumers expect both cooks and TCs to have a repertoire of skills, do a good job, and be considerate. None of us would choose a "cold", un-trained TC or cook. (I was once invited to dinner in a wealthy home where the hostess served turnip soup—that is, water and turnips untainted by a hint of spice or broth! Such a disappointment! She was on a special diet, we were hungry!) Action and service are not enough from the consumer's vantage point. Imagination, sensitivity, and good taste are essential components of expertise.

David Berliner (1991) compares expertise in general to expertise in teaching. His findings are relevant to the training of TCs; that is, 1) an expert teaching consultant is like any expert, no matter what happens, no matter which ingredients are available, an expert can make the recipe work, present the result with panache, and satisfy the consumer's need for nutrition, esthetics, and comfort; and 2) expertise is neither oracular nor mysterious. Rather it is the mastery of a combination of ingredients, seasoned with a dose of experience and creativity.

Expertise may take years to develop, but effectiveness can be taught and learned. In fact, we have discovered through our training of Lead Graduate Teachers, that the cooking analogy to consultation can be quite effective, once the essential ingredients and reliable techniques have been identified. Then, with practice and supervision, the novice TC will have time to acquire the experience and exploit the creativity that appear to be the *art* of consultation.

Essential Ingredients

Effective instructional consultation is based on a broad range of knowledge in education and the related fields of psychology and counseling. The knowledge substratum is multilayered because it must convey both what the teacher needs to do in her/his classroom and what the consultant needs to do in the consultation. Each TC and each teacher must select from a wide variety of concepts, behaviors, and materials to put together an effective consultation or class. Ingredients vary according to the individual's preferences, values, and skills. The happiest combinations in each instance mix well—as do the elements of a good recipe.

In order to be a good instructional consultant, TCs need a broad range of knowledge in pedagogy, cognitive psychology, and academic ethics. They need to be aware of current issues that are changing higher education from outside the academy. They also need to master special skills that have been developed by counseling and educational psychologists to carry out effective consultation.

Regarding issues of teaching, the TC must be aware of and comfortable with the cognitive, affective (feeling level), psychomotor (mental/physical levels), and ethical aspects of teaching and learning and able to explain them when necessary. Bloom's Taxonomy (1956) is useful to analyze cognitive development and the cognitive levels at which a question, test, or course is targeted. David Kolb's (1984) typology of learning styles offers a clear model of differences in cognitive processing. To understand how affect, that is feeling, influences teaching and learning, the Timothy Leary Interpersonal Behavior Circle (1957) is an exciting tool. Freire's (1970) work on power issues in the classroom and the importance of psychomotor and affective learning is requisite. Kohlberg's (1981) scheme of moral development, contrasted with the work of Belenky, *et al.*, (1986) on connected knowing is enlightening, as is William Perry's (1970) typology of how students reason at different stages in their learning development. And, of course, a good grounding in assessment and evaluation is as important to TCs as it is to cooks; works by Angelo and Cross (1993) are excellent. A TC who is conversant in these ideas can offer the teacher tasty tidbits from which to select.

Choosing a Recipe

While instructional consultants don't need a degree in psychology or counseling, they will be more comfortable and more effective if they explore the ingredients essential to what Gazda calls the "helping relationship." These skills include learning to build trust and learning to give effective feedback. They also involve learning to be aware of one's own style of interaction. The "helping relationship" focuses on the needs of the helpee rather than the needs of the helper. If we are to define consultation on teaching as a helping relationship, it is necessary to avoid confusing it with three other processes: therapy, supervision, and advising.

TCs need to understand that consultation on teaching is not the same as psychotherapy, even though consultation tends to be therapeutic. Issues dealt with in the consultation process encompass teaching issues and the teacher's responses and needs in that environment. Therapy treats personal life challenges. Nevertheless, an expert TC is sensitive to the teacher's affective side and is willing to help a teacher work through issues that do come up in relation to the classroom. TCs may want to listen to and support teachers who choose to discuss personal issues, but prefer to encourage them to pursue further assistance through the proper channels.

Instructional consultation is also different from advising. Advising in the university setting is usually limited to helping a student or faculty member proceed along a prescribed sequence of requirements—an undergraduate major, a graduate program, or a tenure-track faculty line.

Advisors work on the next step the student or teacher needs to take; TCs work on the teacher.

Finally, consultation differs greatly from supervision. The purpose of consultation is to assist the teacher; the goal of supervision is to evaluate the teacher. Consultation tends to make teachers feel more comfortable and able to work toward improvement. Supervision, unfortunately, is likely to create mistrust and resentment. Consultation is designed to help teachers perform better in the classroom, while the goal of supervision is to decide whether or not the teacher should be in the classroom.

If consultation is not therapy, advising, or supervision, what is it? Remember that it is more like cooking. TCs, supported by their background knowledge, create a warm, safe environment, use certain interactive skills, and nurture their teachers. Like the cook, the TC is focused on satisfying the consumer's hunger and thirst for a pleasant and productive experience.

A Recipe That Works

Have you ever noticed how guests seem to congregate in the kitchen, while the living room remains empty? They know at an unconscious level that the environment is warm and nurturing. Just being there brings up the warm feelings associated with Mom, warm cookies, and milk after school. That is the kind of ambiance a TC needs to establish. While cookies and milk aren't *de rigueur*, there are verbal ways to create the same feeling. It's important for the TC to establish a growth producing environment in which the teacher can relax, explore new ideas and generate creative solutions. The TC needs to know how to establish trust, build rapport, focus on the teacher's needs, establish open communication, and clarify goals for the process. Consultation sessions need to be comfortable. They should be welcoming times of exchange, comparison and selection. Some advice that has worked for me is given in Appendix A.

Establishing Trust

Trust refers to the relationship between the TC and the teacher that allows the teacher to participate fully in the consultation process. Although it may seem that building trust between two people requires years, the TC can build trust very deliberately by setting up clear boundaries for the consultation process. The TC needs to explain her/his credentials, clarify the reason for which the teacher is participating in the consultation, assure the teacher of the confidential and non-evaluative character of the process, set the interactional norms for the process, and help to determine the goals for the session. In other words, building trust means creating safety for the teacher to explore her/his teaching process.

Credentials are important because the teacher needs to feel confident that the TC knows what she or he is about. They may include teaching a regular course or perhaps a methods course in the same content area as the teacher. Of course, it is not necessary to be in the same field in order to do a successful consultation; other areas of expertise might include experience in faculty/TA development, educational counseling, counseling psychology, or training in videotape consultation. Faith in the TC's skill is essential no matter what the reason for the consultation might be.

To build trust the TC needs to assure the teacher of confidentiality. No information should be given to the teacher's supervisors, to other teachers, nor should it be used in any written correspondence about the teacher. TCs can build trust and rapport by mentioning that they know the consultation process might seem intimidating and that they have been through similar experiences. TCs can assure teachers that they are there to support, assist, and to focus on the teacher's needs. Open communication can be easily established by making sure that comments point toward the positive solution of perceived problems.

Another ingredient of a safe environment is an understanding and awareness of who is in control. A teacher who is aware that she or he is not going to be judged, graded, evaluated, and reported, is much more likely to be able to profit from the consultation process.

Discussing the rules or norms for the consultation process also creates safety and makes the teacher more comfortable. In our consultation process, adapted from David Way's (1988) video recall method, we state very clear rules for interactions. The teacher chooses what to discuss. The TC follows, clarifies, ties together common strands that appear, and offers assistance when requested. It is important to make it clear that the sessions are non-evaluative. That is, if the teacher asks, "How did I do?" the response is, "What do you think?" Teachers are encouraged to take responsibility for their own self-evaluation and self-improvement and to clarify their own goals.

Clarifying Goals

TCs and teachers need to establish goals for the consultation process. The goals need to be more precise than "teacher improvement." In my consultation work with teaching assistants, I identify my personal end goal for the consultation. The end goal is to have them attain a quality that I call "teacher comfort." Teacher comfort is a state of mind in which the teacher can actively teach, focus on the material and the students, move easily from one activity or interruption to another, integrate what is happening at the moment with what has already occurred or will occur, accept student questions, challenges, hostility, and enthusiasm appropriately, and move on to the next subject, method, technique, example, or student. Teacher comfort is similar to the self-assurance of an expert chef. It is built on knowledge experience, creativity, and perseverance. For example, Julia Child's recipe for Hollandaise lists several pages describing how to correct the sauce when the process doesn't work.

Teacher discomfort, on the other hand, is an internal experience in which the teacher is led astray by a too active and too negative internal dialogue. The teacher is unable to pay attention to students' needs, responses, and questions. If the teacher's internal dialogue keeps repeating that s/he is incompetent, should quit teaching, doesn't know what s/he is doing, or that students are unprepared or worse, teacher discomfort is the result. The teacher is the most important person in the classroom and if s/he is not at ease, teaching and learning suffer.

My view of teacher comfort is aligned with Berliner's description of expertise. Experts have a wide range of knowledge, options, strategies, techniques, solutions, communication strategies, and patience brought about by understanding that allows them to function optimally even in difficult or stressful situations. As a TC, the issue of teacher comfort can be addressed directly. For example, David Way's article on videotape recall demonstrates how teachers' feelings, perceptions, and thought patterns influence their performance. I encourage teachers to work toward teacher comfort by addressing the aspects of their teaching with which they are truly uncomfortable. Teachers first determine what makes them most uncomfortable. Then, we work together to help them find ways to relieve the discomfort. The concept of teacher comfort helps teachers, whether they are beginners or experienced, clarify why they are not happy with their classrooms and how they might go about improving the situation.

When the TC helps the teacher delineate goals for the session, another level of trust is attained. The teacher comes to understand that the TC's role is to help open up options, identify strengths and weaknesses, and assist her/him with generating and implementing a plan for improvement. Once these aspects of the consultation are clear, the TC must respect them in order to maintain trust.

Interactions between TCs and teachers. TCs need to determine what role they want to play in the consultation process and how they prefer to work with teachers. For example, the TC could be a listener/reflector, a giver of feedback, or a resource person. The TC could choose to talk a lot or to talk very little. In our training, we encourage

TCs to be active listeners, not to discuss their own issues, examples, or successes; but rather to encourage the teacher to do most of the talking, analyzing, and planning.

A useful tool to teach TCs to interact with teachers is Gazda's Continuum of Unhelpful to Helpful Responses (See Appendix B). Gazda and his group devised the scale for "helpers," (that is, for teachers and counselors) to help their "helpees." It is a good guide for TCs to study, learn to apply, and follow when interacting with teachers in a consultation. Trainers can use it to rate TCs' responses in a training session. Or, TCs can use it to listen to and analyze their own responses via audiotape or videotape. A TC who operates at Gazda's levels from 1.0 - 2.0 is considered to be ineffective and may even be hurtful. A TC who is able to operate at a 2.5 - 3.0 level may be supportive, but if s/he stays at that level, is not necessarily helpful. Skilled TCs function at a 3.5 - 4.0 level and consequently help teachers to move toward realizing desired goals.

Obtaining and using data for and from the teacher. The TC and teacher need to come to an agreement about how data on the teacher's performance, materials, and student response is to be gathered. In brief, various methods are useful. A combination of several—classroom observation, a data collection instrument, student feedback, a teacher's log, or a videotape of classroom teaching—is helpful. The TC and teacher also needs to decide how to process and use feedback that is received. For example, if a written instrument is used to collect data from students on the teacher's classroom performance, all the responses should be typed to protect students' anonymity before giving them to the teacher. Teachers should be assured that any information collected or any discussions held will be absolutely confidential. Notes on sessions may be returned directly to the teacher. See Appendix C for a sample Videotape Notes Form.

The intended outcome of the process. The TC needs to be clear about the intended outcome of the consultation process. Of course, the universal intended outcome is teacher improvement, but what form will it take? The TC may want to end the consultation process with the teacher having a written plan for improvement, a new syllabus, a list of articles or books to read, or an agreement for the teacher to return to a future consultation session. Teachers' goals vary. Some decide to take voice lessons, others decide to switch from lecturing to discussion. Some try to figure out ways to obtain more feedback from their students, while others need help with writing and grading tests. The TC's role is to help the teacher clarify, lay out and carry out her/his plans for success. In the end, it is hoped that the teaching consultant, the teacher, and the students know that their artful use of the recipe worked.

References

Angelo, T. A., Cross, K. P. (1993). *Classroom assessment techniques: A handbook for college teachers.* San Francisco: Jossey-Bass.

Belenky, M. F., *et al.* (1986). *Women's ways of knowing: The development of self, voice and mind.* New York: Basic Books.

Berliner, D. (1991). Educational psychology and pedagogical expertise: New findings and new opportunities for thinking about training. *Educational Psychologist, 26,* 145-155.

Bloom, B. S. (1956). *The taxonomy of educational objectives.* New York: Longmans, Green.

Freire, P. (1970). *Pedagogy of the oppressed.* New York: Seabury Press.

Gazda, G. M., Walters, R. P., & Childers, W. C. (1975). *Human relations development: A manual for health science.* Boston: Allyn and Bacon.

Kohlberg, L. (1981). *The philosophy of moral development: Moral stages and the idea of justice.* San Francisco: Harper & Row.

Kolb, D. A. (1984). *Experiential learning: Experience as the source of learning and development.* Englewood Cliffs, NJ: Prentice Hall.

Leary, T. (1957). *Interpersonal diagnosis of personality: A functional theory and methodology for personality evaluation.* New York: The Ronald Press.

Perry, W. G., Jr. (1970). *Forms of intellectual and ethical development in the college years: A Scheme.* New York: Reinholt and Winston.

Taylor-Way, D. (1988). Consultation with video: Memory management through stimulated recall. In K. G. Lewis & J.T. Povlacs (Eds.), *Face to face: A sourcebook of individual consultation techniques for faculty/instructional developers* (pp. 159-191). Stillwater, OK: New Forums Press.

Appendix A

Best Six Bits of Advice

1. Remember that you build trust by focusing sincerely on the needs of the teacher.
2. Don't be an oracle. Any cheap and quick advice you can think of in two seconds, the teacher has probably already tried and rejected.
3. Interject stories about your own experience only if they might truly enlighten the situation. If you only have 60 minutes with the teacher, s/he wants the attention to be fully directed on her/his problem.
4. Don't be a private detective. You don't have to know everything about the teacher's students, course, tests, evaluations to help. What you do need to know is exactly what is bothering the teacher at the moment.
5. Trust that the problem, feeling, frustration, the teacher mentions is truly a concern. The teacher came to see you because s/he has "hit the wall" and doesn't know what to do next.
6. Help the teacher generate alternative solutions. If s/he cannot do this, give a couple of suggestions. For example, if s/he thinks the students are dumb and lazy, her/his only solution might be to criticize them. You might provide solution number 2: "How about handing out a midterm evaluation?" or solution number 3, "How about giving one-minute papers that ask students to write down questions they have?"

Appendix B

Graduate Teacher Program Continuum of Unhelpful to Helpful Teaching Consultant Responses

Poor Response	Unhelpful Response	Supportive Response	Response that Creates Movement
1.0 1.5	2.0 2.5	3.0 3.5	4.0 4.5
A response in which the [Teaching Consultant] attends to neither the content nor the surface feelings of the [teacher]; discredits, devalues, ridicules, or scolds the [teacher]; shows a lack of caring for, or belief in the [teacher]; is vague or deals with the [teacher] in general terms; tries to hide his/her feelings or uses them to punish the [teacher]; reveals nothing about himself/herself or discloses himself/herself exclusively to meet his/her own needs; passively accepts or ignores discrepancies in the [teacher's] behavior that are self-defeating; ignores all cues from the [teacher] regarding their immediate relationship.	A response in which the [TC] only partially attends to the surface feelings of the [teacher] or distorts what the [teacher] communicated; withholds himself/herself from involvement with the [teacher] by declining to help, ignoring the [teacher], responding in a casual way, or giving cheap advice before really understanding the situation; behaves in a manner congruent with some preconceived role he/she is taking, but is incongruent with his/her true feelings; is neutral in his/her nonverbal expressions and gestures; is specific in his/her verbal expressions (e.g., gives advice or own opinions) or solicits specificity from the [teacher] (e.g. asks questions) but does so prematurely; does not voluntarily reveal, but may briefly answer questions regarding his/her own feelings, thoughts, or experiences relevant to the [teacher's] concerns; does not accept discrepancies in the [teacher's] behavior but does not draw attention to them either; comments superficially on communications from the [teacher] regarding their relationship.	A response in which the [TC] reflects the surface feelings of the [teacher] and does not distort the content; communicates his/her openness to entering a helping relationship; recognizes the [teacher] as a person of worth, capable of thinking and expressing himself/herself and acting constructively; communicates his/her attention and interest through his/her nonverbal expressions or gestures; shows that he/she is open to caring for and believing in the [teacher]; is specific in communicating his/her understanding but does not point out the directionality emerging for [teacher] action; shows no signs of phoniness but controls his/her expression of feeling so as to facilitate the development of the relationship in a general manner; reveals his/her own feelings, thoughts, or experiences relevant to the [teacher's] concerns; makes tentative expressions of discrepancies in the [teacher's] behavior but does not point out the directions in which these lead; discusses his/her relationship with the [teacher] but in a general rather than a personal way.	A response in which the [TC] goes beyond reflection of the essence of the [teacher's] communication by identifying underlying feeling to the [teacher's] welfare; is intensely attentive; models and actively solicits specificity from the [teacher]; shows a genuine congruence between his/her feelings (whether they are positive or negative) and his/her own behavior; communicates these feelings in a way that strengthens the relationship; freely volunteers specific feelings, thoughts, or experiences relevant to the [teacher's] concerns (these may involve a degree of risk taking for the [TC]); clearly points out discrepancies in the [teacher's] behavior and the specific directions in which these discrepancies lead; explicitly discusses their relationship in the immediate moment and helps to generate options.

Appendix C

Graduate Teacher Program Videotape Notes Form
University of Colorado at Boulder
Graduate Teacher Program
Graduate School

Confidential Report

Name:_____

Department:_____

Date Observed: _____

Videotape Consultation With:_____

1. How do you feel today's class went?

2. Do you have any problems with the class?

3. Are there any other observations you have about the videotaping?

4. There are three areas that can be examined to help teachers improve their teaching:

    a.   Behavior: Behaviors are visible actions which we could observe if we shut off the sound and watched. An example of a specific behavior is anything that the teacher is doing (i.e., movement, writing on board, asking questions, etc.). If you watch the tape at home, you might want to study your teaching behaviors and decide if there are things you would like to work on.

    b.   Thinking: A teacher's thinking is most clearly reflected in the course's organization. The course's organization reveals the teacher's thought processes in that it demonstrates whether the order of topic presentation is logical and sequential; whether the reading material complements the classroom activities; and whether the methods of evaluation are consistent with the goals of the course. The organization of the course can be analyzed at the semester, syllabus, course, or class level either at the beginning, middle or end of each segment. Another indicator of the amount of thinking that a teacher does about the course being taught is the way s/he handles unexpected questions or other incidents. It is a good idea to go over the "thinking"/organizational aspect of your course with your supervisor.

    c.   Feeling level: This level includes the thoughts, self-talk, internal dialogue, or emotional experience that you are having or experiencing internally as you teach. The affective process is invisible on the tape and to the observer. You are very aware of this, but your students and I can't see or guess what you're feeling. Some argue that a teacher's feelings while teaching are the most important events occurring in the classroom. If a teacher feels threatened or insecure then he/she may lash out at her students, sometimes in inappropriate ways. Conversely, if a teacher is comfortable and confident, he or she will be able to meet the needs of her students more effectively. One of the goals of the Graduate Teacher Program for you in the videotape consultation process is identifying your teaching comfort zone. Learning how to become comfortable as your teach, or in other situations you will experience as a teacher, will improve your effectiveness as a teacher.

So as we work today, I'd like for you to recall how you're feeling or what your self-talk was as you were teaching this class.

5. What feelings were important to you while you were teaching that were not visible to me?

Personal Bag of Tricks

It's important to develop your personal "bag of tricks" that addresses alternative teaching behaviors that you want to learn to use in the classroom.

If your issue is _____, then you develop a bag of tricks that helps, for example:
1.
2.
3.
4.
5.

If your issue is _____, then you can:
1.
2.
3.
4.
5.

Thanks for inviting me into your class, I enjoyed working with you. If you have any questions or comments about this feedback feel free to let me know.

Consultant's name

4. The First Meeting with the Client

Bette LaSere Erickson and Mary Deane Sorcinelli

*F*aculty make contact with instructional consultants for a variety of reasons. Among the calls we recently received, for example, were the following:

I'm wondering if you can help me with a problem I'm having in my large class. Students talk constantly, and I find it very distracting. And some students complain that they can't hear. Does anyone else have this problem? What should I do?

Do you have a minute to talk? I'm thinking about trying some new assignments this semester, and I'd like to know what you think before I commit myself in the syllabus.

I'm going to be teaching freshmen for the first time in years, and I thought you might be able to help me avoid making some terrible mistakes.

One of my colleagues suggested I talk to you. Can I set up an appointment?

I attended your workshops in August, and I really got a lot out of them. You mentioned then that you work with faculty during the semester, that you observe their classes and get feedback from students. Do you have time to do that for me this semester?

The first thing to note about consulting with faculty is that *they* start the process, and they start in different places. Although we can identify questions we typically ask and issues we usually discuss early in our consultations, our initial meetings vary considerably from one person to the next depending on what faculty want to discuss.

The way we conduct the first consultation meeting also varies depending on how comfortable that instructor appears to be. Although consultation services are available on a voluntary basis on most campuses, faculty volunteer to work with us on their teaching more or less freely. Those who request consultation after attending a workshop or participating in some of our other activities already have some basis for trust; they are usually ready and eager to get down to the business of talking about their courses and their students. This is not always true for faculty who call because they're not happy about student evaluations or because a dean or department chair has urged them to contact us. Understandably, these faculty often want to talk more generally about teaching—to find out what sort of people we are, what beliefs we hold, and to what extent we can be trusted to appreciate them—before they say too much about their particular concerns.

Keeping in mind that faculty call on us with different agendas and different levels of trust and confidence in us, establishing a working relationship is an important early concern. Because we find that easier to do in person, we usually try to schedule at least one face-to-face meeting with faculty at the outset.

Agenda for the First Meeting

Although our consulting styles tend to be informal and conversational, we nonetheless have an agenda for the first meeting. We want to find out what brought the instructor to us and as much as we can about the course he or she wants to discuss. At the same time, we want to share enough about ourselves and our beliefs to assure faculty that we really do believe there is more than one way to teach effectively, that we're interested in helping them find strategies and methods that work for them, and that we can be trusted. And, of course, we want to plan next steps.

We typically begin by asking an open-ended question, one that invites the instructor to establish the starting point for our work together. *What's on your mind? What brings you here? How are your classes going? What is going on in your teaching? What would you like to talk about?* Responses vary, of course, and set these meetings going in different directions. Some want us to look at a syllabus or an assignment or an exam. Others want to talk about activities for getting students more actively involved, or they want to try some collaborative learning activities, or they want to find ways to monitor students learning more closely. Still others might need to talk about a negative relationship with a chair or stresses at home before they are ready to talk about teaching. We try to tailor our initial conversation based on faculty responses to our opening questions.

Although our initial meetings with faculty often take

off in different directions, they nonetheless eventually converge on a common point. Regardless of whether we're asked to review a syllabus or to brainstorm involvement activities or to find out how a course is going, we usually need to know more about their courses and their students if we are to help. Sooner or later, then, the first meeting finds us asking questions about the context for the course, about the students who enroll, and about goals, methods, and evaluation procedures.

Again, we start with an open-ended request, something like *Can you tell me more about the course?* Not only does the open-ended question allow faculty to tell the stories of their courses in their own ways, but what they choose to talk about reveals something about what they deem important for us to know. We ask follow-up questions such as those included in Appendix A to fill in the gaps, and we almost always ask to see copies of course materials—the syllabus, the texts, discussion questions or activities, assignments, quizzes and exams. Such materials—especially the questions posed in the text, for class discussion, and on evaluation measures provide pretty good indicators of what actually goes on in a course and reveal the extent to which course goals, instructional activities, and evaluation procedures are integrated.

Collecting Information

Time for the first meeting often runs out before we've learned as much as we'd like to know about how faculty think about their courses. Sometimes we need to schedule a second meeting to talk more about the course before discussing other consultation activities. More often, we assume we can continue conversations about the course and simultaneously begin collecting other information. In any case, before the first meeting concludes, we discuss what our next steps will be and schedule those.

For faculty who contacted us wanting to find out how their courses are going, scheduling next steps requires deciding what information to collect and when to collect it. In addition to reviewing course materials, we usually try to observe at least one class, to videotape another, and to collect feedback from students. We press for scheduling these activities quickly—within a week, if possible—because the sooner we complete these assessment procedures, the more time is left for addressing whatever concerns they might reveal. At the same time, we try to be sensitive to faculty reactions. If a person seems uneasy, we might suggest "Maybe I could sit in on a class and we could meet afterwards to discuss it. Then we can decide what other information you might like to have." We are likely to jettison any activity about which an instructor has

serious misgivings. For example, watching videotapes of their classes is an extremely valuable experience for many, but being videotaped is very distressing—even debilitating—to others.

Not all requests for consultation lead directly to comprehensive assessment activities or to commitments to collaborate over time. Faculty sometimes ask, for example, that we observe a single class and provide feedback afterwards. These are somewhat troublesome requests because it's difficult to say anything important—never mind, accurate—about a class without knowing how students are reacting. We've also found that relying solely on observed behavior is frequently misleading. On the other hand, a single observation may be all a person wants to risk. Talking about expectations for the class and for the feedback session afterward can make the observation and feedback more productive. Key questions might include: *What do you hope will happen during class? What have you asked students to do as preparation? What should they be doing during class? What do you hope students will take away from the session? How is this class similar to or different from most class meetings? Is there anything in particular that you'd like me to focus on during class?*

In other cases, initial requests to brainstorm ideas or to review course materials often lead to continuing collaboration. Sharing what we knew about our freshmen—the initial request of one professor—led to a semester-long project in which we tried to track how students reacted to course activities and what they learned from them. Going over a syllabus with another led to a collaborative effort to experiment with different strategies for helping students learn from reading, and to assess the results. Brainstorming about activities or assignments or policies on a variety of matters often leads to visiting classes in which faculty try them out, collecting feedback from students about how they work. Sometimes, we plan and schedule these semester-long activities during the first meeting. It's possible to do that when, for example, faculty become interested in monitoring student learning from particular kinds of activities or schedule activities one step at a time. Visiting a class and providing feedback afterward often leads to planning another classroom experiment and another visitation. Whether the commitment is to work together for an entire semester or to visit a single class, we try to schedule the next step during the first meeting.

Confidentiality

Sometime during the first meeting, we make it a point to explain our policies about confidentiality. On both our campuses, any data we collect belong to the instructor.

Although instructors may do what they wish with information we collect, we cannot share it with anyone without explicit permission from the instructor. While most campuses have a similar policy, there are some differences in the details. On one of our campuses, for example, the consultant does offer to prepare a descriptive report for faculty, outlining the data collected, the strengths and areas for improvement identified, the strategies employed for improvement, and the results of the process. Because these reports reflect a relatively careful and comprehensive view of their teaching, many faculty choose to submit these reports in tenure dossiers or annual reviews. On the other campus the Faculty Senate has stipulated that such letters may not be included in personnel files because the absence of such letters might be misconstrued as a lack of interest in teaching. Obviously each campus culture is different so faculty (and the consultant) need to be clear from the outset about who will own the data, what kinds of reports might be produced, and how requests for data from chairs or personnel committees might be handled.

Over the years, we've found that some combination of the above strategies help to create a useful and productive first meeting. Ultimately though, if you can begin to establish a collaborative relationship and to develop plans for consultation that grow out of the elements of teaching, learning, and academic life that are of concern to the instructor, you are off to a good start.

Appendix A
Questions for the First Meeting

The following is a series of questions for use in the first meeting. You need not ask every question; in fact, you will want to pick and choose among them, depending on the needs and concerns of the faculty member with whom you are meeting. We have found that an extended initial interview can prove to be of value not only to you but also to the faculty member being interviewed. When asked to examine and clarify their values, attitudes, and approaches to teaching, faculty members often report that they find the task both enjoyable and beneficial.

Questions about the course:
1. What course do you want to talk about? What can you tell me about it?
2. How does the course fit in the curriculum? Do students take it for general education credit? Is it an elective or a requirement for the major? Are there prerequisites?
3. What do you hope students will learn in the course? What topics are included? What should students be able to do with their knowledge of those topics?
4. What do you expect students to do as preparation for the class? Do students generally come to class prepared in the way you expect?
5. What about evaluation procedures? How do you measure their learning? What are tests, quizzes, papers, and other assignments like? What counts toward their final grades? How much?

Questions about students:
1. What can you tell me about the students who enroll in this course? What about their backgrounds, preparation, majors, motivations? Do students who take this course seem fairly similar in their learning styles or are they widely different?
2. If we could eavesdrop on students describing this course, what might we hear? How do you think they'd describe the course goals and your expectations? What would they say about class meetings and assignments? What would they say about evaluation procedures?
3. Is there anything about the course that students find especially challenging? Interesting?
4. What kind of relationship with students do you try to establish? How satisfied are you with your relationships with students?
5. Have you modified your teaching in any way because of the needs of students coming here?

Questions about the instructor:
1. How long have you been teaching? What's one of the best teaching experiences you can remember? What's one of the worst?
2. How long have you taught this course? How have you changed the course since the first time you taught it? Any recent changes?
3. What do you think are your teaching strengths?
4. What would you like to improve or change in your teaching?
5. What would you like us to focus on this semester?

5. Collecting Information Using Class Observation

Karron Lewis

"Classroom observation gives us a view of
the climate, rapport, interaction, and
functioning of the classroom available
from no other source."

Evertson & Holley, (1981, p. 90)

*T*hough classroom observations are extremely time-consuming, in many cases they are a very necessary part of instructional consultation (Lewis, 1986). In this chapter we will look at: (1) why classroom observations are an important part of instructional consultation, (2) the types of information that can be obtained through in-class observations, (3) integrating observation data into the consultation process, (4) discussing the observation process with faculty members, (5) some characteristics of effective in-class observers, (6) some of the limitations of in-class observations, and (7) some "tools" that might be used to help guide one's in-class observations.

Why Are In-Class Observations an Important Part of Instructional Consultation?

In-class observations can provide a wealth of information about what is affecting the teaching-learning process. Simpson, Dalgaard and Parker (1982) indicate that there are "four major steps in the consultation process: (1) developing an understanding of the factors which the instructor views as critical to successful teaching; (2) comparing what the instructor claims to do with what is actually done, by means of observation, student interviews, and consultation; (3) exploring and using alternative teaching strategies based on the instructor's new conceptualization; (4) evaluating the 'success' of new concepts and strategies in helping to create an instructional

environment consistent with desired educational outcomes" (p. 183). Direct in-class observation plays an integral part in steps two and four.

In my more than 15 years as an instructional consultant, I have found that faculty members are usually profoundly interested in receiving feedback from in-class observations. Through my notes, observation checklists and forms, they are able to catch a glimpse of what actually happens in their classroom without having to bring in a videotape recorder—which many find obtrusive. They also have an opportunity to think about and discuss why they are doing what they are doing; not something most of them do frequently. Because the teaching-learning process is so complex, it is difficult to get a complete picture of what is happening and why, unless one has access to an outside observer.

Without some knowledge of what actually happens in a faculty member's classroom, it is difficult to correctly interpret some of the comments you might read on student evaluations. For example some students in a class might indicate that they think the faculty member doesn't respect their contributions and only accepts one point of view, that is, her own. After observing one or two classes, you discover that her verbal interactions are rather abrupt and that she tends to re-state student comments and then pose questions or offer alternative explanations. By encouraging her to give some positive reinforcement to the student making the comments and modify the way in which she states her own remarks, she can probably get the students to see that she is trying to help them broaden their thinking skills rather than "putting them down." Without actually witnessing the teacher-student exchanges it is almost impossible to help the faculty member address this problem.

L. Dee Fink notes, "The quality of the teacher's classroom behavior also has a major effect on the students' reaction to the course on a day-to-day basis. This refers to characteristics such as the clarity of their explanations, the enthusiasm they show for the subject, the rapport they develop with students, and the degree to which they are organized and prepared for class on a regular basis" (1984, p. 111). In addition, this quality is affected by several other contexts such as: (1) the characteristics of the classroom and when the course is scheduled, (2) the relationship between the teacher and the students and between the students and the teacher, (3) the departmental or institutional actions and attitudes toward teaching, and (4) the activities and events taking place in the teacher's non-professional life (Fink, 1984).

Information That Can be Obtained Through In-Class Observations

"A dilemma that faces the observer is the tendency to make inferences or draw conclusions from scanty evidence not necessarily supported by other data" (Boehm and Weinberg, 1977, 10). Thus, observers need to focus on observable behaviors when acquiring data from in-class observations. From those observable behaviors, inferences may then be made by the consultant and faculty member together as to what they mean or imply. In addition, observers need to choose observation techniques that will result in "the collection, analysis, and presentation of accurate, objective, useful, and persuasive data which can help teachers to change their own behavior" (Acheson, 1981, 1). Let's look at some of the kinds of information one can obtain from in-class observations:

Use of media. Media can enhance teaching or, if used incorrectly, can interfere with learning. The physical skills needed to use the media can be observed (for example, Does the instructor know how to turn on the overhead projector? Does the instructor stand in front of the image, blocking students view? Does the instructor write large enough and clearly enough on the board for students in the back of the room to read what is written?) as well as effective use of the chosen media to enhance the lecture or discussion (for example, Does the instructor have too much on the overhead transparency? Is the image on the screen large enough to read easily? Do the words or images help students understand the concepts being discussed?). The variety of media used can be observed (for example, slides, overhead projector, computer generated images, video-or audio-tape, and so forth) and their appropriateness for that particular lesson can be discussed.

Speaking style. An instructor's speaking style can enhance or detract from learning in a class. An observer can note the volume, pitch, expressiveness and intensity of an instructor's voice. Vocal mannerisms such as "uh"

or "ok" can also be noted. I worked with one faculty member who always sounded like he was bored with the class and the content. The observable manifestations of this apparent boredom were that he spoke very softly, his body was not held erect, and his eyes were often half shut. Though the content of the course was inherently very interesting, this lack of vocal and physical energy rubbed off on the students, some of whom fell asleep.

Variety of teaching techniques used. Teaching is not necessarily standing in the front of the classroom and talking. Because many faculty members have not been exposed to other teaching techniques, that may be what they think teaching is. An observer can note the use of questioning, small group techniques, case study techniques, and other techniques and document student reaction to these different techniques.

Non verbal gestures and mannerisms. Sometimes an instructor's unintentional gestures or non-verbal mannerisms detract from the teaching-learning process. We've all seen the instructor who jingles the change in his pocket or the one who paces back and forth and back and forth. Other mannerisms that can sometimes be distracting are: pushing hair back from face, sliding glasses up on nose, scratching (head or other areas), playing with a piece of chalk or a pencil, looking at the floor or ceiling when answering a question (or throughout the whole class session), and so forth. Observers who document the number of times these things happen provide substantial evidence that such gestures or mannerisms need to be modified. On the other hand, non-verbal gestures used appropriately can provide emphasis and heightened meaning to the words being said. These should also be noted by the observer.

Teacher/student rapport. Though this cannot be observed directly, one can infer good or poor rapport from the student and instructor interactions (verbal and non-verbal). An instructor who has developed a good rapport with the class typically talks to the students before and after class, asks questions of the students during class, and listens intently to student comments and questions. This instructor probably knows the names of most, if not all, of the students and calls on them by name. Poor rapport is often evidenced when the instructor and students don't talk before and after class, when the instructor talks "down" to the students, and when students aren't given an opportunity to ask questions or participate in other ways during the class session.

Organization of content. In lower-division courses and courses in the observer's area of expertise, it is usually easy to determine whether or not the content is presented in an organized manner and what the organizational form is. This becomes more difficult as the courses become more specialized. Nevertheless, even in advanced or specialized courses, if the observer takes notes and records what seems to be the most important points, these can be discussed with the instructor and compared with notes taken by the students to help the instructor analyze the structure and organization of the content discussed.

Attentiveness and note-taking. The attentiveness of students can be observed fairly accurately. (Heads on desks, eyes closed, reading other materials and the like are all indications of inattentiveness.) Notetaking activities can also be monitored and frantic notetaking or no notetaking can provide clues about the pace and complexity of the material being covered.

Student participation levels. Noting the number of students who participate and which students participate most can be especially informative for faculty members who are using discussion and case study techniques. Verbal flow charts (discussed later under observation tools) can be used to determine such things as: Does the instructor call on female and male students equally? Are students allowed to talk to each other, or does all of the interaction begin and end with the instructor? Do one or two students dominate the discussion? Since active student participation promotes learning, focusing on this aspect of the classroom interaction is very important.

Instructor utilization of physical space. The physical layout of a classroom can enhance or detract from effective teaching and learning depending on how the instructor utilizes that space. Long narrow rooms with desks bolted to the floor and one blackboard in the front will require a different kind of teaching style than one with movable chairs and tables and blackboards on two or three of the walls. Where does the instructor spend most of his/her time? How does the physical layout make it more difficult or relatively easy for students to work in small groups? What does the instructor do to reduce the "distance" between him/her and the students in the back of the room to bring them into discussions and make them feel they are a part of the class? Are there any "blind" spots (e.g., desks behind pillars, lighting on the boards, physical distance from the front of the room) that make it more difficult for students to see and hear what is going on? How comfortable or uncomfortable are the chairs/desks for a 50-minute class vs. a 75-minute class or a three-hour class? Often these things aren't even considered by instructors until they find them to be a problem.

Integrating Observation Data into the Consultation Process

The instructional consultation process varies somewhat from consultant to consultant and from institution to institution. What is described below is one institution's version of integrating data into the consultation process.

Before going to a classroom to observe, consultants typically spend time with the faculty member getting to know them, analyzing past student evaluation data and comments, looking at the syllabus and objectives for the course, and possibly reviewing the textbook(s). Prior to my first observation, I always ask faculty members if there are any things in particular that they want information about. Often they will cite something students have said about their presentation style or lack of organization and I try to focus on that to make sure I can provide descriptions of the relevant action(s) and perhaps some alternatives to discuss with them at the end of the class.

Since one classroom observation does not give a representative picture of the variety of teaching and learning activities that occur in a class, I always try to observe a class at least three times, often sequentially. By observing sequential classes I am able to see the transition (or lack thereof) from one class to the next, and I get a good sense of whether or not the faculty member's stated objectives are being met in class. I also ask the faculty member what the students are supposed to do to prepare for the classes and I attempt to do those things too (for example, read the chapter, watch a video, and so forth).

All of this pre-observation information helps me decide what tools I might use to ensure that the data gathered reflects the faculty member's concerns. While there are a wealth of tools from which one can choose, they can be broadly categorized as follows. (Examples of each of these types of tools are appended to this chapter.)

Narrative systems. These systems contain no preset categories. An attempt is made to record broad segments of behavior using the syntax of those being observed, for example, *In-Class Observation Form*, field notes, diaries.

Descriptive systems. These systems usually have preset categories but call for the collection of detailed descriptions within each category with attention to the context and multiple aspects of the behaviors observed, for example, *First Class Observation Form, Music Ensemble Teaching Analysis Form.*

Category systems. These types of systems contain closed, preset categories which are used to tally (descriptive) or rate (evaluate) samples of behavior, for example, *Cognitive Interaction Analysis System* (CIAS), checklists, rating scales, selective verbatim techniques.

Technological systems. These systems can be used to record events verbatim, for example, videotape, audio tape, photographs.

Visual systems. These systems contain a diagram or drawing made by the observer which is used to tally teacher-student interactions, illustrate visualized concepts, depict student- or teacher-produced objects, for example, seating chart records, discussion flow charts, drawings of student artwork or a demonstration apparatus.

Usually, I use a narrative system during my first in-class visit because such methods provide a great deal of flexibility concerning what is recorded and when it is written down. Then, depending on the faculty member's concerns and taking into account what I see during the first observation, I may select another tool to use during my next two visits. As soon as possible after each observation (preferably immediately after class) I try to get together with the faculty member to provide some reinforcement for things well done and briefly discuss one or two things I noticed that related to the student comments. Then, after each class I make copies of my notes to send to the faculty member along with a brief description of what I saw happening in the class. I also send copies of any checklists, rating scales or special observation forms that I used. I ask the faculty member to call with any questions or comments about what I've written.

After attending three classes, I ask the faculty member to make an appointment so we can analyze my observations together and determine what might be most productive to work on. We choose one or two things, determine how change might be accomplished (for example, notes to self in big letters, rehearsing lectures beforehand, practicing writing larger on the board, more eye contact with the students, and so on), decide how long the faculty member wants to work on these changes before I return to class to observe again, and set a date for the next observation. Then, the cycle begins again.

Whenever possible, it is invaluable to show evidence of change by using checklists or rating scales, along with your notes. The progressive movement of check marks from one column to another or ratings from a lower rating to a higher one, tend to make an impression on the faculty member and show visual evidence of success. Because changing the way one teaches is often a slow painstaking process, any evidence you can provide that the changes are really making a difference is very valuable. (Note: This is also an excellent way to document your impact on the teaching of a particular faculty member.)

Most consultants decide which observation techniques to use and what to help the faculty member focus on based on student feedback and evidence of student learning. Usually I get student feedback shortly after my first set of three observations to verify that what I am seeing is similar to what they are experiencing. (Often I use the TABS—Teaching Analysis By Students—short form for the student feedback because it provides quantitative as well as qualitative data.) I like to get feedback from the students again after the instructor has had some time to work on the skills and techniques we've identified. Usually, this latter feedback is more positive than what was gathered the first time. (See Chapters 6 through 8 for other methods of collecting information from students.)

Discussing the Observation Process with Faculty Members

Prior to going into an instructor's classroom, it is a good idea to discuss the logistics (for example, where the observer will sit) and how or whether the observer will be introduced to the students. I find my presence in the classroom and finding a way to explain my presence to the students can be somewhat traumatic for some faculty members. (One client asked me to say that I was doing research on different teaching styles rather than to tell the students I was consulting with him.) Also, because I tend to write continually, I warn the faculty members of that so they won't think I'm finding a rash of inadequate things to write down.

After the first time I observe a class, especially if the class is rather small, faculty members often say that my presence made them nervous. Usually that nervousness is apparent only to them and not to the students or to me. I always reassure them that they "didn't look nervous" and they generally report that they become less and less nervous each time I come.

After an observation, most of the faculty with whom I have worked are very interested in seeing my notes, checklists, and comments concerning what happened in the class. A majority of them immediately want to see the checklists or rating scales (if used) because this provides a very quick idea of what I thought was done well and what might need work. Next, they look for the organization of the notes I take as well as their content completeness. Most are surprised at the completeness and detail of my notes and many have said the notes reassure them that they actually are conveying the ideas they had hoped they were. Finally, they move to reading my comments on things that I observed relating to the student behavior, teacher mannerisms, and so forth. They often find this information most helpful in the long run, because it usually focuses on teaching techniques and behaviors. (I frequently use the *In-class Observation Form*, Appendix A, for recording my notes, the time, and additional comments during my first observation.)

As a consultant in a large research-oriented university, I find that a number of my clients prefer that my observations be as objective as possible. They seem to like some of the checklists and rating scales as much or more than my written notes. This phenomenon may not be true in other types of institutions where research is stressed much less. I find that this phenomenon also varies somewhat depending on the faculty member's discipline; for example, Liberal Arts or Fine Arts faculty seem to prefer narratives and visual systems while those in the hard sciences often prefer numerical data. The main thing to keep in mind is that the instrument or approach used during the observation must suit your purposes, the instructor's learning style and/or discipline, and the culture of your institution.

Some Characteristics of Effective In-Class Observers

As human beings, we are always observing things in a total perspective. Seldom do we focus on the "way in which a bird hops," rather we just note the total movement. This is one of the main things we have to overcome as we prepare to observe faculty and students in a classroom setting. It is very difficult to move from focusing on everything to focusing "only on those specific behaviors which, when isolated, might be the key to gaining insight, to changing a behavior or to solving a problem" (Acheson, 1981, p. 1). We must learn to use techniques that will help us identify and record significant behaviors that can be heard and seen in a learning environment.

One of the first steps in becoming an effective in-class observer is to "discover experientially the difference between random and focused observation, and descriptive and judgmental observation" (Hilsen & Rutherford, 1991, p. 253). Focused, descriptive observations can lead to changes in behavior, whereas random, judgmental observations often make the faculty member defensive. For example, you might say "I had trouble following your organization because you didn't use sequential numerals and letters when you wrote the main topics on the board" rather than "Your lecture was very unorganized; you need to work on that." Practice noting and writing down behaviors of teachers and students in as much detail as possible. From these behaviors, inferences can then be made by the faculty member. For example, rather than just writing "the students looked bored," you can add "because some were reading materials from other classes, some were sleeping, some were drawing pictures in their notes," and so forth.

After observing classes for many years, Hilsen and Rutherford (1991) have developed a list of some of the behaviors of effective classroom observers.

These include but are not limited to:

a. Get to class early and observe student and teacher entrances to determine their relationship.
b. Note classroom environment, physical setting, and atmosphere.
c. Take notes on process (organization, techniques, format, delivery, and so on).
d. Quantify as much as possible:
   - Record communication patterns—for example, gender of students asking and answering questions, level of questions being asked, teacher-group, teacher-student, student-student, and so forth (using the *Cognitive Interaction Analysis System* or other system—see section under "Tools").
   - Count number of student questions, responses, input.
   - Calculate "wait-time."
e. Note facial expressions and body language of teacher and students.
f. Watch class disperse. Note whether anyone stays after to talk to the teacher and how the teacher responds. Note groups that form to discuss doing homework together, and so forth.
g. Give brief positive reinforcement to teacher after class with thanks for asking you to come and observe.

In addition, effective classroom observers have a variety of techniques and "tools" in their repertoire. Depending on the class being observed, the discipline, the objectives of the teacher, and the like, one may need to vary the kind of data gathered. The "tools" provided later in this chapter are a sample of ways to gather "hard data." Examples of when each might be appropriately used will be presented with each one.

Some Limitations of In-Class Observations

In-class observations provide a wealth of information that really cannot be acquired any other way. However, there are some limitations and cautions to keep in mind. First and foremost, each of us approaches classroom observation with our own biases, training and beliefs about effective teaching and our observations only represent one version of what happened. Wilkerson says, "In order to serve as an effective observer of the teaching behavior of another person, you must first carefully examine your beliefs about effective teaching and learning. Before the observing, you might ask yourself the following questions:

- What do I think is essential in the classroom process for learning to occur?
- Is there anything distinctive about this particular subject or these students that might alter the usual process of learning?
- When I say effective teaching, what standards am I using to determine effectiveness, e.g., student learning, a set of teaching behaviors, student enjoyment, and so on?" (1988, p. 96).

Another thing to keep in mind when observing is that, while many things may be happening at once, we are only capable of observing one, or at most two, activities/incidents at one time. We may scan the students to determine attentiveness or note-taking activities, or we may focus on the instructor to note behaviors and write down what is being discussed. We cannot do both. Thus, knowing what questions the instructor has about his or her teaching and being cognizant of the instructional and observational objectives for that class session can help us determine which behaviors and activities are most important in this particular situation.

To alleviate as much bias as we can, it is imperative that we try to reduce the impact of our biases on the process by:

- Involving the instructor in planning for the observation (for example, what are the objectives, teaching philosophy, questions to be answered, and so on),
- Collecting data about the classroom and what happens in it from a variety of sources (for example, multiple observation methods, student input, videotapes, and so on),
- Providing continuous feedback to the instructor about what was observed and together interpreting the impact of those behaviors and activities on student learning.

Tools

In their review of observational methodologies in the third edition of the *Handbook of Research on Teaching*, Evertson and Green (1986) describe four broad types of observational tools from which one might select depending upon the objectives and goals of the observation. Each of these broad types enables the observer to collect descriptive or evaluative data. I have added a fifth type, visual systems, which I find useful in some situations.

Brief descriptions of these were given earlier and they are listed here to refresh your memory.

- Narrative systems
- Descriptive systems
- Category systems
- Technological systems
- Visual systems

Samples of each of these types of systems along with a brief description of how they might be used are provided on the following pages.

Narrative Systems

These systems contain no preset categories. The observer makes an attempt to record broad segments of behavior using the syntax of those being observed. Other types of narrative systems include field notes and diaries. The example included is the *In-Class Observation Form* (Appendix A). Many people with whom I have talked use a system similar to this, though most do not have a form for recording their notes and comments. This form, appropriate for use in almost any situation, includes a section for recording the time, the lecture notes, and observer comments.

Time. Most people say they try to record the time every fifteen minutes or whenever the topic or activity changes. This provides information about the amount of time spent on an activity or a particular topic of the lecture. Knowing how much time elapsed for such things can help faculty members gauge how much time they will need for similar activities/topics or it can let them know that they are spending too much time on some things and not enough on others.

Lecture notes. The section for lecture notes is usually used to record notes taken as though you were a student in the class. This provides information about the organization of the lecture or discussion and where there may have been gaps in logic or unclear transitions. I often record instructor and student questions in this area too.

Observer comments. This area of the form is used to record observations about the instructor's presentation style (for example, voice volume and expression, gestures), the use of AV aids (for example, size of print on overheads or on the blackboard, appropriateness of videos or films, organization of blackboard/overhead presentation), instructor/student rapport (for example, reinforcement, non-verbal cues, willingness to ask and answer questions), and the like.

Descriptive Systems

These systems usually have preset categories but call for the collection of detailed descriptions within each category with attention to the context and multiple aspects of the behaviors observed. The examples included are:

1. **First Class Observation Form. (Appendix B)** This form may be used during the first observation done in a classroom to help the observer focus on some of the general aspects that influence the classroom climate. It also provides a way for the observer to document the type of class (for example, number of students, level of students, course title, and so on) and provide a brief description of the physical facilities. (Note: I typically use this form and the In-class Observation Form during my first class visit.)

2. **Classroom Visit Instrument (Consolidated).** (Appendix C) This form provides a number of general categories followed by some examples of behaviors and activities to look for. The observer is then free to describe what was observed as it relates to each of the broad categories.

3. **Musical Ensemble Teaching Analysis Form.** (Appendix D) Though this form is also a type of "category system", it prompts the observer to provide detailed descriptions of behaviors that justify each rating. In this respect, it is quite descriptive. (Note: Because this form deals with a very specialized field and teaching method, some knowledge of that field and the methods used is desirable in order to provide the most effective feedback.)

Category Systems

Category systems contain closed, preset categories which are used to tally (descriptive) or rate (evaluate) samples of behavior, for example, objective observation systems, checklists, rating scales, selective verbatim techniques.

The examples included here are:

1. **Lecture Evaluation Form.** (Appendix E) This form is a rating scale with some space left to the side for written comments. This kind of form can be used over several observations to show change (hopefully improvement) over time. The items for this form are from Harry Murray's (1983) list of effective teaching behaviors based on research in social science courses and are somewhat restrictive in nature, but I find it works well and may alert instructors to things they could be doing to make their lectures more effective.

2. **Checklist of Teaching Skills.** (Appendix F) This form is a checklist with space for written comments. Though this form is very long, it provides a broad look at the skills typically associated with effective teachers. I have added the category "Sometimes" between "Yes" and "No." This allows me to indicate to the instructor that, yes, they did this, but it was not done consistently.

3. **Teaching Through Discussion.** (Appendix G) This form is also a checklist with spaces for clarification and elaboration of what was observed. A unique part of this form is the Attachment page on which jargon and possible unclear terms are defined. This enables all observers who use this form to understand what the developers of the form were thinking when they wrote the various entries.

4. **Reinforcement Analysis Form.** (Appendix H) This form is a selective verbatim form. Using this form the observer focuses almost exclusively on the kinds of verbal and non-verbal reinforcement used by the instructor. This form is especially useful when a class has been videotaped.

5. **Cognitive Interaction Analysis System (Expanded Version).** (Appendix I) Objective observation systems such as this one have been used to gather data in classrooms since the early 1970's. Though some people find them a little unwieldy, once learned, they can provide a great deal of specific data about what happens in the classroom. I find this particular system to be very helpful if, after my first general observation, I identify one or more of the following situations:

   - the instructor is not using "wait time" effectively,
   - the instructor is asking a series of questions rather than just one at a time,
   - the instructor asks a good higher level question, but when no one answers immediately, changes the question to a lower level,
   - the instructor tends to provide few verbal cues or examples.

Faculty members typically are very impressed with the amount of data collected with this system and the numerically designated categories provide some "hard data" that is especially appreciated by faculty in the sciences and engineering. A detailed description of this system and how it is used may be found in Lewis and Povlacs (1988), Lewis (1986), and Lewis and Johnson (1990).

Technological Systems

These systems can be used to record events verbatim. The verbatim records are then usually analyzed using some of the other systems discussed here. Examples of these systems are:

1. **Videotape recordings.** Videotape recordings enable observers to preserve both the visual and verbal aspects of a class session. These recordings may then be viewed by both the observer and the instructor and critiqued using one of the other types of pencil and paper forms. One of the big advantages of videotaping a class session is that the videotape can then be looked at several times in order to critique specific skills or activities. Videotapes may also be saved to show progress over time.

2. **Audiotape recordings.** Audiotape recordings are somewhat less disruptive to a class session than are videotape recordings because the tape recorder can be placed on the desk at the front of the room. In addition, the instructor can audiotape him/herself for self-analysis. The audiotape can be played over and over or transcribed to facilitate analysis and can be saved to show progress over time. The main disadvantage is that there is no visual record of the class.

Visual Systems

These systems contain a diagram or drawing made by the observer which is used to tally teacher-student interactions, illustrate visualized concepts, depict student- or teacher-produced objects, and so forth. One example is included here.

1. **Interaction Diagram.** (Appendix J) When observing a case study or discussion oriented class session, it is useful to find out how the teacher interacts with the students and which students participate most often. A discussion flow chart may be used to diagram and keep track of this interaction. On the figure, the arrows show the direction of the interaction while the small parallel lines indicate the number of times such interaction occurred. This kind of chart can help the instructor see things such as: whether s/he is facilitating equal participation by all students; whether males or females are interacted with most often; whether students talk to each other and how much; and so forth.

References

Acheson, K. A. (1981). Classroom observation techniques. *IDEA Paper No. 4*, Center for Faculty Evaluation & Development: Kansas State University.

Boehm, A. E., & Weinberg, R. A. (1977). *The classroom observer: A guide for developing observation skills.* New York: Teachers College Press.

Evertson, C. M., & Green, J. L. (1986). Observation as inquiry and method. In M. C. Wittrock (Ed.), *Handbook of research on teaching (3rd ed.).* (pp. 162-163). New York: Macmillan Publishing.

Fink, L. D. (1984). The evaluation of college teaching. *To Improve the Academy, 3*, 109-118.

Hilsen, L., & Rutherford, L. (1991). Front line faculty development: Chairs constructively critiquing colleagues in the classroom. *To Improve the Academy, 10*, 251-269.

Lewis, K. G., (1986). Using an objective observation system to diagnose teaching problems. *The Journal of Staff, Program, & Organization Development, 4*(4), 81-90.

Lewis, K. G., & Johnson, G. R. (1990). *Monitoring your classroom communication skills.* (Unpublished, programmed workbook.) Austin, TX: Center for Teaching Effectiveness, The University of Texas at Austin.

Lewis, K. G., & Povlacs, J. T. (Eds.). (1988). *Face to face: A sourcebook of individual consultation techniques for faculty/instructional developers.* Stillwater, OK: New Forums Press.

Murray, H. G. (1983). Low inference classroom teaching behaviors and student ratings of college teaching affectiveness. *Journal of Educational Psychology, 75*, 138-139.

Simpson, D. E., Dalgaard, K. A., & Parker, C. A. (1982). Instructional improvement through individual consultation. *To Improve the Academy, 1*, 181-189.

Wilkerson, L. (1988). Classroom observation: The observer as collaborator. In E.C. Wadsworth (Ed.), *A handbook for new practitioners* (pp. 95-98). Stillwater, OK: New Forums Press.

Additional Readings

Bergquist, W. H., & Phillips, S. R. (1975). *A handbook for faculty development* : Vol. 1. Washington, DC: The Council for the Advancement of Small Colleges.

Bergquist, W. H., & Phillips, S. R. (1977). *A handbook for faculty development*: Vol. 2. Washington, DC: The Council for the Advancement of Small Colleges.

Flanders, N. A. (1970). *Analyzing teaching behavior.* Reading, MA: Addison-Wesley Publishing Company.

Johnson, G. R. (1987). Changing the verbal behavior of teachers. *The Journal of Staff, Program & Organization Development, 5*, 155-158.

Rosenshine, B., & Furst, N. (1973). The use of direct observation to study teaching. In R. M. W. Travers (Ed.), *Second handbook of research on teaching* (pp. 122-183). Chicago: Rand McNally.

Simon, A., & Boyer, E. G. (Eds.). (1970). *Mirrors for Behavior II: An anthology of observation instruments*: Vols. A & B. Philadelphia, PA: Classroom Interaction Newsletter. (ERIC No. ED 031 613).

Observation Tools

Available from the Center for Teaching Effectiveness, University of Texas at Austin, Main Building 2200, Austin, TX 78712-1111.

- *Questioning Skills Analysis Form* (category and descriptive)
- *Stimulus Variation Rating Form* (category - rating scale)
- *Music Private Lesson Teaching Analysis Form* (category - rating scale and descriptive)

- *Beginning Acting Class Feedback/Evaluation Form* (category - rating scale)
- *Oral Presentation Evaluation Form* (category - rating scale)

Available from the Faculty Development and Instructional Services Center, Appalachian State University, 155 Whitener Hall, Boone, NC 28608.

- *Teaching Through Lecture* (category - checklist)

Appendix A

In-Class Observation Form
Center for Teaching Effectiveness
The University of Texas at Austin

Instructor:_____   Date:_____

Course:_____   Time:_____

Room:_____   #Students:_____

Time	Lecture Notes	Observer Comments
Reprinted with permission.		

Appendix B

First Class Observation Form
Center for Teaching Effectiveness

Instructor: _____ Date:_____ Observer: _____

Course Number: _____ Title:_____ Meeting Time: _____

Level: ___ Freshman ___ Sophomore ___ Junior___ Senior ___Graduate_____

No. Students: _____ Building/Room #: _____ Description of Room:_____
_____

Where students congregate:_____

Subject for the Hour:_____
Method:

THE INSTRUCTOR:
    Speaking style:

    Use of movement/gestures:

    Enthusiasm:

    Handouts:

THE STUDENTS
    Attentiveness (beginning vs. end):

    Questions:

    Evidence of understanding:

    Notetaking:

GENERAL COMMENTS:

Appendix C

Classroom Visit Instrument (Consolidated)
University College
UndergraduatePrograms
Classroom Visit

Faculty Member:_____ Course & Section:_____

Date:_____Length of visit: _____ Place:_____ Visitor:_____

Number of students present: _____

Classroom: Note any inadequate aspects of the classroom (size, temperature, acoustics, lighting, etc.)

_____

_____

Instruction: Comment on the presentation of the material: points to be covered and their relevance to class session, knowledge of subject matter, organization of lecture, explanation of terms and concepts.

_____

_____

Instructor/Student Rapport: Comment on student involvement and interaction with the instructor: opportunities for students to ask questions, answers to questions, guidance of class discussion, openness to suggestions and ideas.

_____

_____

Style of Presentation: Comment on gestures, physical movement, pitch and tone of voice, eye contact with students, use of resources such as blackboard, audio-visual media, handouts and other materials, demonstrations, student presentations and group activities, and the integration of various elements of the class session.

_____

_____

Syllabus: Comment on the syllabus and other written materials provided by the instructor. (Please refer to the University College Syllabus Construction Handbook.)

_____

_____

General Comments: What part of the class seemed particularly to enhance the learning process? What specific suggestions can you give for improving this particular class?

_____

_____

From the University of Maryland University College Peer Visit Program Reprinted with permission.

Appendix D

Musical Ensemble Teaching Analysis Form

Instructor:_____   Date:_____

Class: _____   Observer:_____

5 - Strongly Agree	4 - Agree	3 - Disagree	2 - Strongly Disagree	1 - Not Applicable

The Instructor

1. Uses rehearsal time efficiently.
   (Please give examples of instructor behavior that made you rate as you did.)   1   2   3   4   5

2. Is well prepared for rehearsal.
   (Please give examples of instructor behavior that made you rate this as you did.)   1   2   3   4   5

3. The instructor's conducting technique effectively communicates musical ideas.
   (Please give examples of instructor behavior that made you rate this as you did.)   1   2   3   4   5

4. The choice of musical material is appropriate and challenging.
   (Please give examples of instructor behavior that made you rate this as you did.)   1   2   3   4   5

5. Challenges student to maximum achievement in rehearsals.
   (Please give examples of instructor behavior that made you rate this as you did.)   1   2   3   4   5

6. Challenges the students to maximum achievement in performance.
   (If you have not heard this ensemble in a performance, please omit this question.)   1   2   3   4   5

7. Is fair and impartial when dealing with the students.
   (Please give examples of instructor behavior that made you rate this as you did.)   1   2   3   4   5

8. Verbal instructions in rehearsals are concise and clear.
   (Please give examples of instructor behavior that made you rate this as you did.)   1   2   3   4   5

9. Instills a sense of pride in members of the ensemble. (Please give examples of instructor behavior that made you   1   2   3   4   5
   rate this as you did.)

10. Instructor showed enthusiasm about teaching this ensemble. (Please give examples of instructor behavior that   1   2   3   4   5
    made you rate this as you did.)

11. Taught materials and gave assignments consistent with the stated objectives of the ensemble. (Please give   1   2   3   4   5
    examples of instructor behavior that made you rate this as you did.)

The Ensemble

1. There are clearly stated objectives for the ensemble.   1   2   3   4   5
2. Materials used are consistent with the objectives.   1   2   3   4   5
3. Students appear to enjoy being in the ensemble. (Please give examples of student bahavior that made you rate   1   2   3   4   5
   this as you did.)

Primary Conductor Strengths:

Primary Conductor Weaknesses

Suggestions for improvement:

Form adapted from student Teacher/Course Evaluation - (Ensembles/Labs) used at Berklee College of Music. Adapted by the Center for Teaching Effectiveness, The University of Texas at Austin. Reprinted with permission.

Appendix E

Lecture Evaluation Form

Lecturer's Name _____   Date _____

Topic _____   Observer _____

Please mark an "X" in the space that best represents your evaluation of the lecture.

	Poor	Adequate	Good	Excellent
Enthusiasm				
Speaks expressively or emphatically				
Moves about while lecturing				
Gestures with hands and arms				
Shows facial expression				
Uses extemporaneous delivery				
Clarity				
Uses concrete examples of concepts				
Gives multiple examples				
Points out practical applications				
Stresses important points				
Repeats difficult ideas				
Interactions				
Addresses students by name				
Encourages questions and comments				
Talks with students after class				
Praises students for good ideas				
Asks questions of class				
Task Orientation				
Advises students regarding exams				
Provides sample exam questions				
Proceeds at good pace for topic				
Stays on the theme of the lecture				
States course objectives				
Rapport				
Friendly, easy to talk to				
Shows concern for student progress				
Offers to help students with problems				
Tolerant of other viewpoints				
Organization				
Puts outline of lecture on board				
Uses headings and subheadings				
Gives preliminary overview of lecture				
Signals transition to new topic				
Explains how each topic fits in				

Suggestions for improving lecture:

Center for Teaching Effectiveness, The University of Texas at Austin
Reprinted with permission.

Appendix F

Checklist of Teaching Skills*

Instructor:_____ Class_____

Observer:_____ Date:_____

Directions: Respond to each of the following statements by checking the blank which corresponds to your observation.

Yes = Observed   No = Not observed; would have been appropriate   NA = Not applicable

	Yes	No	NA	Comments
Importance and Suitability of Content				
1. Students seemed to have the necessary background to understand the lecture material.				
2. The examples used drew from students' experiences.				
3. When appropriate a distinction was made between factual materials and opinions.				
4. When applicable, appropriate authorities were cited to support statements.				
5. When appropriate, divergent viewpoints were presented.				
6. A sufficient amount of material was included in the lecture.				
Organization and Clarity				
7. Stated the purpose of the class session.				
8. Presented a brief overview of the content.				
9. Made explicit the relationship between today's and the previous class session.				
10. Defined new terms, concepts and principles.				
11. Arranged and discussed the content in a systematic and organized fashion.				
12. Asked questions periodically to determine whether too much or too little information was being presented.				
13. Presented clear and simple examples to clarify very abstract and difficult ideas.				
14. Used alternate explanations when necessary.				
15. Explicitly stated the relationships among various ideas.				
16. Periodically summarized the most important ideas.				
17. Slowed the word flow when ideas were complex and difficult.				
18. Did not often digress from the main topic.				
19. Summarized the main ideas.				
20. Related the day's material to upcoming sessions.				
Use of Media				
21. Writing on board/overhead/slides was legible.				
22. Information presented on board/overhead/slides was organized and easy to follow.				
23. The AV-materials used added to the students' comprehension of the concept(s) being taught.				
24. The AV-materials were handled competently (e.g., the instructor did not walk in front of the image for overhead or slide projector; the instructor spoke to the class, not the screen or board; etc.).				
Use of Questions				
25. Asked questions to see what the students knew about the lecture topic.				
26. Addressed questions to individual students as well as the group at large.				
27. Used questions to gain students' attention.				
28. Paused after all questions to allow students time to think of an answer.				
29. Encouraged students to answer difficult questions by providing cues or rephrasing.				
30. When necessary, asked students to clarify their questions.				
31. Asked probing questions if a student's answer was incomplete or superficial.				
32. Repeated answers when necessary so the entire class could hear.				
33. Received student questions politely and enthusiastically.				
34. Requested that very difficult, time-consuming questions of limited interest be discussed before or after class or during office hours.				

Teaching Skills Checklist - Continued

Interaction

	Yes	No	NA	Comments
35. Established and maintained eye contact with the class.				
36. Listened carefully to student comments and questions.				
37. Facial and body movements did not contradict speech or expressed intentions (e.g., waited for responses after asking for questions).				
38. Noted and responded to signs of puzzlement, boredom, curiosity, etc.				
39. Encouraged student questions.				
Individual Style				
40. Voice could be easily heard.				
41. Voice was raised or lowered for variety and emphasis.				
42. Speech was neither too formal nor too casual.				
43. Speech fillers (e.g., "ok now", "ahmm", etc.) were not distracting.				
44. Rate of speech was neither too fast nor too slow.				
45. Wasn't too stiff and formal in appearance.				
46. Wasn't too casual in appearance.				
47. Varied the pace of the lecture to keep students alert.				
48. Spoke at a rate which allowed students time to take notes.				

Comments:

* Adapted from material in Improving Your Lectures from the University of Illinois at Urbana-Champaign. Reprinted with permission.

Appendix G

Teaching Through Discussion
Faculty Development and Instructional Services Center
Appalachian State University
RESULTS OF THE SYSTEMATIC OBSERVATION:

Y= Yes   N= No   ⌐ No opportunity to observe   *= See attachment for example

MECHANICS

Y N 1. Group is appropriate size (< = 15).

Y N 2. Group is arranged so all can see and hear one another.

Y N 3. Instructor attends to the physical needs of the group.*
Needs observed:_____

Y N 4. Instructor usually speaks in a clear voice.

Y N 5. Instructor's verbal behaviors distract from discussion.*
Verbal behaviors observed: _____

Y N 6. Instructor usually maintains eye contact equally among students.*
Physical behaviors observed: _____

Y N 7. Instructor usually calls students by names.

Y N 8. Instructor's physical behaviors distract from discussion.*
Physical behaviors observed: _____

Y N 9. Instructor models good listening habits.*

PREPARATION

Y N 10. Instructor provides a common ground prior to discussion.*

Y N 11. Instructor uses specific means to assure that students come prepared.

ROLE OF TEACHER

Y N 12. Instructor states specific goals and objectives of the discussion at the beginning of the session.

Y N 13. Instructor states issues/topic at beginning of session.

Y N 14. Instructor uses specific means to involve students initially in the discussion.*
Method used: _____

Y N 15. Instructor paraphrases ambiguous comments for clarification.

Y N 16. Instructor repeats significant contributions for emphasis/reinforcement.

Y N 17. Instructor remains silent after some students' contributions.

Y N 18. Instructor sometimes uses nonverbal cues to direct discussion.*

Y N 19. Instructor admits not having an answer.

Y N 20. Instructor admits losing control of discussion.

Y N 21. Instructor periodically restates goals and objectives.

Y N 22. Instructor makes opportunities for all to participate.*

Y N 23. Instructor makes opportunities for quiet individuals to contribute.*

Y N 24. Instructor corrects wrong statements without penalizing contributor.

Y N 25. Instructor prevents or terminates discussion monopolies.*

Y N 26. Instructor accepts silence in the group.

Y N 27. Instructor encourages students to express differing opinions and to challenge each other.

Y N 28. Instructor mediates conflicts or differences in opinion.

Y N 29. Instructor voices own opinion later in discussion so as not to bias or dominate with own views.

Y N 30. Instructor encourages students to examine a variety of points of view before drawing conclusions or making judgments.

CONCLUSION

Y N 31. Instructor summarizes students' contributions.

Y N 32. Instructor draws together the various points made in contributions and relates them to the goal of the discussion.

Y N 33. Instructor helps students to relate discussion concepts learned in lecture, or to new learning situations, or to students' own lives, etc.

Observer's Comments:

Attachment to "Teaching Through Discussion"

<u>Examples of behaviors that may be observed:</u>

Question #3   "Needs observed" may include: the temperature of the room; ventilation; level of lighting; level of sound; acoustics; break in long sessions, etc.

Question #5   "Behaviors observed" may include: excessive clearing of throat; "fillers" such as "um", "you know", "well, like...", etc.

Question #8   "Movements observed" may include: excessive pacing, fidgeting, tapping, gesturing; playing with chalk, etc.

Question #9   "Good listening habits" may include: eye contact with the speaker; not interrupting the speaker; thwarting interrupters (e.g., by interrupting them and asking the original speaker to complete his/her thought); praising infrequent contributors when they do speak; "drawing out" reticent contributors with silence or by asking for elaborations, implications, etc.

Question #10   "Common ground" may include: pictures, slides, video film recordings, tapes, charts, flow charts, diagrams, maps; stories, personal anecdotes, current event items, assigned readings; or demonstrations, games, simulations, role-playing, debates, etc.

Question #11   "Specific means to insure that students come prepared" may include: a question about who did the reading/etc.; or may take the form of impromptu reports or summaries at the beginning of the session; or the instructor may do an activity in class to insure that all have experienced a common event.

Question #14   "Specific means to involve students initially in the discussion" may include: asking for a show of hands (i.e., pro and con regarding an issue) then asking specific students to defend/support their opinion; asking several students to paraphrase or summarize portions of the event; having students participate in an activity (i.e., simulation or role-play); breaking students into subgroups of 3 or 4 (to discuss a specific issue, generate a list, identify concepts, etc.), then have them report their results; going around the table to establish opinion; etc.

Question #18   "Nonverbal eyes" may include: looking, pointing, smiling, nodding, or maintaining eye contact; keeping silent.

Question #20   "Admits losing control of discussion" may include statements such as "How did we get here? or "A tangent has taken us too far from the major issue—let's get back to the original question." or "Although this is mildly interesting, it is not going to help you understand the topic at hand, which is—."

Question #22   "Makes opportunities for all to participate" may include: the items from Question #14.

Question #25   "Prevents or terminates discussion monopolies" may include statements such as "We've been hearing from the same people for 10 minutes now—Mary, with whom do you agree?" or "This seems to have turned into a debate between Jane and Fred..." or "Tom, you've given us several good points, but now let's hear what some others have to say."

Appendix H
Reinforcement Analysis Form

Instructor: _____   Date: _____

Class: _____   Observer: _____

Write the words and/or phrases used as reinforcers (praise) during the lesson.

Verbal Reinforcement   **# times said**

1. _____   _____
2. _____   _____
3. _____   _____
4. _____   _____
5. _____   _____
6. _____   _____
7. _____   _____
8. _____   _____

Non-Verbal Reinforcement

1. _____   _____
2. _____   _____
3. _____   _____
4. _____   _____
5. _____   _____
6. _____   _____

Number of times the teacher repeated a student's answer (to indicate acceptance of it, to make sure the whole class heard the answer, etc.)   _____

Number of times the teacher referred to a positive aspect of a student's previous answer. (Delayed Reinforcement)   _____

Number of times a student's answer should have been reinforced, but wasn't.   _____

Number of times instructor indicated student's answer was almost correct. (Qualified Reinforcement)   _____

Evaluation of ability to use reinforcement/praise effectively and at appropriate times.

Poor			Average		Excellent
1	2	3	4	5	

Center for Teaching Effectiveness, The University of Texas at Austin. Adapted from K. Lewis, et al. (1973). Microteaching: Gateway to Performance. Texas A&M University. Reprinted with permission.

5. Collecting Information Using Class Observation / 47

Appendix I

Cognitive Interaction Analysis System (Expanded Version)

1 - Accepting Student Attitudes
   1h - Use of Humor
   1f - Affective Instructor Comments

2 - Positive Reinforcement

3 - Repeating a Student Response
   3f - Giving Corrective Feedback
   3b - Building on a Student Response

4 - Asking Questions
   4c - Knowledge/ Comprehension Level
   4e - Application (Example) Level
   4a - Analysis Level
   4y - Synthesis Level
   4j - Evaluation (Judgment) Level
   4f - Affective Questions
   4s - Process or Structure Questions

4r - Rhetorical Questions
4p - Probing Questions

5 - Lecturing
   5v - Simultaneous Visual & Verbal
   Presentation
   5e - Using Examples/ Analogies
   5r - Reviewing
   5x - Answering a Student Question
   5m - Mumbling
   5t - Reading Verbatim from
   Text/Overhead/ Board/Slide

6 - Providing Cues
   6m - Focusing on Main Points
   6d - Giving Directions
   6c - Calling on a Student
   6s - Giving Assignments/Process
   6v - Cues with Visual Presentation

7 - Criticism of Student Answer/Behavior

8 - Cognitive Student Talk
   8c-8j - Answers to Teacher Questions
   8n - Student Doesn't Know Answer
   8q - Student Question
   8h - Student Laughter
   8g - Students Working in Groups
   8i - Students Working Individually

9 - Non-cognitive Student Talk

0 - Silence
   0b - Writing on Board/ Overhead
   w/o Talking
   0m - Mumbling (a general low roar)
   0l - Listening/Watching

Typical Sequence of CIAS Coding

Sequence	Comment
6s	This sequence indicates that the instructor began by giving the students an assignement (6s)
6s	or indicated a procedure which they should follow in completing an assignment.
6d	Directions for completing this process were then given (6d). The instructor then told students what
6d	they were going to be covering that day in lecture (6). This is followed by the instructor calling
6	on a student (6c) who then asks a question (8q).
6c	
8q	
4a	In this sequence the instructor asks a question which would be classified as being at the
4a	Analysis level (4a). The question is then followed by silence or "think time" (0), and finally,
0	the question is answered by a student (8a).
0	
8a	
8a	
8q	When the students ask a question, it is recorded as 8q. The instructor's answer to that question
8q	is recorded as 5x. This provides information about whether the instructor is
5x	spending adequate or too much time—which is more often the case—in answering each student's question.
5x	
4e	This sequence shows that the instructor asked a question at the application level (4e)
4e	and it was answered by a student (8e). The instructor then praised the studen's answer (e.g., "That's right Joe!"),
8e	repeated the student's answer so the rest of the class could hear it, and then used
8e	the student's answer to explain the concept further (3b).
8e	
2	
3	
3b	

Copyright 1990 by Lewis and Johnson. Reprinted with permission.

Cognitive Interaction Analysis Observation Form
Center for Teaching Effectiveness

Instructor:_____ Date:_____ Class:_____

No. Students: 22

Time: 9:04		Topic: Handing papers		
0	4s	4s	0	4s
6s	4s	4s	4s	4s
6s	0m	4s	4s	4s
0m	0m	4s	8s	0m
6s	4s	4s	0	0m
4s	4s	0m	4s	4s
0m	4s	4s	4s	4s
4s	4s	0m	4s	2f

Time: 9:06		Topic: (same)		
4s	4s	0m	6	6
4s	4s	6s	6	6
4s	0m	6s	0m	6
4s	0m	6	7	6
4s	8	6	7	0
0m	4s	6	7	0
0m	8	6	6	6
4s	4s	6	6	0

Time: 9:09		Topic: giving handouts		
0	6s	0	6s	5t
0	6s	5	5t	5
0	6s	5	5t	5
0	6s	5	5t	5
0	6	5	5t	5
6d	0	5	5t	5
0	0	5	5t	5
0	0	6s	5t	5

Time: 9:12		Topic: Going over assign		
5	5r	5	5	5
5	5r	5	5	6m
5	5	5	5	6m
5	5	5	5	5
5	5	5	5	5
5	5	5	5	5r
5	5	5	5	5r
5	5	5	5r	

Time 9:14		Topic: Prob. w/original		
5	5	5	6d	5
5	5	5	5	5
5	5	5	5	5
5	5	5	5	5
5	5	5	5	5
5	5	4r	5t	5
5	5	4r	5t	5
5	5	5	5t	5

Time: 9:16		Topic: (same)		
5	5	5v	5	5
5	5	5v	5	5
5	5	5v	4s	5
5	5	5v	4s	5
5	5	5	5	5
5	5v	5	5	5
5	5v	5	5	5
5	5v	5	5	5

Comments: Really could ask more questions. Students seem like they would enjoy participating more. Examples of the types of communication being discussed would help students understand the nuances of the forms.

NOTE: One category is recorded every three (3) seconds or whenever a change in the interaction occurs. Thus, each "block" of codes represents approximately 2 minutes of class time. When reading these codes you read down each column of numbers in each "block" and then go to the block below it; as illustrated by the arrows on the sheet above.

Cognitive Interaction Analysis Matrix
Second number of pair

Categories Tallies		1	2	3	4	5	6	7	8	9	0	Total
	1	4	0	1	3	1	1	0	1	0	0	11
	2	0	0	1	8	1	5	0	1	0	0	16
	3	2	7	19	25	8	4	0	5	0	1	71
	4	1	1	0	88	5	3	0	56	0	14	168
First Number of pairs	5	0	1	0	15	89	10	0	0	0	0	115
	6	0	0	0	15	6	89	0	0	0	0	116
	7	0	0	0	0	0	0	0	0	0	0	0
	8	3	7	50	6	1	1	0	28	0	0	96
	9	0	0	0	0	0	0	0	0	0	0	0
Total Tallies	0	1	0	0	8	4	3	0	5	0	4	25
		11	16	71	168	115	116	0	96	0	25	618
% Total Time		1.8	2.6	11.5	27.2	18.6	18.8	0	15.5	0	4.0	

Percentages		Ratios		Totals	
SC=	4.05%	STC=	1.00	Q= 80	
TT=	80.42%	SSSR=	0.29	cf= 52	
ST=	15.53%	TSSR=	0.58	r= 16	

SC = % Silence
TT = % Teacher Talk
ST = % Student Talk

STC = Student Talk Cognitive
SSSR = Student Steady State Ratio
TSSR = Teacher Steady State Ratio

Q = # Questions
CF = # Corrective/Feedback
R = # Reinforcements

NOTE: By entering the data in a computer-generated matrix, additional information can be obtained. For example, in the class given above the teacher talked 80.42% of the time and the students talked 15.53% of the time. In a 50-minute class, that translates to 40 minutes of teacher talk and about 8 minutes of student talk. In cell 4-8, we see that the students immediately answered 56 of the teacher's 80 questions. Because of the number of questions asked and the rapid student responses, we can infer that this was probably a review session. (For additional information on how to interpret this data, see Lewis & Johnson (1990).)

APPENDIX J

Interaction Diagram

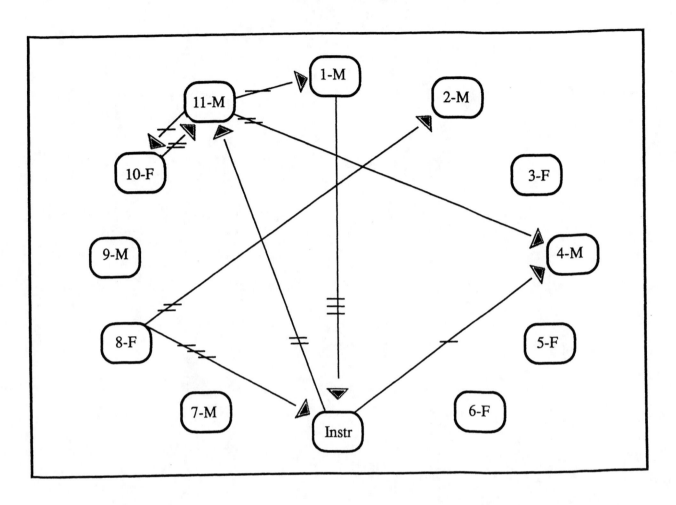

6. *Small Group Methods for Collecting Information From Students*

Richard Tiberius

*E*ducational consultants are discovering that group methods of data collection are among their most valuable tools for improving teaching and learning. Market researchers and social science researchers have used them profitably for over fifty years.

In the context of the data collection literature, "group" refers to an interacting group. The information collection methods selected for this article therefore all include interaction as a central feature. The size of such groups is determined by the requirement that participants interact. They are usually small, from three to six members, but can be considerably larger if organized to permit interaction. They include focus groups, interview methods, brainstorming, quality circles, leaderless discussion groups, and nominal group methods.

This review tends to read like a consumer's report since it presents strengths and weaknesses of each method and suggests appropriate uses. Readers who are regular users of consumers' reports should not be misled. The opinions expressed here are my own, one experienced user, not the results of a broad survey of users. Second, these methods of data collection are not finished products like video cassette players. They do not display stickers warning the customer against tampering with their insides. To the contrary, each of these methods has been "customized" many times over, with benefit to the user, to suit local conditions and needs. My advice is to take from any of the methods whatever suits you and do not hesitate to modify a method so that it fits your needs more precisely.

Methods have been assigned to categories based on the relationships between students, teachers and consultants inherent in each method. Such relationships are the single most important characteristic of these methods. The first cluster, Moderated Group Interaction, include techniques that employ interaction among students to gather information, moderated or facilitated by someone other than the teacher. Face-to-Face Methods feature direct conversations between teachers and students. These are planned and organized by consultants and often facilitated by consultants as well. Leaderless Discussion Groups also use group discussion for gathering information but are not facilitated by an educational consultant or faculty colleague (although students often fulfill the role spontaneously). Nominal Group Methods are groups in name only. Participants interact indirectly through exchange of summaries either written or on a computer network.

Moderated Group Interaction

"Moderated" groups are guided or conducted by a moderator or interviewer whose purpose is to make sure that the appropriate information is elicited under the proper conditions. By design the teacher is absent from these groups.

Brainstorming

Brainstorming sessions are designed to "storm" a problem by generating lots of ideas from a group. The moderator explains the rules of the brainstorming session and then describes the problem in specific terms. For example, what could be done to make this course more helpful to your learning? Students are encouraged to contribute ideas just as they pop into their heads, without deliberation on their feasibility; students are encouraged to express their ideas even if they seem far fetched, or are just variants of ideas already given. Even a small twist in what has already been said may contain the key that unlocks an important idea for another person. The group is explicitly admonished against saying anything negative about anyone's idea no matter how zany it may appear. The facilitator writes down the group's contributions. The method works by silencing the critic that each of us carries within us in order open the creative floodgates to new ideas. Later there is time to sort through the ideas selectively.

Focus Group Interviews

Over the last fifty years the uses of focus groups have expanded so dramatically and the procedures have become so varied that today virtually any small group interview procedure that is guided by a moderator has been called a focus group. I will use Patton's (1990) phrase "focus group interviews" to indicate that I am not distinguishing focus groups from other types of group interviews. The focus group interview was originally called a focused interview. It was designed to evaluate audience reactions to radio programs in the early 1940's (Merton, 1987). While listening to a program the audience would indicate a point of positive or negative feeling by pushing a red or green button respectively. Audience responses and the time position of each response were recorded on paper tape. When the program ended each group member focused on her or his reactions and explained them to the moderator.

The typical focus group includes six to twelve members and lasts from half an hour to two and a half hours (Steward & Shamdasani, 1990; Patton, 1990). Interviewers must be experienced and skilled at interviewing since they must promote a psychological climate in which members will feel comfortable about disclosing information.

The interview may be highly structured (directive) or unstructured (non-directive) depending on the kind of information that is needed. For example, if the objective is to discover issues that are important to students, an unstructured approach is probably appropriate. Unstructured interviewing is not constrained by a set of specific questions. The interviewer might open with a few general questions such as "Is there anything that could improve the teaching of this course? After that, the skilled interviewer is free to follow student leads and to pursue topics of real importance to students as opposed to ones which the designers of the questions only guessed would be of importance to students. An unstructured session that has been well prepared and led is characterized by lively conversation among students and little direction by the interviewer. The interviewer guides discussion so that each issue raised is discussed, encourages contributions from all members, explores differences of opinion, summarizes the views of the group and checks out accuracy of the summaries. The success of unstructured interviewing is very much dependent on the skills of the interviewer.

On the other hand, a structured interview might be more appropriate if the purpose of the interview is to confirm the findings of a questionnaire, explain questionnaire results that are confusing, or reconcile two contradictory sets of opinion. A structured interview is guided by a series of more specific or directive questions. A typical directive question might be "On the questionnaire about half the class said that Dr. X was not very organized and the other half said he was organized. Frankly, we're puzzled. It would be helpful to hear people representing both sides of the issue. Can I see by a show of hands, if we have representatives from each viewpoint? How many see Dr. X as organized? How many see him as not very organized? Would someone who thought the lecture was well organized please tell me in what way?"

The structured interview follows a questioning strategy, usually a list of predetermined questions. The questions undoubtedly restrict students' responses but the strategy often includes some flexibility for the interviewer to follow up interesting leads.

Recommendations for Use

Brainstorming is particularly suited to idea-generating, such as generating teaching problems or solutions to those problems. The major strength of this method is the richness of ideas that are generated. On the other hand, brainstorming would not be a very useful information gathering technique for clarification of teaching problems or for developing cooperation and commitment to a solution. Since participants are explicitly prohibited from interacting critically, their contributions remain at a rather shallow level. There is no discussion process during which ideas could be modified to accommodate to the realities of the classroom, differences in opinion are not reconciled and there is not much room for subtlety. Brainstorming lacks these typical advantages of discussion methods. Indeed, participants engage only in the minimal interaction of building on one another's ideas.

Focus group interviews, particularly in their less structured forms, are especially useful for goals such as exploring the issues that are important to students (as a basis for designing a questionnaire), fine-tuning teaching, and obtaining a deep understanding of the subtle aspects of teaching such as those involved in the teacher-student relationship. Structured interviews are more suited to situations in which the evaluator has a very specific idea of what to find out and is not as concerned with what students want to say. Structured interviews can also be used to follow-up hunches that have been gathered using a broader spectrum feedback method. They are not particularly well suited to finding out what is on students' minds, a purpose for which unstructured interviews are better suited.

The success of the unstructured interview is more dependent on the skill of the interviewer, while the success of the structured interview is more dependent on the quality of the questions and how well the group interaction is managed.

The advantages of focus group interviews arise from the synergy of interaction. Interactive groups are often lively and enjoyable to both group members and interviewers. A sense of security and trust grows in such a group as each member begins to feel that she or he will not be singled out by the interviewer and as it becomes clear that the focus is on understanding perceptions and not on assigning blame. Under such conditions, respondents speak freely and frankly, dare to disagree, and stimulate one another with ideas. Such groups are capable of generating rich information, concrete anecdotes, subtleties of meaning and deep explanations. Moreover, group methods are more efficient than single interviews,

and more productive than questionnaires. Students seem able to talk more easily than they write.

Interaction has some advantages for the interviewers, too. They can probe interesting issues, reconcile subtle differences of opinion, elicit specific examples of teacher behaviors and quotations with which to enliven the information, and observe non-verbal responses such as facial expressions, body movements and sighs that may contradict the verbal message. Finally, group interaction produces information in an easily understandable form—coherent sentences and even stories, rather than percentages, marks on a continuum, or mere phrases.

Additional advantages are peculiar to unstructured interviews. Unstructured groups are free from the constraints inherent in the vocabulary and conceptual framework of the interviewer. Students are able to respond in

---

Box A: Procedures for Unstructured Focus Group Interviewing

Step One. The group facilitator and the teacher talk so that the facilitator becomes familiar with the teacher's aims, methods, evaluation.

Step Two. The facilitator visits a class to observe the context for the feedback that s/he will get from the students. Near the end of the class, the teacher introduces the facilitator and asks for the students' cooperation. The facilitator explains to the students that s/he would like to gather a random sample. S/he chooses names using some method that is open to the class such as picking from a pile little strips of paper on which names have been written. S/he calls out the names and arranges a time to meet with those students who were called. S/he then explains to the rest of the class how the information from the group will be summarized, a copy returned to the student group for validation and then given to the teacher. The teacher and facilitator will then sit down and discuss the feedback in order to improve the teaching.

Step Three. At the meeting with the students the facilitator assures students as to the confidentiality of the information; takes a quick turn around the group to elicit all the points before any of the points are discussed; discusses the points one at a time; encourages each student to comment on every point raised; reminds students that it is more important to discover the range of opinion than to strive for consensus. The facilitator continually summarizes the views of the students and checks out the summary with the students.

Step Four. The facilitator summarizes the information from her or his notes and gives a copy to the teacher. Much of the organization of the information has already been done with the students in the small group.

Step Five. After the teacher reads the summary s/he sets up a meeting with the facilitator for a discussion of the issues raised, the teacher's reaction to it, and what can be done to improve the teaching. Of course, the summaries contain suggestions for improvement as well.

Step Six. The teacher conveys to the class the results of the discussion session including a plan for improvement of the course.

Step Seven. After several class meetings, another sample is drawn from the class to evaluate the improvements. This session provides feedback on the improvement process itself.

their own colorful language, qualify their responses, reject and rephrase the questions. It is well known that students will answer an interviewer's questions even if they do not believe that the questions are the important ones to ask. Moreover, even if the questions are important from the students' point of view, rigid adherence to those questions by the interviewer could stifle students from volunteering important elaborations.

Interaction, the main feature of focus group interviews, has disadvantages as well. Information may be biased by the dominant influence of one or two group members, especially if those members are perceived as more powerful than the others. The first speaker may influence what others say. Subsequent respondents are often reluctant to contradict their fellow students for fear of "messing things up." Students who hold minority views are also reluctant to voice their disagreement. In addition, group data is inherently difficult to summarize and interpret because each member of the group tends to go her or his own way unless the interviewer constrains them by asking specific questions or refocusing. But constraining the group threatens the very freedom essential to the success of the focus group interview.

The skilled, experienced interviewer can overcome these biases to some extent. Bias stemming from students' influence on one another can be reduced by taking a quick turn around the group, asking each student to state a point before any of the points are discussed; discussing the points one at a time; encouraging each student to comment on every point raised; and ensuring students that you are more interested in discovering the range of opinion than in arriving at a consensus. The task of summarizing the messy data that is elicited from a group can be made easier if the interviewer continually summarizes the views of the students during the interaction, reads notes back to them and asks them if the summary is correct. These and other suggestions are mentioned in the description of an unstructured interviewing process given in Box A.

Other limitations are not so easily overcome. The data from one group may not generalize to the entire class, while interviewing a statistically reliable number of sample groups is often too costly. Even skilled interviewers may unwittingly introduce bias by the way they ask questions or respond to student discussion. A seemingly innocent statement by the interviewer like "That's interesting" (while beginning to take notes on a pad) can change the course of the conversation radically. Finally, unless a tape recorder is used, the writing speed or summarizing ability of the interviewer limits the quantity and quality of the information that can be communicated to the teacher and thus compromises the instructional improvement process that is based on this information.

There are some disadvantages specific to the unstructured interview. The lack of structure leaves the unskilled interviewer free to pressure students, perhaps unwittingly, to confirm her or his beliefs about the teaching or, at least, to focus on the topics that s/he sees as important rather than those that students would like to pursue. There is a tendency for unskilled interviewers, without the guidance of structured questions, to strive for consensus at the expense of ignoring disagreements and to slight minority views in summarizing results. The accuracy, importance to students, and representativeness of the information (important to faculty) is thus critically dependent on the skill of the interviewer in unstructured interviewing.

Teacher and Students, Face-to-Face

The potential for rich communication through face-to-face meetings is obvious. Student comments, phrased in their own words, and augmented by their gestures and facial expressions, have a powerful effect on those who are privileged enough to witness them live. Moreover, the intensity with which views are held and contested, the subtle differences of opinion, the enormous amount of good will, the energy—all of these characteristics of the lively small group—are very difficult to communicate to the teacher in written text.

Unfortunately, face-to-face interaction tends to inhibit both students and teachers. Typically, teachers become defensive about criticisms of their teaching and students are wary of speaking freely for fear of embarrassing their teachers. To be successful, feedback methods based on face-to-face dialogues between teachers and students must reduce the potential for embarrassment. At least three devices are used for this purpose in contemporary methods: arranging a sufficient number of meetings between the teacher and the same group of students to develop a sense of comfort and trust; arranging the interaction so that students can communicate by proxy, that is, discuss the opinions of their classmates rather than their own views (by this device, students do not have to take personal responsibility for the comments); and structuring meetings using a pre-circulated agenda. The pre-circulated agenda allows both teachers and students time to get control of their emotions and get used to the issues that will be discussed.

Advisory Groups

A small group of students can mediate between the teacher and the rest of the class by meeting periodically with the teacher. Methods based on such continual contact between teachers and a group of students have been used in higher education for at least twenty years. Parent et. al. (1971) describe a successful experience with such a method, using groups of six to ten students. A similar method, described in The Network Newsletter of College Teaching, (September, 1987) defines a three-member student group which is called an "advisory committee." The method became widely known more recently as a Japanese management technique called Quality Control Circles. Cross and Angelo (1987, pp. 160-161) have spelled out the steps of a procedure for quality circles which they have modified for use by instructors to improve teaching. Their procedure puts the onus on the teacher to select those aspects of the instruction on which the group will focus. I have modified their procedure in order to allow both teachers and students to share the responsibility for developing the agenda. The steps of this modified version are given in Box B.

Advisory groups utilize three devices for reducing embarrassment: meeting frequently, discussing what others have said, and pre-circulating an agenda. And since students are closer to their peers than are either teachers or consultants, they can more easily understand their peers and can speak to them more freely. Cross and Angelo (1987) also remind us of the importance of compensating the students in some way for their time and energy; buying their lunch is one good way.

One weakness of advisory groups arises out of the use of volunteers. Volunteers may not be well enough connected to the class to gather issues widely. And even if

---

Box B: Steps for Organizing Student Advisory Groups

Select the Groups. Obtain a volunteer group or several groups of five to ten students. About three meetings per semester have been found to be adequate. Half of the students should be changed each time, retaining some students for continuity of process.

Prior to the Meeting. A week prior to the meeting students are asked to submit to the teacher a single sheet describing issues that the student feedback group would like to raise. The student advisory group gathers these issues on their own, by talking with students. At the same time the teacher gives her or his agenda of issues to the advisory group.

At the Meeting.
    Introduction. New members of the group are introduced. Going by an old principle of exchanging feedback, the person who is in the most vulnerable position speaks first to an issue. The teacher usually speaksfirst to issues raised by the advisory group and vice versa. It is a good idea to rotate from teacher to student ideas throughout the meeting.
    Understand and suggest. The object of the discussion is to clarify the issues from everyone's point of view, and then to suggest ways to enhance strengths and remedy problems.
    Someone should take notes. It is a good idea if the teacher takes notes since s/he will probably have to implement the decisions, but anyone who has an efficient recorder will do.
Notes are circulated for validation. The teacher and students get a copy of the notes taken at the meeting for validation. That is, they can edit the notes if they think that the recorder missed something or misrepresented something.

Teacher communicates to the class. By communicating to the entire class the conclusions from the feedback session and the actions s/he will take, the teacher motivates the class to look positively at the efforts she is making.

Follow up. At a subsequent meeting, in addition to the usual new issues, time is set aside to gather reactions to the actions that were taken after the previous meeting.

they faithfully represent class views at the beginning of their relationship with the teacher, they may come to adopt the teacher's point of view over time. It is therefore recommended (Cross and Angelo, 1987) to rotate some of the members of the group, although rotating sacrifices continuity.

Face-to-Face Focus Groups

In face-to-face focus groups the teachers do not interact with the same students over and over again, as in advisory groups, so that the potential for embarrassing confrontation must be overcome by other means. One contemporary consulting method, Alliances for Change (Tiberius, et al., 1993 and Chapter 13 of this book), features a two-stage arrangement whereby students discuss the problems and issues that were raised by random selection of their classmates in a prior group. This prior group, called the Agenda Group because it sets the agenda for the face-to-face group, is conducted by an educational consultant or peer consultant in the absence of the teacher. The main purpose of the face-to-face focus group is, therefore, not to raise new issues but to help the teacher understand and address the issues that have been defined previously. The group endeavors to clarify, elaborate, illustrate and address the teaching issues on the agenda.

Box C contains the steps of a method that has worked well (see Tiberius, et. al., 1993).

Recommendations for Use

Face-to-face methods are particularly powerful for changing students' and teachers' attitudes or perceptions. Teachers who hold cynical attitudes toward students, for example, are more likely to be affected positively by direct dialogue with students than by indirect methods. Hearing others speak in their own words and seeing their facial expressions is motivating, both for teacher and students. The process instills in students a sense that the teacher cares about their welfare and convinces teachers that what they do is important to students. The process enhances both the teacher's and the students' commitment to the changes that are agreed upon. Class attitudes toward the teacher may be affected, too, mediated by the representatives of the group, who extend the teacher's caring attitude into the class as they ask questions of their classmates. In addition to the effect on attitudes, face-to-face groups offer a useful forum for sorting out conflicting claims, understanding issues in depth, clarifying subtleties and generating ideas that have been shaped by the students' input.

Face-to-face methods are excellent complements to such methods as brainstorming and nominal group meth-

---

Box C: Procedures for Face-to-Face Focus Groups

Step One. Determine an agenda of important teaching and learning issues both from students and from the teacher. This can be accomplished by various means: another focus group, a questionnaire, Nominal Group Techniques, Delphi or Small Group Interactional Diagnosis.

Step Two. The teacher chooses a group of about six students from those who raise their hands in class in response to a request for volunteers to help improve the instruction. The teacher hands out copies of the agenda to the volunteers and invites them to a meeting to discuss the agenda.

Step Three. A facilitator meets with the teacher and the volunteers to clarify the issues, analyze them, and decide what actions to take. The same rules should be followed as recommended for the advisory group. The teacher should speak first to issues raised by students and vice versa. Someone should take careful notes throughout the process.

Step Four. The notes are typed, copied, and handed out to both teacher and the group for validating and editing.

Step Five. The teacher discloses to the entire class both the issues and the plans for changes. The teacher asks the class for comments.

Step Six. At the end of the course, the class is surveyed to assess the successfulness of the changes.

Box D: Steps of Small Group Instructional Diagnosis (SGID)

Step One. A discussion is scheduled between the teacher and the facilitator who is going to conduct the SGID for the purposes of acquainting the facilitator with the teacher's style and of reaching an agreement as to how the SGID will be conducted.

Step Two. A regular class meeting is selected for the procedure, during the middle of the term. The instructor teaches as usual for the first part of the period, then introduces the facilitator, and leaves the facilitator alone with the students for the last 25 to 30 minutes. The facilitator explains the SGID process and her or his role, emphasizes that information will be given only to the instructor, and points out that students will have an opportunity to directly affect the remainder of their course. The facilitator then asks them to divide themselves into groups of about five and to select one person from each group to act as recorder and spokesperson. The groups discuss the following questions, which the facilitator puts on an overhead or chalkboard: "What do you like about the course?" "What do you think needs improvement?" "What suggestions do you have for bringing about these improvements?" After 10 minutes of discussion, the facilitator asks the spokesperson from each group to report one response to each of the questions (more than one round can be made if time and class size permit). The facilitator writes the responses on the board, being sensitive to minority views. When a statement is not shared by most, the facilitator requests a show of hands and records the vote. A copy of the statements on the board is made for the facilitator to share with the instructor.

Step Three. The instructor and facilitator discuss the students' comments, the instructor's reaction to them, and strategies for improvement. They also discuss what the instructor should say to the students. This step is the most difficult in the process. The facilitator should be supportive, warm, sensitive, understanding, nonjudgmental, and an active listener.

The facilitator role requires that s/he operate on several levels. On the first level, the facilitator is a communication channel with primary concern for conveying the students' sentiments in such a way as to avoid defensive reactions from the instructor that may block the flow of information. On the second level, the facilitator is an information source, perhaps sharing her or his own teaching experiences or telling the instructor about various resources and techniques. On the third level, which only should be incorporated by the more experienced, the facilitator gives possible interpretations of student reasoning and concerns. S/he may hypothesize about the instructor's teaching strategies for the instructor's reaction and reflection.

Step Four. The instructor uses the first ten minutes of the ensuing class period to clarify comments that were unclear and summarize the students' comments to allow students to correct distortions and check for accuracy. The instructor should offer some reactions to the comments and perhaps outline intended changes or adaptations.

---

ods (described below). The latter can efficiently elicit a set of themes which are then clarified through a face-to-face focus group. What is the role of the educational consultant in this process? Teachers who have been prepared for conducting face-to-face groups may not require the assistance of a consultant but inexperienced teachers certainly do. Teachers and students rarely have the kind of training in group facilitation that would enable them to ensure that everyone contributes, to reconcile disparate views, to work against pressures to conformity and dominance of a minority, to organize information into a form that is un-

derstandable, to ferret out subtle issues, to summarize accurately and so on. Such information gathering and summarizing skills benefit from some training and experience. Educational consultants need to help teachers acquire these skills. For example, I suggest that the consultant lead the first two advisory committee meetings to model the process and take pressure off the teacher.

After more than twenty years of using focus groups to gather evaluative feedback, my perception is that an educational consultant can make important contributions to the process: by convincing teachers to try the procedure (for example, using demonstrations at workshops), by coordinating the process, and by facilitating the groups. Recently, my colleagues and I have attempted to work out a method whereby teachers can form partners and carry out the roles of consultation required by this method for one another (See Tiberius et. al, 1993). Where this has been successful, our roles have changed from "expert" consultants to facilitators who demonstrate the process at workshops, answer questions and evaluate it for research purposes.

Arranging and participating in face-to-face groups takes time. Even face-to-face focus groups which meet only once take at least three hours of faculty time.

Leaderless Discussion Groups

Leaderless discussion is a misnomer to some extent since students often assumes a leadership role when none is officially assigned. Indeed, facilitators who arrange so-called leaderless groups often instruct the groups to name a scribe or a reporter. Reporters, feeling the responsibility to report the information accurately, will often ask questions and summarize positions, two leadership behaviors. Gradually, they drift into a full leadership role. Nevertheless, the absence of teachers or consultants has a liberating effect on the group — students tend to say what they want, in their own language, talk rapidly, excitedly and with an astonishing degree of candor.

The absence of skilled group leadership leaves such groups highly subject to bias due to influence by dominant members or by first speakers. It is important, therefore, if you are going to use leaderless groups for the purpose of gathering information to improve teaching, to use many of them so that their numbers will counteract the bias. The procedure described below, for example, breaks up the entire class into leaderless groups.

Small Group Instructional Diagnosis

The acronym "SGID" stands for Small Group Instructional Diagnosis, a procedure for improving instruction based on a technique for gathering information in the classroom. Designed by Dr. D. Joseph Clark at the University of Washington more than fifteen years ago (Clark & Bekey, 1979; Clark, 1982), the method keeps growing in popularity. In fact, a few years ago, at the annual conference of the American Educational Research Association, when a speaker who was talking about SGID asked the audience how many are aware of SGID being used on their campus, more than half (about 30 people) raise their hands.

SGID uses a combination of a leaderless small group

discussion followed by an unstructured, whole class interview, and it retains some of the advantages of each. The outcome of these information gathering processes is a rather brief list, but there is plenty of discussion in the SGID process before the list is generated. The discussion, both among students and between students and the facilitator, allows for misinterpretations to be corrected and provides the kind of contextual statements and qualifications that aid understanding.

Conducting this process requires the help of a consultant or an experienced colleague. The teacher should not perform it on her or his own class. Dr. Clark (1982) describes the method in five steps. These steps are summarized in Box D and the SGID approach is further discussed in Chapter 15.

Recommendations for Use

There are compelling reasons why consultants might want to encourage teachers to use SGID. Because it draws the entire class into the process, it can have a profoundly positive effect on the class attitude toward the teacher and can enhance their sense of responsibility for improving the teaching-learning process. Teachers typically report that their students are flattered when teachers show so much interest in their opinions, particularly if the teachers also make improvements based on those suggestions. Students often continue to contribute helpful suggestions and feedback long after the SGID process has ended.

SGID is designed to elicit information that is clearly stated, important to students, and representative of the class. Student discussions serve both to clarify responses and to filter out unimportant ones, so that the suggestions that reach the facilitator are usually clearly articulated and important to students. Furthermore, since the material is generated in leaderless student groups, there is little inhibition to speaking frankly. Although the process of interaction is subject to the usual distortions from pressure to conformity and influence of early speakers and by dominant speakers, just as in any group interaction process, the presence of many groups in the class tends to cancel out these distortions. Conducting one SGID in a large class is the equivalent of conducting many unstructured interviews simultaneously. Finally, SGID includes several opportunities for two-way communication to correct errors of misinterpretation: after the list is on the board, the facilitator can clarify any item that she or he is not clear about. These interactions between facilitator and students provide the facilitator with an understanding of the context of students' suggestions. The teacher also has an opportunity to check out his understanding of the information during the beginning of the ensuing class.

On the other hand, SGID is probably not suitable to every teacher nor to every teaching problem. Not every teacher has the courage to allow her or his weaknesses to be aired aloud in front of the entire class and then to follow-up with a face-to-face discussion with that class. If the teacher is intimidated by this level of exposure the consultant should suggest more private methods, ones which draw information from individual questionnaires or from small samples of the class and that allow teachers to make improvements without raising the entire class' awareness.

Second, I would not recommend SGID for the experienced teacher whose teaching problems are subtle and difficult. Subtle problems of personality, differences in student views which are difficult to reconcile, and other complex or subtle problems require discussion. SGID may be useful as a first step in the process of discovering such problems. But once it is known that the problems are complicated, personal, or subtle I would recommend moving to a procedure that utilizes periods of face-to-face dialogue between the students and the consultant and even between students and the teacher. These latter methods can elicit the kinds of stories and detailed explanations that could reconcile opposing views, communicate subtleties of meaning or convey important contextual information.

There is a trade-off here between breadth and depth. The SGID polls the entire class, but the depth is limited to rather simple statements of the most important issues. I have witnessed difficult issues become more and more confused with each new speaker until the facilitator gave up and simply restated the original confused statement. Of course, there is an opportunity, described in step four (Box D), for teachers to clarify brief comments by discussing them in the whole class. Such discussion could flesh out the teacher's understanding of the issues, but whole-class discussion is an awkward format in which to try to unravel subtleties and reconcile discrepancies within ten minutes, as I mentioned before.

Nominal Group Methods

Nominal Group methods take their name from the fact that participants constitute a group in name only. They do not actually interact in the usual sense of people in conversation. The process was originally used to achieve consensus in policy decisions but has more recently been applied to curriculum development and teaching improvement. (Delbecq et. al., 1975; O'Neil & Jackson, 1983).

The Nominal Group Technique

The Nominal Group Technique begins with the for-

mulation of a question. The question must be carefully worded and rather broad since only one question is asked. The group leader puts this question to a small group of participants and asks them to write, on paper, privately, as many responses to it as they can. If the purpose is to gather information to improve teaching, an appropriate question might be, simply: "What are the ways in which Dr. Jones' teaching can be improved?" Although group members are physically in the same room, possibly at the same table, they do not interact with one another in answering the question. When students have finished writing their responses, the group leader asks each student in turn to read out one of her or his contributions, which the leader writes on a flip chart. When every student has contributed once, the group leader begins with the first student and goes around the group again until every contribution from every student's list is exhausted.

In the second step the list of contributions is clarified and overlapping ones are eliminated. This step also excludes discussion except that which is directed at clarification of listed items. Finally, the leader conducts a successive voting procedure by which participants rank the items. The top five ideas are copied down by the group leader and communicated to the teacher.

The Delphi Technique

The Delphi technique (Delbecq et. al., 1975) is a specialized form of Nominal Group method that has been widely used in business and educational settings for achieving consensus. The Delphi technique has been developed for the purpose of eliciting, from a group of highly selected participants, a consensus supported by explanations. The participants are often people selected because of their special expertise in a field. Often such people cannot be gathered for a face-to-face meeting. The advantage of the Delphi is that people do not have to travel to the same location in order to interact.

Members of the group never meet face-to-face. They interact entirely on paper, by means of a succession of questionnaires. The first questionnaire might ask a group of alumnae to list the material from the program that they found most relevant to their current practices. Responses to the first questionnaire are summarized by the evaluator. Typically such summaries are returned to the participants who are asked to rank them for importance. This second iteration of the questionnaire may include follow-up questions as well. The alumnae in my example might be asked to "Rank the various facts and concepts that were judged by the group to be most relevant to your practices," and then to "Give some suggestions for improvement of the program."

A third iteration might return both the ranked list of relevant facts and concepts and the suggestions for improvement to the alumnae and then ask them to rank the latter for potential effectiveness. In this third iteration alumnae may be given the opportunity to change their responses to previous questions if they would like. The evaluator can add as many iterations as the patience of group members will permit. At each phase each participant gets the opportunity to view and respond to the product of all of the participants in the sample. The final product is, therefore, not just one list but several connected lists: for example, a list of material deemed relevant, suggestions for improvements, and a list of any other helpful responses that the evaluator requested, all ranked for importance.

Recommendations for Use

Enthusiasts of Nominal Group Techniques (see Lomax & McLeman, 1984) point out that since the students generate their ideas privately, these techniques produce a wide range of ideas and little opportunity for the biases that plague interactive groups. The techniques also have mechanisms for sorting out trivial suggestions from important ones. Although students do not interact in the usual sense, they do respond to the contributions of other students in clarifying and assigning priority. A student may assign top priority to a suggestion that she or he did not even think of while writing a list but which rang "true" when it was written.

Finally, the product of a Nominal Group process is a discrete list which need not be analyzed or summarized further. It can be communicated to the teacher with much greater ease than the messy product of real group interaction.

Nominal Group Techniques (NGT) do not fare so well with regard to other information qualities such as representativeness of the information that they elicit. In the absence of a sampling mechanism the consultant cannot assume that the opinions of one small NGT group reflect those of the entire class. Indeed, the key to recruiting respondents for a Delphi procedure is the exclusivity of the group. It is mailed out to a highly selected group, only after their cooperation is obtained. For example, one might choose to define a group as students with a certain grade point average.

The range of opinion is even more restricted in the NGT compared to the Delphi. Since the NGT selection process reduces the items to five, items which are of moderate importance to all of the students will be dropped in favor of items of great importance to a few students. And there seems to be no way to increase the number of

alternatives without encumbering the process. The Delphi does not need to reduce the number to five, so items which are of moderate importance to a large number of respondents will be retained as well. The number of items can be increased limited only by the motivation of the group.

The NGT seems to be most usefully applied to achieve a quick consensus around a single question, especially when there are serious conflicts among the participants in their initial opinion or glaring power differences among participants. An appropriate situation might be a meeting of students to select criteria for a teaching award given by students, under circumstances in which there were strong differences of opinion among members of the group.

The most memorable occasion on which I used the NGT was not an instructional one but it was strikingly successful. I was requested to chair a meeting of the Ontario Medical Association and the teachers of clinical communication skills. Its purpose was to generate ideas for a response to the growing frequency of malpractice litigation. There were huge opinion and power differences among members of the group. The conversation would likely have polarized around two or three dominant persons had I used a discussion technique. The nominal group technique succeeded in flushing out all of the ideas from the group. When these were written on the board in simple language, shorn of their ideological baggage, participants found that they were able to agree on the level of priority for most of the items.

I would not recommend the NGT for gathering information to improve teaching performance unless it were coupled with a focus group or other discussion method. The information is too spare to be very useful to teachers, unless, of course, the consultant is able to supplement the method with interpretation, elaboration, rich anecdotes and a deeper understanding of the situation. The Alliances for Change procedure (Tiberius, 1993, and Chapter 13 of this book), for example, uses the NGT as a prior group to set the agenda for a focus group, as mentioned above. A class questionnaire could produce results similar to those of the NGT with the added advantages that it would reflect the entire class opinion and the questions could be worded expertly to reflect key dimensions of teaching. Responses to questionnaires can be ranked for importance, too.

I would use the Delphi procedure for respondents who cannot be gathered together easily, like students from different campuses, alumnae, respondents who would not behave well in face-to-face discussions, or for larger units of analysis than a course, such as an entire program or part of one.

Conclusion

I began this article by contrasting the methods of data collection with technological devices such as cassette players. I invited you to feel free to tamper with the methods. I want to leave you with a concluding thought by extending my analogy. If I had reviewed not data collection methods but cassette recorders manufactured over the last ten years, my statements about the recorders would still be accurate. But virtually no one today is using any of the data gathering methods in their original form. I invite you once again to pick up the phone and call the people currently using these methods. Find out their latest modifications and variations. Learn how various disadvantages have been overcome and advantages have been enhanced. And experiment yourself.

References

Clark, D. J., & Bekey, J. (1979). Use of small groups in instructional evaluation. *Professional and Organizational Development Quarterly*, *1*(2), 87-95.

Clark, D. J. (1982). The history of SGID development. *SGID Newsletter*, 1(1), 1-4.

Cross, K. P., & Angelo, T. A. (1988). *Classroom assessment techniques: A handbook for faculty*. Ann Arbor, MI: National Center for Research to Improve Postsecondary Teaching and Learning, University of Michigan.

Delbecq, A. L., Van de Van, A. H., & Gustafson, D. H. (1975). *Group techniques for program planning: A guide to nominal group and delphi processes*. Glenview, IL: Scott, Foresman.

Lomax, P., & McLeman, P. (1984). The uses and abuses of nominal group technique in polytechnic course evaluation studies in higher education. *Studies in Higher Education*, *9*(2), 183-190.

Merton, R. K. (1987). Focused interviews and focused groups: continuities and discontinuities. *Public Opinion Quarterly*, *51*, 550-556.

Network Newsletter of College Teaching. (1987). Vol *1*(1), 2. Carbondale, IL: Southern Illinois University.

O'Neil, M. J., & Jackson, L. (1983). Nominal group technique: A process for initiating curriculum development in higher education. *Studies in Higher Education*, *8*(2), 129-138.

Parent, E. R., Vaughan, C. E., & Wharton, K. (1971). A new approach to course evaluation. *Journal of Higher Education*, *42*, 113-118.

Patton, M. Q. (1990). *Qualitative evaluation and research methods*. Newbury Park: Sage.

Steward, D. W., & Shamdasani, P. N. (1990). *Focus groups: Theory and practice*. Newbury Park: Sage.

Tiberius, R. G., Sackin, H. D., Janzen, K. R. & Preece, M. (1993). Alliances for change: A procedure for improving teaching through conversations with learners and partnerships with colleagues. *The Journal of Staff, Program, and Organization Development*, *11*(1), 11-23.

7. *Collecting Information Using Videotape*

Eric Kristensen

*U*sing videotape in instructional consultations is a cost-effective way to work with teachers on their teaching. Both in terms of time and money (especially time) videotape is an elegant tool which, when used correctly, can cut to the quick of the teaching and learning process in almost any classroom. The cost-to-benefit ratio in these terms is very favorable.

This chapter discusses many issues the consultant needs to consider. Skills need to be acquired, equipment procured, and the context properly prepared for a videotaping program to succeed. There are also times when it might be more appropriate to observe a teacher in person, or to distribute survey instruments to students rather than to videotape. This chapter examines some possible choices that face instructional consultants and offers some advice from my years of experience using videotape in instructional consultation.

A conceptual guide for each stage of the videotape consulting process can be useful. For example, to make the decision whether or not to videotape a teacher's class, the question of effectiveness should be addressed. In terms of making a videotape for teaching analysis, a goal should always be transparency and simplicity. In the tape reviewing process, I find that a teacher-based rather than a consultant-based approach is more useful.

Considering Videotape's Effectiveness

New teachers benefit most clearly from videotaping. Teachers who are experimenting with a new teaching technique or developing a new course benefit about as much. Another place where videotape is useful is when a teacher confronts a teaching problem, and attempts to discover the source of the problem and generate solutions.

For new faculty who have little experience teaching and who have only recently made the transition from being a student, videotaping teaching is often a revelatory experience. It can dramatically shorten the learning curve needed to become an effective teacher. I would say that, on average, a person using videotaped instructional consultation and feedback can learn within one year what would normally take two or three years of teaching. This is an important factor to consider when working with new junior faculty members who are often under pressure to do research, publish articles, write a book or two, and teach upwards of five or six new courses in a two or three year span. Getting teaching under control as early as possible will allow the faculty member to manage time more effectively. Once teaching becomes manageable, faculty are better able to bring research and writing to the forefront of their efforts. In general, it is in their own interest to quickly learn as much as possible about teaching.

For more experienced faculty, the teacher that they see on the video screen is one which is more familiar than the one encountered by the new teacher. Rather than the revelation that a new teacher experiences, the experienced faculty member sees a confirmation of the teacher that he or she has become over the years. Videotaping is very effective for these teachers when they are interested in trying new techniques and analyzing the results in the classroom, developing a new course, or finding the solution to a teaching problem that has come to their attention.

Videotaping is not always the best method of instructional consultation. If videotaping is required by a superior because of bad evaluations, the emotional tension of the situation can become overwhelming when combined with the stress of watching oneself teach on videotape. In this case perhaps administering a student evaluation of teaching would provide much more useful information and become an effective first step in solving the problems a teacher may have. In other cases, it might be more useful to engage colleagues in observation in order to facilitate departmental or interdepartmental communication. Sometimes videotape can work well here, but asking a group of faculty members to watch someone else's two hour class on tape may not be the most effective way to achieve this end. The consultant should be aware of the teacher's goals when he or she asks to be taped, and consider whether or not videotaping is the most effective way to achieve these goals.

In every situation, setting ground rules for working with teachers and their videotapes is necessary in an effective videotaping program. For example, if a teacher is asked by a department chair to work on teaching and make a videotape, is it reasonable for the teacher to bring along the department chair to watch the tape? If you do not make clear what your ground rules are, such an event may occur (and actually happened to me once). So in order to be effective, you will need to determine your ground rules and make sure they are reasonable and flexible. (Sample ground rules are included in Appendix A.)

In most instances, the benefits of videotaping far outweigh the costs. It is an efficient and effective tool for the instructional consultant, and allows the faculty member to observe and criticize himself or herself and the students without someone else's interpolation or interpretation. It offers an invaluable opportunity to observe students without the distractions caused by the immediate concerns of teaching a class in real time. The experience of watching one's class on tape is immediate and powerful, and direct evidence of change is easily observed and monitored with subsequent tapings.

Making the Tape

This section discusses important goals and decisions related to making the tape.

The Ideal of Transparency

The overall goal of making a videotape for instructional analysis is "transparency." A tape is transparent when it seems to flow seamlessly, without creating in the viewer futile urges to push the camera around so that it can catch an expression, notice a gesture, catch up on people we haven't seen for a while or follow the action. In order to avoid this problem, it is imperative that you keep your eye on the monitor or the viewfinder at all times. Unless the operator remembers this, it is all too easy to let the eyes wander around the room and catch the action without moving the camera. Later, the tape reviewers will feel like they have missed many important moments in the class and wind up frustrated with the time and effort spent. Remember that the teacher and a consultant will watch the tape later on; make it for them.

Another way to enhance transparency is to take the time to introduce the viewers to the teacher and the class at the beginning of the tape. Record the teacher and slowly pan the students during the opening moments of the class, then spend about five minutes recording the teacher. This allows the consultant to discuss a number of important issues with the teacher during the start of the consultation. During the class, spend about half the time recording the students' involvement in class. This may sound excessive, but this strategy will pay handsomely later in the consultation.

Keeping It Simple

Another aspect of transparency concerns the teacher's experience of the taping itself. Be mindful and respectful of the teacher's time, energy and need for concentration on the task at hand: teaching the class. Ask permission to get into the room early and set up before class arrival if possible. Stay out of the way, take care of scheduling and other details with the teacher after class if at all possible. Try to "blend into woodwork," be unobtrusive but effective. You can make it easy for students, too, and help put them at ease. Never say, "Don't pay any attention to me" because by doing so they usually will! I have found a simple announcement to students about the tape and why it is being made to be effective yet unobtrusive. Sometimes a teacher will mention the taping ahead of time or right at the beginning of class; nevertheless, I usually make a three part statement that says, for the record, that: I am from the teaching and learning office; at the teacher's request we are making the tape so that he or she can see himself or herself teach; and that the tape is confidential but members of class may watch it by calling the center. This lets students know that the "administration" is not checking up on the professor, that they can see it if they want (which generally puts them more at ease), and answers the question of why we are taping this class without getting into specific reasons. Otherwise every student will be wondering if they will be on "60 Minutes" or the admissions office's next promotional videotape.

Some Technical Considerations

Because it is so important to catch students on the tape, the camera should not be set up at the back of the room and simply pointed it at the teacher. Set up at the side of a room, where you will be able to catch a fair number of students' faces and expressions as well as the teacher's. Mount the camera on a smoothly operating tripod, and use your zoom lens carefully, balancing close shots of students with long shots of groups of students. If the teacher uses the blackboard, be sure to document this as well.

The camera may make some students nervous, especially at first. But in my experience, a relatively still and quiet camera person will become "part of the furniture" after the first five or ten minutes. Some teaching centers have special rooms set up with one or more remote controlled cameras mounted near the ceiling, and avoid the use of camera operators in the room. In my experience, however, the intrusion is quite minimal once the class settles in and students start to work. It is also important to keep a balance between following the action and observing the reactions of others in the room. In all cases, it is extremely helpful to have a small video monitor with which to shoot the class. Staring for an hour into a small camcorder eyepiece is a sure recipe for eye strain and headache. Classroom lighting is usually less than ideal for the video camera, but modern camcorders make easy work out of a once difficult problem. Using a recorder that will record decent images in low light with high definition will solve most problems. (See equipment list in Appendix B.) If the teacher turns out the room lights and switches on the overhead projector, lighting problems increase.

There are a number of pedagogical issues to discuss with the teacher later, but a little foresight and planning can help minimize your problems. Always ask teachers how they set up their classes, including a question about use of the overhead projector. Many times teachers will be happy to compromise, and leave some or all of the room lights on so that you can catch the students on tape. In fact, they may realize that being able to see the students is preferable after all, and that the students can still see the slides quite well.

It is often difficult to hear well on tapes made in large and noisy classrooms. In these situations, the teacher can sometimes hardly be heard above the din of forty or fifty students rustling their papers and shuffling their books. Hearing student comments and questions can be an even greater problem. Microphones pick up sound far differently from your ear. The microphone (mic) generally picks up all sounds without regard to their origin or function, whereas the ear uses highly sophisticated aural processing techniques that tend to screen out unwanted sounds from our "hearing," or conscious focus. Thus, taping on location presents special problems. Large rooms with hard surfaces make recording good sound almost impossible. You can mitigate this problem by using a wireless mic for the teacher. Student contributions are still a problem, but multiple mics with a mixer may help. Obviously, the complexity of the task increases. Establishing good relations with the AV professionals on your campus can save you many headaches as you go about your work! A special room set up for taping can obviate many difficulties. Also many modern auditoria are better suited for sound recording than older ones, but never take it for granted that you will be able to hear well on the tape you have made. Always be as prepared as you can: ask the teacher about the room set up, find out if there is a class in the room beforehand, and get there early. (I have often started setting up equipment in the hall outside the classroom while there is an earlier class going on inside. It helps to get a start by getting the camcorder on the tripod, putting the tape in and doing other simple tasks ahead of time.)

Videotape Consultations

I saw myself on tape for the first time in 1979 when I was a young teaching assistant in graduate school. While watching the tape I experienced a deep fascination with the unfolding class which had an uncanny, almost out-of-body quality to it. To my complete surprise, I experienced my teaching persona as confident, thoughtful and coherent compared to my internal experience of feeling that the class was jumbled, disjunct and confusing in the extreme for students. In class I would always be juggling at least three or four tracks of information at one time: keeping a log of my progress through the class outline, responding to students' questions and their looks of confusion, and making sure that what I was saying was coherent, intelligible, and most of all, accurate. My problems seemed enormous, and I needed lots of help. What I actually found from watching the tape was that I did present ideas carefully and logically, but students were still confused. I had problems in that class, but they were discrete and manageable rather than global and overwhelming. What I remember most about the consultant was that she seemed concerned with me and my goals for the class. I felt like she really cared about me as a teacher and encouraged me to make my own judgments about my teaching and set the pace at which I comprehended important teaching concepts.

Teacher-Based Collaborative Consulting

Underlying my work with teachers through the years has been an unwavering commitment to the people who are called to the vocation of teaching. It is clear to me that we teach best by example, and that my consulting practice with teachers is the most important vehicle for teaching other teachers about teaching. Therefore I consider collaborative, client-based consulting a foundation upon which I base my teaching consultation practice. As a faculty development professional I am here to serve teachers. I can do this best by addressing their needs and concerns, always starting with their perceptions of a situation. Find out what they would like to explore in their teaching as well as their concerns. For a consultant to be truly effective it is important that he or she feels, in some small way, like an ally in the teacher's work. My agenda as a faculty developer is important, but it is subservient to the teacher's agenda. The more I lose sight of my client's concerns, the less effective I become. This is an attitude which I bring to every teaching consultation I do.

In order to understand what our clients experience while watching tape, it is helpful for a consultant to review a videotape of himself or herself teaching, giving a seminar, or running a discussion in order to have a first hand experience of what it feels like. The knowledge and personal authority gained by being able to say, "I was anxious when I taped myself, but found that the benefits of videotaping far outweighed the initial fear," is invaluable in giving potential videotape clients confidence in your judgment that it would be beneficial to tape a class. A consultant who is client-based should also be aware of his or her skills in observation, listening, empathy, interpersonal communication and tact. If there are major deficiencies in any of these areas, work to improve them is indicated. Teachers, particularly new or young teachers, can have profound psychological experiences while reviewing a tape of their class. They may confront lifelong personal fears and anxieties concerning adequacy, family relationships, being liked by others, and so on. For example, I find that it is quite common for teachers who have never before seen themselves on tape mention how much they are reminded of siblings and parents. Just as frequently, I find that new teachers are amazed at how effective they really are in the classroom (as I was).

In a collaborative teacher-based consultation it is important to consider whether one should watch a tape before the tape review session. Of course, if you made the tape yourself the point is moot. But if a staff member made it for you, you may want to consider not watching it in advance. The advantage here is that you can learn about the class and the students directly from the teacher. In the consultation, they are the experts on their class. The consultant is already seen as an authority figure with many answers (especially with new and young teachers), so there is no need to exacerbate this problem. In addition, this approach allows the consultant to stay fresh because there is constantly something new or perhaps unexpected around the corner in each class. In addition, the teacher now has the benefit of experiencing the class in real time allowing the consultant to put himself or herself in the place of the students during the review process.

The benefits of watching tapes ahead of time include the ability to think through approaches to serious problems, if there are any, and to have "tools" ready ahead of time. It could also shorten the meeting because it may be easier to focus quickly on major issues, and can possibly be a more efficient use of time. There are pitfalls, however, including a skewed power relationship between teacher and consultant. By watching the tape in advance, one can easily impose assumptions and criteria onto a class and form inaccurate assumptions and opinions, however subtle or unconscious. The consultant can easily, even unconsciously, take the opportunity for discovery away from a client allowing the teacher to become passive and less engaged or invested in outcomes and solutions.

In a teacher-based consultation a collaborative process of discovery unfolds for both client and consultant as you watch the tape together. In my experience this becomes a very important shared, collegial experience. With this approach, the teacher also remains the "expert" on the class. The consultant must ask the teacher about later outcomes of events in early parts of class, providing the teacher and the consultant the opportunity to observe whether these perceptions are correct or not. The consultation has more of an opportunity to be truly guided by the teacher's agenda, because the consultant has less opportunity to form opinions ahead of time.

Practical Advice for Creating a Collaborative, Teacher-Based Consultation

My advice for effective consultations has the following eight points.

Create a Setting of Comfort for the Teacher

A setting which closely resembles a private living room is usually best. Make sure that doors can be closed, your meeting can proceed uninterrupted and that privacy is assured (be mindful of windows which look out into halls). The room should be comfortable enough for two to sit for two hours without feeling cramped. Fresh air, natural light, and windows help. My deck and monitor are set up in my office, in a cozy alcove away from my desk. A table to lean and write on between our two chairs also provides a good spot to place the remote tape controller. Informality and a comfortable location can help put a teacher at ease.

Establish a Comfortable Climate

Find out what this teacher is interested in knowing about their class. Learn about the course and the students in this class. What purpose does the course have in the undergraduate or department curriculum? What are students supposed to learn? What do they generally learn? Asking questions about the students signals your intent to observe them and their behavior in class. Ask the teacher whether she or he has questions or concerns about the class. What do they think they will see? It can be helpful to focus on one or two main questions that the teacher raises. If none is offered, you can always observe students' behavior in class and infer how they may be learning in class.

Let the Teacher Show You the Tape

Give the remote control to teacher. Mention that he or she can stop the tape at any time to discuss questions or comments that arise. Let your client know that if you have a comment or question, you will suggest a pause. The teacher should have (literal) control of tape.

Allow the Teacher to React

At first, clients are usually fascinated and intently watch themselves. If you stop the tape after five or ten minutes, and ask "What do you see?" you will get lots of information about the teacher's initial concerns. It is important to acknowledge these concerns and answer them honestly. A client might mention, for example, "It really bothers me that I keep touching my hair. Doesn't it bother you?" If it is distracting, say so while remembering the dictum that the first step to changing a habit is recognizing that it is there! This is important feedback; it allows a teacher to bring immediate concerns about their appearance and presentation ability to the surface. In general, a little nervousness is harmless enough, but watch out for the nervous "twitch" or repetitive habit that is distracting to everyone in the room. If there is a problem, tell them that the process of ridding oneself of a habit is difficult but entirely predictable: one becomes overly conscious of the habit, then self-consciously tries to replace the habit over time. If there really is no problem, tell them so. "No, I didn't notice that at all" or "I noticed it, but it didn't distract me from what you were saying." An important fact to keep in mind when working with clients is that one hears one's own vocal timbre differently from others because we hear a great percentage of our own voice through our skull's bony structures. When played back on tape we hear our voice through the air, as others hear us. This can be disconcerting for some people, but there is a clear physical reason for this phenomenon. You should work on any important but "peripheral" concern which could otherwise detract from the entire consultation. Once the air is cleared of that concern, you have a better chance to focus teachers on their students and the learning atmosphere they create in their class.

Observe the Students

Some of the main questions that you've teased out in the beginning of the consultation may be concerned with student learning. As you watch the tape, it usually becomes clear to the teacher that this focus offers the richest and most profound feedback. What is happening in class? How are students reacting to the teacher's questions, lecturing, explanations, board work, and so on? What expressions do students show in their faces? Why? What is it like for the teacher to sit in on his or her own class?

Observe the Teacher

There are limits to how much anyone can learn in one session. When I first started out in instructional consultation, I would see many teaching issues worthy of analysis and discussion. With time I learned to acknowledge the glazed look on the client's face and realize that I had overstepped the limit to how much someone could learn in one sitting. In my experience, this varies greatly from teacher to teacher, and often depends on how much experience and confidence they have in the classroom.

I have learned to limit the scope of consultations as needed, and to focus on what is most important from the teacher's perspective. When starting out as a teacher, learning one important lesson is more than enough, let alone two or three. For example, a teacher notices that students become passive, bored and sleepy during the lecture. What can be done? This is more than enough work for the next few months! Keep in mind that professors have a lot of work in addition to whatever it is you have in mind for them. Appreciate the work and energy it takes to teach, and adjust your sights accordingly and develop attainable goals with your client.

Summarize

Together, go over the main themes of the consultation. What teaching strengths were evident? Which weakness was most important? Decide together to work on a manageable number of concerns, offering help and support. Helping a teacher to set an attainable goal is a very useful role for the consultant.

It can help to make another tape in two, three or four

weeks. You can often actually see change, which helps to demonstrate the efficacy of reflection on teaching practice and the efficiency of the videotaping and consulting process. If a client doesn't have a sense of cause and effect in teaching (typical among first time teachers), it is invaluable for them to see actual, observable change happen. You can demonstrate that teaching isn't such a mystery after all. You can reflect on it rationally, make changes, and see results. At this point other activities may be indicated to support the teacher's reflection and learning process, such as student evaluations of teaching and classroom assessment techniques.

Humility is the Most Important Lesson

There have been many times when, in the middle of a difficult consulting situation the tape will run for ten, fifteen, even twenty minutes straight and the teacher will suddenly pause the machine and understand, without any intervention from me, exactly the issue I tried to raise earlier but with no success. Such is the nature of videotape reflection: it allows teachers to become students in their own classes and gives them the means to grasp, in an essential way, the learning environment they have created and the power to reflect on it and change it.

Appendix A

Ground Rules for Videotape Consultations

Recruiting

I have found that good recommendations from faculty colleagues combined with a personal conversation or telephone call is the best means for recruiting teachers to take advantage of videotaped instructional consultation. At the start of a taping program, the most adventurous faculty typically volunteer to be videotaped. Many of these volunteers are simply curious to see themselves teach. Other times they are faculty who face some unexpected challenges in a class such as instituting a new course, or changing an old one to meet new curricular needs.

If your campus has a new faculty orientation, sponsoring discussions about teaching can be an extremely effective way to build trust with new faculty. If faculty are new to teaching or new to the institution, a good opportunity exists to engage them in this form of instructional development. As mentioned in this chapter, videotape can shorten the learning curve for new teachers and provide experienced faculty an opportunity to reflect on comfortable routines in the context of a new school and department.

Confidentiality

Credibility relies upon maintaining the strictest confidentiality concerning instructional and other professional development activities with faculty members. Even in the face of pressures to report results to supervisors, which can even come from the teachers themselves, consultants must maintain the strictest confidentiality. Only teachers themselves should report outcomes to a supervisor. With the permission of instructor you may choose to report that faculty member has engaged in consultation, but nothing else. Why? If a consultant divulges this confidential information and his or her analysis of it, I believe that he or she would quickly become the campus "teaching police," a role not helpful for credibility with faculty.

Teachers' Use of Classroom Tapes

In my program teachers are asked to watch their tapes privately with me first. After they have seen it with me, they are free to take it home, show it to their chair, or do anything else as long as there remains a legitimate educational use for the tape. If a teacher wants to show the tape to their chair with me present, I tell them that in order to make that session most productive, it would be helpful to determine what the main teaching issues are in the class and then show only those portions of the class which are clearly relevant to that issue. In a sense, then, we will use the private session to prepare for the meeting with the teacher's supervisor.

I have very little experience with teachers watching their tapes at home alone. The few experiences I have had so far have been somewhat negative in that teachers, once they saw the tape, canceled their appointments for the consultation much more often than teachers who had not seen the tape. Taking two hours, or even one hour, out of a busy schedule can seem overwhelming given the demands that many of our faculty have upon their time. So far, I have found the incentive of seeing the tape for the first time to be a real help rather than a hindrance, and faculty have almost never questioned me about it.

If teachers do want to watch first at home, I usually am able to avoid this by using a format which is not common in home machines, i.e. S-VHS or Super VHS. The tape will fit in a normal VHS machine and run through the mechanism just fine, but the electronic content of the tape creates a more or less unusable picture on normal VHS machines. It is a high resolution format, which I find useful for many reasons during the consulting process (see next section). It also gives me the opportunity to say that the teacher could not use it on their home machine, but if they like it after they see it I am more than happy to have a copy dubbed onto a regular VHS tape.

Appendix B

Basic Video Equipment List

For getting out and doing on-location taping in small classrooms, you could start with a minimum complement of equipment, including:

- high quality, durable, commercial-grade camcorder (I use S-VHS)
- good tripod
- small video monitor
- multi-outlet power strip
- extension cords and connecting cables
- carrying case or cart to help carry the equipment

If you want to record in large, noisy rooms you will need extra audio equipment including:

- mic for the teacher (wireless is best) plus receiver
- pressure zone mic for picking up the students
- portable audio mixer for connecting the two mics

For your playback setup in the office, include:

- high quality monitor with good sound and a picture large enough to see well, but not so big as to be intimidating
- stand for the monitor that places the screen at chair height
- heavy duty commercial VCR (I prefer one which contains a digital frame memory, so that when pausing the tape for long periods the picture remains on the screen)

8. Collecting Information Using Student Ratings

Michael Theall and Jennifer Franklin

*A*s instructional consultants, we are often called on to provide faculty with general information about their teaching. Sometimes we are asked to assess the effectiveness of a new teaching method or the net effect of a new course. Sometimes we are asked to help faculty improve their overall teaching performance or to sharpen particular skills. And, on occasion, we are asked to help a faculty member prepare documentation for a portfolio or a promotion and tenure dossier. While each of these situations places different demands on both the consultant and the client, there is one similarity: the need for information which can inform and guide the process. In this chapter, we concentrate on data from one specific source, students, and on one specific kind of information, data collected with student ratings questionnaires.

Student opinions have a legitimate place in all of the situations noted above. With care, valid and reliable data can be collected for use in these situations. Although it is not difficult to construct valid and reliable instruments, the most common errors we have encountered involve either questionable data, misinterpretation of results, or invalid use of the data. One problem lies in the assumption that student ratings data gathered with any and all questionnaires can be used in the situations we have listed and in many other situations as well. While it is generally true that student ratings data can be used for teaching improvement, for administrative decision-making, for program development, for institutional research, for classroom research, or for investigation of questions about evaluation and college teaching, it does not follow that all data are equally useful.

Because instructional consultants may be asked to review and interpret ratings data for any or all of these purposes, it is critical that we both understand the differences and be able to explain them to our clients. What makes the difference? When are ratings useful? Reliable? Valid? What kinds of data can we collect? Under what circumstances can other sources of information be used?

What are the dangers we should avoid? Finally, how can we help faculty to best use the information available to them? The focus of this chapter is on these kinds of questions and on practical guidelines for instructional consultants' accurate and effective use of student ratings data.

What Do We Know About Student Ratings?

The first question asked in any discussion of student ratings is whether or not student opinions are worth considering. The fact is that there is clear and consistent evidence that students are valid and reliable raters of the instruction they receive if: 1) the instruments and methods used to collect data are appropriate; and 2) there is no deliberate attempt to subvert the process.

We have included references for those who would like to read more about student ratings, but the literature can be briefly encapsulated. In over forty years of investigation, researchers have verified what common-sense tells us: that the people in the best position to report what goes on in a classroom are the people who are there for the full length of the term and who witness and/or take part in the process. They are uniquely qualified to comment on the quality, usefulness, and outcomes of their experiences (that is, they are *valid* raters), and they are very consistent in the ratings they give (that is, the data they generate are *reliable*).

Whether the reports of ratings results are useful and beneficial or pointless and destructive depends largely on what the students are asked to report and on how the data are analyzed, reported, and interpreted. Often, problems with validity and reliability are more closely related to the users of the data than to those who provide it. For example, current concerns about gender and ratings appear to have much more to do with course assignments and the attitudes of faculty and departments than with supposedly prejudicial student attitudes. We have all heard the complaint that ratings are "just a popularity contest," and someone almost always makes the comment that they know an unnamed professor who "pushed up his ratings by giving high grades." These comments are not supported in the literature. Our feeling is that good teachers ought to be popular. The terms are not mutually exclusive! Good teachers must understand their subject and must be able to explain its concepts in terms students can understand. Good teachers can also be charismatic, or extraordinarily attentive to students, or good story tellers, or very organized, or good discussion leaders; but in the end, *students value the outcomes of the instruction they pay for*. If students feel they have learned a lot, they will be satisfied and react positively to the teacher and the course. If they feel they haven't learned anything, charisma and good stories won't make a difference. Likewise, even if unearned higher grades could lead to better ratings (and there is clear evidence they don't), who is at fault in the grade-inflation scenario: the students, the ratings system, or the professor who is trying to manipulate the process? We emphasize that the results of student evaluations can be productively used if: 1) there is a match between the intent of the evaluation, the kinds of data collected, and the way in which results are reported; and 2) the users of the results are trained in interpretation. Here's an example which illustrates both of these points. Let's assume that the purpose of collecting student ratings is to gather data for teaching improvement. It follows that the instrument(s) used should provide data that can help to improve teaching. Questions should focus on the processes of instruction and the behaviors of the teacher and not on vague or overly broad issues. For example, an item like "The instructor was well prepared" coupled with an agree-disagree response scale is marginally useful to the teacher for several reasons. First, even if we assume that the students are in a position to accurately judge this issue (a major assumption in this case), it is difficult to tell on what basis the students judged preparedness and whether they shared a definition of the term. Second, the item contains the word "well" as a qualifier of the word "prepared". How "well" is "well?" Does a choice of the response "agree" mean the same as the response "strongly agree" when the word "well" doesn't appear? Next, would two teachers interpret these responses similarly or would their own definitions of preparedness be based on totally different concepts? One might say, "I prepared for hours," while another said, "I have a Ph.D. and spent years preparing to teach this subject." And finally, with reference to item 2 above, what if the data were then given to an administrator even though the original purpose of the evaluation was teaching improvement? Would the data be used to make some decision about the quality of the instructor's teaching? What definitions would the decision maker use and would this person be knowledgeable enough to know that the "preparedness" item was suspect or to correctly interpret the statistics presented in the evaluation report?

Faculty and staff who are instructional consultants are frequently called on to assist in the interpretation of these kinds of data. The next section reviews some qualifications that are necessary if the consultant is to be effective in this role.

Consultant Qualifications

There are many critical components in successful consultation. Because of the specificity of this chapter, we will discuss only knowledge and process factors which relate to consultation involving the use of student ratings data. General interpersonal and consultative skills, the dynamics of the consultation process, the institutional variables beyond the consultant's control, and the use of other kinds of student data are discussed elsewhere in this book. Three areas of expertise are important for instructional consultants: knowledge of the technical aspects of evaluation and the ability to apply this knowledge to real situations; knowledge of pedagogy and how to assist others with their teaching; and political and practical knowledge. These areas are discussed below.

Evaluation Knowledge (Technical and Applied)

We believe that the first critical component of consultant success for providing feedback with ratings is solid knowledge of the literature dealing with instructional design, college teaching, faculty evaluation, faculty development, teaching improvement, and social/psychological measurement.

Consultants must be able to assess the quality of questionnaires, to interpret results, and equally important, to know when results are not interpretable. Consultants will probably have to assure clients that ratings can be reliable and valid and they will also have to defend ratings against the many myths which surround them. Consultants must know how to select or construct instruments and how to administer evaluations. They must be able to determine if samples are adequate and if results are due to real events, chance, or error variance. All these activities require grounding in survey and research methods and while statistical skills are essential, advanced levels of highly sophisticated knowledge are not required.

A second important component of success goes beyond the direct knowledge discussed above and involves the consultant's skill in performing the tasks which are part of the process. Consultants often become involved in extended working relationships with clients. In these cases, "book knowledge" is not enough. The consultant must be able to transfer some of this knowledge to the client and to participate in the development/improvement process. It's one thing to suggest that a teacher become familiar with the taxonomy of instructional objectives (by itself, this probably won't result in anything productive anyway) and quite another to be able to write good objectives and to get a faculty member to appreciate the direct value of objectives in good instructional design as well as their indirect value in the improved ratings which may result.

Teaching Consultation Skills

Faculty may come to consultants with specific questions about teaching techniques or with disappointing ratings which can be a catalyst for improvement efforts. However ratings are introduced into the process, the consultant must be able to explain how they work, what their limitations are, and how they can be used.

Consultants will have to draw inferences from the data and make suggestions about teaching strategies and techniques. Consultants will have to deal with results having implications for testing, assessment, and classroom research, and in doing so, may have to help faculty further investigate their teaching processes and outcomes. Given valid and reliable data from ratings as well as other information gathered in interviews, examination of materials, exam results, and other sources, consultants must be able to draw conclusions and to construct productive programs for improvement. Understanding what dimensions of teaching are measured by which items and how these dimensions contribute to student learning are prerequisites for consultants. Faculty clients need specific information about their strengths and weaknesses and about a variety of instructional methods and strategies, if they are to increase their repertoire or design and development skills.

Without a substantial base of theoretical and applied knowledge, the consultant is limited both in ability to provide significant assistance and in credibility as a valuable and productive colleague.

Practical and Political Awareness

Since instructional consultation does not occur in a vacuum, there are some practical and environmental issues which impact on the process. Some of these issues are within the control of the individuals involved and some are not, but both consultant and client are at a great disadvantage if institutional resources, practices, and policies prevent or interfere with collecting useful data, providing resources for improvement, and delivering tangible rewards for excellent teaching. For example, if the only ratings process supported by the institution (in principle and with finances) is untested, inefficient, and invalid, then the consultant has little useful information to work with and s/he will have to either use poor information or devise and somehow support collection of better data. In these cases, the consultant may have to help the faculty member develop better data and further, may have to overcome resistance even to the ideas of evaluating and improving teaching. These tasks will be very difficult without institutional support.

There is also the great danger that the diminished opportunities for productive and successful consultation will eventually result in negative views of the process. The comment, "Well, we tried that and it didn't work," has often been made about educational innovations from consulting to computers; but more often than not, the lack of success in innovative programs does not stem from bad ideas or limited potential of the programs themselves, but rather, from a failure to provide the kinds of resources the program needs. Unfortunately, many faculty and administrators think of student ratings only in terms of questionnaires, pencils, machine-readable answer sheets, and a little anonymous help from the computer center. The same mistake is made with teaching improvement efforts when a faculty member is assigned responsibility for an improvement program and then given only a little released time and a work-study student as resources. The implications of these conditions are that consultants must have or must be able to obtain support—publicity, credibility, finances, space, staff, access to decision makers, formal title and unit designation. Consultants (or those who might be appointed as consultants) must know what kinds of support will be required and must bring issues of proper support into discussions either at the planning stage or at the initiation of the program. Consultants must also have influence—ability to influence policy and process. They must be aware of the institutional/organizational climate and politics and be able to influence decisions made about the nature and extent of the programs that are proposed and the support that they require.

Operations, Processes, and Guidelines

Given the basic needs and preconditions described above, let us now move to the more concrete issues of collecting and using ratings data.

Policy and Procedures

The most critical part of the student ratings process does not involve questionnaires or data analysis. Rather, it is the development of clear, accepted policy about ratings and their use. *The most common course of action we have seen is also the most common error: to begin the process not with agreement on purpose but by selecting or developing a ratings questionnaire.* Several problems are frequently embedded in this approach. First, until we determine what the process is supposed to accomplish and how and by whom the results will be used, we won't know what questions to ask. Second, the approach is often institution-wide and in conflict with college, school or departmental processes already in place. Third, the question of comparing individual performance against some standard has not been addressed either in terms of what kind of comparisons will be made or in terms of what standards will be applied. Are there institutional norms (e.g., the average rating on a given item is 3.67)? Are all faculty expected to get "...at least a 3.5 rating on the overall instructor item" or even more inappropriately, are decisions made on the basis of small numerical differences in ratings results (e.g., "...a 3.7 is better than a 3.5")? Fourth, there is no agreement about what constitutes good/effective teaching, about how the various aspects of teaching performance will be considered, or about whether some aspects will be weighted more heavily than others. Fifth, distinctions have not been made between formative (revision and refinement) and summative (judgment and decision making) uses of the results. Finally, the consequences of good or poor performance have not been specified.

Despite the potential problems and pitfalls, there are many benefits to be gained from a well designed ratings system. But in any discussion of ratings process, it is critical to keep in mind that student ratings are only part of what is required to put in place truly functional and effective systems for faculty evaluation and development. In the following section, we provide a matrix which outlines the relationships of various kinds of data and some common functions of ratings.

Instruments and Questionnaires

Assuming that the above issues have been addressed, the next question has to do with instrumentation. In choosing questionnaires, form should follow function. Consultants will review ratings for formative and summative purposes and the principal concern is to avoid confusing the functions with the kinds of data collected. Even if the consultants and clients have to live with current mechanisms for data collection, analysis, and reporting, consultants still have to be able to sort through the results for clients. Ratings data can be concerned with the processes as well as the outcomes of teaching and learning; but, because process is affected by the situation in which the teaching takes place, data about specific behaviors are usually more appropriate for teaching improvement use than for personnel decision making. Likewise, personnel decisions should be informed by information that is least susceptible to situational factors such as class size, required/elective status of the course, and so on.

The following matrix (Figure 1) is intended to clarify the issue of the most appropriate data for each purpose.

The columns of the matrix represent four general areas in which ratings data can be used. "Improving teaching" refers to some organized effort to enhance performance over time and requires the analysis of ratings results, some actions leading to improvement, and future evaluation to assess the effect of the interventions. The second column concerns use of data for "Understanding a particular situation" such as the effect of a teaching strategy or the exploration of the overall success of a new course, or some other attempt to investigate teaching and learning with respect to a particular event. The "Classroom or other research" column includes classroom research or investigations into teaching, learning, evaluation, or other issues as part of a more formal process. Finally, the last column deals with "Judging teaching performance" for personnel decision-making.

On the left side of the matrix, eleven kinds of information are listed. Ten are categories of information often collected with ratings instruments. The first four either provide overall ratings or deal with course components. Five through nine provide details about the instructor or the students. Ten and eleven are included because they are so frequently collected and are so influential. In the body of the matrix, each kind of information is rated with respect to its usefulness for the four general functions identified in the columns. (The rating scale is provided at the bottom of the page.)

Differences between investigative uses of the data (the first three columns) and the administrative function (column four) are immediately apparent. There is universal

Figure 1: Usefulness of Students' Ratings Data for Various Purposes

Data from questionnaire	Improving teaching	Understanding a particular situation	Classroom or other research	Judging teaching performance
1. Global or overall judgment items (e.g., overall rating of teacher, course & amount learned)	1	2	5	5
2. Averaged scores from groups of items (e.g., assignments, texts, syllabus)	2	3	5	5
3. Course components (e.g., assignments, texts, syllabus)	3	4	4	1
4. Course Information (e.g., workload, required/elective)	3	3	4	*
5. Specific teacher skills (e.g., speaking, discussion leading, questioning)	5	5	5	1
6. Specific teacher behaviors (e.g., providing assistance, punctuality, returning exams)	5	5	5	1
7. Student demographics (e.g., class level, GPA)	3	4	5	*
8. Student attitudes (e.g., motivation, effort, attributions)	4	5	5	1
9. Additional, specific items providing further detail or dealing with unique characteristics of the class or the instruction	5	5	5	*
10. Teacher knowledge and preparation	2	2	2	1
11. Narrative comments	4	5	4	#

SCALE				
1	2	3	4	5
barely useful				extremely useful

*   possible use depending on the situation

\#   possibly useful if the sample is sufficient, if comments are transcribed, and if some analysis is performed which accurately reflects the meaning, balance, and implications of the comments agreement in the evaluation literature that personnel decisions should be based on information which is: 1) general or overall in nature; 2) most resistant to variance; and 3) most able to allow accurate and fair comparisons. Global ratings and weighted factor scores (average scores of statistically confirmed groups of items assessing similar concepts, then assigned a relative weight and importance in decision-making) are best for this purpose. But pay special attention to the remaining ratings in column four. Consultants should know, and clients should be warned that the remaining kinds of data are not appropriate for administrative decision-making because these data can be misinterpreted and misused.

For example, does a low rating on discussion-leading (number 5) mean poor teaching when the course in question is a required, large enrollment (over 100 students), introductory course taught in an amphitheater or auditorium? Obviously this situation does not provide opportunities for seminar-type discussion and the instructor's lower ratings on an item like "regularly led productive discussions" should not negatively influence a decision about this person's performance.

On occasion, course data may help to clarify a personnel decision. The starred items in column four indicate such situations. For example, in the course mentioned above, overall ratings might be taken as evidence of poor performance if they were below some general department norm or criterion. But we know that large enrollment courses and required courses are often rated a bit lower than other courses. We also know that these courses are more difficult for beginning students. Enrollment information, required/elective status, and student data such as class level would help to identify the course as one where a reduced overall rating might be expected, possibly preventing misinterpretation. A consultant should be able to point out such issues to a client so that the client can take appropriate action.

The ratings of course "workload" and "difficulty" are legitimate for some purposes (for example, determining if there is a match between the students' prior preparation and the content of a course, and assessing instructional design issues) but the typical correlations between these items and overall ratings are near zero. "Heavy" workload and "extreme" difficulty do not automatically mean good or bad teaching even though many people often make this mistake in interpretation. We can, however, use these ratings in conjunction with other information. If freshmen students (who may not be skilled at note taking) reported a "difficult" course, and also reported that the instructor: 1) did not speak clearly; 2) presented information at too fast a pace; and 3) did not indicate which information was

of major or minor importance; then we might try to help the instructor adapt the course content and class lectures to better suit the needs of these students. We might also suggest peer assistance programs, training in note taking and study skills, special work sessions, assignment reviews, or videotaping lectures so that students could spend more time on difficult points.

Specific information like that in categories five through nine is particularly useful in all functions requiring detailed understanding of the teaching/learning situation. Note that only for research functions are overall ratings are just as valuable as the specific items. This is because they allow us to more accurately judge the effects of the specific skills or behaviors in question: something of more immediate interest to researchers in search of dependent variables than to those who seek to alter teaching strategies in order to increase their effectiveness. Ten and eleven are special cases. We discourage the use of students' estimation of knowledge or preparation because we do not feel that students are in the best position to provide this information. At best, students only make inferences based on their observations of classroom behavior; this is a problem because, for example, there is no standard for "preparation." Recent research indicates that many new teachers overprepare but still do not teach effectively. More experienced professors may spend little time preparing for a class they have taught several times but students would not know how much time was spent at any given instance. To the question whether data from this kind of item provides us with useful information not better supplied by other sources, the answer is "No."

Narrative comments can be either general or specific, but they are separated from other data to stress the point that great caution must be used in their interpretation. Our experience has been that, on average, ten percent of the students in a class will include written comments. When we deal with quantitative information, we stress that any report based on less than a 50 percent response rate should not be used for personnel decision-making. Why, then, should we use a 10 percent sample for the same purpose?

While we acknowledge the value of narrative comments for all other purposes, we strongly argue against the use of these comments for personnel decisions unless three conditions hold: 1) the sample is greater than 50 percent for classes with more than 30 students, 70 percent for classes with 10 to 29 students, and 80 percent for classes with 5 to 9 students; 2) student anonymity is protected; 3) a valid technique (such as content analysis) is used for characterizing responses; and 4) the administrator who uses the narrative comments does not give them unwarranted weight simply because they are verbal rather than quantitative. Unfortunately, research and anecdotal information suggest just the opposite. Faculty and administrators are often more influenced by a single well-turned phrase than by quantitative data reflecting the opinions of an entire class.

Logistics

One of the biggest headaches for faculty and consultants is that the instruments used in the student ratings process may vary by department and that additional requirements for data collection may be imposed by a school-wide or institutional level evaluation process. Consultants may have to work with unvalidated questionnaires or data which are difficult or impossible to interpret, and faculty may have to use more than one questionnaire for each course. Further, if the existing forms are general and the faculty member wants data for teaching improvement, the only recourse is to devise another means of collecting that data.

We believe that it is possible to serve many functions with a single instrument (or a short and a long form of the same instrument) as long as the capacity exists to analyze and appropriately report data. To fully serve an institution, it may be necessary to develop and use several different coordinated questionnaires and to employ an institutional or college/school set of "core" items. These demands can only be met if the ratings process includes a data management system which can accommodate custom forms and produce custom reports. Instructional consultants may have to make recommendations about developing these various forms and ultimately, may have to be familiar enough with the forms to assist faculty interpret results in the context of each department's policies for ratings use.

The system we use, the Teacher-Course Evaluation Project (TCEP) materials and Course Evaluation System (CES) software, was specifically designed to provide data for multiple purposes: teaching improvement, personnel decision-making, student course selection, institutional studies, and basic research. The TCE Project's principal function is teaching improvement and the questionnaire has its roots in instruments such as the TABS (Teaching Analysis By Students) instrument developed at the University of Massachusetts Clinic to Improve University Teaching, the IDEA (Instructional Development and Effectiveness Assessment) system developed at Kansas State University, and other nationally distributed instruments. CES software was developed to allow direct analysis and reporting of ratings results in several report formats, and to generate data for research. TCEP-CES is in use in a variety of postsecondary settings from large-scale evaluation programs to individual uses in teaching centers. (See appendices for samples of TCEP forms.)

At the beginning of each term, faculty choose either the 40-item questionnaire or a shorter version using a few items extracted from the long form. Analysis of the 40-item TCEP questionnaire automatically provides two reports: an item-by-item report which also includes the instructor's self ratings (if the instructor completed a survey), and an abbreviated report containing only the items usable for personnel decisions. Both reports go to the instructor, but the administrator would receive only the short report from the faculty member or, if requested as department policy by faculty vote, from the evaluation office. If the faculty member chooses to use the short form, only the administrative report is produced and distributed as before. Results are used administratively in accordance with department or school policies and for improvement purposes, the individual can choose to deal with a consultant or to review results privately. TCEP results can be used at mid-term for consultation purposes, making end-of-term or subsequent evaluations useful in assessing the success of teaching improvement interventions.

TCEP allows additional questions to be asked on a one-time basis, or for specialized questionnaires and affiliated reports to be designed. These allow for departmental differences within a school or for differences within departments (for example, graduate vs. undergraduate instruction). Such questionnaires and reports are developed based on faculty input and department needs, while policies for the use and interpretation of results are developed concurrently.

Whatever system is used, the basic requirement for good practice remains the same: namely, that use and interpretation of student ratings data should be guided by the needs of the situation and the users of the data. There is no one form or process which will serve every need: the main task of instructional consultants is to assist faculty in choosing and using reliable and valid data in reliable and valid ways.

Conclusion

Instructional consultants face a wide range of tasks relating to the use and interpretation of student ratings data. The variety of forms, purposes, reports, policies, procedures, and situations with which consultants are involved means that breadth of knowledge and experience are important characteristics for success. When the institution supports sound evaluation process and provides resources for teaching improvement, the consultation process can have a positive and lasting impact on students, faculty, and the institution.

Additional Readings

Braskamp, L. A., Brandenburg, D. C., & Ory, J. C. (1984). *Evaluating teaching effectiveness: A practical guide.* Beverly Hills, CA: Sage Publications.

Centra, J. A. (1979). *Determining faculty effectiveness.* San Francisco: Jossey Bass.

Doyle, K. O. (1983). *Evaluating teaching.* Lexington, MA: Heath.

Marsh, H. W. (1987). Students' evaluations of university teaching: Research findings, methodological issues, and directions for future research. *International Journal of Educational Research, 11,* 253-388.

McKeachie, W. J. (1994). *Teaching tips: Strategies, research, and theory for college and university teachers* (9th ed.). Lexington, MA: D.C. Heath.

Theall, M., & Franklin, J. (Eds.). (1990). Student ratings of instruction: Issues for improving practice. *New Directions for Teaching and Learning, no. 43.* San Francisco: Jossey Bass.

Theall, M., & Franklin, J. (Eds.). (1991). Effective practices for improving teaching. *New Directions for Teaching and Learning, no. 48.* San Frncisco: Jossey Bass.

Weimer, M., Parrett, J. L., & Kerns, M. (1988). *How am I teaching? Forms and activities for acquiring instructional input.* Madison, WI: Magna Publications.

Attachments

Sample Forms from the Teacher-Course Evaluation Project (TCEP):

1. TCEP standard instrument on machine-readable answer sheet.

2. TCEP Teacher's self-evaluation form.

3. A typical, short form usable in the TCEP-CES system.

Note: These forms do not differ greatly from several other carefully developed and validated questionnaires. The items and emphases are similar to those in other forms and are guided by the same literature on teaching and evaluation. In TCEP-CES, however, custom forms and customized analyses and reports of results can be developed to meet individual needs and to generate usable data for multiple purposes. TCEP-CES is available to any institution but is not sold as a commercial or retail product. Contact the authors for information.

TCEP   Teacher-Course Evaluation

INSTRUCTOR'S NAME	DO NOT MARK IN THIS AREA	QUESTION I.D.	YEAR CODE	T E	KEY NUMBER

COURSE NUMBER

COURSE NAME

INSTRUCTIONS: Your instructor has specially requested the TCEP questionnaire form in order to get more detailed and useful feedback. Your responses are anonymous. Please write any comments on the blank paper provided.

☞ USE BLUE INK, BLACK INK, OR A #2 PENCIL ONLY

THE INSTRUCTOR

Which of the options to the right best describes how often the event described in each item below occurs in THIS class:

KEY: A = almost always
B = more than half of the time
C = about half of the time
D = less than half of the time
E = almost never or
F = ITEM NOT APPLICABLE

The instructor:

1. communicates the purposes of class sessions and instructional activities.
2. speaks clearly and audibly when presenting information.
3. presents information at a rate I can follow.
4. indicates which information is essential and which is minor.
5. uses examples and illustrations which help clarify the topic being discussed.
6. shows important relationships among the topics being treated in this course.
7. inspires excitement or interest in the subject matter of this course.
8. relates course material to relevant real life situations when possible.
9. asks questions which challenge me to think.
10. provides opportunities for me to bring up or discuss issues related to the course.
11. develops an atmosphere of respect and trust in the classroom.
12. manages classroom discussions so that they are a useful part of my learning experience.
13. presents activities and materials appropriate for my level of experience and ability.
14. clears up points of confusion for me.
15. provides assistance on an individual basis outside of class when I need it.
16. gives me regular feedback about how well I am doing in the course.
17. states in advance precisely how my performance is to be evaluated.
18. gives tests (exams) that are fair and accurate measures of course skills, concepts, and information as taught.
19. returns exams and assignments quickly enough to benefit me.
20. suggests specific ways I can improve my performance in this course (when needed).
21. makes effective use of class time.
22. is punctual in meeting class and office hour responsibilities.

THE COURSE

23. **The workload for this course is:**
- One of the lightest
- lighter than average
- about average
- heavier than average
- one of the heaviest

24. **The difficulty level of the course activities and materials is:**
- extremely easy
- easier than average
- about average
- more difficult than average
- extremely difficult

Continued ...

Printed in U.S.A.   (C2-VP)   CP92-0840

DO NOT MARK IN THIS SPACE

THE COURSE, cont'd	THE STUDENT

THE COURSE, cont'd

25. The textbook(s) and readings used in this course are:
- (A) among the best
- (B) better than average
- (C) about average
- (D) worse than average
- (E) among the worst
- (F) item not applicable, no textbooks or readings used

26. Rate how well the syllabus, course outline, or other overviews provided by the instructor helped you to understand the goals and requirements of this course.
- (A) unusually well
- (B) better than usual
- (C) about as well as usual
- (D) worse than usual
- (E) not at all or none provided

27. Rate the usefulness of the outside assignments (writings, reports, and special projects) in helping you to learn.
- (A) extremely useful
- (B) more useful than average
- (C) of average usefulness
- (D) less useful than average
- (E) almost useless
- (F) NOT APPLICABLE, no outside assignments

28. Rate how well the various elements of the course (e.g., class activities, textbooks, readings, and outside assignments) worked together in helping you learn.
- (A) very well
- (B) better than average
- (C) about average
- (D) worse than average
- (E) very poorly

29. The course goals or objectives presented by the instructor were met.
- (A) strongly agree
- (B) agree more than disagree
- (C) agree and disagree, uncertain
- (D) disagree more than agree
- (E) strongly disagree
- (F) no goals or objectives were presented by the instructor

OVERALL RATINGS

30. Overall, how much do you feel you have learned in this class?
- (A) an exceptional amount
- (B) more than usual
- (C) about as much as usual
- (D) less than usual
- (E) almost nothing

31. What is your overall rating of this instructor's teaching effectiveness?
- (A) one of the most effective
- (B) more effective than average
- (C) about average
- (D) less effective than average
- (E) one of the least effective

32. What is your overall rating of this course?
- (A) one of the best
- (B) better than average
- (C) about average
- (D) worse than average
- (E) one of the worst

THE STUDENT

33. My educational background prepared me with the skills and information I need to achieve success in this course.
- (A) strongly agree
- (B) somewhat agree
- (C) mixed feelings, uncertain
- (D) somewhat disagree
- (E) strongly disagree

34. In my own judgement, what I am being asked to learn in this course is important.
- (A) strongly agree
- (B) somewhat agree
- (C) mixed feelings, uncertain
- (D) somewhat disagree
- (E) strongly disagree

35. Overall, I tried to do my best to meet the requirements of this course.
- (A) strongly agree
- (B) somewhat agree
- (C) mixed feelings, uncertain
- (D) somewhat disagree
- (E) strongly disagree

36. The single most important factor determining the grade I expect to receive in this course has been:
- (A) my ability
- (B) my effort
- (C) instructor's teaching ability
- (D) difficulty level of course
- (E) other students in the course
- (F) mainly luck

37. In my program, this course is:
- (A) required - AND in my major area of study
- (B) required - BUT NOT in my major area of study
- (C) elective - AND in my major area of study
- (D) elective - BUT NOT in my major area of study
- (E) other (e.g., non-credit or audit)

38. My class is:
- (A) freshman
- (B) sophomore
- (C) middler (five year or "co-op")
- (D) junior
- (E) senior
- (F) graduate student

39. My overall gradepoint average is: (first quarter freshman use high school overall G.P.A.)
- (A) 1.00 - 1.75
- (B) 1.76 - 2.25
- (C) 2.26 - 2.75
- (D) 2.76 - 3.25
- (E) 3.26 - 4.00

40. I expect to receive a grade closest to:
- (A) A
- (B) B
- (C) C
- (D) D
- (E) F or U (fail or unsatisfactory)
- (F) S (satisfactory)

41. Your gender
- ○ female
- ○ male

TCEP
Instructor's Questionnaire

SECTION I: THE INSTRUCTOR

Use the scale below to indicate how often statements 1 through 22 are true about YOU as an instructor for THIS class.

A = almost always
B = more than half of the time
C = about half of the time
D = less than half of the time
E = almost never   or
F = this item DOES NOT apply to this course

As the instructor, I

1. communicate the purposes of class sessions and learning activities.
2. speak clearly and audibly when presenting information.
3. present information at a rate students can follow.
4. indicate which information is essential and which is minor.
5. use examples and illustrations which help clarify the topic being discussed.
6. show important relationships among the topics being treated in this course.
7. inspire excitement or interest in the content of this course.
8. relate course material to relevant, real life situations when possible.
9. ask questions which challenge students to think.
10. provide opportunities for students to bring up or discuss issues related to the course.
11. develop an atmosphere of respect and trust in the classroom.
12. manage classroom discussions so that they are a useful part of students' learning experience.
13. present activities and materials appropriate for students' levels of experience and ability.
14. clear up points of confusion for students.
15. provide assistance on an individual basis outside of class if students need it.
16. give students regular feedback about how well they are doing in the course.
17. state in advance precisely how student performance is to be evaluated.
18. give tests (exams) that are fair and accurate measures of course skills, concepts, and information as taught.
19. return exams and assignments quickly enough to benefit students.
20. suggest specific ways students can improve their performance in this course (when needed).
21. make effective use of class time.
22. am punctual in meeting class and office hour responsibilities.

36. The primary (most important) mode of instruction for this course is:
A. lecture (by instructor) and examination and/or papers
B. group discussion with team or collaborative projects
C. laboratory, performance, or other "hands on" in-class activities
D. clinical, field work, or practicum off-campus activities
E. independent student research with individual supervision
F. presentations of invited lecturers, videotapes, films, etc with discussion, papers, and/or exams.

37. The main method used for evaluation of student performance in this class is:
A. tests and/or exams only
B. papers and projects only
C. papers and/or projects and tests and/or exams
D. performances, presentations, or demonstrations
E. non-print projects (e.g. constructions or fabrications for engineering; paintings, photographs, drawings for fine arts)
F. assessment of quality of participation in class, groups, or team-work.

38. Compared to other groups of students you have taught, how would you rate this group?
A. among the best
B. better than usual
C. about the same as usual
D. worse than usual
E. among the worst

SECTION IV: Instructional Objectives

Use the scale below to indicate the emphasis you placed in this class on the objectives described below.

A. = very heavy emphasis
B. = moderate emphasis
C. = some emphasis
D. = slight emphasis
E. = no emphasis

Students:

39. gaining factual knowledge (terminology, classifications, methods, trends).
40. learning fundamental principals, concepts, or theories.
41. improving logical thinking, problem-solving, and decision-making.
42. developing psychomotor (kinesthetic, manipulative, or manual) skills.
43. developing skills in organizing ideas and presenting them in written form.
44. opportunities to be creative (imaginative, inventive, original).
45. developing a favorable attitude toward the subject matter.
46. developing skills for leadership, teamwork, and group work.
47. developing knowledge of self; insight; or self-confidence

v. 3.0

SECTION II: THE COURSE

Compared to other college courses at this level (in this or similar disciplines) ...

23. The workload for this course is
   A. one of the lightest
   B. lighter than average
   C. about average
   D. heavier than average
   E. one of the heaviest.

24. The difficulty level of the course activities and materials is
   A. extremely easy
   B. easier than average
   C. about average
   D. more difficult than average
   E. extremely difficult.

25. The textbook(s) and readings used in this course are
   A. among the best
   B. better than average
   C. about average
   D. worse than average
   E. among the worst.

26. Rate how well the syllabus, course outline, or other overviews you provided may have helped students to understand the goals and requirements of this course.
   A. unusually well
   B. better than usual
   C. about as well as usual
   D. worse than usual
   E. not at all or no such information was provided.

27. Rate the usefulness of the outside assignments (writing, reports, and special projects) in helping students to learn
   A. extremely useful
   B. more useful than average
   C. of average usefulness
   D. less useful than average
   E. almost useless
   F. outside assignments were not a significant part of instruction

28. Rate how well the various elements of the course (e.g., class activities, textbooks/readings, and outside assignments) worked together in helping students learn.
   A. very well
   B. better than average
   C. about average
   D. worse than average
   E. very poorly

29. The course goals or objectives as you presented them were met.
   A. strongly agree
   B. agree more than disagree
   C. agree and disagree, uncertain
   D. disagree more than agree
   E. strongly disagree

30. Overall, how much do you feel students learned in this course?
   A. an exceptional amount
   B. more than usual
   C. about as much as usual
   D. less than usual
   E. almost nothing

31. What is your overall rating of your teaching effectiveness (in this course/section) compared with other college instructors?
   A. one of the most effective
   B. more effective than most
   C. about average
   D. less effective than most
   E. one of the least effective

32. What is your overall rating of this course?
   A. one of the best
   B. better than average
   C. about average
   D. worse than average
   E. one of the worst

SECTION III: OTHER INFORMATION

Please answer the following items:

33. Your rank: (leave blank if not applicable)
   A. full professor (including emeritus)
   B. associate professor
   C. assistant professor
   D. instructor
   E. lecturer (including adjunct, senior, and part-time)
   F. teaching assistant

34. Your years of experience teaching
   A. less than one
   B. one to two
   C. more than two but less than five
   D. five or more but less than eight
   E. eight or more but less than twelve

35. Years of experience, con't:
   A. more than twelve but less than twenty
   B. twenty or more

Teacher-Course Evaluation Questionnaire

1. The instructor inspired interest and excitement in the content of the course
   A. strongly agree
   B. agree more than disagree
   C. agree and disagree (uncertain)
   D disagree more than agree
   E. strongly disagree

2. The course goals or objectives presented by the instructor were met.
   A. strongly agree
   B. agree more than disagree
   C. agree and disagree, uncertain
   D. disagree more than agree
   E. strongly disagree
   F. no goals or objectives were presented

3. Rate how well the various elements of the course (e.g., class activities, textbooks/readings, and outside assignments) worked together in helping you learn.
   A. very well
   B. better than average
   C. about average
   D. worse than average
   E. very poorly

4. Overall, how much do you feel you have learned in this course?
   A. an exceptional amount
   B. more than usual
   C. about as much as usual
   D. less than usual
   E. almost nothing

5. What is your overall rating of this instructor's teaching effectiveness compared with other college instructors you have had?
   A. one of the most effective
   B. more effective than average
   C. about average
   D. less effective than average
   E. one of the least effective

6. What is your overall rating of this course?
   A. one of the best
   B. better than average
   C. about average
   D. worse than average
   E. one of the worst

7. The workload for this course is:
   A. one of the lightest
   B. lighter than average
   C. about average
   D. heavier than average
   E. one of the heaviest.

8. The difficulty level of the course activities and materials is:
   A. extremely easy
   B. easier than average
   C. about average
   D. more difficult than average
   E. extremely difficult.

Please respond to questions 9, 10, and 11 using the following scale
   A. strongly agree
   B. agree more than disagree
   C. mixed feelings (uncertain)
   D disagree more than agree
   E. strongly disagree
   F. no opinion or do not understand the question

9. My educational background prepared me with the skills and information I need to achieve success in this course.

10. In my own judgment, what I am being asking to learn in this course is important.

11. Overall, I tried to do my best to meet the requirements of this course.

12. In my program, this course is:
    A. required - AND in my major area of study
    B. required - BUT NOT in my major area of study
    C. elective - AND in my major area of study
    D. elective - BUT NOT in my major area of study
    E. other (e.g., non-credit or audit)

13. My class is:
    A. freshman or sophomore
    B. junior or senior
    C. 5th year student
    D. masters program
    E. 6th year student (e.g., Ed. S.)
    F. doctoral program

14. I expect to receive a grade closest to:
    A. A
    B. B
    C. C
    D. D
    E. F or U (fail or unsatisfactory)
    F. S or P (satisfactory or pass)

Your written comments are welcome. Please use the reverse side of this questionnaire..

v. 1.0

9. *Data Review and Follow-Up Consultation*

Bette LaSere Erickson and Mary Deane Sorcinelli

When we work with faculty, we usually collect relatively comprehensive information about their teaching. We talk with them about course goals and methods, about the students enrolled in their courses, and about specific questions or concerns they may have. We collect and review samples of course materials—the syllabus, exams and quizzes, paper assignments, discussion questions, case studies, problem situations, and other materials that provide focus for class activities. We observe at least one class and often videotape another. We solicit student reactions via questionnaire, structured discussion groups, or some other classroom assessment technique.

We come then to a pivotal event in the consultation process, the meeting in which we review the information with the instructor and develop plans for responding to it. First on the agenda is sifting through the information to identify instructional strengths and areas that need attention. Equally important are selecting a focus for efforts to improve or experiment in the course and initiating a plan of action. We share below some strategies we have used to facilitate the data review and to provide follow-up consultation as faculty try out new techniques and practices.

Reviewing the Data

Preparing for the Review Meeting

Most faculty want and need time to review videotapes and student feedback independently before meeting to discuss them. In some cases, it makes most sense simply to give faculty the videotape, the students' feedback, and any other information we've collected and send them off to draw their own conclusions. Other times, providing structure for the independent review reassures and saves time. For example, faculty new to the consultation process sometimes ask "What should I be looking for?" or "What will we talk about when we meet?" Questions such as those listed in Appendix A provide direction through student ratings and classroom videotapes. Often, because we do not want to take all of our meeting time to look at videotape, we ask faculty when they are reviewing the tape independently to select a segment or two—one they like best, one they like least, or one they regard as representative of their teaching—to discuss during the review meeting.

While faculty are studying their videotape and student feedback, we are preparing for the review meeting as well. As we've gained consulting experience, we've become able to more readily discern patterns emerging from the information. The data review form (Figure 1) provides a useful way to sort through the various pieces of information at hand. We typically look at each source of information separately, teasing out teaching strengths and problems. We make note of the evidence that supports our tentative conclusions. Finally, we focus on a few teaching strengths and areas for improvement that we'd like to touch on in the review session. Some questions we ask ourselves include: Which strengths can we best build on to increase this instructor's effectiveness? In what ways can we provide reinforcement for what is working well? For which problems does the instructor (and the consultant) have the skills and resources to deal with? Which problems can we tackle immediately and which would better be postponed until the instructor has some initial success?

Figure 1: Data Review Form		
Strength	Evidence	Strategies
Problem	Evidence	Strategies

Opening the Conversation

Despite the fact that we identify some issues for consideration, when we meet to discuss the information collected we always begin with an open-ended question, something like: What did you make of all this? When you reviewed all this information, what stands out for you? Where would you like to start? Some responses take us by surprise, of course. The person whose student evaluations are terribly negative says, "I was pleased to see that the course seems to be going okay." Another worries about the one student who said the course moved too slowly but ignores the many who complain the pace is too fast. Faculty who have been videotaped often begin with observations about their physical appearance—dissatisfaction with their weight, voice, gestures, posture. Although these early responses may not be where we would choose to start the conversation, most faculty eventually go beyond them. In any case, the open-ended invitation puts faculty in control of the review process, and their responses reveal what they are ready to hear and to address.

Identifying Strengths and Areas That Merit Attention

What stand out for most faculty are the criticisms, the shortcomings, the negatives. Although a few seem blind to their teaching problems, most faculty in a very short time are able to come up with a long list of things they need to improve. Consequently, we usually find we must be more assertive and insistent in getting faculty to acknowledge their strengths. We ask: What things seem to be going well? What segment on the videotape did you like the best and why? What do students say is very good or excellent? What do you think are positive aspects of this course? We offer our own thoughts about the same questions, using student comments, course materials, videotape, and observation notes to illustrate and elaborate.

We've learned not to underestimate the importance of identifying strengths or to shortchange the time we spend talking about them. It's not just that we want to make faculty feel good, although we see no harm in that. Over the years we've seen that although faculty tend not to make dramatic changes in their teaching, they will expand or generalize those activities, assignments, and skills which they currently use if those practices seem to be working fairly well. In any case, we spend a good deal of time highlighting which class activities, assignments and teaching skills promote learning. We point them out specifically in the videotape, in our observation notes, in the course materials, and as they are reflected in student evaluations. Along the way, we talk about learning theory and research

so that faculty may deepen their understanding about why these practices are effective. Whenever we can, we encourage faculty to adapt and expand their use of those skills and activities that work well for them and their students.

The exploration of all this information rarely proceeds in an organized fashion. Conversation jumps back and forth between strengths and problems as we look at the different sources of information—student evaluations, observation notes, videotapes, course materials and samples of student work. We find it helpful for faculty and for ourselves to pause from time to time to review and summarize what we identify as strengths and what we think needs attention. As the review winds down, we begin thinking about next steps.

Selecting a Focus and Planning for Action

Before concluding the review meeting, we urge faculty to select a focus for their efforts to improve or to experiment. Without a focus, some faculty attempt to try too many new things and discover they do not have time to think about any carefully enough. Others recognize more quickly that they do not have time to do all the things they might like to do, they begin to feel overwhelmed, and they respond by doing nothing. We often ask, Where would you want to start? What do you think you'd like to focus on first? Faculty typically respond with something like: "I'd like to work on getting students more involved" or "I agree that their inability to distinguish major and minor points is probably a key to a lot of things, so I guess I should start with that" or "Well, we have an exam coming up so it's probably a good time to try to address their concerns about evaluation procedures."

Once faculty have identified a focus for their improvement efforts, we shift quickly to developing a plan for action: "All right, let's start by trying to think of something you might try in the next class. What do you have planned for that session?" "OK, when is the exam because we'll need to work back from that in terms of reviewing the questions and thinking about ways to prepare students." Whenever possible we press for coming up with something faculty can try in the next class or within the week, including a strategy for getting feedback on how it worked. Often the assessment strategy involves scheduling a visit to the class or arranging to collect some feedback from students, which leads in turn to scheduling another meeting.

Some programs offering consultation services operate on the assumption that the consultant's work with faculty will usually conclude with the data review meeting. Under that assumption, outlining a plan for action is a much larger task, one that calls for brainstorming more ideas and for planning beyond the next week or two. Both our programs assume that consultation really only begins with the data review meeting, and we stress ongoing collaboration as faculty experiment with alternative activities and practices. We do not feel the same pressures to cover all the data, to brainstorm all the alternatives, or to plan very far ahead. We emphasize instead getting started, trying something, getting feedback on the results, and providing follow-up consultation.

Follow-Up Consultation

We are convinced the most important work we do begins after the review meeting when we consult with faculty as they test new ideas and practices in their classes. Work during this phase is highly individual, which may explain why it is so rarely discussed in the literature on instructional consultation. We can identify tools for earlier phases of the consultation process—interview protocols, observation guides, sample questionnaires, steps and procedures for analyzing and synthesizing data. It is more difficult to codify practices and procedures for providing continuing consultation, and we have few tools. We describe instead four general strategies or approaches we have used in working with faculty.

Use of Experimental Cycles

By far the most common strategy we use engages us in cycles of planning, testing, and getting feedback. We meet with faculty to plan a class activity or an assignment. We observe or videotape the class and perhaps collect feedback from students. Then we meet with the instructor to discuss how the activity worked—what went well, what needs refinement, what variations or alternatives merit testing. The feedback discussion leads, in turn, to planning the next class or the next experiment, which begins a new cycle.

For example, a communications professor with a small class of sixteen students was struggling to engage them in discussion. We suggested that he divide the class into groups of three or four students, give each group a question or problem, and ask them to prepare a group response within a specified time. We then observed the next class. The results were dramatic. Students discussed the task with animation and enthusiasm while the instructor moved from group to group, monitoring student progress. When time was up, the instructor reconvened the class and asked for comments. The room suddenly grew silent and the instructor felt compelled to jump in to offer conclusions. In reviewing the class, the instructor immediately saw a problem with the way the groups had been reconvened: they had no structure for summarizing and reporting their discussion. We suggested that he might ask every group to designate a reporter. Then each group (or a sample of them) could report answers or conclusions before the instructor offered feedback or comments. We went back to visit his class the next week. Sure enough, a simple refinement in his use of small groups—assigning a reporter—allowed each group to collect their thoughts and sort them out with their group before venturing a contribution to the whole class.

Use of Colleagues

Building on the fact that colleagues are for many faculty the most credible sources of inspiration about teaching, we sometimes arrange for faculty to visit other classes and for us to meet with them afterwards to discuss their observations. Initially it was frustration in consulting with a mathematics professor that lead us to try this strategy. He insisted that working problems at the board was the only way to teach mathematics; yet student performance on exams and feedback on evaluations clearly indicated the strategy was not working. He countered every alternative we proposed with "Well, I suppose you could do something like that in the humanities or the social sciences but I don't think it would work in the hard sciences." Finally, he agreed to visit classes taught by a colleague and to meet afterwards to discuss teaching techniques used. In the end, he incorporated several of the techniques in his own courses.

Typically we identify the classes to visit and make the arrangements with the host instructor, mostly because over the years we've come to know several good teachers who are willing, and oftentimes flattered, to be asked to open their classes to visitors. Whenever possible, we also sit in on the class so that our conversation afterwards is about a shared experience and thus can be more specific. During the follow-up conversation, we try to identify skills and techniques the visiting instructor might fruitfully adapt for his or her class. Sometimes the host instructor attends the follow-up discussion but usually not because the conversation is less about the person observed than about how the observer might adapt ideas in his or her teaching.

Another way we take advantage of the expertise and experiences of colleagues is in faculty development workshops. We usually offer two or three campus-wide workshops per semester, approximately two hours in duration. Although we sometimes bring in outside speakers, most of the sessions are led by our own faculty. Topics such as teaching large classes well, dealing with troublesome behaviors in the classroom, teaching in the diverse class-room, and getting students to talk have drawn large audiences. The focus of such sessions is always on sharing concrete strategies that faculty have tried in a variety of disciplines. For example, to demonstrate how she overcomes the passivity of students in her 300 student class in adolescent psychology, one faculty member had workshop participants try out a writing-to-learn exercise. She asked them to write about when they were aware of their entry into adolescence, to share their reflections with another participant, and to compare their markers of adolescence with those in the research literature that she covered in her class. At the end of the workshop she distributed handouts with written instructions, directions, and samples of writing exercises she uses.

Through both visits to colleagues' classes and participation in workshops led by good teachers, we've found that faculty can learn about teaching from peers within and outside of their departments. The science professor who welcomes a classroom visitor seeking fresh ideas for teaching can become a source of motivation for change. And the psychology professor who lets faculty experience a writing-to-learn exercise and paired discussion clarifies how active learning in large classes can work across the disciplines.

Use of Students

Along the way we've learned that improvement can result from getting ongoing feedback from students themselves. Student feedback through diagnostic questionnaires such as the Teaching Analysis By Students (TABS) and through structured discussion with students using Small Group Instructional Diagnosis (SGID) are two good methods of obtaining this information. But there are other sources of feedback that we've found valuable. Some are indirect. For example, we've reviewed the results of student tests and exams with faculty to determine whether expectations were reasonable. We've shared observation notes with instructors, to illustrate that students reading newspapers, whispering, and failing to take notes may mean that students are not "with them." For more direct feedback, we've used strategies like the "minute paper." An instructor in sociology was convinced that our suggestion that she provide students with an outline of what would be covered in class was "spoon feeding." When we asked students to take five minutes at the end of a class to write down the most important things they learned in class and what important questions remained unanswered, they struggled with the task. Their responses provided the instructor with a much better sense of how well students were learning what she was teaching. She now outlines

key ideas on the board or on a transparency, reviewing them periodically and summarizing them at the end of class.

McKeachie (1994) also has outlined some ideas for gathering feedback from students that we've passed on to faculty. For example, in multi-section courses some of our faculty have asked each section to elect a representative to meet with them to tell them how the course is going. Because the representatives can begin the conversation with, "Some students say....," we find the comments are usually quite candid. McKeachie also suggests the use of individual conferences with students outside of class. Our faculty report that in one-on-one or small group discussions, students raise issues that indicate possible problems in instruction and that faculty can then use these discussions as cues for improvement.

Use of Print Materials

When we started consulting with faculty in the 1970's, little had been published about college teaching practices. Today, that literature grows more robust each month, and printed materials play an increasingly significant role in our consultations as sources of ideas and techniques. For example, we sent to one professor with whom we're working an article on small group techniques in science classes, to another a piece on content mapping, and to a third a chapter on writing multiple choice questions. Subsequently, we met with each to work out details for adapting the techniques in their classes.

While we tend to use published materials as sources of ideas which we then meet to discuss, some programs rely even more heavily on printed materials. Wilson (1986), for example, describes a program at the University of California at Berkeley that creates and distributes Personal Teaching Improvement Guides for faculty. Faculty who participate begin by administering the Student Description of Teaching, a questionnaire that asks students to indicate how descriptive each of 24 statements is of the teaching in the class. Faculty receive summaries of students' responses to all items. In addition, an "intervener" reviews the results, identifies the four items students rated as least descriptive of teaching in the class, and creates a Personal Teaching Improvement Guide by selecting four Teaching Improvement Packets from a library of packets corresponding to each of the 24 questions.

The Teaching Improvement Packets are interesting both in their development and in their contents. To create the packets, outstanding teachers at Berkeley agreed to administer the Student Description of Teaching and to be interviewed about the items students said were most descriptive of their teaching. The packets for each item includes general suggestions for improving performance as well as specific ideas contributed by faculty representing a range of disciplines. The packet on explaining clearly, for example, includes seven general recommendations such as "Use lots of concrete and memorable examples." The meat of the packet, however, comes from faculty who describe what they actually do. An economics professor, talking about finding concrete examples, says "In talking about inflation and price controls, I'll use the Prince tennis rackets or Sony Walkmans rather than apples or a general product." Each of the 24 packets includes a handful of general suggestions and dozens of specific illustrations. (For a large compendium of such suggestions see Davis, 1993).

In both the Berkeley program and in our own experience, faculty find written materials more useful when they include specific illustrations of activities and assignments even when the illustrations come from different fields. The economist who refers to Prince tennis rackets or Sony Walkmans rather than apples or a general product clarifies the meaning of concrete or memorable examples in a way that faculty from widely different disciplines can understand.

Conclusion

Although consultation on improvement strategies may continue longer than a semester, we usually take stock of progress near the end of the term. We may recollect information through class visits and videotape. We sometimes ask students to indicate changes they might have noticed in faculty members' teaching and additional improvements they would suggest. We then review the information collected over the semester with faculty to assess both progress made and changes still in process.

In some cases, this final review concludes our work together. Faculty report that they have accomplished their goals, that no new problems have emerged, and that they are satisfied with their teaching. In other cases, faculty find that they have made some headway but that they are interested in further improvement efforts. In those cases, we may continue working with faculty over the course of several semesters. For example, one business professor began exploring the benefits and drawbacks of multiple choice and essay exams, of short reaction and longer term papers. He found that it took a full academic year to rethink and refine his measures of student learning. A mathematics professor who worked with us some five years ago still gives us a phone call once a semester or so to ask us to observe a class or collect student feedback as part of a "progress check."

We have no illusions that our approach to consultation as ongoing collaboration with faculty as they experiment and evaluate alternative practices is the only effective way to work toward improving teaching and learning. However, we are convinced that this approach provides faculty with a model for how to assess, develop, and refine their teaching throughout their academic careers. However this process of feedback and follow-up consultation is modified to meet local needs and resources, it should be an important part of almost any teaching consultation program.

References

Davis, B. G. (1993). *Tools for teaching*. San Francisco: Jossey-Bass.

McKeachie, W. J. (1994). *Teaching tips: Strategies, research, and theory for college and university teachers* (9th ed.). Lexington, MA: D. C. Heath.

Wilson, R. (1986). Improving faculty teaching: Effective use of student evaluations and consultants. *Journal of Higher Education, 57*, 196-211.

Appendix A

Guide for Analyzing your teaching

This guide can help faculty to sort through various sources of information, especially feedback from student questionnaires and classroom videotapings. You might ask faculty to jot down notes and bring them to the review session as a way of getting discussion started and focusing on their perception and concerns.

Identifying Strengths

1. In reviewing your student ratings, identify the five items with the most responses in columns 1 and 2 (little or no improvement needed).

2. Read students' responses to the open-ended questions about what they liked best and least about the course and your teaching of it. Make a list of things mentioned frequently (e.g., "really cares about students," "tests are fair"). Then read the comments again, tallying the number of students who mention each item on your list.

3. After you've reviewed the videotape at least once, identify a segment that you think captures one of the better moments in this class.

And/Or

4. Identify segments of the videotape that you think illustrate or explain students' favorable responses to the items you identified in questions 1 and 2 above.

Identifying Areas That Merit Attention

1. In the student ratings, identify 3-5 items with the most responses in columns 3 and 4 (improvement needed and considerable improvement needed).

2. After you've read students' written responses to the question about what they liked best and least about the course and your teaching of it, list the things mentioned most frequently (e.g., "I'm not interested in the subject matter," "exams are unfair"). Read the comments again, tallying the number of students who mention each item on your list.

3. Identify one segment of the videotape that you are not completely happy about or one that you would like to talk about for some other reason.

10. *Collaborative Consultation for International Faculty*

Erin Porter and Ghislaine Kozuh

*T*he Center for Teaching Effectiveness at the University of Texas at Austin works with faculty and other teaching staff to enhance the quality of instruction on our campus through workshops, seminars, and orientations as well as through individual consultations. Because classrooms are extremely complex environments, considerable sleuthing often is required to determine why things go wrong and to find solutions that satisfy both disappointed students and frustrated instructors. With international faculty, the problems can be even more difficult given the additional language and culture factors. For this reason, we have found it helpful to combine the expertise of a faculty development specialist with that of a consultant with training in English as a Second Language (ESL) and inter-cultural expertise. A collaborative consultation approach helps to meet the needs of a growing number of international faculty concerned with teaching in American university classrooms.

Nationwide, international faculty are becoming increasingly important. The national trends are evident at The University of Texas at Austin. Three hundred thirty-two non-citizen faculty (both tenured and non-tenured) taught at the University of Texas in Fall 1992, with the highest percentages in math and physics (16 percent and 15 percent respectively). International faculty represent approximately 10 percent of the total (3,000+) UT Austin faculty. University records indicate that about forty new international faculty are hired annually.

As the international faculty numbers increased on our campus, so did their requests for Center services. During school years 1991-1992 and 1992-1993, Center consultants have assisted twenty-four international teaching faculty, over 17 percent of the annual consultation load. Five of the internationals participated in our collaborative consultation program.

Preliminary data from several large institutions (University of Washington, University of Minnesota, Texas Tech University, University of Pittsburgh, University of Michigan, and others) indicates that their faculty development centers deal with three to four international faculty per year. When institutions lack a centralized or even a systematic program, it is generally the staff of the International Teaching Assistant Program or the English as a Second Language Institute that offers tutorials, consultations, and workshops on an ad hoc basis.

Due to the complex needs of international clients and their increased consultation requests, we designed a collaborative consultation process. It features collaboration between a pedagogical consultant and a language consultant who work with the instructor in an individualized program. This collaborative consultation works on the assumption that all faculty, including internationals, are entitled to services that achieve the best possible instructional result.

The Collaborative Consultation Model

Collaborative consultation is "an interactive process that enables people with diverse expertise to generate creative solutions to mutually defined problems" (Idol, et al. 1986). As indicated earlier, we use collaborative consultation so that language proficiency, cultural, and teaching needs of international clients are met. As co-consultants we collaborate on the recommended consultation program for the client, meeting regularly to discuss our observations, reviewing and assisting the client through the phases.

The phases cited by Nyquist and Wulff (1988) and others resemble the five stages included in our model for collaborative consultation with international faculty. It is important to note that the sequence of the five stages is not exclusively chronological, thereby allowing consultants to move back and forth from stage to stage as required. The additional variable in our model features collaborative interaction between two consultants who design and implement an individualized program for international faculty (see Figure 1 and Appendix A). A case study journal illustrates how this model has functioned with an international client at our Center (see Appendix B).

Stage I: Comprehensive Data Collection

Faculty clients, including internationals, contact the faculty development specialist at the Center for assistance with classroom teaching. During that initial telephone call, a consultant is assigned based on the client's needs and time constraints. In a preliminary interview with the consultant, the client describes classroom problems, teaching issues, and other concerns. At the next meeting, the client shares data about course materials, student evaluations, peer evaluations, and a self-evaluation of teaching skills; the client's view of his or her problem is our focus. At this point, two to three classroom observations are scheduled or a videotape session at the Center. Appendices C through G illustrate the type of information the consultant requests from clients. We believe that the same data forms should be used for each faculty client whether or not he or she is an international faculty member.

Stage II: Data Analysis and Interpretation

On the basis of the data, the faculty consultant makes an initial determination whether the English language proficiency of the international faculty member is a factor contributing to problems with teaching. If this seems to be the case, the language consultant reviews the comprehensive data collected by the faculty consultant. After the client has received a personal and confidential evaluation, a plan of action is initiated. The client and the co-consultants interpret the data together and construct a general program framework. In this three-way meeting with the client, the faculty consultant discusses the teaching issues then defers to the language consultant who discusses language proficiency, cultural issues, and the language program design. The client's endorsement of all aspects of the program is crucial to the success of the consultation. The two consultants discuss with the client the best option of four approaches: (1) language and pedagogy concurrent or parallel programs, (2) language and pedagogy programs in sequence, (3) language and pedagogy alternating programs, or (4) an exclusive language or pedagogy program. At the end of this three-way meeting, the two consultants briefly review the details of the client/consultant collaboration.

Stage III: Program Design

The collaborative consultation process interfaces two areas: (1) the English language program and (2) the pedagogy program. The ESL consultant works with the client on language proficiency issues and the faculty developer works on teaching issues. Generally, international faculty communication problems related to low proficiency in

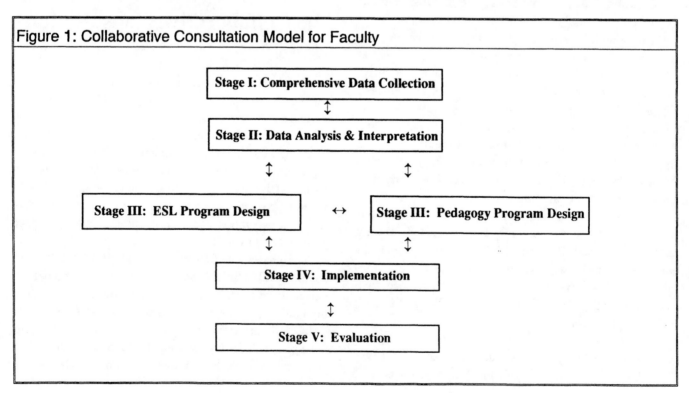

Figure 1: Collaborative Consultation Model for Faculty

Stage I: Comprehensive Data Collection

↕

Stage II: Data Analysis & Interpretation

Stage III: ESL Program Design   ↔   Stage III: Pedagogy Program Design

Stage IV: Implementation

↕

Stage V: Evaluation

English are addressed before teaching issues, but any of the four options listed in Stage II are applicable. A detailed description of the ESL Program Design is provided below because this information is the most unique addition to the consultation model.

Language program design. New international faculty sometimes cite pronunciation and the lack of English idioms and academic colloquialisms as primary concerns, but students often attribute communication difficulties to a foreign accent. It is important to help the client understand that to communicate effectively, much more are required than linguistic accuracy and idiom knowledge. Second language acquisition theory, accent reduction programs, and advanced level ESL training currently focus on the primary importance of suprasegmentals (intonation, stress, pauses, and so on) in contrast to the traditional emphasis on accuracy in grammar and in vowel and consonant production. Whereas sporadic errors in grammar, pronunciation, or vocabulary may be irritating, they do not usually account for serious misunderstandings or antagonisms (Canale & Swain, 1980).

More serious problems occur when sociolinguistic rules are broken such as when an instructor asks an inappropriate question, is too apologetic or indirect, and so on. Then social patterns of usage are violated and may have negative consequences because they are interpreted as rudeness, unfriendliness, or reflective of character flaws, and often result in negative stereotyping. Sociolinguistic rules reflect the value systems of the culture in question that are not usually made explicit and are intuitively acquired with the language during childhood. Native speakers are not always aware of such rules, because they may assume that the norms for their behavior are universal and that these behaviors are the only acceptable ones (Stewart & Bennett, 1991).

Thus, communicating effectively with students in another culture requires mastery of the social rules, the appropriate nonverbal behaviors, and the cultural values of the target language besides grammar, syntax, and pronunciation. The cultural diversity of the American university classroom is adding to these requirements in terms of every faculty member's communication skills and sensitivity to cultural differences. The American student body of undergraduates now includes large numbers of Hispanics, Asian Pacific Americans, African Americans, and more mature students returning to the classroom. If the consultation process is to be successful, the client must have realistic expectations and needs to understand the second language acquisition process and the role of the language consultant as guide in that process.

The first step in the language program is an evaluation of English proficiency based on a videotaped lesson and/or the language consultant's class observation. The language proficiency consultant does a diagnostic analysis of the client's speech patterns to identify the problems that may contribute to communication difficulties, for example, (1) pronunciation of certain vowels, diphthongs, consonants, and consonant clusters, long and short vowel sounds; (2) syllabification, word stress; (3) suprasegmentals: intonation, rhythm, blending, speech connectedness, and appropriate pauses; (4) use of articles, plural and past tense forms, prepositions, and so on; (5) use of conventional rhetorical patterns; (6) use of appropriate interactive strategies; (7) non-verbals; and (8) command of cultural information and referents (Morley, 1992). Faculty are generally impressed with the fact that for the first time ever they themselves now know where their problems lie and that they can learn strategies for monitoring speech patterns and compensating for language difficulties.

Next, the ESL consultant prioritizes language problems and proposes an individualized program for improvement. Materials and activities to be employed in the program, such as extensive audiotaping and videotaping, are reviewed with the faculty member. Finally, the language consultant and the client prepare a schedule for tutorial sessions, periodic progress assessments, classroom observations, and so on (See Appendix B). Due to the individualized nature of the instruction, we do not use a specific textbook for the tutorial sessions, but instead we select a variety of materials. Videotapes are supplied by the Center where some videotaping and all playback appointments are conducted. However, faculty clients do need to have their own audiotape recorder. Some faculty find work in the language laboratory very helpful; others prefer to make tape-recordings of pronunciation exercises, dialogs, or short presentations. Still others may want more short videotaped sessions where they can experiment with presentation styles, pacing, organizational language, and so on. They may want to examine the styles and language of exemplary professors in our Center videotape library. The ESL consultant is careful to help the client select the most potentially beneficial materials and activities.

Pedagogy program design. The pedagogy program design follows a classic faculty development approach that is tailored to the needs of each client. A pedagogy program includes some or all the following activities: (1) client in-depth self-evaluation of teaching skills, (2) classroom observations, (3) client/consultant review of observations, (4) a review of course materials, that is, syllabi, exams, handouts, overhead transparencies, lecture notes or outlines, and so on, (5) videotaping of classroom teaching, (6) client/consultant review of videotapes, (7) telephone conferences about particular classroom issues or problems, and (8) reviews of mid-semester and/or end-of-semester student evaluation forms, that is, Teaching Analysis by Students (TABS), Small Group Instructional Diagnosis (SGID), or our campus-wide Course Instructor Surveys (CIS), and so on.

Stage IV: Implementation

The activities and methodologies used in this stage are designed for each specific client as described earlier. Consultants exchange ideas as the project advances; they discuss which strategies are proving most effective with client's approach to problems, types of materials, and pace of work, any improvements in the classroom, and other needs that have come to either consultant's attention.

The frequency of collaboration or sharing is determined by the program option determined in Stage II: a concurrent, sequential, parallel, or exclusive approach. Discussions are most involved in the concurrent and sequential formats. Questions for discussion typically include: (1) At what point is the client prepared for work with the other consultant? (2) What areas must the co-consultant continue to build on? and (3) What combinations of activities will be most helpful for this client? At the completion of Stage IV, written and/or oral reports are provided for the client with possible recommendations for additional assistance. If the client follows-up by contacting the other consultant and is motivated to continue work, then the collaborative consultants and client return to and implement Stage III as needed.

Stage V: Evaluation

At the conclusion of the process, each consultant has a data file about the client and the work accomplished during the consultation; these files are held at the Center for future reference. Evaluation documentation includes summary reports, client file letters, lists of materials used, a review of recent student evaluation forms, and so on. The consultation process closes when consultation objectives are met or the client decides to discontinue.

Limitations and Benefits of Collaborative Consultation

A primary limitation of the collaborative consultation process is that the Center is not funded to provide these specialized consultation services; consequently, we have met the demand by maximizing our collaborative assets and contact hours. We believe that meeting and documenting the special needs of international faculty clients are

among our growing responsibilities. In view of the limitations described above, guidelines for the allocation of consulting time are as follows: (1) a visiting professor or scholar receives a maximum of ten hours and (2) a full-time or tenure track faculty member receives as much time as schedules allow up to a maximum of 30-40 hours per semester. Tutoring may continue for one or more semesters at the rate of one or two hours per week.

Other challenges in dealing with international clients include (a) the client resists the idea that his/her classroom English proficiency is problematic for students; (b) the client feels that language proficiency is the only issue to address; (c) the client resists adaptation of his/her cultural concepts about teaching methodologies; (d) the faculty member is a reluctant client sent by a chair or dean; (e) the client does not follow the agreed approach; (f) the client finds cultural adjustments to the American university classroom extremely difficult; or (g) the client terminates contact before consultation objectives have been achieved. For example, the client may be quite satisfied with the progress attained and may intend to continue these efforts on his or her own.

The Center's collaborative consultation process continues to develop. We are aware of "glitches" that need to be addressed. For example, the sequential referral from the language consultant to the faculty consultant has not worked well. Perhaps the source of this problem is the client's presumption that language is the only issue when it is not. To address this, the language consultant recommends additional work with the faculty consultant through a written referral to the client.

We believe the benefits of the program far outweigh the limitations. The co-consultation process is able to address the client's needs more fully and to provide a personal approach. Our clients are impressed when two experts from different backgrounds provide a well-coordinated data interpretation and plan of action. The faculty consultant interprets the faculty member's classroom performance and the language consultant identifies linguistic and cultural barriers to effective classroom communication. Consequently, the collaborative consultants (a) are less "expertise blind" to the possible alternatives for each client, (b) construct a balanced evaluation of client needs, (c) provide the international client with an integrated approach for faculty development, and (d) share credit for successes and responsibility for failures.

The shared responsibility of co-consultants is handled easily in our Center due to physical proximity of office space, specific areas of expertise of each consultant, similar attitudes about the importance of teaching effectiveness, confidence in the professional qualifications of the other consultant, and a strong sense of cooperation. The responsibilities of each consultant are clearly understood and the boundaries not contested.

From this cooperation we offer the following caveats when working with international faculty: (1) be sensitive to the personal dignity, image, and prestige of international faculty and their level of achievement; (2) consider the effects of gender differences in other cultures on your client-consultant relationship; (3) remember your role as a consultant—you provide a service outside the client's discipline; (4) explain fully the ramifications of client confidentiality; (5) avoid premature assumptions that international faculty issues are language and/or culture based; (6) consider the effects of student responses or reactions to international faculty in terms of prejudice, racism, and so on; and (7) avoid overestimating the severity of language and/or culture differences.

Measuring the effectiveness of this collaborative consultation approach is problematic since the severity of language difficulties varies as does the investment of time and effort of the individuals in the program. In some cases, progress comes quickly and international clients are content with fewer than ten hours of tutoring. As with any faculty development procedure, the motivation of the client often determines the effectiveness of the process. The amount of improvement also varies depending on the context; communication in controlled conditions such as practiced presentations will be better than that in the more spontaneous conditions of classroom teaching.

We have not yet done a full scale evaluation of this program given the small sample of participants, but informal comments and referrals indicate that participants find the program of great value. Course Instructor Surveys (CIS) — student evaluations of course and instructor — are scored by the Measurement and Evaluation Center each semester upon the request of teachers. Surveys of the semesters before and after consultation would yield useful data on our program's effectiveness. However, accessing this client data is problematic because: (1) not all departments require CIS's of their faculty; (2) faculty may choose not to release the CIS results; (3) new or visiting faculty have not taught here prior to working with us; and (4) the Center consultants have no direct access to CIS results and must rely on clients to voluntarily furnish this data.

Client Evaluations of the Collaborative Consultation

At this time, we have received four complete *Consultation Process Evaluation Forms* from the five interna-

tional clients who have completed the collaborative process. On question one, all four clients strongly agreed that the consultation process was very helpful. For question two, three clients strongly agreed that the consultant provided specific assistance with teaching ideas; the fourth client indicated that she had concentrated on language in the consultation. In question three, all four clients agreed that the materials/resources provided were adequate for their needs. For question four, all strongly agreed that the consultation process was personalized to meet their specific needs. All four clients responded "yes" to questions six, eight, and nine on the evaluation form; they agreed that the consultation process had correctly identified their strengths and weaknesses as teachers, had helped them improve their teaching, and that they would recommend the consultation process to peers. On question seven, three clients said that the length of our consultation process was sufficient to accomplish their goals as teachers; the fourth client said "No, because language learning is a life-long process for foreigners."

Clients' written responses to questions five and ten were also very favorable. One client stated, "This was extremely important and helpful!" The most helpful aspects to another client were the "identification and correction of my pronunciation problems," "videotaping and discussion of my presentations in class," and "information on how the American education system works." This client indicated that he would refer peers to this program to seek assistance with "language difficulties" and "an opportunity to review and improve your teaching." Another client commented about the "identification of my specific problems in spoken English" and the need for "some consultation in teaching, regardless their mother language and nationality." These four clients had assessed their improvement based on feedback from students and peers.

Conclusions

The collaborative consultation model meets the needs of international faculty who have multiple problems, one of which is communicative competence in English as a second language. Unfortunately, ESL has long been associated with remediation and therefore may be perceived on campus as a non-academic field. This perception is gradually changing as state legislatures, in response to pressures from students and their parents, consider English proficiency requirements for international faculty. It is important that the ESL discipline be presented as a valid area of professional development—at least equivalent to total quality management training, computer workshops, professional seminars, and so on. A second problem is the lack of commercially available ESL material specifically for international faculty making it necessary to use materials for international teaching assistants and other advanced second language (L2) learners. Whereas the (L2) needs of international faculty are similar to those of ITAs, their heavier classroom and professional responsibilities engender more sophisticated communication functions. Advanced level ESL interactive computer programs need to be developed for faculty clients with pronunciation practice for speakers of different L1 backgrounds including extensive work on suprasegmentals, sociolinguistic and strategic competencies; cultural information with associated problems to solve; American rhetorical patterns; and so on. Third, techniques and materials from related disciplines such as speech pathology (Anderson-Hsieh, 1991) and speech communication should also be explored.

Finally, the collaborative consultation model has the potential to meet the needs of international faculty in the areas of language, pedagogy, and culture. This comprehensive, integrated program and coordinated case management has become a valuable service for the Center at The University of Texas at Austin. Certainly similar programs could be developed at other large institutions where internationals will increasingly constitute the faculty corps of tomorrow.

References

Anderson-Hsieh, J. (1991). *Teaching discourse intonation through visual feedback.* Paper presented at TESOL, New York.

Canale, M., & Swain, M. (1980). Theoretical base of communicative approaches to second language teaching and testing. *Applied Linguistics,* 1(1), 1-47.

Idol, L., Paolucci-Whitcomb, P., & Nevin, A. (1986). *Collaborative consultation.* Rockville, MD: Aspen.

Morley, J., (1992). *Rapid review of vowel & prosodic contexts.* Ann Arbor: The University of Michigan Press.

Nyquist, J., & Wulff, D. (1988). Consultation using a research perspective. In E. C. Wadsworth (Ed.), *A handbook for new practitioners.* Stillwater, OK: New Forums Press.

Stewart, E., & Bennett, M. (1991). *American cultural patterns: A cross-cultural perspective.* Yarmouth: Intercultural Press.

Weimer, M., Parrett, J., & Kerns, M. (1988). *How am I teaching? Forms and activities for acquiring instructional input.* Madison: Magna Publications.

Additional Readings

Babcock, N. L., & Pryzwansky, W. B. (1983). Models of consultation: Preferences of educational professionals at five stages of service. *School Psychology, 21,* 359-366.

Damico, J. S. (1987). Addressing language concerns in the schools: The SLP as consultant. *Journal of Childhood Communication Disorders,* 11(1), 17-40.

Davis, W. E. (1991). International teaching assistants and cultural differences: Student evaluations of rapport, approachability, enthusiasm and fairness. In J. D. Nyquist, R. D. Abbott, D. H. Wulff, & J. Sprague (Eds.), *Preparing the professoriate of tomorrow to teach* (pp. 446-451). Dubuque, IO: Kendall-Hunt.

Evertson, C. M., & Green, J. L. (1986). Observation as inquiry and method. In M. C. Wittrock (Ed.), *Handbook of research on teaching* (3rd ed.). New York: Macmillan Publishing.

Lewis, K. (1988). Individual consultation: Its importance to faculty development programs. In E. C. Wadsworth (Ed.), *A handbook for new practitioners.* Stillwater, OK: New Forums Press.

Monoson, P. K., & Thomas, C. F. (1993). Oral English proficiency policies for faculty in U.S. higher education. *Review of Higher Education, 16,* 127-140.

Porter, E., Meyer, D. K., & Hagen, A. S. (1993). *Creating an exemplary teaching videotape library for faculty development.* Manuscript under review.

Povlacs, J. T. (1988). The teaching analysis program and the role of the consultant. In K. G. Lewis & J.T. Povlacs (Eds.), *Face to face: A sourcebook of individual consultation techniques for faculty/instructional developers* (pp. 81-101). Stillwater, OK: New Forums Press.

Taylor-Way, D. (1989). Using video recall for improving professional competency in instructional consultation. *To Improve the Academy, 8,* 141-156.

Thomas, C. F., & Monoson, P. K. (1991). Issues related to state mandated English language proficiency requirements. In J. D. Nyquist, R. D. Abbott, D. H. Wulff, & J. Sprague (Eds.), *Preparing the professoriate of tomorrow to teach* (pp. 382-392). Dubuque, IO: Kendall-Hunt.

Wilkerson, L. (1988). Classroom Observation: The observer as collaborator. In E. C. Wadsworth (Ed.), *A handbook for new practitioners* (pp. 95-98). Stillwater, OK: New Forums Press.

ESL Resources

Axtell, R. E. (1991). *Gestures: The do's and taboos of body language around the world.* New York: John Wiley & Sons, Inc.

Center for Teaching and Learning. (1992). *TAs and professors as a teaching team: A faculty guide to TA training & supervision.* University of North Carolina at Chapel Hill.

Center for Teaching Effectiveness. (1992). *Teachers and students.* University of Texas at Austin.

Dauer, R. M. (1993). *Accurate English: A complete course in pronunciation.* Englewood Cliffs, NJ: Regents/Prentice Hall.

Gburek, J., & Dunnett, S. (Eds.). (1986). *The foreign TA: A guide to teaching effectiveness.* Buffalo: State University of New York at Buffalo.

Gilbert, J. (1984). *Clear speech.* Cambridge: Cambridge University Press.

Goodale, M. (1987). *The language of meetings.* Hove, Great Britain: Language Teaching Publications.

Handschuh, J., & Simounet de Geigel, A. (1985). *Improving oral communication : A pronunciation oral communication manual.* Englewood Cliffs: Prentice-Hall.

Morley, J. (1987). *Current perspectives on pronunciation.* Ann Arbor: University of Michigan Press.

Osgood, C. (1991). *The Osgood files.* New York: Fawcett Crest.

Rooney, A. (1986). *Word for word.* New York: G. P. Putnam's Sons.

Smith, J., et al. (1992). *Communicate: Strategies for international teaching assistants*. Englewood Cliffs: Prentice Hall.

Stern, D. A. (1992). *The sound and style of American English*. Los Angeles: Dialect Accent Specialists, Inc.

Swan, M., & Smith, B. (Eds.) (1991). *Learner English: A teacher's guide to interference and other problems*. Cambridge: Cambridge University Press.

Appendix A
COLLABORATIVE CONSULTATION MODEL FOR FACULTY
Program Design Model for International Faculty Clients

I. COMPREHENSIVE DATA COLLECTION
A. Client data — (i.e.) initial interview
B. Student Date — (i.e.) semester evaluation forms
C. Consultant data — (i.e.) first classroom observation

II. DATA ANALYSIS AND INTERPRETATION
A. Review all available data
B. Request a collaborative consultation
C. Co-consultants interpret data together
D. Mutual agreement on program design

III. ESL PROGRAM DESIGN
A. **Focused Data Collection**
   1. Speech analysis
      a. Grammatical competence
      b. Sociolinguistic competence
      c. Strategic competence
B. **Plan of Action**
   1. Recommended language tutorial
   2. Client/Consultant contract

a n d / o r

III. PEDAGOGY PROGRAM DESIGN
A. **Focused Data Collection**
   1. Client data — (i.e.) syllabi, class handouts
   2. Student data — (i.e.) mid-semester evaualtion
   3. Consultant data — (i.e.) videotape sessions
B. **Plan of Action**
   1. Review client objectives
   2. Recommendations for faculty activities
   3. Client/Consultant contract

IV. IMPLEMENTATION
A. Tutoring and/or consulting
B. Constant plan adaptation
C. Co-consultant progress reports
D. Formative evaluations
E. Repeat step for program design

V. EVALUATION
A. **Summative evaluations**
   1. Language review reports
   2. Teaching progress reports
   3. Comparison of videotaped series
B. **Final written reports**
   1. Client file letter
   2. Summary of classroom observations
   3. Recommendations for additional tutoring/consulting

Center for Teaching
Effectiveness, the
University of Texas at
Austin

Reprinted with
permission

Appendix B

The Collaborative Consultation Process: A Case Example

The following case has been adapted to illustrate how the collaborative consultation process works with an international client. This case is based on actual consultation activities as described in consultants' notes and client records; however, references to department and nationality have been changed to ensure client confidentiality. The content was recorded for our use and was not reviewed by the client. Our written reports to the client are less specific and less evaluative in tone.

Stage I: Comprehensive Data Collection

Initial inquiry to the Center. The department chair telephoned the Center's director who suggested that the faculty member call the faculty development specialist directly. The case information provided by the chair concerned student complaints made directly to him. Many finance majors complained about unclear lectures, the difficult mathematics used in the course, the instructor's poor English skills, as well as the instructor's demeaning attitude toward the class. Of the 30 students enrolled, 10 had dropped the class.

Shortly thereafter, the instructor made an appointment with the faculty development specialist. (See *Consultation Client Referral Form, Appendix C*.)

Initial interview with faculty consultant. The initial interview revealed that this instructor had been in the U.S. for five years. He had been a teaching assistant at a research university for one semester working with small groups of students. He stated that he did not like the University of Texas students because they were not motivated and had poor attitudes toward the class. The consultant noted English language problems during this one-on-one conversation, that is, monotone delivery, intonation and articulation problems, generally low level of clear English speech patterns, and limited English vocabulary during conversation. A videotape session at the Center with a follow-up review was scheduled.

Preliminary data review by the two consultants. The faculty consultant contacted the language consultant to briefly review the available data and they decided that a collaborative consultation approach would be the most helpful for this client. The consultants discussed possible program formats and concluded that English language proficiency was a serious concern and would require immediate, concentrated attention. The language consultant would be available to start tutorials immediately. Both consultants would be involved in videotaping and critiquing a short lecture, followed by a session to map out further strategies.

Videotaping. A 25-minute segment of a lecture the client had prepared for his class was videotaped.

Stage II: Data Analysis and Interpretation

Videotape playback with both consultants and the client. The co-consultants found serious problems with overall intelligibility due primarily to monotone intonation and syncopated speech patterns. Comprehensibility was also impaired by frequent grammatical errors, poor eye contact, insufficient volume, and non-standard rhetorical patterns of information organization. The client agreed with the consultants that work on language skills, especially in the areas of articulation, intonation and stress should be a priority. The faculty consultant would observe at least one class to observe teaching and interaction with students.

Faculty consultant observation of client's class (further data collection). The behaviors observed were classified according to *Evaluation of Classroom Skills* (Appendix D):

Content
- Multiple mistakes in the mathematical calculations; would erase, start over, erase again, in a very repetitive pattern.
- Many formulas were incorrect the first time they were written on the board.
- He seemed to be confident of his knowledge of the material.

Organization
- He did not present an overall organizational framework for the material.
- Transitions between formulas were inadequate.
- He referred to a diagram on the board as he explained how to approach problem solution.
- He summarized the material in conclusion.

Interaction
- He did not attempt to reach out to students or to

connect with their experiences with concrete examples.

- He consistently ignored student questions and demonstrated limited understanding of the few questions he did allow during class.
- He stopped the lecture periodically to ask: "Are there any questions?"
- He answered students' questions about homework both before and after class.
- Students were verbally and non-verbally hostile toward the instructor during the class.

Verbal/Non-verbal

- He had his back to the audience most of the time, thereby ignoring them and further reducing his intelligibility.
- His presentation lacked enthusiasm and expressiveness.
- His voice was monotonous, soft, and difficult to hear.
- He had little eye contact with anyone in the class.
- He made numerous spelling and grammatical errors.

Use of media

- He erased the formulas and notes on the chalkboard before students had a chance to copy the material.
- He expended considerable effort on drawing and modifying diagrams on the board to supplement his explanations.

Faculty consultant and client discuss the evaluation of classroom skills. The faculty consultant sent the client a written report on the classroom observation consisting of a general summary and some recommendations. In the next meeting, the client and both consultants discussed the findings of the videotaped lesson, the class observation, the student data, and the client data; priorities were jointly established.

Stage III: Program Design

Preliminary design. A preliminary program design was presented for the client's consideration and acceptance. The client wished to work only on his language proficiency due to his time constraints. It was therefore agreed that ESL and pedagogy programs would be handled in sequence starting with ESL tutorials.

ESL program. The ESL consultant discussed goals and realistic expectations for improving English proficiency as well as issues concerning effective communication. The consultant described the methods and materials available, such as the language laboratory, personalized audiotapes, pronunciation textbooks, readings on cultural and pedagogical matters, videotaped pronunciation courses, and so on. Together they outlined a program of

remediation having prioritized the linguistic and communication problems.

Pedagogy program. The client and faculty consultants scheduled a videotaped lesson in his regular classroom without students present. The lecture content was taken from one of the client's last classes.

Stage IV: Implementation

ESL tutorials.

- Discussed interference from client's first language on intonation, rhythm, stress, and vowel length in English. Worked with examples illustrating differences in meaning conveyed by stressing different words in mathematical equations. Practiced listening to recorded lectures and marking the transcript for pauses, primary and secondary phrasal stress.
- Worked on reduced or weak forms, and linking across word boundaries.
- Modeled reading informal texts focusing on intonation, stress, and reduced forms. Studied transitional phrases. Worked on defining terms in finance, organizing information, using transitions, and giving examples. Practiced giving short definitions, both prepared and unprepared.
- Studied the effects of changes in pitch. Recorded text while imposing appropriate intonation patterns and pitch changes.
- Practiced responding to questions and interruptions while paraphrasing information in a text.
- Worked on stressing the correct syllable in polysyllabic words.
- Discussed articles on teaching mathematics in American universities; the role of lecturing in an introductory science course; and interactions between Asian TAs and American students.
- Worked on pronunciation of /i/ and /ey/.
- Videotaped and critiqued a 5-minute lecture. Re-taped and critiqued the same lecture. Discussed strategies to generate interest, the use of advance organizers, the formulation of questions to check comprehension, and ways to get students involved.
- Practiced introduction of lesson that the ESL consultant was scheduled to observe.
- Worked on grammatical problems such as "to be" in passive and progressive constructions, certain modals, word order in questions, and two-word verbs.

Classroom observation. The ESL consultant observed client's class using the form *Observation of English Communicative Competence in the Classroom* (Appendix E). Afterwards she reviewed the self-observation form with the client using the *Teaching Self-Evaluation* form (Weimer, 1988), and the consultant's observation notes.

First, the client and language consultant identified the strengths of the class: the instructor seemed well prepared for the lecture; he returned homework promptly; and he gave individual students the feedback they required.

Second, they discussed ways to improve some problematic areas: substitute transparencies for much of the board work; stand closer to the front of the class and out of the poorly lit area by the board so students can hear and see the instructor better; use concrete examples from current events or students' experiences to generate interest and introduce the material; prepare a selection of questions to incorporate into the lecture.

Next, the ESL consultant and the client watched a videotaped class of an experienced faculty member in a similar field. They examined the way new topics were introduced, what strategies were used for creating interest and involvement, what transitions were used between topics, and how students participated in the class.

Pedagogy program. Videotape help session; client and faculty consultant. The client presented the first 20-25 minutes of his last lecture in his regular classroom. After videotaping the segment, it was discussed, improvements were tried out, and the segment was videotaped again. The client and consultant returned to the Center to view the videotape and to evaluate the first and second versions of the lesson. The client was encouraged to comment on his improvements in both language and teaching. He agreed to continue the collaborative consultation for the spring semester. (See the *Written Report Evaluation Form,* Appendix F.)

Stage V: Evaluation

ESL Program. Client and language consultant discussed areas of improvement and prioritized remaining problems.

ESL consultant referred client to the faculty consultant for the final sessions in the semester.

Summary by Collaborative Consultants. The number of consultation hours for this client were divided as follows: three hours for initial interview and written re-

ports, three hours of classroom observation, three hours for videotape review and collaborative work by the two consultants, and thirteen hours of ESL tutorials. A total of twenty-two consultation hours were spent with this client over the period of one semester.

In discussing accomplishments, non-linguistic factors were pivotal in remedying some of the most severe problems in the classroom; for example, facing the class and maintaining some eye contact, ensuring that the blackboard was adequately illuminated and legible, increasing use of the overhead projector, and using color and overlays on transparencies. The work done on defining terms by restructuring the information and including relevant examples significantly contributed to a better class. The readings on academic and teacher-student relations, as well as texts on classroom techniques seemed to be of considerable interest to this client.

The client returned the *Consultation Process Evaluation Form* (Appendix G), expressing his satisfaction with our program. He stated that the ESL consultant "was very helpful in correcting my pronunciation and intonation." He also indicated that his "student evaluations had improved" and that he tries "to face the students and discuss with students instead of just lecturing." A recent, informal student poll indicated "Dr. X is a bit hard to understand but teaches a good class."

Several additional needs were indicated. Efforts to improve pronunciation whether on phonemes or suprasegmentals did not seem to have much effect overall. The instructor did try to speak more loudly and was convinced that he was monitoring his intonation and speech connectedness with some success. To the language consultant any change was almost imperceptible. The client was not yet comfortable with an interactive class format, nor did he develop a good rapport with this group of students. Consequently, both consultants recommended that he continue work on both language and teaching. Perhaps his goals were met when he received better student ratings that semester; after the semester break he did not contact the Center as agreed.

Appendix C

Consultation Client Referral Form

Initial Client Contact

Date of call: Consultant on call:

Client name: Department:

Campus address: Campus code:

Campus phone: Home phone:

Method of referral to CTE:

Reason for the initial call:

Specific requests by client:

Consultant assignment:

Rationale for assignment:

Consultaion Client Referral Form
Initial Office Visit

Date: Client:

Consultant:

Client & course data:

        Example data: Course number and description:
                                 Description of course:
                                 Years teaching experience at UT Austin:
                                 Other teaching experience:

Client statement of need:

        Example date: Client's self-evaluation of teaching strengths and weaknesses:
                                 Instructor's methods of teaching:
                                 Instructor's perception of consultation objectives:

Plan of action:

Additional commetns:

Note: Both of these forms are kept on computer disk to provide as much flexibility for space and content as needed for each client or consultant.
Center for Teaching Effectiveness, The University of Texas at Austin. Reprinted with permission.

Appendix D
Evaluation of Classroom Skills

CONTENT

	1	2	3	4	5	(Excellent)
Main ideas are clear and specific	1	2	3	4	5	(Excellent)
Sufficient variety in supporting information	1	2	3	4	5	
Relevancy of main ideas was clear	1	2	3	4	5	
Higher order thinking was required	1	2	3	4	5	
Instructor related ideas to prior knowledge	1	2	3	4	5	
Definitions were given for vocabulary	1	2	3	4	5	

ORGANIZATION

	1	2	3	4	5	(Excellent)
Introduction captured attention	1	2	3	4	5	(Excellent)
Introduction stated organization of lecture	1	2	3	4	5	
Effective transitions (clear w/ summaries)	1	2	3	4	5	
Clear organizational plan	1	2	3	4	5	
Concluded by summarizing main ideas	1	2	3	4	5	
Reviewed by connecting to previous classes	1	2	3	4	5	
Previewed by connecting to future classes	1	2	3	4	5	

INTERACTION

	1	2	3	4	5	(Excellent)
Instructor questions at different levels	1	2	3	4	5	(Excellent)
Sufficient wait time	1	2	3	4	5	
Students asked questions	1	2	3	4	5	
Instructor feedback was informative	1	2	3	4	5	
Instructor incorporated student responses	1	2	3	4	5	
Good rapport with students	1	2	3	4	5	

VERBAL/NON-VERBAL

	1	2	3	4	5	(Excellent)
Language was understandable	1	2	3	4	5	(Excellent)
Articulation and pronunciation clear	1	2	3	4	5	
Absence of verbalized pauses (er, ah, etc.)	1	2	3	4	5	
Instructor spoke extemporaneously	1	2	3	4	5	
Accent was not distracting	1	2	3	4	5	
Effective voice quality	1	2	3	4	5	
Eye contact with students	1	2	3	4	5	
Confident	1	2	3	4	5	
Enthusiastic	1	2	3	4	5	

USE OF MEDIA

	1	2	3	4	5	(Excellent)
Overheads/Chalkboard content was clear and well-organized	1	2	3	4	5	(Excellent)
Visual aids can be easily read	1	2	3	4	5	
Instructor provided an outline/handouts	1	2	3	4	5	

Center for Teaching Effectiveness, The University of Austin at Texas
Reprinted with permission

STRENGTHS:

WEAKNESSES:

Client Name:_____ Date: _____

Department: _____ Phone: _____

Center for Teaching Effectiveness, The University of Texas at Austin

Appendix E

Observation of English Communicative Competence in the Classroom

Teacher: _____ Date: _____

Lesson Topic: _____

CTE Consultant: _____

Pronunciation *

•Clear, precise articulation of consonant and vowel sounds	1	2	3	4	5
•Consonant combinations both within and across word boundaries, elisions, assimilations, etc.	1	2	3	4	5
•Neutral vowel use, reductions, contractions, etc.	1	2	3	4	5
•Syllable structure, phrase groups, linking words across word boundaries	1	2	3	4	5
•Features of stress, rhthym, and intonation	1	2	3	4	5
•Features of rate, volume, and vocal qualities	1	2	3	4	5

Oral Communication *

•Overall clarity and precision of speech	1	2	3	4	5
•General vocal effectiveness	1	2	3	4	5
•Overall fluency and ongoing planning and structuring of "speech" as it proceeds	1	2	3	4	5
•Overall intelligibility	1	2	3	4	5
•General command and control of grammar	1	2	3	4	5
•General command of appropriate vocabulary	1	2	3	4	5
•Expressiveness of nonverbal behaviors	1	2	3	4	5

Conventional Rhetorical Patterns

•Orientation to topic: interest level, advance organizers	1	2	3	4	5
•Clarity to main ideas	1	2	3	4	5
•Coherence: transitions, connectors, summaries	1	2	3	4	5
•Illustration: examples, audio and visual aids	1	2	3	4	5
•Conclusion: summary, preview of next class, etc.	1	2	3	4	5

Strategies for Interaction

•Culturally appropriate tone and idiom	1	2	3	4	5
•Verbal and non-verbal encouragement of student participation	1	2	3	4	5
•Questions at various levels of complexity	1	2	3	4	5
•Individualization: using names, reinforcement	1	2	3	4	5
•Adequate wait time	1	2	3	4	5
•Comprehension checks, attention to signals of miscommunication	1	2	3	4	5
•Command of strategies for clarification	1	2	3	4	5

* Joan Morley, Rapid Review of Vowel & Prosodic Contexts. Ann Arbor: The University of Michigan Press, 1992

Center for Teaching Effectiveness. The University of Texas at Austin. Reprinted with permission

Appendix F

Written Report Evaluation Form

In order to assist us in the evaluation of how our time is spent in the CTE, we request that you complete this evaluation form about the written report/s given to you:

Classroom Observation: _____ **Mid-semester Report**_____

Consultant: _____ **Hours spent on report/s:** _____

Please circle one answer for each statement:
   The scale is from 1 (strongly disagree) to 5 (strongly agree).

1. I have read the report/s and they were useful.   1   2   3   4   5
   Comments:

2. The report identified my teaching strengths and areas for improvement.   1   2   3   4   5
   Comments:

3. The report provided me information to use for teaching improvement.   1   2   3   4   5
   Comments:

4. The report conference with my consultant explained the written comments well.   1   2   3   4   5
   Comments:

Please give detailed answers to the following questions.
5. What was the most helpful part of the written report?

6. Was the conference about the report more helpful than the written report? Why? Why not?

7. What changes would you make in the written report form?

8. Would you prefer options to a written report? Can you give specific suggestions?

Thank you for your responses. Please return your response form through the campus mail:

Consultant: _____
Center for Teaching Effectiveness
12100.

Name: _____ Department: _____

Appendix G

Consultation Process Evaluation Form

To assist us in the evaluation of how our time is spent in the CTE, we request that you complete this evaluation form about the total consultation process you followed.

Consultant: _____

Total hours spent in consultation: _____

Please circle one answer for each statement:
   The scale is from 1 (strongly disagree) to 5 (strongly agree).

1. I found the consultation process at the CTE very helpful.   1 2 3 4 5
    Comments:

2. The consultant provided me with specific assistance on teaching ideas.   1 2 3 4 5
    Comments:

3. I feel that the consultation helped me to improve my teaching.   1 2 3 4 5
    Comments:

4. The consultation process was personalized to meet my specific needs.   1 2 3 4 5
    Comments:

Please give detailed answers to the following questions.

5. Which aspect/s of the consultation process were most helpful for you?

8. Was the length of the consultation process sufficient to accomplish your goals as a teacher? Why? Why not?

9. After consultation, do you think that your teaching has improved? What measurements are you using? (CIS form results, promotion/tenure, etc.).

10. Would you recommend the CTE consultation process to peers? Why? Why not?

Thank you for your responses. Please return form through campus mail:
Consultant:
Center for Teaching Effectiveness, 12100.

Form developed by Erin Porter, Faculty Development Specialist, Center for Teaching Effectiveness, The University of Texas at Austin.

Reprinted with permission.

11. Consulting with Faculty in Small Groups

William C. Rando

My purpose in this chapter is to explore the wonders and worries of consulting with faculty in small groups. We can define a small group consultation technically as work with between five and fifteen participants. But the real definition of small-group consultation goes well beyond numbers; it is revealed in the principles which allow small groups of faculty to work and learn. As a consultant, I have found that the faculty members I work with get much more out of group work when I focus my attention and skills on small-group principles rather than on specific lessons or outcomes. In other words, if the group is functioning, learning happens. In this chapter I discuss four major principles: 1) faculty interaction, 2) faculty interdependence, 3) process awareness, and 4) group independence.

After exploring the four principles, I look at some of the rewards and challenges of working with small groups. Finally, I provide a model for developing small groups according to the consultant's goals and program limitations.

Enacting the Principles of Small-Groups with Faculty

As I enact small-group principles in my own work, I gravitate toward the role of facilitator. As a facilitator, I allow faculty members to do the work and gain the benefits of experience. My contributions come in the form of interventions, that is, comments or actions designed to move, shift or reorient the group. For example, an intervention can slow the group down, speed it up, help it reflect, allow it to reframe a problem, or stop the action altogether. Interventions are designed to support one or more of the principles of small-group functioning.

Throughout the chapter I use examples of interventions from groups that I have convened in the past. A brief description of those groups will clarify the purpose of my interventions:

Faculty Focus Groups: For an hour each week, faculty members can drop by to raise current problems/questions and to get feedback from other faculty.

Case Seminars: Faculty members read teaching cases and attend discussions.

Program for Reflective Practice: Faculty members form small groups for on-going reflection on complex teaching problems and significant personal teaching development.

Faculty Interaction

The most basic principle of a small group is that participants be able to interact. Faculty members must communicate with each other for the benefits of a group to emerge. A consultant can use the amount of communication among participants as well as the quality of interaction to assess the success of the group.

To encourage communication in the group, consultants may select an optimal number of faculty members (somewhere between five and fifteen), arrange meeting rooms so that everyone can see and hear each other, provide name tags, do personal introductions and explicitly state his/her desire for participation. Once the group's work has started, the consultant may maintain participation by drawing out quiet members, "Susan told us about her difficulties with class discussion. Alan, how do you feel about what Susan said?" The consultant may also want to set limits on more vocal members in the name of broader participation, "Sarah, I'd like to hear from a few other people before I come back to you." Some consultants like to set up rules of participation like the "rule of three" in which each member allows at least three other members to comment before jumping in again. Others start (or end) their meetings by "passing the talking stick" — an opportunity for each member to speak uninterrupted.

Focusing on the quality of interaction is more complex. While some consultants use civility or a "happiness index" as the standard, a healthier (and ultimately more productive) standard is honest and active involvement. Active involvement means that faculty members are allowed to express a full range of ideas and emotions including anger, disagreement, and conflict. Honest and active involvement is a good quality standard because it is an ideal. In other words, faculty groups are more likely to thrive when they are striving for a goal (involved participation) rather than avoiding a problem (passivity).

The consultant's most powerful tool in moving faculty toward active involvement is modeling. So, for instance, in a faculty focus group in which faculty members' comments are superficial, I demonstrate active involvement with a probing question or disagreement. Thereafter, others are more likely to become more critically involved.

Faculty Interdependence

The second principle asserts that faculty members working in small groups should experience interdependence; that is, they should hold themselves and each other responsible for the group's functioning. This is sometimes difficult for faculty who prize their autonomy and *inde*pendence.

Interdependence grows naturally as faculty members come to identify with the group's mission and as they come to rely on one another. It is therefore wise for the consultant to introduce opportunities for each experience —identification and mutual reliance—early and, with long-term groups, often. For instance, at the beginning of case analysis sessions, I might put forth my expectations of group members and then ask each faculty member to do the same. In long-term groups waning faculty involvement requires that I ask faculty members to reassess their involvement and their expectations of others. If a faculty member has become indifferent or unreliable, the consultant can help remaining members produce confrontations that clarify rather then punish.

As with participation, a consultant cannot create interdependence among members of the group but s/he can promote it by requiring faculty members to be dependable and by his/her willingness to be depended upon.

Process Awareness

The third principle of consulting with faculty in small groups is process awareness. Process awareness refers to faculty members' awareness of the norms and assumptions operating in the group. Put another way, process awareness is an active knowledge of what the group is **doing** in addition to what it is saying. For example, I've seen a group start with a complex, personally grueling problem and, in three minutes, turn it into an academic

exercise. Faculty groups that are unaware of this process run the risk of intellectualizing complex issues beyond recognition.

Similarly, it is not unusual for faculty members to decry their students' reluctance to challenge them in class while they themselves do not challenge each other. I have been motivated to comment, "I notice that we don't challenge each other, and I'm wondering how much we really value this kind of confrontation."

On another level, process awareness allows faculty members to see and change destructive but common behavior patterns such as the implicit shutting out of individual group members due to bias or political pressure, or scapegoating.

Faculty members develop awareness by witnessing and discussing the clarifying power of a consultant's process comments.

Functional Independence

The final principle of small-group work is functional independence, which refers to the group's need to develop a life of its own, beyond the intentions of the consultant. The fact that small groups, particularly long-term groups, do develop a "personality" accounts for much of their power and appeal. However, consultants may find this independence a challenging aspect of small-group work. For instance, faculty members in high functioning groups commonly challenge, and even attempt to take authority from, the consultant. Savvy consultants can encourage the group's independence and growth by changing his or her role to suit the learning needs of the group rather than becoming defensive and punitive. Consultants who value obedience over independence are unlikely to facilitate independent learning in their faculty groups.

Summary of Principles

As I participate in a faculty session, I use the principles as a diagnostic tool, asking:

- Are faculty members able to communicate with each other?
- Do faculty members rely on each to make the group work?
- Does the group require everyone to be responsible and available?
- Are group members aware of the group's functioning?
- Have participants demonstrated an ability to address or confront patterns of behavior?
- Has this group demonstrated its own personality and energy?
- Is this group motivated beyond **my** expectations?

In my experience, floundering or low functioning groups tend to be in violation of one or more principles. Once I have discovered the source of the problem, as, for instance, when a group is not process aware, choosing an intervention is relatively easy. I might, in this case, make more process comments and invite other members to do the same. A consultant who designs groups based on these principles possesses a heuristic or program for setting up groups, maintaining healthy functioning, identifying problems, and creating solutions.

Rewards and Challenges of Small-Group Work

Consulting with small groups of faculty creates an infinite number of unique situations and outcomes, many of which have little to do with the consultant's intentions. As a result, small-group work is both highly rewarding and personally challenging. In this section I explore some of the rewards and the major challenge of small-group consulting. First, let me address the rewards.

Energy and High Involvement

Small groups are dynamos; they create a lot of energy and a great deal of heat. Whether a one-time group discussion or a year-long project, a small group's energy often goes well beyond the topic or the task itself. This high level of involvement produces profound learning and change highly unlikely in lectures or even one-on-one.

Community Building

Both full-time and adjunct faculty report needing a sense of academic community. Faculty members feel less isolated in their teaching when they are participating in small groups, developing interdependence and mutual understanding. Friendships and working partnerships are formed, as is a cohesive sense of faculty. Faculty members turn to each other for guidance and collegiality.

Cross-Disciplinary Learning

Related to the issue of academic community is the opportunity created by small groups for cross-disciplinary learning. Academic disciplines are cultures, with their own ways of knowing and doing, but these cultures are not mutually exclusive. So, for instance, the ways of teaching and testing in the sciences can often be revelatory for teachers in the humanities and visa-versa. Small-group work is ideal for academic cross-pollination and the re-

moval of narrow mindedness created by closed disciplinary lines.

Interactive Skill Development

Participation in small-group discussion encourages the development of interactive skills, skills potentially applicable in a faculty member's classroom. The degree to which a faculty discussion acts as a skills-training lab is largely a function of the consultant's skill and willingness to confront the unskilled behaviors of faculty members. For example, a consultant might say, "I notice that we keep cutting each other off...no one gets to finish a thought...does anyone else see this?" In this intervention, the consultant has confronted an ineffective behavior (cutting off) and modeled two interactive skills (focusing on process and checking). The consultant might choose to follow up with, "I'd like to look back at the skills I just used and get your feedback on them." Modeling is even more powerful when it is made explicit. Small groups are well suited for the development of such skills as questioning, listening, clarifying, collaborating, reframing problems and managing process.

Transformative Potential

Adult educator Jack Mezirow (1991) describes a transformation process which reflects the fifth benefit of small group work. According to Mezirow, a transformative experience is one which allows the individual to move outside his/her current ways of thinking and perceiving by reassessing old assumptions. When faculty members are energized and involved, when they can rely on their fellow participants, when they listen and see themselves from new perspectives, and when they experiment with new skills and models of action, then they are open to transformational professional and personal change.

Transformation does not occur when participants are only half present, or when the interaction is filled with defensive posturing, one-upmanship, ego stroking, passive aggression, and war stories. Neither is transformation possible when faculty members and the consultant stay in their heads, passing along generalizations and ideas with no real personal searching. Focusing on the previously mentioned principles allows consultants to create groups that do real work with transformative results.

Summary of Rewards

Every small group of faculty has the potential to achieve these benefits though many, sadly, do not. The role of the consultant in producing learning benefits is somewhat paradoxical in that often the best thing the consultant can do is get out of the way and allow the group to move, struggle, stumble, fall and learn. Our efforts run counter to group learning when we don't allow the group to express and work through its needs, frustrations, and angers. Many consultants, like many faculty members, see it as their responsibility to keep learners from having frustrations, much less expressing them. Skilled facilitation is really a delicate dance between introducing powerful interventions and letting the group discover solutions for themselves.

If working with small groups of faculty has all the benefits I just described, why don't all consultants use them and why aren't their merits more apparent? The answer to both these questions lies in the same issue, control. Fears related to loss of control causes many consultants to create very tight and restricted groups, and keeps many others from engaging faculty in groups at all.

The Challenge of Control

In a study of teaching faculty I completed a number of years ago, one theme came across loud and clear—faculty members run into problems in the classroom when they try to solve problems by attempting to control students' responses. The tendency is no less common among consultants and the results are the same. The problem is an essential one; that is, attempts to control learners in groups destroys the motivation and personal involvement that we know are necessary for learning. Why, then, does it happen?

The tendency to over-control, over-prepare and be over-responsible is fear-based—"This will protect me from failure, criticism, shame"—and ultimately casts a pall over the learning process. This same attempt to control impressions and outcomes stops many consultants from being creative, lively, and risky in their approaches, fearing criticism and, worse, the unknown. Paradoxically, the impulse to control learners moves some consultants to "hold on" and others to "hold back." Either reaction puts a "hold" on learning.

While a full discussion of this issue is beyond the scope of this chapter, two thoughts for addressing control problems will be useful. First, consultants can focus on experiences and questions rather than solutions. The experience might be a case discussion, an interactive game, or a series of probing questions. The goal is to design an experience that involves faculty members fully, allows them to interact, requires them to be involved and dependent upon on another. Second, approach every group meeting as an experiment. Focus on discovery rather than outcomes. Delve into the unknown with faculty groups rather than regurgitating the known and the tried.

Focusing on these two principles is a first step in loosening the reins and creating learning throughout a group's life. The ability to share control of the learning process is essential to any consultant's effectiveness. Consultants concerned with improving their small-group skills can start by reading books and articles on group work, but this approach has significant limitations. Consultants who are serious about working with faculty in groups will want to do actual skill-based training through an existing program or through self-created learning with a group of motivated and talented colleagues. In either case, the key is to find people who are willing and able to give skill-based feedback over an extended period of time.

The Varieties of Small-Group Experience

What are some specific forms that faculty groups take and what kinds of skills does each group require? The model below (See Figure 1) presents two dimensions of small-group consulting on two axes: agenda and expected duration.

Agendas are considered on a continuum from highly structured to loosely structured. Duration is considered from short (one meeting) to long (over a year). Each

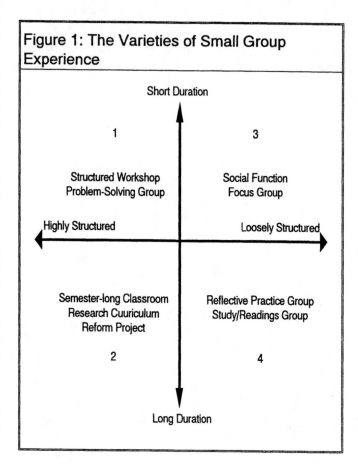

Figure 1: The Varieties of Small Group Experience

Short Duration

1

Structured Workshop
Problem-Solving Group

3

Social Function
Focus Group

Highly Structured

Loosely Structured

Semester-long Classroom
Research Cuurriculum
Reform Project

2

Reflective Practice Group
Study/Readings Group

4

Long Duration

quadrant represents a different type of small group. A discussion of each quadrant appears below along with consultant notes which highlight skills particularly relevant to that quadrant. The notes do not represent definitive lists, nor are they completely discrete. They do focus on the unique aspects of the groups in each cell.

Quadrant One—Highly Structured Agenda/Short Duration

Faculty groups in this quadrant are of the workshop or small-group exercise variety. Faculty members come to gain specific skills or knowledge. A consultant would convene such a group to accomplish the following:

- Introduce faculty members to a new teaching technique.
- Allow faculty members to explore a specific issue or question.

The consultant works in a more defined role, on clearly defined objectives. Experiences are structured, yet open-ended forms will allow faculty members to invest their energy and develop some interdependence. For example, I do a workshop every year on collaborative learning in which I ask faculty members to engage in a series of collaborative exercises. Clearly defined objectives and open communication work in concert.

Consultant notes:

- Use e-mail, posters, and mailing advertisements.
- Express the goals of the workshop early and clearly.
- State expectations prior to the session.
- Stay close to agenda/exercise, give 'em what they came for.
- Intervene quickly, opportunities can be fleeting.
- "Wind it up and let it go" so that faculty members can invest and exert some independence.
- Debriefing is very important.

Quadrant Two—Highly Structured Agenda/Long Duration

A consultant would convene this type of group to accomplish the following:

- Engage faculty in long-term classroom research.
- Work through curriculum reform.

These groups require well defined roles for faculty members, particularly at the beginning. Early communication tends to be highly task oriented. Outcomes are defined. Leadership is important. Consultants may play a number of roles: leader, education specialist, group observer, or resource person. In all roles, the consultant provides process comments as needed to highlight the group's functions or raise awareness. If the consultant

"allows" it, a great deal of off-task learning, such as skill development, will result.

Consultant notes:

- Play an active role in setting up; support a series of reasonable, short-term goals.
- Open a dialogue on issues of commitment and the stresses that pull participants away from completing their tasks.
- Open a dialogue on leadership issues; allow the group to decide.
- Keep the group aware at the process level.
- Be flexible; change roles as needed.

Quadrant Three—Loosely Structured Agenda/Short Duration

Faculty groups in this quadrant have little structure, open communication and varied, spontaneous outcomes. The agenda is often participant-centered as is the majority of the communication. Consultants convene these types of groups in order to:

- Provide support for day-to-day teaching.
- Develop community within faculty.
- Open dialogue on "hot" campus topics.

The consultant acts as a facilitator, intervening only when necessary. Open forums, like faculty focus groups, where faculty members come to discuss current teaching problems would be in this quadrant, as would more social types of faculty gatherings.

Consultant notes:

- Find a comfortable, convenient place and time for interested faculty members to meet and talk.
- Reach faculty members and motivate them to participate.
- Avoid rushing in and "saving" the group by providing ad hoc structure.
- Address silence, hostility, or confusion and reflect on the viability of the open format.
- Bring "hot" issue or tensions out in the open. Allow the group to decide.

Quadrant Four—Loosely Structured Agenda/Long Duration

Faculty groups in this quadrant are of the study-group or learning-group type. A consultant may convene such a group in order to:

- Provide a learning forum for highly motivated faculty members.
- Create a campus think-tank on teaching/learning processes.
- Involve peers in on-going skill development.

Agendas tend to be participant based, though some openness may be sacrificed in order to accomplish a certain, short-term goal. Self-authored teaching cases or other reflective tools such as journals can provide focus and deep insights. Sometimes these groups emerge from short term groups in which members want to continue. Leadership and involvement are constant issues.

Consultant notes:

- Reflect patterns back to faculty members so that they make more informed choices regarding how they spend their time.
- Document progress, patterns, problems for group learning.
- Stay with faculty members as they deal with hostility, hurt feelings, discomfort and anger. Don't avoid.
- Use ad hoc exercises to "pry the group open" if oppressive norms develop.
- Open dialogues on leadership, involvement, membership, etc.
- Risk, risk, risk....

Summary of Model

This model highlights the relationship between a consultant's goals and the types of small groups. It also suggests the types of interventions that will allow groups to flourish. Consultants can add their own considerations to this model to create school and department specific models of designing small-group experiences for faculty.

Conclusion

Working with faculty members in small groups is an exhilarating and deeply rewarding professional activity. I have provided a framework for thinking about and choosing the appropriate type of small-group work. One final word: throughout the chapter I have reiterated that the work of small groups is done by the participants. At the same time I have focused on the critical role of the consultant. This seeming contradiction is the paradox of small-group work. Does a consultant's actions in a small group matter or not? The answer is that they do matter, absolutely. Consultants who "do everything" end up with dead or near dead groups; yet, consultants who hang back miss opportunities to help dying groups learn and grow. A skilled consultant turns a floundering or superficial group into a group that produces meaningful change for faculty. Working with faculty in small groups means committing yourself to your faculty group and then using your own skills to support small group principles.

Reference

Mezirow, J. (1991). *Transformative dimensions of adult learning.* San Francisco: Jossey-Bass.

Part Two:

Programmatic Approaches to Instructional Consultation

Part Two focuses on instructional consultation programs—their structure and components, the kind of data collected, who does the consulting, and the roles and relationships between consultant and client. Part Two begins with an overview of instructional consultation programs in North America, proceeds to describe seven specific programs, and ends with considerations for those who are establishing a consultation program. These chapters should be especially helpful to those who are planning or refining a consultation program.

In Chapter 12, Morrison offers an overview of programmatic approaches to instructional consultation that can be found within the United States and Canada—the parameters of consultation, the essential components of consultation, a short summary of research on consultation. She then offers a typology of six kinds of individual and group instructional consultation programs: traditional, peer consultant, peer partner, developer-led workshop, peer-led workshop, and support group. In Chapter 13, Tiberius describes three related instructional consultation programs—microteaching, laboratory teaching, and Alliances for Change—that use peers as consultants and that include face-to-face dialogue and feedback between teacher and students. For each program, Tiberius highlights strengths and limitations and offers recommendations for use. Smith, in Chapter 14, focuses on one instructional consultation program, Partners in Learning. Also known as the The New Jersey Master Faculty Program, Partners in Learning uses peer consultants and face-to-face dialogue and feedback between a pair of teachers and their students over the course of a term.

A distinctive and popular approach to consultation, Small Group Instructional Diagnosis (SGID), is presented by Lenze in Chapter 15. In SGID, a consultant rather than a peer mediates the process of obtaining feedback from small groups of students. Wilbee (Chapter 16) discusses the Instructional Skills Workshop (ISW) that includes three levels of program: (1) the ISW that focuses on developing fundamental teaching skills and includes three opportunities for videotaped microteaching and feedback within the workshop; (2) the Facilitator Development Workshop that prepares experienced faculty to conduct the ISW at their home institutions; and (3) the Trainer Development Workshop that prepares experienced ISW facilitators to conduct Facilitator Development Workshops. Probably the most versatile of all consultation programs is the Teaching Improvement Process described by Sorcinelli (Chapter 17). Consultants using the Teaching Improvement Process tailor activities to individual teaching needs and problems, and use assessment techniques that are best able to answer clients' questions.

In Chapter 18 Kerwin discusses the instructional consultation program in the University of Kentucky Community College System. In this context, Kerwin observes the strategies that made his program successful, and Part Two concludes with Kerwin providing some general guidelines for establishing peer consultation programs.

From reading these chapters, those who are planning a consultation program and experienced consultants who are refining their consultation programs will have learned about the variety and richness of programmatic approaches, all of which have proven robust across a variety of campuses and institutions. By illustrating the many possibilities, we hope to inspire consultants to devise similarly creative programs that are tailored to suit the needs of their own faculty and their home institutions.

12. *Overview of Instructional Consultation in North America*

Diane E. Morrison

Recent reports on higher education in both the United States and Canada have focused attention on teaching and learning (Boyer, 1987; Study Group, 1984; Smith, 1989). This call for educational reform has occurred during a time marked by dramatic changes in student demographics. Colleges and universities now serve a greater proportion of women students, and have a student population diverse in terms of age, race, ethnicity, socio-cultural background, previous life experience, and educational goals (Smith, 1989).

Greater awareness of the need for teaching enhancement activities accompanies the call for accountability for teaching and learning. There is a recognition that professionals can benefit from the opportunity for feedback on their practice (Schon, 1983), and that colleagues can assist professionals to learn to be more aware of the assumptions underlying their practice (Brookfield, 1991). Instructional consultation is a professional development approach that incorporates feedback on one's teaching and is a structured way for colleagues to help each other enhance teaching and learning in their classrooms.

Parameters of Instructional Consultation

Faculty developers provide consultative assistance to faculty members and teaching assistants in such varied domains as research, scholarly writing, and career planning, in addition to curricular and instructional design and delivery. Consultative assistance also occurs on an informal basis among colleagues in colleges and universities. However, instructional consultation is used here to denote a structured process of inquiry into one's own teaching.

In instructional consultation, a faculty member or teaching assistant, working either individually or in a group setting, elicits and interprets feedback from others in collaboration with at least one other person. In this chapter, that person is referred to as a consultant when working with an individual and as a facilitator when working with groups. The consultant or facilitator is a full or part-time faculty developer, or a colleague who has received training in a particular individual or group-based program. Although faculty developers do not usually describe their services as programs, instructional consultation activities offered by faculty members or teaching assistants are almost always referred to as programs. In peer partner and group-based programs, participants provide consultative assistance to one another. In a few programs, student observers are trained to serve in the consultative role.

Essential Components of Instructional Consultation

Instructional consultation, in my view, has four essential components.

1) *The participant reflects on his or her own teaching and also inquires into the perceptions of others* — namely students, the consultant/facilitator, and in group programs, other participants. This information may be provided as written and/or verbal feedback. Video recording is often used to enhance the feedback process, either as a primary or supplementary source of information.

2) *Instructional consultation is offered as a voluntary activity*, carried out for developmental purposes rather than for personnel decisions such as contract renewal, tenure, or promotion. However, at some institutions, new faculty members or teaching assistants may be asked to participate in an orientation program that includes teaching short lessons and receiving feedback from other participants. Faculty members may also choose to include information about their participation in an instructional consultation process as part of the documentation they prepare for personnel purposes.

3) *Conversations between the participant and those in consultative roles occur at various stages of the program.* Early in the process, these individuals discuss the information gathering procedures. Later, they review the feedback, discuss alternative teaching approaches, and create an action plan.

4) *The whole process occurs within an established time frame, varying on the basis of the specific activities included.* In programs for individuals, the time frame is usually negotiated on a case by case basis. Programs for groups usually have a predetermined time frame. Instructional consultation, as defined in this chapter, always includes information gathering and analysis. However, after the initial phase is completed, there may or may not be assistance provided during a follow-up skill enhancement phase.

Research on Instructional Consultation

Menges points out that "[r]esearch on feedback to teachers relies primarily on student ratings as the source of feedback information" (1987, p. 83). Cohen (1980) conducted a meta-analysis of studies that examined the effectiveness of student ratings as a feedback mechanism. He found that feedback from student ratings was much more effective in promoting teaching improvement when used in conjunction with consultation than when student rating information was provided on its own.

Menges and Brinko (1986) conducted an update of Cohen's meta-analysis. Reviewing thirty empirical studies, they found, as had Cohen, that faculty members' post-feedback ratings were substantially enhanced when instructional consultation was provided in addition to student rating information. More recently, another study replicated these results, within a system-wide peer consultant program (Rozeman & Kerwin, 1991). Anecdotal reports reinforce these findings from experimental research. Specifically, Menges indicates that "participants report high satisfaction, more interaction with other faculty members, increased motivation, and renewed interest in teaching" when involved in instructional consultation with colleagues (1987, p. 91).

In summary, empirical studies show that student ratings can have a positive impact on teaching improvement when combined with instructional consultation. Many institutions now use student ratings for evaluation purposes (Seldin, 1989). However, comparatively few institutions report that they supplement student ratings with instructional consultation (Erickson, 1986).

A Typology of Instructional Consultation Programs

Although studies show that instructional consultation can work, relatively little research has been conducted into understanding the way it works. As an early step in my own research, I examined descriptive literature on institutional and system-wide programs. On the basis of a review of existing research literature, a close reading of published program descriptions, and my own experience in the field of faculty development since the late 1970s, I developed a typology of instructional consultation programs.

This typology is offered as a framework for thinking about the range of programs currently offered in the field. Planning groups can use the typology to guide their discussion of such questions as: what approach will fit the needs of different groups of faculty or teaching assistants, what approaches may have been overlooked in an existing program, and what strengths and limitations will likely be present if the institution chooses one program type over another.

The first dimension of the typology describes the role relationship between the consultant/facilitator and the participant. This dimension includes three identifiers: developer as consultant, peer as consultant, and peer as partner. The second dimension, method of program organization, is based on two identifiers—programs organized for individuals or for groups. When the two dimensions are com-

Figure 1: Instructional Consultation: A Typology of Programs

Method	Role Relationship		
	Developer as Consultant	Peer as Consultant	Peer as Partner
Individual	Traditional	Peer Consultant	Peer Partner
Group	Developer-led Workshop	Peer-led Workshop	Support Group

bined, six different instructional consultation program types are identified.

Many institutions that offer instructional consultation provide what I have identified as the *traditional* program type where full- or part-time faculty developers offer services to individual faculty members or teaching assistants. There are also a number of peer-based models available in colleges and universities across North America. These differ from the traditional approach in at least one of three ways: 1) faculty members or teaching assistants are provided with training to offer *peer consultant* services for their colleagues on a one-to-one basis; 2) two participants work together as *peer partners* within an established program; or 3) faculty members or teaching assistants provide consultative assistance to each other within one of the group-based program models, that is, *developer-led workshop*, *peer-led workshop*, or *support group*.

A consultant or facilitator who is a full- or part-time faculty developer may experience greater expectations of providing expert advice than may someone who is another faculty member or teaching assistant providing assistance for a colleague. These expectations may be held by either or both the consultant and the participant, and also by other institutional personnel, including those who make program funding decisions. The role relationship dimension can also be viewed as a continuum rather than as a set of discrete, mutually exclusive categories. For example, programs offered by part-time faculty developers may be closer to the "peer as consultant" identifier than to "developer as consultant."

Some consultation programs are designed as mentor programs, where a new faculty member or teaching assistant works with an experienced person who serves as a coach. A mentoring program may be called a peer partner program at an institution; however, unless each person is engaged in structured inquiry into his or her own teaching a mentoring program is viewed in this typology as a peer consultant program not as a peer partner program.

No hierarchy of programs is implied in this typology; indeed, it appears that each of the program types has particular limitations as well as strengths. Nor is it expected that an institution's instructional consultation services will evolve in any particular order or pattern. Also, some institutions offer a variety of types of programs, others offer only one type of program.

Relatively little research has been conducted on specific instructional consultation programs, and no systematic comparative research on programs was identified. An in-depth comparative study of instructional consultation programs seemed warranted and timely. Therefore, I re-

cently undertook a study of eight instructional consultation programs reflecting a range of program types, with four programs offered on an inter-institutional basis. One hundred and fifty-five interviews were conducted during site visits to seventeen colleges and universities in both Canada and the United States. The study provides institutions of higher education with information based on the considerable experience of selected colleges and universities that have been using instructional consultation, and particularly peer-based approaches.

Each of the six types of instructional consultation is described briefly below. The comments on strengths and limitations are informed by my field-based research.

Individual Consultation Programs

Traditional Programs (The consultant, a developer, works with individuals.)

In what I refer to as the traditional type of instructional consultation, a full- or part-time faculty developer provides assistance for an individual faculty member or teaching assistant using a variety of techniques of information-gathering and analysis. The faculty developer is often expected to have a broad-based understanding of teaching and learning. Descriptions of this type of program are numerous with many of the articles describing services provided at research universities. For detailed descriptions of several programs, see Lewis (1988).

The consultation process used in the 1970s at the University of Massachusetts at Amherst and the University of Rhode Island has been an important resource for many of the institutions that offer instructional consultation for individuals. Detailed information about this process is provided in Bergquist and Philips (1975, 1977), in Melnick and Sheehan (1976) and in Chapter 17 of this book.

One of the strengths of this program type is that the full- or part-time faculty developer is available to work with each participant in a highly individualized and intensive way. The faculty developer usually can draw on knowledge about a wide variety of teaching and learning situations. In addition, this person often has developed a fairly wide repertoire of consultative skills. Several of these faculty developers have also provided valuable assistance for the evolution of peer-based models offered for individuals and/or for groups.

In this program type, instructional consultation is usually portrayed as a private activity. The private nature of the traditional approach, in addition to being an advantage for some individuals, can also be one of the limitations of this model. Unlike some of the other approaches, the participants do not have the opportunity to work closely with other faculty members or teaching assistants who are also engaged in structured inquiry into their own teaching practice. The private and confidential nature of this model does not readily facilitate conversations about teaching amongst faculty members or teaching assistants. However, some programs have enhanced the traditional consultation process by the addition of group activities (for example, Erickson & Erickson, 1988).

Peer Consultant Programs (The consultant, a colleague, works with individuals.)

Peer consultant programs are usually offered by a small team of faculty members or teaching assistants who provide services to individuals on an occasional basis. The kind of activities provided by peer consultants for their colleagues are often quite similar to those offered by faculty developers. However, many peer consultant programs emphasize a particular configuration of activities such as video review, analysis of student feedback from a common rating instrument, or the use of a specific interview process. Most peer consultants also conduct classroom observations.

Although the peer consultants do not need to be experts about teaching and learning in a wide range of settings, they do need to have expertise in the inquiry processes used within their particular program. These programs usually include fairly extensive preservice training and on-going development activities for the peer consultants. For a detailed description of one peer consultant program, the Teaching Consultation Program, see Kerwin (1985, 1987, 1989, and Chapter 32 of this book). Peer consultant programs are also offered at several major Canadian universities, including the University of Alberta and the University of British Columbia. Another peer consultant model is the video recall process, used in graduate teaching assistant programs at such places as Cornell University and the University of Colorado at Boulder and described in Taylor-Way (1988). Most peer consultant programs for faculty match consultants and participants across departments. However, some peer consultant programs are offered by experienced teaching assistants who provide consulting services for other teaching assistants within their own departments.

A few institutions offer *student observer programs*, where an undergraduate student is selected to work with a faculty participant. The student is not taking the course for credit, but attends all of the classes and meets regularly with the faculty member. These programs offer training and development activities for the student observers to help them enhance their observation and feedback skills. I cluster these programs with the peer consultant program type as the student observer works in a collegial fashion with the faculty participant. For a detailed description of one student observer program see Helling and Kuhlman (1988). Student observer programs are also offered at Carleton College, Minnesota, and Brigham Young University, Utah.

The peer consultant program type shares many of the strengths and limitations of the traditional consultation service as both program types are organized around a private discussion of one's teaching with one other person. This type also has the benefits of close, personal attention to the individual, but lacks structured opportunities for sharing the consultative experience with others. An additional strength of the peer consultant program type is that the number of faculty members or teaching assistants who can participate in the program is greatly expanded. I also hypothesize that peer consultant programs for faculty are perceived as "faculty-owned."

Another strength is that developmental and evaluative activities are regularly provided for the peer consultants. Preservice and inservice training activities, combined with a clearly defined set of activities, help maintain program consistency across a team of consultants. However, having a recommended set of activities can be one of the limitations of the peer consultant program type. The peer consultants may not have the time or encouragement to experiment with inquiry techniques used successfully in other programs.

Peer Partner Programs (Colleagues are partners for each other.)

In Peer Partner Programs, colleagues work together as partners within a structured set of inquiry-based activities. As with the student observer approaches, it is very important to have a designated program coordinator. In peer partner programs, there are usually orientation activities for prospective participants. Individuals are encouraged to choose partners from the people who have attended the orientation, or to find their own partners from amongst colleagues at the institution. Sometimes, the program coordinator is asked to propose partner matches. In some programs, partners work concurrently in both the participant and helper roles. In other cases, only one of the partners is in the role of helper at one time, with the pair reversing their roles during another semester.

The peer partner programs do not require that participants have either broad-based knowledge about teaching, or expertise in the consultative role. Instead, these programs tend to rely more on mutual inquiry processes into teaching and learning. Partners work together to increase their understanding of the experiences of the learners in their courses. Some of the institutions that offer peer partner programs target the services more for experienced faculty members than for new faculty members or teaching assistants. The Partners in Learning program is described in Golin (1990), Katz (1989), Katz and Henry (1988), Smith and LaCelle-Peterson (1991), and in Chapter 14 of this book; the Alliances for Change program is described in Tiberius et al. (1993) and in Chapter 13 of this book.

As with other programs for individuals, the peer partner program type has the strengths and limitations that are associated with a private focus on one's teaching and learning. However, some peer partner programs include a group activity with partners meeting together regularly throughout the duration of the program. Peer partner programs appear to have other strengths in common with the peer consultant type, including the potential for wide-based participation and for faculty ownership of the program.

A potential weakness of this program type is that the partners do not need to have broad-based expertise in either teaching and learning or in consulting. Their observations and comments may be based primarily on their own experiences, and may not provide a particularly broad view of the teaching and learning enterprise. Peer partner programs can counter this potential limitation by focusing on joint inquiry into the students' experiences in the courses.

Some peer partner programs rely heavily on verbal input from students rather than on student rating forms, finding that interview procedures can enrich the nature of the student information collected. These student interview formats provide an opportunity for expanding the conversations about teaching and learning, not only between the two partners, but also between the participants and the students. Of course, these individual and group student interview procedures can also be adapted for use within the other types of instructional consultation programs offered for individuals or for groups.

Group Consultation Programs

Group programs considered within this typology are limited to those that specifically include feedback on one's own teaching. In the group-based approaches, participants serve in consultative roles for one another within a variety of leadership configurations. In developer-led workshops, the facilitator is a full - or part-time developer; in peer-led workshops, the facilitator is a faculty member or teaching assistant who has participated in training activities related to the particular program being offered. Support group programs, the third type, usually involve members sharing the leadership responsibilities.

In addition to different leadership models, there are several ways that information about one's teaching can be gathered and analyzed within group-based programs. The most widely used approach, often referred to as microteaching, involves each group member teaching a short lesson and then receiving feedback from the other participants who have been learners in the teaching event. Video recording is often used to enhance the feedback review.

Early microteaching approaches were used within teacher education programs, with the teaching exercise focused on specific skills such as questioning (Allen & Ryan, 1969, and Chapter 13 in this book). Microteaching, as it is used in instructional consultation programs in higher education, differs in several ways from the approaches initially used within teacher education programs. In higher education, the microteaching activity is generally used within a workshop setting rather than within a teacher certification program. Each participant has considerable latitude in his or her choice of teaching event. The facilitators and participants provide feedback on the basis of their experiences as learners in the lesson, not as experts in teaching and learning. Role reversal enhances the opportunities for learning. In addition to receiving feedback on their own teaching, the participants also learn from observing other teachers, from articulating their own experiences as learners in each lesson, and from reflecting on and discussing the feedback provided by other participants.

In a second design, the participants do not teach at the workshop. Instead, feedback is based on samples of teaching practice that each person provides. The sample may be in the form of a video recording or a transcript of a case situation that has occurred in the participant's own class. In a third workshop design, each participant gathers information from students and/or observers in their own teaching environment, using such tools as classroom assessment techniques. The participants then bring samples of the information collected for analysis and interpretation with the other participants.

The major distinction amongst the group-based program types is not in the specific information sources that are used (that is, teaching each other within a workshop, bringing videos or transcripts from one's teaching, or bringing samples of feedback gathered from students or observers). Rather, as in the services for individuals, the distinction between these three program types is based on the role relationship of the group facilitator and the participants. Each of the three group-based program types is described briefly below along with comments on their strengths and limitations.

Developer-Led Workshops (The facilitator, a developer, works with groups.)

Sometimes the developer-led workshops occur within a larger institutional program such as an orientation workshop for new faculty members or a teaching certificate program for faculty members or teaching assistants. Some institutions provide developer-led workshops in conjunction with a consultation program for individual faculty; some institutions offer stand-alone workshops on an occasional basis. For descriptions of two developer-led workshops see Erickson and Erickson (1988) and Smith and Schwartz (1988).

There is often a close overlap of this program type with peer-led workshops; that is, a program offered at a campus or within a consortium may be offered both by faculty developers and by a team of colleagues trained as workshop facilitators.

The strengths and limitations of both the developer-led and peer-led workshop types are very similar, especially when the program includes microteaching. Both types are discussed together within the next section.

Peer-Led Workshops (The facilitator, a colleague, works with groups.)

As described earlier, peer-led workshops may be organized on the basis of a variety of workshop designs. The most prevalent model, however, is microteaching with participants teaching short lessons to each other and then receiving written, verbal, and video feedback. Program descriptions of peer-led workshops that emphasize microteaching include the Instructional Skills Workshop Program (Morrison, 1985) and the Course Design and Teaching Workshop of the Great Lakes Colleges Association (Nowik, 1983). Peer-led workshops are also offered for teaching assistants at such places as Cornell University, the University of Colorado at Boulder, and Stanford University.

One of the limitations of a model based on teaching one's peers is that the teaching events occur within a workshop or course setting removed from the individual's class environment. However, this program feature also has benefits. Teaching one's colleagues in a workshop setting can provide a safe yet challenging environment for experimentation and expansion of one's teaching repertoire. The workshop is a teaching laboratory, a place to practice skills that can later be transferred to one's own teaching setting.

A major strength of both the developer-led workshops and the peer-led workshops is the interaction and discussion about teaching and learning that occurs among the participants. The effectiveness of this type of program is linked to the facilitator's skills, as well as to the specific design of the program. In these workshops, it is important to foster an environment where the participants draw on each other as resources rather than relying primarily on the workshop facilitator for feedback and consultation.

As with the peer consultant programs, facilitators of peer-led workshops may not have the time or encouragement to incorporate ideas from models offered successfully at other institutions. However, peer-led workshops also have some advantages over developer-led workshops, similar to advantages of a peer consultant program over a traditional one. When a team of facilitators is available to lead workshops, program access can be substantially increased. Also, having a team of colleagues serving as workshop facilitators may help insure that the program is perceived as "owned" by the participants.

Support Groups (Colleagues, meeting in groups, are partners for each other.)

Although support groups may be organized for a variety of purposes, in this typology support groups have a particular focus. Participants work together to support their individual efforts to gather and analyze feedback for teaching enhancement. The leadership is usually provided from within the group's membership, and a number of different activities can be used. In one model, each participant brings a sample of teaching or feedback from a specific course, and elicits assistance from the others in interpreting the information collected. Group members may also visit each other's classes, provide direct feedback on their observations, and discuss ways that the faculty member can build on teaching strengths as well as address weaknesses raised in the feedback.

Although I have not linked classroom assessment techniques with any one particular type of instructional consultation program, individuals interested in using classroom assessment techniques sometimes form support groups to supplement their individual work (Angelo & Cross, 1993). Another example of a support group is found in some of the peer partner programs. In addition to the two faculty members working together as partners, the pairs of program participants may meet together on a regular basis to discuss the feedback and learnings from their individual work in the program (see Golin, 1990, and Chapter 14 in this book).

One limitation that can occur with support group activities is the difficulty of sustained involvement if there is not sufficient program structure for participants. Also, although members may state their interest in visiting each other's classes and in discussing feedback on teaching, this interest may be difficult to translate into action if it is simply an optional activity.

A major benefit of this program type rests with the collegial relationships that are established within these support groups. The informal setting of this program type seems to help facilitate in-depth conversations about the individuals' teaching experiences—their strengths as well as their weaknesses.

Changes in Instructional Consultation

Examining different types of instructional consultation programs offered across institutions can help us reflect on how this type of approach has evolved over the last two decades. The range of activities described in published program descriptions, along with my own interviews, suggest to me that instructional consultation has changed since its introduction into higher education in the 1970s. More people are now involved as participants and as leaders, and a greater variety of approaches are used across institutions. There also appears to be a move towards more open inquiry into one's teaching practice conducted in collaboration with colleagues and with students.

Workshops that include microteaching have been provided by some faculty developers since the early 1970s. In the early literature on faculty development, there is a description of a Teaching Laboratory model (Bergquist & Phillips, 1975). However, the growth of peer-led workshops has had a substantial multiplier effect in terms of numbers of participants in group-based models. The introduction of peer consultant and peer partner models has also expanded access to instructional consultation. These models provide settings for faculty members and teaching assistants to actively experiment with their teaching. The expanded use of peer-based approaches suggests to me that *instructional consultation can be viewed as collaborative and active learning for faculty members and teaching assistants.*

A number of faculty developers report that they have had little opportunity for formal training in instructional consultation (Lenze & Menges, 1993). However, in the literature describing both peer-led workshops and peer consultant programs, a central feature is the provision of training and development opportunities for consultants or facilitators (Morrison, 1985; Kerwin, 1985; and several chapters in this book). These programs also often provide participants with orientation activities about giving and receiving feedback.

The growth of peer consultant, peer partner, and peer-led workshop programs has not only expanded access to instructional consultation, but has provided a testing ground for initial training, on-going development, and evaluative activities for peer consultants, workshop facilitators, and coordinators of peer partner programs. As the peer-based models often involve a team of consultants or facilitators, developmental activities usually occur within a group setting. A few peer-based programs are offered across several institutions with training and on-going development opportunities provided on an inter-institutional basis. Many of the training activities for these programs are based on an experiential and active learning model. Thus, a second change in instructional consultation can be described as *a shift towards training for consultants, facilitators, and coordinators as collaborative and active learning.*

My review of published descriptive materials and my own research in the field suggests that there is a third change occurring through the increased use of qualitative inquiry methods. Some programs now use student interviews in addition to, or instead of, student rating instruments. Written responses based on open-ended questions are also regularly used to gather formative feedback from students.

These various open-ended inquiry techniques invite students to generate feedback themes rather than respond to pre-set categories. These formats also provide an opportunity for faculty members and teaching assistants to hear positive feedback from students, in the students' own words. Participants report that this feedback can be very reinforcing. Some programs, such as Alliances for Change, also involve students in the discussion and interpretation of feedback gathered anonymously in the course. Participants indicate that students appreciate the opportunity to engage in these interviews and conversations about teaching and learning, and that these activities can also help improve classroom dynamics and discussions.

In addition to the increasing use of student interviews, there also are changes in the way classroom observation is conducted. For example, in Partners in Learning (a peer partner program), one partner visits the other person's class and interviews a few students one or more times over for the duration of the course. The two partners are involved in extended conversations about teaching and learning stimulated by the classroom observations and student interviews. The student observer programs also involve regular observations and conversations over the duration of an entire course. These extended observation approaches could be described as a move towards a more ethnographic inquiry approach. The use of qualitative materials to document teaching effectiveness in teaching portfolios appears to mirror the use of qualitative research approaches in instructional consultation. This third change can be described as *a shift towards instructional consultation as collaborative inquiry that draws on qualitative as well as quantitative research techniques.*

With the increasingly diverse student population found in many colleges and universities today, faculty members and teaching assistants face considerable challenge in their classrooms. We cannot rely on the small numbers of faculty developers in our institutions to provide adequate support for individuals interested in intensive teaching enhancement activities. Nor should we do so, as many advantages can be gained by expanding the number of faculty members and teaching assistants who work together in structured inquiry processes for the enhancement of teaching and learning. Individuals who serve in consultative roles within peer-based programs say that their work with these programs has had an important impact on their own teaching.

I predict that those of us interested in faculty development in higher education will continue to experiment with collaborative and active learning approaches and with qualitative research techniques to enhance the practice of all types of instructional consultation. We also need to find more ways to exchange information on the various models that have evolved over the last two decades. This book is one resource that may trigger more conversations about this kind of professional development approach. As more institutions offer these services, particularly the peer-based programs, more faculty members and teaching assistants will be able to benefit from the cross-fertilization of ideas across programs and institutions.

References

Allen, D. W., & Ryan, K. (1969). *Microteaching*. Reading, MA: Addison-Wesley.

Angelo, T. A., & Cross, K. P. (1993). *Classroom assessment techniques: A handbook for college teachers*. San Francisco: Jossey-Bass.

Bergquist, W. H., & Phillips, S. R. (1975, 1977). *A handbook for faculty development*. (Vols. 1-2). Washington, DC: Council of Independent Colleges.

Boyer, E. L. (1987). *The undergraduate experience in America*. New York: Harper and Row.

Brookfield, S. D. (1991). *Developing critical thinkers: Challenging adults to explore alternative ways of thinking and acting*. San Francisco: Jossey-Bass.

Cohen, P. A. (1980). Effectiveness of student-rating feedback for improving college instruction: A meta-analysis of findings. *Research in Higher Education, 13*, 321-341.

Erickson, B. L., & Erickson, G. R. (1988). Notes on a classroom research program. *To Improve the Academy, 7*, 19-22.

Erickson, G. R. (1986). A survey of faculty development practices. *To Improve the Academy, 5*, 182-196

Golin, S. (1990). Four arguments for peer collaboration and student interviewing: The Master Faculty Program. *AAHE Bulletin, 43*(4), 9-10.

Helling, B. B., & Kuhlmann, D. (1988). The faculty visitor program: Helping teachers see themselves. In K. G. Lewis & J. T. Povlacs (Eds.), *Face to face: A sourcebook of individual consultation techniques for faculty and instructional developers* (pp. 103-119). Stillwater, OK: New Forums Press.

Katz, J. (1989). Turning professors into teachers. *Journal of Staff, Program, and Organization Development, 7*(1), 3-6.

Katz, J., & Henry, M. (1988). *Turning professors into teachers: A new approach to faculty development and student learning*. New York: ACE/Macmillan.

Kerwin, M. A. (1985). The Teaching Improvement Process. *Journal of Staff, Program, and Organization Development, 3*(1), 10-11.

Kerwin, M. A. (1987). Teaching behaviors faculty want to develop. *Journal of Staff, Program, and Organization Development, 5*(2), 69-72.

Kerwin, M. A. (1989). Analyzing student-perceived teaching behavior using the teaching analysis by students questionnaire (TABS). *Journal of Staff, Program, and Organization Development, 7*(3), 115-119.

Lenze, L. F., & Menges, R. J. (1993). *Materials for training instructional consultants*. Paper presented at the meeting of the American Educational Research Association, Atlanta.

Lewis, K. G. & Povlacs, J. T. (Eds.). (1988). *Face to face: A sourcebook of individual consultation techniques for faculty/instructional developers*. Stillwater, OK: New Forums Press.

Melnick, M. A., & Sheehan, D. S. (1976). Clinical supervision elements: The clinic to improve university teaching. *Journal of Research and Development in Education, 9*(2), 67-75.

Menges, R. J. (1987). Colleagues as catalysts for change in teaching. *To Improve the Academy, 6*, 83-93.

Menges, R. J., & Brinko, K. T. (1986). Effects of student evaluation feedback: A meta-analysis of higher education research. Paper presented at the meeting of the American Educational Research Association, San Francisco. (ED 270 408)

Morrison, D. E. (1985). The Instructional Skills Workshop Program: An inter-institutional approach. *To Improve the Academy, 4*, 75-83.

Nowik, N. (1983). Workshop on course design and teaching styles: A model for faculty development. *To Improve the Academy, 2*, 143-158.

Rozeman, J. E. & Kerwin, M. A. (1991). Evaluating the effectiveness of a teaching consultation program on changing student ratings of teaching behaviors. *The Journal of Staff, Program, and Organization Development, 9*(4), 223-230.

Schon, D. A. (1983). *The reflective practitioner: How professionals think in action*. New York: Basic Books.

Seldin, P. (1989). How colleges evaluate professors 1988 vs. 1983. *AAHE Bulletin, 41*(7), 3-7.

Smith, D. G. (1989). *The challenge of diversity: Involvement or alienation in the academy?* (ASHE/ERIC Reports No. 5.) Washington, DC: School of Education and Human Development, The George Washington University.

Smith, M. & LaCelle-Peterson, M. (1991). The professor as active learner: Lessons from the New Jersey Master Faculty Program. *To Improve the Academy, 10,* 271-278.

Smith, R. A., & Schwartz, F. (1988). Improving teaching by reflecting on practice. *To Improve the Academy, 7 ,*63-84.

Study Group on the Conditions of Excellence in American Higher Education. (1984). *Involvement in learning: Realizing the potential of American higher education.* Washington: U.S. Department of Education, National Institute of Education.

Taylor-Way, D. (1988). Consultation with video: Memory management through stimulated recall. In K. G. Lewis & J. T. Povlacs, (Eds.), *Face to face: A sourcebook of individual consultation techniques for faculty/instructional developers* (pp. 159-191). Stillwater, OK: New Forums Press.

Tiberius, R. G., Sackin, H. D., Janzen, K. R., & Preece, M. (1993). Alliances for Change: A procedure for improving teaching through conversations with learners and partnerships with colleagues. *Journal of Staff, Program, and Organization Development, 11*(1), 11-23.

13. *Microteaching, Teaching Laboratory, and Alliances for Change*

Richard Tiberius

*T*his chapter deals with three programs that provide instructional consultation to faculty: microteaching, the teaching laboratory, and Alliances for Change. As part of each program, faculty receive feedback either from students or from peers acting as students. Strengths and weaknesses of each program are presented along with recommendations for use.

Microteaching

Microteaching was developed in the 1960s by Dwight Allen and Kevin Ryan (1969) at the Stanford Teacher Education Program. The theory behind microteaching is that teaching can be broken down into a number of specific component skills which can be isolated and practiced separately. Microteaching is a training device that focuses on the classroom in microcosm, a highly simplified version of the classroom, which allows the teacher to demonstrate one teaching skill and immediately afterward receive constructive feedback from the group who are acting as students. The feedback process is in the form of written evaluation ratings from students that are collected by a facilitator and reported to the teacher. Moreover, the teacher can then repeat her or his demonstration of the same component, taking into consideration the feedback, and gathering feedback on her or his improved performance.

In the early programs, the teacher did not choose the skills to be practiced. The skills were selected by the program designers and reinforced by handouts explaining them to the teachers. Allen and Ryan (1969) used a list of components that they believed were helpful in college teaching:

- stimulus variation—the ability to vary the pattern of instruction, that includes such elements as the instructor's movement around the classroom, gestures, voice level, and the ability to draw attention to important points.
- set induction—the ability to prepare a class for learning, often done through an analogy, a demonstration, or a leading question.
- closure—as a complement to set induction, the ability to bring a learning activity to a close in a way that not only summarizes the activity but also draws it together into a new conceptualization.
- silence and nonverbal cues—the ability to use nonverbal messages to move a class discussion.
- reinforcement of student participation—the ability to use both verbal and nonverbal messages to encourage and control student participation.
- questioning—the ability to ask clear, stimulating questions.
- use of examples—the ability to use both verbal and visual examples at appropriate times in a discussion. (p.3).

There have been hundreds of variations in the format of the microteaching session since the original Allen and Ryan book on the subject. Some practitioners have used videotape, others just verbal feedback; the duration of the teaching sample varies from five to fifteen minutes; and so on. But the basic sequence is what is important: teach, analyze and reteach. Appendix A presents the steps of a typical microteaching session.

Strengths

Microteaching reduces the threat to the teacher and therefore the reluctance to accept feedback. The teacher can focus on a single component of teaching rather than having to cope with an unpredictable and complex classroom situation; the teacher is given the opportunity to correct poor performances immediately; the consultant or supervisor who discusses the feedback with the teacher can encourage the teacher, can help the teacher interpret the feedback and construct improvements. In addition, the component skills approach itself is welcomed by many teachers because it simplifies the overwhelming complexity of teaching by breaking it down into learnable skills.

Weaknesses

Because microteaching is focused on a specific set of teaching performances it is more limited than other procedures for teaching improvement. For one thing, it is limited to classroom teacher performances rather than subtleties of teacher student relationships or attitudes. Second, it is focused on the performance—what the teacher does—rather than the effect it has on the students' learning (Bergquist & Phillips, 1975, p. 107). Third, the teaching practice episode is too short to allow teachers to demonstrate some of the more subtle aspects of teaching, such as creating an accepting class climate.

It is also quite time consuming. If the procedure happens to offer precisely the behaviors that the teacher would like to improve, then the time might be well spent, but there are hundreds of specific teaching behaviors, and it is likely that the teacher will not be learning the most relevant skill for her or his particular situation. Moreover it would take several of these microteaching sessions before the teacher will have covered a significant number of the most useful components of teaching.

Recommendations for Use

Microteaching uses real students. The use of real students is recommended when the skill that is selected for practice requires student roles that are difficult for faculty to enact. For example, in a group consisting of only senior physician-teachers, one teacher wanted the group to simulate medical students on their first day so that he could teach a basic concept. But his peers were unable to put aside their knowledge. Their level of questions and manner of reacting to the sample teaching were so unreal that the session was not very useful. This kind of teaching performance requires real students. On the other hand, if the faculty can easily enact the roles, then I would use faculty peers as students and reap the advantage of the role reversal experience, as practiced in the laboratory teaching procedure (see below).

Although the components of teaching performance are specified by the designers of the program in advance of the teaching session, there is no need to stick with the components of teaching identified by Allen and Ryan. I

recommend that designers choose components appropriate to their setting.

Laboratory Teaching

Following Bergquist and Phillips (1975) I have distinguished between microteaching and the teaching laboratory. The teaching laboratory is a modification of the microteaching procedure. The teaching laboratory procedure requires teachers to present samples of their teaching illustrating skills of their own choosing rather than ones taken from a set of standard skills. Also, members of the group are seldom real students. They are faculty peers acting as students. Thus, laboratory teaching features a role reversal aspect—faculty learn the students' point of view by taking on the role of students.

The main information gathering tool is the interview. Actually, there are two interviews, one that is conducted by a facilitator and aimed at gathering information about the teacher's performance and another that is conducted by a second facilitator and is aimed at gathering information about the first facilitator's performance.

Appendix B is a format I have used often with good results. It is a modified version of one that was used by Dr. LuAnn Wilkerson at the Harvard Medical School.

Strengths

The teaching laboratory provides feedback on specific aspects of teaching. It also allows teachers to choose the particular aspect of their teaching that they want to improve. Another advantage, one which has been very powerful in teaching laboratory sessions that I have run, is the opportunity for role reversal. Normally teachers do not have a chance to take the students' role in the teaching-learning relationship. The insight that they gain from it has been astounding to me. I remember teachers telling me how antagonized they felt by a particular style of teaching. Their negative, even hostile, reactions made them look with more understanding at similar behaviors in their students. Bergquist and Phillips point out (1975, p. 109) that not only receiving feedback but learning to give feedback in the teaching laboratory is an important learning experience for faculty.

Finally, it is encouraging for teachers to see that other teachers have similar problems. The discussions and even friendships that grow out of laboratory teaching should be counted among its advantages.

Weaknesses

Since the teaching laboratory focuses on traditional classroom skills, it is limited to examining the performance aspects of teaching, and rather short performances at that. There is much more to teaching than brief, skilled performances. And it is these other aspects, like rapport and trust, that are the forte of focus groups. In addition, since laboratory teaching usually does not use real students, the question arises as to whether the peer teachers who are acting as students are actually performing as real students would.

Recommendations for Use

Although the teaching laboratory sessions that I have witnessed at the college level seldom use real students, there is no reason why they could not use them more often if there was good reason to. There is a trade-off between the use of real students versus peers. Peers provide teachers with the advantage of role reversal experience and use of real students provides more valid student responses. As I stated above, I recommend using real students when the skill that is selected for demonstration requires student roles that are difficult for faculty to enact. I cited the example of a group consisting of only senior physician-teachers in which one teacher wanted the group to simulate medical students on their first day so that he could teach a basic concept. But his peers were unable to put aside their knowledge in order to react like real students. But if the faculty can enact the roles that they are asked to, then I would recommend that faculty peers take the roles of students in order to benefit from the experience of role reversal, as I mentioned before.

The teaching laboratory is especially recommended for beginning teachers or teachers who have specific problems of teaching performance such as closing the lecture or dealing with difficult students in the small groups. But I would not rule it out as a valuable experience for more senior teachers as well because role reversal can be a very powerful tonic for teachers who have long forgotten how it feels to be a student.

Alliances for Change

The explicit aim of the Alliances for Change procedure is for faculty "to identify strengths and weaknesses specific to their teaching and learning situation, negotiate remedies for the weaknesses, and reinforce the strengths" (Tiberius, et al., 1993). But the implicit agenda is to help teachers and students enhance their understanding of one another, become more collaborative and begin to view teaching and learning as a process of dialogue rather than a transmission of information.

The central feature of the Alliances procedure is a face-to-face conversation between teachers and small groups of students. It is designed to provide the conditions for a successful face-to-face dialogue between teachers and students and then to use that dialogue as the basis of teaching improvement.

The design of the procedure is very conscious of time. It requires a about eight to ten hours in total. A summary of the steps is in Appendix C.

Strengths

Alliances for Change requires partners to help one another simultaneously. One advantage of this is that it enables teachers to be more empathic toward one another since they are each going through the experience of giving and receiving feedback. Teachers have remarked that they would not have been so understanding and appreciative of their partner's effort to gather feedback from students if they had not been engaged in the same process themselves. One teacher remarked that when he felt like criticizing his partner for a sloppy job of gathering information he looked at the product of his own effort, and shut his mouth. Another advantage is that teachers are less anxious about the process of receiving feedback from someone who is in exactly the same situation.

Another strength of Alliances lies in the separation of the two types of groups which enables each group to be designed optimally for a single function. The information gathering (agenda) group is composed of a randomly selected sample of students and is facilitated by the partner, in the absence of the teacher. The conversation group is composed of volunteer students and includes the teacher. The conversation groups have had an enormous impact on teachers, according to testimonials from both the teachers and the students. Teachers have spoken about a sense of rejuvenation for teaching.

Weaknesses

The most serious weakness of the procedure lies in advertising the procedure to faculty. Most of the faculty who observe a demonstration of the procedure are persuaded of its value and many sign up to try it. Moreover, faculty who have tried it find it very valuable. But workshop coordinators have not yet discovered means of advertising the procedure to interest faculty in attending demonstrations. Perhaps the phrase "face-to-face" sounds confrontive to faculty. Perhaps the requirement for two groups sounds like it will be a lot of work. It may be useful to think of a broader, more "programmatic" approach such as employed by Partners in Learning (see Chapter 14), including departmental commitment and monthly meetings, would be a useful device to stimulate participation in Alliances.

Recommendations for Use

Alliances shares with other methods that use face-to-face groups the capacity to have a powerful effect on teacher and student perceptions and attitudes. It has been designed to uncover subtle aspects of teaching, particularly those involved with the teacher-student relationship. I recommend its use for experienced teachers who are willing to make an eight hour commitment to teaching improvement in order to fine-tune their teaching but who are not willing to commit the considerably more time required of such programs as like Partners in Learning.

References

Allen, D. W., & Ryan, K. (1969). *Microteaching*. Reading, MA: Addison-Wesley.

Bergquist, W. H., & Phillips, S. R. (1975). *A handbook for faculty development*. (Vol. 1). Washington, DC: The Council for the Advancement of Small Colleges.

Tiberius, R. G., Sackin, H. D., Janzen, K. R., & Preece, M. (1993). Alliances for Change: A procedure for improving teaching through conversations with learners and partnerships with colleagues. *The Journal of Staff, Program, and Organization Development, 11*(1), 11-23.

Appendix A

Summary of the Steps of a Typical Microteaching Procedure

Step One. Teacher presents a five-minute lesson, which demonstrates a particular teaching skill, to a group of three or four students. Students' are not the only observers; the teaching may also be observed by a teaching consultant or supervisor, and may be videotaped.

Step Two. After the session the students complete a brief feedback form and then leave the classroom.

Step Three. The teacher and consultant discuss the teaching, referring to the forms and video when appropriate.

Step Four. The teacher has a brief time to redesign the session, making corrections based on the discussion of the feedback.

Step Five. The teacher teaches the session again to a different group of students and gathers new feedback.

Appendix B

Summary of the Steps of the Teaching Laboratory

The teaching laboratory is a practice teaching exercise in which a volunteer teacher has an opportunity to teach a simulated class.

The focus of the teaching should be a tiny sample of a natural teaching sequence, such as outlining the plan of a clinic day, eliciting questions, or summarizing a lecture. The teaching laboratory is, as the name implies, a method for close examination and critique of a small piece of teaching.

During the teaching laboratory you will have the opportunity to act as a teacher, a consultant, or a student in the teacher's "class." The following guidelines are offered toward effective use of your time in this session:

a. One person should volunteer to act as teacher, a second as consultant, and the rest as students. Ideally the group should be small (e.g. six participants) and there should be sufficient time available, so that everyone will have at least one opportunity to be the teacher and the consultant.

b. The teacher and the consultant meet briefly (a few minutes), aside from the group, to discuss the focus of the teaching laboratory lesson and to agree on goals the teacher wishes to achieve.

c. The teacher sets the stage by providing background information to the members of the group who are acting as students. The teacher briefly (e.g., in two minutes) describes such features as the type of group, its place in the educational sequence, characteristics of the learners, or whatever information is important to their role as learners.

d. The teacher conducts the lesson in five to ten minutes. The consultant notifies the teacher at one minute before his or her time is up and stops the teacher at the end of the teaching time.

e. The consultant leads a feedback session of the teaching for ten minutes. The teacher is allowed the privilege of making the first comments since he or she is in the most vulnerable position.

f. The group critiques the consultant's performance for about five minutes.

g. The entire process is repeated with a different teacher and consultant.

h. If time permits, the teacher should re-teach the episode, taking advantage of the feedback from his or her first teaching session. Steps two through six are repeated for the second attempt.

Appendix C

Summary of the Steps of Alliances for Change

1. After a workshop demonstrating the method, teachers choose partners with whom they will work.

2. Each member of the pair interviews the other concerning her or his teaching expectations, methods, and evaluations.

3. Each member of the pair observes the other's teaching, usually just once.

4. Each member of the pair conducts a focus group interview with a random selection of students drawn from the other teacher's class. The purpose of these groups is to strike agendas of teaching issues that will be discussed in subsequent groups. The outcome of the "agenda" groups, as these groups are called, is summarized, written in a brief report and returned to the students for validation. Then each partner gives a copy of her or his report to the other teacher. The group is a true focus group. The group focuses on two simple questions: what aspects of the teaching and learning should stay as they are (because they are helpful to your learning as it is); and what aspects need improvement to make them more helpful to your learning?

5. The teacher may obtain a broader class response by conducting a written class survey, asking the same two questions. This step may be omitted.

6. The full class response is summarized and combined with the agenda group report. Each teacher takes copies of this combined report to class and calls for volunteers to join the teacher in a meeting for the purpose of helping the teacher interpret it and make suggestions for improvement. This second type of group is called a "conversation group."

7. The teacher briefly tells the class the results of discussion with the conversation group and then discloses how s/he plans to address the problems and to maintain the features that were considered successful. A brief opportunity for questions from the class is useful at this point.

8. At the end of the course all students in the course are asked to complete a "final questionnaire" to find out whether they perceived any improvement in the areas that were addressed.

14. *Partners in Learning: Breaking Down the Barriers Around Teaching*

Myrna Smith

*P*artners in Learning, the most comprehensive consultant-based teaching improvement procedure available, has the goal of enhancing the quality of communication between faculty and students and among faculty. The assumptions underlying the procedure are: first, that faculty who communicate with one another and with their students on a regular basis will break down the barriers around teaching by becoming aware of specific problems that can then be resolved; and second, that once students and faculty become active collaborators rather than antagonists, faculty—perceiving the students differently—will make broad changes in their approaches to teaching.

The procedure, first described by Joseph Katz and Mildred Henry in *Turning Professors into Teachers* (1988), was developed by them during the 1970s and 1980s. In the late 1980s Katz brought the procedure to New Jersey under the name The New Jersey Master Faculty Program. The procedure is now being used at colleges across the country, usually under the name Partners in Learning.

The Four Program Components

Classroom Observation

The faculty pair constitutes the fundamental unit of the program; two faculty members agree to work together for a period of time. To begin breaking down the barrier around teaching, one partner observes a class taught by the other for a semester, quarter, or a given number of weeks; then the two switch roles. The frequency of the observations may vary, depending upon the involvement of the partners. For intense work the observations might occur every week or even every class period for a few weeks. The observing faculty member needs to become knowledgeable about the class, the students, the class work, and the evaluation in order to engage in a meaningful dialogue with the observed teacher.

Student Interviews

Each faculty member interviews two or three students from the observed class. The student interviews, like the faculty observation, occur regularly over time, each lasting from thirty minutes to an hour. Questions range from the general in initial interviews to specific queries about the particular student's learning in later interviews. Some faculty, particularly those less skilled in interviewing techniques, have found group interviews more useful. Because the goal of the interviews is to bring light to the question, "How do students learn?," faculty do not ask direct evaluative questions, such as "Is Professor X a good teacher?" (For a fuller discussion of student interviews and other details about the program see Golin, 1990, Finkelstein and Smith (undated), and Smith and LaCelle-Peterson, 1991.)

Collegial Discussion

The faculty pair further breaks down the barrier around teaching by meeting regularly to discuss the observations and the student interviews. They meet as two colleagues who have collected data on a small, applied research project that focuses on what is happening in the class and on how student learning is promoted or hindered. If the program is campus-wide, the pair's discussions can spill over into the group meetings of all the campus participants.

Coordination

Finally, on each campus where there is a program, one or two campus coordinators take care of the logistics of recruiting participants, matching up pairs, and scheduling campus group meetings. While the classroom observations, students interviews, and collegial discussions are central to the process of learning about teaching from the perspective of the participating faculty members, collegial leadership by the campus coordinators is essential to the success of the program as a whole. The campus coordinators may act as liaisons to a state or regional director, who in turn may conduct coordinator meetings, plan special events of interest to the campuses, and lobby administrators to support the program.

Strengths

In addition to specific lessons about teaching that faculty can learn from one another and from their students, faculty learn the importance of understanding their students' perceptions and thoughts, and gain insight into what affects student learning. Faculty also have the opportunity to observe teaching styles different from their own. An evaluation of the New Jersey Partners in Learning, then called the New Jersey Master Faculty Program, showed that the process of thoughtful interaction with others who care about teaching has a rejuvenating effect and lessens the feeling of isolation (Rice & Cheldelin, 1989).

By visiting the class a number of times, the partner gradually becomes "invisible" to the class and can observe the class without interfering with its dynamics. Often after many visits to the class and discussion with the students, the partners become more attuned to educational issues and develop skills in discussing them.

The wide-ranging interviews with students provide faculty with information about the context within which their students live and learn. Exchanges of personal information have enabled teachers to perceive students as "individuals with complicated lives and with aspirations and expectations that may not coincide with those of the instructor who may have viewed his class as a faceless 'them' (Finkelstein & Smith, no date). Once teachers perceive the students differently, they are more open to change.

Weaknesses

The main weakness of the program is that it requires time and commitment from faculty without any clear goals. In contrast to most faculty development workshops, faculty may come away, after several hours of invested time, with no new techniques that can be tried in their classes. Neither will they receive any "help" from an "expert" about something that should be modified in their teaching. Since the product emerges from the process, faculty must invest with no guaranteed pay off, and the "interest" may be at too low a rate for some faculty. This drawback can be alleviated if an experienced person interviews students in front of a group of faculty. How much

students have to say about their own education generally surprises faculty.

Another potential weakness emerges when one member of the faculty pair is perceived to be (or actually is) an inferior teacher. In such cases the better teacher can become the "expert" with the answers to help remediate the inferior teacher. When this happens, Partners in Learning loses its special collegial quality and becomes more like traditional mentoring procedures.

Another issue that may be construed as a weakness is time. Regularly observing classes, interviewing students, and meeting with a colleague takes time. Katz and Henry believe it to be worthwhile "if one takes into consideration the educational benefits that can be derived from the work."

Since the procedure invites users to modify it, other weaknesses can be overcome by user modification. As noted above, faculty who are not skilled in individual interviewing techniques may interview students in a group of three or four. Faculty who do not want to commit for an entire semester may agree to observe and interview for five weeks. If the pair becomes concerned that the six students being interviewed represent some bias, the observer can interview the entire class or any number the pair agrees upon.

Conclusions

In the first three years of the New Jersey program, participants wrote essays at the end of each semester, many of which were published in a booklet. Eugene J. Cornacchia of Saint Peter's College included in one essay this comment about his experience: "Another discovery I made was how much one can gain from observing a colleague in the classroom. For nearly twelve weeks I watched as a colleague brought chemistry to life, a task I believed was impossible. A kind of synergy developed between us that reinvigorated both of us. I was able to translate some of my colleague's techniques into useful classroom strategies for my own course. Additionally, I hopefully provided some useful suggestions and input for my colleague. The program represents a powerful new approach to faculty development and an invaluable source of information and techniques for the improvement of college learning" (Morrissey, 1990).

Paul Genega of Bloomfield College wrote about what he learned from observing his colleague's history class: "One of the most enjoyable parts of the [Program] was the contact I had with students, as I occupied a third position in the class, not the instructor, but not really another student. In part, I became someone students could blow off steam with, someone who would listen. I made it a point to never champion nor criticize [my colleague] and I think this neutral position was valuable to the students and me. I wasn't judging them; I was simply interested in how the course was going, how they were learning. The pairing of instructors with different roles seems like such a wonderful idea to me, something which higher education might use more often" (Morrissey, 1990).

These two comments, typical of participants who sincerely involved themselves with the program, show how the barriers around teaching, both between faculty and among faculty and students, can be broken down.

References

Finkelstein, M., & Smith, M. (Eds.). (no date). *Partners in Learning*. South Orange, NJ: New Jersey Institute for Collegiate Teaching and Learning, Seton Hall University.

Golin, S. (1990). Four arguments for peer collaboration & student interviewing: The Master Faculty Program. *AAHE Bulletin, 43*(4) 9-10.

Katz, J., & Henry, M. (1988). *Turning professors into teachers: A new approach to faculty development and student learning.* New York: ACE/Macmillan.

Morrissey, P. (Ed). (1990). *Essays by coordinators and participants in the New Jersey Master Faculty Program: Perspectives for exploring the ways in which faculty and students think and learn.* Princeton: The Woodrow Wilson National Fellowship Foundation.

Rice, R. E., & Cheldelin, S. I. (1989). *The knower and the known: Making the connection. Evaluation of the New Jersey Master Faculty Program.* South Orange, NJ: New Jersey Institute for Collegiate Teaching and Learning, Seton Hall University.

Smith, M. J., & LaCelle-Peterson, M. (1991). The professor as active learner: Lessons from the New Jersey Master Faculty Program. *To Improve the Academy, 10,* 271-278.

15. *Small Group Instructional Diagnosis (SGID)*

Lisa Firing Lenze

Testimony from experienced consultants about the Small Group Instructional Diagnosis suggests that this method is a consultant's best friend. Why do consultants have such faith in this feedback method? Perhaps because it is one of the few methods that encourages students to discuss the teaching and learning they experience in a course while the course is in session.

Small Group Instructional Diagnosis, or SGID, was originally developed by D. Joseph Clark at the University of Washington's Biology Learning Research Center and was later supported by a grant from the Fund for the Improvement of Postsecondary Education. It is a small group interview method for collecting feedback from students, midway through the academic term, in order to improve teaching and learning. Clark's SGID involves an instructional consultant, a willing instructor, and the instructor's students. Five basic steps comprise the SGID process, and three tasks describe the work involved for the consultant.

SGID Step One: Initial Conference

During the initial conference in which the SGID is discussed, the consultant and instructor typically review the purpose and the steps of the SGID, make plans for the

student feedback session, and set a date for an instructor feedback session.

When explaining the purpose of the SGID, it is usually a good idea to talk about the formative nature of the information generated during the SGID. Although instructors are accustomed to gathering student feedback for evaluative purposes, they are less familiar with feedback gathered solely for improving the instructor's teaching.

Reviewing the SGID steps outlined here is a relatively simple task. Sometimes consultants have a handout that details each step in the process, so that instructors have a clear description of the SGID.

Making plans for the student feedback session entails talking about the questions the consultant will ask students to answer in small groups and discussing logistics for the feedback session. When the instructor and the consultant talk about questions, the consultant may offer two options. First, the instructor may use the common SGID questions—three general, open-ended questions about strengths, weaknesses, and suggestions (see Consultant Task A below). Alternately, the instructor may design questions to get feedback on specific aspects of his or her teaching.

Discussing the logistics is simply a matter of reviewing the amount of time allotted for the SGID (usually 25-30 minutes at the end of a designated class period), determining how the consultant will be introduced, and determining a date for the class visit (usually around the

---

Figure 1: Sample Directions for the SGID Feedback Form

Directions

Please answer the following questions about the teaching-learning experience in this course as specifically as you can. When answering questions, please use concrete examples to help clarify what you mean. Specific examples will be most useful to the instructor in making changes.

Do **not** write any names on this feedback form. All comments will be reported in group summary only. This form will not be given to the instructor; it will be used by the facilitator to compile a written report. At the end of class, please give this form to the facilitator. Thank you.

middle of the academic term). Before adjourning, the instructor and consultant set a time for the instructor feedback session, to take place shortly after the student feedback is gathered.

Consultant Task A: Prepare Question Sheet

Prior to meeting the instructor's class, the consultant must prepare for the classroom feedback session. This includes constructing a feedback sheet on which the students will respond and figuring out the logistics of the 25-30 minute session.

Formats for feedback forms vary from consultant to consultant, but two pointers may be helpful. First, the form needs directions. Directions are important for reminding students of what type of feedback is useful to instructors. A sample set of directions is presented in Figure 1.

Second, the form needs questions. The standard, general questions used for conducting an SGID are listed in Figure 2. However, when instructors design their own questions (or even their own forms), the body of the feedback form may look more like the sample in Figure 3.

Before the feedback session, the consultant must also calculate the time constraints. That is, given the amount of time the instructor agreed to leave for the feedback session (usually 25-30 minutes total) and the already allotted time for an introduction to the SGID (usually five minutes), how much time should be allotted for the students to talk in groups? And given the number of student groups (usually three to five students per group), how much time should be allotted for each group to report to other groups? Planning for these logistics ahead of time makes the feedback session run smoothly.

SGID Step Two: Student Feedback Session

The feedback session is the time when students generate information, in the instructor's absence, about their experience in the course. Through small group work and a synthesizing discussion, the consultant gathers information to compile a written report. Specifically, this step might proceed in the following manner.

Sitting in on the beginning of class. The consultant attends class on the designated day and reminds the instructor of the agreed upon time to begin the SGID. The instructor teaches until 25 minutes remain in the period; then the instructor introduces the consultant and leaves the room.

Introducing the SGID. The consultant takes about five minutes to explain her or his association with the instructor and emphasizes that the instructor is engaging in this activity voluntarily because the instructor cares about improving the teaching and learning in this class. When describing the purpose and procedure of the SGID, the consultant may elect to put the procedures for the next 25 minutes on the board, or overhead, with time limits.

Forming small groups. The consultant asks students to form small groups (usually of three to five students) and choose a recorder. She or he distributes the feedback forms, one to each person, and reads through the directions, stressing the importance of helpful feedback. For about 10 minutes, students talk about the questions on the feedback form, and the recorder writes positive and constructive responses with specific examples on the designated group feedback form.

Facilitating large group discussion. At the end of the 10-minute small group period, the consultant facilitates a large group discussion for the remainder of the class. Usually, each group reports one positive and one constructive comment. The consultant notes all responses on a blackboard or overhead so that students can see the consultant's notes. (If the consultant elects to use the blackboard, asking a student to copy everything on paper allows the consultant to take the notes along at the end of the period.) After each comment, the consultant takes a vote on how many groups agree with the comment and makes some note of the numbers.

Concluding the feedback session. Toward the end of the session, the consultant summarizes the main comments and reviews what will happen next, including the time frame in which the instructor will receive feedback. The consultant again gives credit to the instructor for inviting the students to participate in this form of feedback, thanks students for their participation, and collects the feedback forms for analysis.

Figure 2: Standard Questions for the SGID Feedback Form

1. What do you like about the course?
2. What do you think needs improvement?
3. What suggestions do you have for bringing about these improvement?

Consultant Task B: Prepare Written Report

In the time between the feedback session and the next meeting with the instructor, the consultant prepares a written report. Just as the feedback forms vary from consultant to consultant, so do formats for written reports.

The simplest report lists the answers students gave for each question with an asterisk next to those items mentioned by more than one group and, next to those items that engendered debate, a ratio of groups-that-agree to groups-that-disagree. More labor-intensive reports include a written summary of student comments by topic. In this type of report, the instructor does not see all the comments, but gets a sense of what the group as a whole said.

Often, the feedback from students and the vulnerability of the instructor dictates the format for the report. If students had an equal number of positive and constructive points to make and the instructor is very open to feedback, a list report may serve the purpose well. On the other hand, if students had many more critical comments to make than positive feedback to offer and the instructor is already anxious about receiving feedback from students, a report written in prose might be more appropriate.

SGID Step Three: Instructor Feedback Session

Once the consultant has completed the feedback report, she or he meets with the instructor to discuss the report. In this meeting, the two discuss the content of the report, the instructor's reactions to the report, and instructional strategies and procedures to continue or change.

During this step, the instructor is very vulnerable. Consider that the consultant heard, first hand, what students said; the instructor did not. The consultant put together the written report; the instructor is reading it for the first time. Since the instructor may be very anxious about this meeting, it is important to remind the instructor that the report is open to interpretation and to encourage the instructor to raise questions about issues in the report that do not make sense.

In addition to creating a comfortable tone and setting for this meeting, the consultant must engage the instructor in a meaningful, non-threatening conversation about the written report. The consultant is best prepared for conducting this discussion if she or he has received some practice-based training with feedback. For information and materials about giving information to instructors, see other chapters of this book.

Before concluding the session, the consultant might help the instructor think about what to say to students and how to say it. Paying some attention to this during the

---

Figure 3: Alternate Questions for the SGID Feedback Form

Clarity of teaching in lectures:

Think about whether the instructor's examples are helpful.
Think about whether the instructor explains the material clearly.
Think about how the instructor helps you understand difficult material.

  1. What about the instructor's lecture is most clear and helpful?
  2. What do you suggest the instructor do to enhance the clarity of lectures?

Quality of discussion in small groups:

Take into account the quality of the instructor's organizing questions for discussion.
Take into account whether sharing information in small group discussions helps you learn.
Take into account the instructor's role during discussions.

  1. What about small group discussions is most helpful to your learning?
  2. What do you suggest the instructor do to enhance learning in small groups?

meeting gives the instructor a head start on preparing the actual verbal report.

SGID Step Four: Clarification Session

During the next class period, the instructor devotes five to ten minutes to discussing the feedback students provided. The instructor summarizes the main points of the report and asks students to clarify those comments the instructor found unclear. The instructor then concludes the session with a statement about the changes she or he plans to implement before the end of the course.

Consultant Task C: Contact Instructor

Once the instructor takes the written report out of the consultant's office, the instructor is alone in her or his efforts to make instructional changes. A phone call from the consultant inviting the instructor back to talk about the clarification session or the process of making changes in teaching is often welcomed. This extra step of making contact on a separate occasion, rather than simply using the instructor feedback session to arrange a follow-up meeting, often engenders a perception of genuine, long-term interest.

SGID Step Five: Follow-up Conversation

The consultant and the instructor meet to discuss the outcome of the clarification session and to reinforce commitment to the changes the instructor proposed for the course. It is during this meeting that instructors are most likely to request information, materials, or further consultation about how to implement changes in their classes.

Most consultants report that instructors react favorably to the SGID. The information students generate is often unlike any feedback instructors have received from students. It is concrete, confirming, constructive, and thoughtful. The SGID facilitates a conversation between students and instructors that may well deem the SGID an instructor's best friend.

Additional Readings

Bauer, G., & Tanner, M. W. (1993). Insights into ITA instruction in problem-solving courses through student perceptions at midterm. In K. G. Lewis (Ed.), *The TA experience: Preparing for multiple roles* (pp. 401-409). Stillwater, OK: New Forums Press.

Bennett, W. E. (1987). Small group instructional diagnosis: A dialogue approach to instructional improvement for tenured faculty. *The Journal of Staff, Program, and Organization Development, 5,* 100-104.

Clark, D. J., & Bekey, J. (1979). Use of small groups in instructional evaluation. *Professional and Organizational Development Quarterly, 1,* 87-95.

Coffman, S. J. (1991). Improving your teaching through small-group diagnosis. *College Teaching, 39,* 80-82.

Redmond, M. V., & Clark, D. J. (1982). Student group instructional diagnosis: A practical approach to improving teaching. *AAHE Bulletin, 34*(6), 8-10.

White, K. (1991). Mid-course adjustments: Using small group instructional diagnosis to improve teaching and learning. *Washington Center News, 6,* 20-22.

16. *Instructional Skills Workshop Program: A Peer-based Model for the Improvement of Teaching and Learning*

Judy Wilbee

*I*n the community college system of British Columbia, most faculty are hired based on their expertise or content knowledge of their discipline, whether this is in the vocational, technical or academic area. Many faculty begin their careers as educators with part-time instructional contracts where they have minimal responsibility for the overall educational process other than the specific course or unit which they are teaching. As most students and faculty development practitioners will tell you, content competence does not necessarily provide the instructional expertise required to ensure quality educational experiences. Until recently, little regard has been given to the professional development needs of new faculty in acquiring the theory and practical skills of teaching adults.

In the late 1970s, Doug Kerr, a faculty member at Vancouver Community College, Vancouver, British Columbia, designed the Instructional Skills Workshop (ISW) to help new vocational instructors make the transition from industry to the classroom. The workshop was found so desirable and useful it was quickly made available to instructors in all disciplines and at all stages of their careers. Since that time the ISW has evolved into a three-tiered peer-based program which includes preparing trainers who train facilitators who head the campus-based ISW. In the ISW, teachers help teachers, with colleagues facilitating, not teaching each other. Administrative support for the ISW program provides an opportunity for colleges to demonstrate commitment to faculty professional development and for faculty and administration to attain the mutual goal of improving the teaching and learning in their classrooms.

Overview of the Program

The Instructional Skills Workshop Program is a comprehensive approach to faculty development which offers the following features:

- equally usable by both new and experienced instructors,
- relevant to instructors from a broad range of disciplines,
- intensive experiential learning design,
- voluntary participation by institution and individuals within institutions,
- implementable by faculty at the local level,
- highly flexible and adaptable,
- infinitely expandable.

The program is designed on the assumption that the capacity for dramatic improvement in the quality of instruction resides with instructors currently functioning in the system. The program, designed around the "design-instruct-feedback-redesign" microteaching model concentrates on the development of the instructional skills of each individual participant.

The program consists of the following three levels:

1. *Instructional Skills Workshop* concentrates on the development of the fundamental skills of writing instructional objectives, preparing lesson plans, designing pre-and post-assessment strategies, and conducting instructional sessions. Sessions on such topics as cooperative learning, learning styles, classroom research, classroom assessment and stages of group development are also conducted during this four-day workshop.

2. *Facilitator Development Workshop* prepares experienced instructors to conduct the Instructional Skills Workshop at their own institutions. The focus of this five-day workshop is on facilitating the giving and receiving of both positive and growth feedback.
3. *Trainer Development Workshop* provides experienced ISW facilitators an opportunity to practice and improve their facilitator skills in order that they may lead the Facilitator Development Workshop.

Instructional Skills Workshop

The goals of the Instructional Skills Workshop are that participants: learn to use instructional objectives to inform learners about what they are expected to learn; write useful, practical lesson plans; conduct highly participatory classroom sessions; competently use common instructional aids (chalkboard, overhead projector and screen, flip chart); use good questioning techniques during a classroom session; use simple techniques during lesson to test teaching; evaluate what has been learned in relation to performance objectives; and provide objective behavioral feedback.

The ISW uses a learner-centered model of instruction with a laboratory approach to the improvement of teaching and learning. It is an intensive 24-hour experience generally spread over four days and limited to five participants with one or two facilitators. On day one of the workshop participants are introduced to: information related to the theory and practice of teaching the adult learner; techniques for motivating students; selection and writing of useful instructional objectives with accompanying lesson plans; techniques for eliciting learner participation; and suggestions for evaluation of student learning. On each of the following three days, each participant teaches a "mini-lesson." The instructor receives oral, written and video feedback from the other participants in the workshop about the effectiveness of his/her lessons and then, using the feedback as the raw data, the participant develops strategies for improvement. Given the limited time available to participate in teaching enhancement activities, the opportunity to teach and receive feedback three times increases the probability of participants incorporating new learning.

A challenge for all educators is to capture learner interest and in the ISW participants are encouraged to engage actively as learners and to give and receive honest, non-judgmental feedback. Participants are encouraged to experiment with different teaching techniques and to utilize different learning domains—psychomotor, cognitive and affective.

The ISW is structured on the experiential learning model of David Kolb, which emphasizes the direct experience of the participant. It is based on the premise that experience precedes learning and that learning, or meaning, from any experience comes from within the learner. Experiential learning occurs when individuals engage in an activity, reflect or look back on the experience, extract useful information from the analysis, continue through the cycle again, and re-engage in the activity in a new and different way. Information without demonstration, practice, and coaching will not enable transfer or integration to an instructor's repertoire of teaching techniques. The ISW encourages reflection and examination of one's teaching practices and provides feedback focused on process rather than on the specific content of the lesson.

Mini-Lesson Basics

While there are a number of effective instructional models, the mini-lesson for the ISW has the following five lesson basics:

- Bridge-in
- Instructional Objective
- Pre-test
- Participatory Learning
- Post-test

Participants are urged to incorporate these lesson basics into each mini-lesson.

Bridge-In

While it is the students' responsibility to learn, bridging-in provides a meaningful link between the objective of the lesson and its value to the learner. It is sometimes referred to as the "hook" or "motivator," or simply, that intermediate step when the learner puts aside private thoughts and tunes into class. The "bridge-in" will vary depending on the subject material and learning context. In extension and recreation courses, participation is voluntary, so learners are usually already motivated. A few words to learners about how the task helps to achieve their goals is usually sufficient. Motivating students in academic, career, and vocational programs where the course is required makes "bridging-in" especially important.

Instructional Objective

An instructional objective can be thought of as a statement indicating what students will be able to do at the conclusion of instruction. Generally, this "doing" will be something that is assessable and/or observable. Clearly defined objectives constitute a basis for the selection of content and design of instructional materials or techniques. They create a basis for determining when the instructional purpose has been accomplished and provide the learner with the means to organize efforts toward accomplishment of the learning tasks.

Pre-Test

The pre-test determines what the learners already know. This ensures that teaching starts at the right point in the subject material, that is, not above or below the current "know-how" of the students. The pre-test may be an informal question/answer process, or a more formal test given to all students. For the purpose of mini-lessons, the question/answer method is most appropriate. A mixed group of adult learners can include people who already possess the information or abilities you intend to teach to the entire group. In this case, you can share the teaching role with the learners instead of taking sole responsibility for their learning.

Participatory Learning

Whenever possible, instructors should endeavor to have students actively involved in achieving the desired learning outcomes. Effective learning generally results from activities that are sequenced from simple to complex, from known to unknown, from general to specific, from concrete to abstract and chronologically.

Psychomotor skills are best mastered through repeated practice combined with feedback. Concepts and theories frequently evolve as a result of discussion, debate or dialogue. Changes in attitude result from the integration and synthesis of new information by the learners—a process that is gradual and difficult to measure.

Strategies for participatory learning also depend on the students' sophistication—how well they have "learned to learn." If the students are skilled in the process of learning, it may be best to plunge them into a discovery learning situation with little guidance. On the other hand, if they lack confidence and/or competence as learners, a more structured approach may be required.

Opportunities for participatory learning can be limited by the setting. For example, a sequence of activities appropriate to an academic classroom might be useless in a laboratory or on the shop floor.

Finally, the decision to facilitate participatory learning will depend on the level of knowledge, skills, and attitudes the students bring to the instructional session.

Post-Test

The type of test depends on the instructional objective:

students being tested on their math will be given a knowledge test while students being tested on their ability to service an engine will be given a skills test. In a mini-lesson, questions that test knowledge or knowing could be multiple choice, true/false, matching, completion of short answers or identification of items on a diagram. Skill or "doing" questions could use checklists or rating scales; attitudinal or feeling questions could use an attitude scale or an essay. The post-test for the mini-lesson will be short.

The Mini-Lesson Cycle

A mini-lesson should be a complete instructional segment and should deal with topics that will provide new learning for the participants. The instructor should not ask the participants to play a role such as imagining that they are in the third month of a class dealing with quantum mechanics or to assume an imaginary identity. Feedback to the instructor is based on one's genuine experience of being a learner in the lesson.

There is often resistance to the 10-minute time frame of the mini-lesson, after all classes are normally at least 50 minutes long. However, this time limit forces editing and concise planning and there is more than sufficient data generated during 10 minutes of instruction on which to provide feedback. If the lesson was longer, the feedback could not focus as well on specific teaching strengths or areas for growth. The aim is to identify areas for improvement without overloading and to give participants the confidence to work toward that improvement. While it is unlikely an instructor in a class would teach solely in 10-minute components, using this five-part instructional model will help faculty with their lesson design as they prepare for their regular classes.

This learner-centered approach, requiring participants to design and instruct their colleagues, is in keeping with an adult education model of instruction. The focus is on the adult learner. When participants articulate their personal experiences as learners, they become more sensitive to themselves as learners which enables exploration and consequent discussion of teaching. This focused reflection can result in increased sensitivity to learners within their own classrooms.

While the actual instructional time in a mini-lesson is only 10 minutes, the total time needed, including planning and feedback, is 40 minutes. This is divided into four sections.

Preparation: 10 Minutes

During this time the facilitator consults with the instructor in selecting a feedback form, discusses points to be observed, and provides support and reassurance. The instructor sets up teaching space in preparation for the lesson.

Lesson: 10 Minutes

The instructor teaches the mini-lesson to other participants. The facilitator videotapes the lesson, makes observations, and prepares for a feedback session.

Written Feedback: 7 Minutes

The facilitator hands out the selected feedback form (see Appendices for samples) and gives any required directions to participants. The facilitator then provides reassurance to the instructor and may provide video feedback.

Verbal Feedback from Learners: 13 Minutes

The facilitator conducts an oral feedback session, she/he may use video for emphasis and ensures that the instructor receives and understands the comments of the participants. The facilitator also records/summarizes feedback for the instructor and participants give their written feedback form to the instructor.

The Feedback Session

With the aid of a feedback form and using verbal, written and video resources, the facilitator ensures that the individual who taught the lesson receives feedback that is balanced and appropriate, identifying strengths as well as areas in need of improvement. Participants are urged to engage actively as learners while the other participants teach, and to give honest, helpful, non-judgmental feedback that is positive in nature and encourages growth in the individual. The risk of presenting to one's peers is offset by the support from the group members.

Giving Useful Feedback

Constructive feedback is descriptive rather than evaluative. It describes behavior you can see, not inferences about causes of behavior. By describing one's own reactions, the giver lets the instructor accept or reject feedback. If the giver avoids judgmental language, the instructor may not react defensively to suggestions. Several basics characteristics of effective feedback are listed in Figure 1.

Constructive feedback has the following characteristics:

- It is specific rather than general, because specific information helps the receiver focus on immediate behavior. General feedback confuses and lacks impact.
- It is directed toward behavior that the receiver can change, as frustration is often increased when a person is reminded of a shortcoming he or she cannot control.
- It is solicited rather than imposed, because feedback is most useful when the receiver has a question the observers can answer.
- It is well-timed and given as soon as possible after the observation or reaction. This way, the person can relate to the facts and emotions of the situation and make better use of the feedback.
- It is checked to ensure understanding. The receiver is encouraged to rephrase the feedback to ensure understanding.
- It does not overload. If the individual is overloaded, it reduces the possibility that he or she may use the feedback effectively.
- It considers the needs of the receiver and giver. To be classed as "helping feedback" the information should be given as an offering, not as something forced upon the other person. The intention is to share ideas and information, not give advice.
- It is given in a caring manner.

Figure 1: Feedback Basics	
Feedback is less likely to work when it is:	**Feedback is more likely to work when it is:**
Evaluative	Descriptive
Generalized	Specific
Focused on personal characteristics	Focused on behaviors
Focused on unchangeable characteristics	Suggestive of or allows for change
Focused on the giver's needs	Focused on receiver's needs
Dogmatic	Open to discussion

Receiving Feedback

The Instructional Skills Workshop teaches participants to receive feedback effectively. Some guidelines include:

- Request specific information. For example, the instructor in a mini-lesson may have a specific question on the clarity of the objective.
- Paraphrase what you hear. By paraphrasing, the receiver is able to put the feedback in his or her own words and then check for understanding.
- Make eye contact with the giver. This acknowledges the giver of the information and suggests a willingness on the part of the receiver to be open and to hear the feedback.
- Accept all feedback. This does not require agreement on the part of the recipient, just an openness to consideration.
- Ask for specifics if unclear. This indicates a willingness to achieve clarity.
- Feedback does not have to be given or received verbally. It can be communicated through gestures, eye contact, stance, and distance between people. Participants are encouraged to give honest experiential responses and to refer to what is actually seen or heard, not to why the observer thought it happened. In an Instructional Skills Workshop both giver and receiver can check with others on the accuracy of the feedback and determine if this is an impression of one person or if it is a shared impression.

Facilitator Development Workshop

During the Facilitator Development Workshop, participants acquire and practice the skills needed to facilitate the Instructional Skills Workshop. This workshop, consisting of a maximum of five participants, is conducted during five consecutive days and is led by a peer trainer who has received additional training in group process skills.

The goals of the Facilitator Development Workshop are the same as those of the Instructional Skills Workshop with the addition of acquiring the skills of facilitating feedback. This additional goal includes leading the group in both positive and growth producing feedback that is understood, accepted and usable by the instructor. This allows the participants the freedom to make some points that seem important to them, directing the group to focus on the basic ingredients of the mini-lesson, managing overall time and process during the first two-thirds of the cycle, and using video resources effectively.

As in the Instructional Skills Workshop, each participant prepares and conducts three 10-minute mini-lessons and receives oral, written and video feedback on each mini-lesson. In addition, each participant has three opportunities to develop the skills needed to lead the group feedback sessions on other participants' mini-lessons and to use the video equipment to identify specific strengths and limitations of the instructional sessions conducted.

Because of the intensity of the workshop, it is critical that participants be freed from their day-to-day responsibilities during the workshop and that all participants attend all sessions. There are also evening assignments which include some reading and preparation of the following day's mini-lesson. During the first four days, the participants develop and practice facilitator skills. On the fifth day, the participants work together with other individuals from their own institution to plan implementation of the program.

Activities During the Facilitator Development Workshop

During the Facilitator Development Workshop, the participants will experience a number of roles and be involved in a variety of activities:

Instructing

- presenting a mini-lesson on each of days two, three, and four;
- experimenting with different instructional techniques and teaching different learning domains (cognitive, affective and psychomotor).

Facilitating

- leading a feedback session on each of days two, three, and four;
- experimenting with different facilitator techniques.

Receiving Feedback

- achieving clarity on the learner's response to one's own mini-lessons (strengths, areas for growth);
- achieving clarity on the instructor's and other participants' response to one's own facilitation of feedback sessions.

Being a Learner

- being a learner in mini-lessons presented by other participants;

- formulating a personal response (both written and verbal) as a learner in a mini-lesson.

Filming

- being a video operator for others' mini-lessons.

Giving Feedback

- communicating directly to the instructor and facilitator one's personal experience in the mini-lesson and in the feedback session;
- clarifying where requested by the instructor and facilitator;
- providing a balance of positive and growth-related feedback useful to the instructor and the facilitator.

Setting Personal Goals

- weighing expectations in relation to the goals of the workshop;
- formulating a personal goal for each day.

Group Process

- taking responsibility for the progress of the group towards its goals;
- giving formative evaluation of the workshop itself;
- helping to create an environment conducive to learning.

During the Facilitator Development Workshop, participants will receive theme sessions on learning styles, learn methods for obtaining student feedback as a method of formative evaluation (such as Classroom Assessment Techniques and Small Group Instructional Feedback) and study the stages of group development.

Suggested Criteria for Selecting the Instructional Skills Facilitator Team

Any college participating in the Instructional Skills Workshop Program is asked to select a team that is balanced in terms of gender and ethnicity and from as broad a range of disciplines or program areas as is possible. Facilitators should be volunteers and should meet the following criteria:

- demonstrated competence as an instructor,
- credibility with fellow instructors,
- strong commitment to his/her own instructional skills development,
- strong desire to be involved in a peer-based faculty development program,
- availability to conduct Instructional Skills Workshops, and

- prepared to be available for the entire week of Facilitator Training and to complete homework assignments each evening.

Trainer Development Workshop

This workshop prepares the individual who has completed the Facilitator Development Workshop and has led several Instructional Skills Workshops to lead the Facilitator Development Workshop. Often this five-day workshop is conducted using the apprenticeship model with an experienced trainer working along side the trainee.

External Support Structures

To maintain and enhance the system-wide impact of the ISW Program, the facilitators hold an annual residential institute called "Potlatch" (from the West Coast Indian gift-giving tradition). Potlatch is an advanced level leadership development program for ISW facilitators. It provides an opportunity for participants to strengthen their understanding of the theories and concepts underlying experiential instructor development activities as well as become familiar with new developments in the ISW Program. The emphasis in the program, and at Potlatch, is on the exchange of ideas among the facilitators and on sharing the gifts of knowledge, talent and energy that each one has to offer. The annual institute provides an opportunity to focus not only on instructional development but on helping facilitators acquire skills in personal and organizational development.

Benefits of the Instructional Skills Workshop Program

Many organizations have a policy statement for the ISW facilitators which insures the activities are developmental and confidential. Any data collection is at the request of a faculty member with all materials collected becoming the personal property of the instructor. While the workshops are funded and supported by the administration, it is not perceived as part of the authority structure of the organization. Attendance at an ISW is voluntary and may be encouraged, but it should never be imposed. All records, videotapes and workshop proceedings are kept confidential. The ISW is developmental not remedial. It should not be connected to summative evaluation procedures. Because the workshop utilizes a laboratory approach to instruction that encourages exploration and risk-taking within the context of the mini-lessons, any suggestion of an evaluation component could destroy the effectiveness of the workshop.

In addition to facilitating workshops, ISW facilitators often assist in a variety of other activities related to the improvement of instruction. These include classroom observation visits, videotaping of a class, involving students as a means of eliciting feedback to an instructor, as well as individual consulting/facilitating.

It is not a requirement of all individuals who participate in a Facilitator Development Workshop to conduct an ISW. For seasoned faculty, participation may be a renewing and revitalizing activity, providing a new interest in the teaching and learning process. Those charged with the responsibility of evaluating faculty can enhance their ability to provide growth-producing constructive feedback. The workshop also improves one's competence and confidence in working with small and large groups. Being a workshop facilitator may provide the opportunity for individuals to demonstrate their leadership ability or prepare themselves for fulfilling a mentoring role for new members. The reward for being a facilitator is personal and professional. The growth and the internal satisfaction that evolve from being involved in a helping, caring relationship with one's colleagues are the primary benefits of the Program.

The ISW Program can help educational institutions address the needs of our diverse student population and build a community of scholars with a shared vocabulary and knowledge base. It can increase interest in instructional as well as discipline-based development activities. Utilizing a learner-centered model for teaching helps to address the needs of minorities, re-entry students, women and groups with special needs. Developing the skills of faculty in giving and receiving both affirming and growth feedback improves their ability in acknowledging the unique learning needs of all learners. Building community is accomplished through the development of a sense of colleagueship, team learning, self-discovery and through learning new approaches to assist others. Relationships are established as participants work and learn in an atmosphere of trust and support. Participation in a workshop creates an opportunity for new faculty to discover the unique culture and value system of the organization.

Support for the ISW Program provides an opportunity for administration to demonstrate commitment to the shared goal of improving teaching and learning. Politically, faculty and administration will often focus on that which divides; the ISW focuses on that which brings together.

Additional Readings

Bergquist, W. H., & Phillips, S. R. (1975). *A handbook for faculty development.* (Vol. 1). Washington, DC: Council for the Improvement of Small Colleges.

Kerr, D.W. (1980). *The Instructional Skills Program.* Unpublished Ministry of Education major paper, University of British Columbia, Vancouver.

Cariboo College ISW Facilitators (1982). *Facilitators policy paper.* Unpublished manuscript.

Kerr & Mason (1980). The Instructional Skills Program in British Columbia. *Pace Newsletter, 10*(4), 9.

Kolb, D. A. (1984). *Experiential learning: Experience as the source of learning and development.* Englewood Cliffs, NJ: Prentice-Hall.

Kort, M. S. (1993). Improving teaching and learning. *Facilitator Development Workshop for the Instructional Skills Workshop: Handbook for Participants.* Ministry of Skills Training and Labour and the Centre for Curriculum and Professional Development, Province of British Columbia.

Morrison, D. (1985). The Instructional Skills Workshop Program: An inter-institutional approach. *To Improve the Academy, 4,* 75-83.

Appendix A

Instructor:_____Observer: _____

Lesson #:_____ Topic: _____ Date: _____

Please record your comments regarding the instructional session that you have just observed. Be as specific as you can. Describe behaviours wherever possible. Try to avoid using judgmental terms and making inferences.

1. Clarification of purpose, objectives and structures:

2. Pre-assessment:

3. Choice of instructional activities:

4. Use of instructional aids:

5. Questioning techniques and encouraging participation:

6. Post-test for learning:

7. Closure:

Judy Wilbee, Centre for Curriculum and Professional Development
Reprinted with permission

Appendix B

Sample Feedback Form Instructional Skills Workshop
Suggested questions to aid participants in completing form

Instructor:_____Observer: _____

Lesson #: _____Topic: _____Date: _____

Please record your comments regarding the instructional session that you have just observed. Be as specific as you can. Describe behaviours wherever possible. Try to avoid using judgmental terms and making inferences.

1. Clarification of purpose, objectives and structures:
   - Was the objective(s) clearly written and displayed?
   - Did the objective include a performance criteria?
   - Were learners clear about the general purposes of the lesson?
   - Did learners understand how they were expected to learn?

2. Pre-assessment:
   - Did the instructor conduct a pre-assessment?
   - Was the pre-assessment specific enough?
   - Was the instructor able to adjust the lesson to learners' knowledge?

3. Choice and delivery of instructional activities:
   - What were the actual techniques used?
   - Did the technique(s) used lead to appropriate learning?
   - Did learners have a chance to practice and demonstrate desired skills?
   - Was there a high degree of learner participation?
   - Was more than one common technique used?
   - What other technique(s) could have been used?

4. Use of instructional aids:
   - Did the aid add to or detract from learning?
   - How was the instructor positioned relative to the aid?
   - Could you easily read the instructor's writing?
   - What other aid(s) could the instructor have used?

5. Questioning techniques and encouraging participation:
   - How often did the instructor use
     - closed questions?
     - open questions?
     - rhetorical questions?
     - probing questions?
   - How did the instructor deal with incorrect answers?
   - How often did the instructor direct the same questions at two or more learners?
   - Did the instructor do anything else to encourage participation?
   - Did the instructor provide enough support?

6. Post-test for learning:
   - Did the instructor conduct a post-test?
   - Did the post-test accurately measure achievement of objective(s)?
   - Did the post-test come as a surprise to learners?

7. Closure:
   - Did learners find out how well they had learned?
   - Was there a sense of completion to the lesson?
   - Did the instructor summarize the lesson?

Judy Wilbee, Centre for Curriculum and Professional Development
Reprinted with permission

Appendix C

Sample Mini-Lesson Feedback Form
Instructional Skills Workshop

Instructor: _____ Observer: _____

Lesson #: _____Topic: _____ Date: _____

Please record your comments regarding the instructional session that you have just observed. Be as specific as you can. Describe behaviors wherever possible. Try to avoid using judgmental terms and making inferences.

1. What did the instrctor do that helped the participants to learn?

2. What did the instructor have the participants do that helped them learn?

3. What could the instructor have done differently to help the participants learn?

4. What could I, as a learner, have done differently to have helped myself learn in this situation?

Judy Wilbee, Centre for Curriculum and Professional Development
Reprinted with permission

17. *The Teaching Improvement Process*

Mary Deane Sorcinelli

*M*any colleges and universities have instituted faculty development programs to assist instructors with various aspects of instruction. The variety of resources that a program is able to make available can have a great impact on what actually is happening in the classroom. However, many faculty developers and faculty members have found that one of the best ways to eventuate positive and lasting changes in teaching is through individual consultation.

One consultation process which *A Handbook for Faculty Development* describes as "lying very nearly at the heart of faculty development" (Bergquist & Phillips, 1977) is the teaching improvement process developed in 1972 at the Clinic To Improve University Teaching, University of Massachusetts at Amherst. This model, pioneered by Michael Melnik, Dwight Allen, and colleagues, with the financial support of the W.K. Kellogg Foundation, has been further developed, disseminated, adapted, and studied by instructional development programs at colleges and universities across the country (Bergquist & Phillips, 1977; Erickson & Erickson, 1979, 1980; Kerwin, 1985; Povlacs, 1988; Sorcinelli, 1977, 1982).

This individualized, voluntary, and confidential process allows instructors to work with a trained teaching consultant to identify teaching strengths and problems and to develop strategies for improvement. Typically conducted over the course of a semester or longer, the process includes four phases: 1) assessment of teaching (for example, interviews, class observation, videotape, student feedback, and self-assessment), 2) analysis of information (for example, review of the aforementioned sources of data to identify teaching strengths and problems), 3) improvement efforts (for example, using cycles of planning an activity, trying it out and collecting feedback, using the resources of the instructor, consultant, colleagues, students, and print or video material), and 4) a final review (for example, end-of-semester observation, videotape, and student feedback). As initially designed, the process focuses on the improvement of teaching skills and behaviors, offering "perhaps the most powerful methodology yet conceived for the actual improvement of in-class teaching" (Bergquist & Phillips, 1977, p.78). At the same time, because of its versatility, the process also can address a variety of issues related to course and curriculum development, the assessment of student learning, and professional and career development.

Beyond its versatility, at least four other aspects of the teaching improvement process make it a powerful tool for teaching improvement. First, the process is voluntary. Research and practice show that mandatory improvement programs for "problem" teachers do not work (Sorcinelli & Cunningham, 1991). Second, the process is individualized so that faculty member and the faculty member alone decides whether and with whom to share that information. Third, the process is systematic, yet flexible enough to accommodate different goals, levels of courses, methods, and teaching styles. Finally, the process is collaborative. While some teachers can improve their teaching after receiving feedback in isolation, change is far more likely if a consultant or knowledgeable colleague can help interpret information, provide encouragement, and suggest teaching improvement strategies.

References

Bergquist, W. H., & Phillips, S. R. (1977). *A handbook for faculty development.* (Vol.2) Washington, DC: Council for the Advancement of Small Colleges.

Erickson, B. L., & Erickson, G. R. (1980). Working with faculty teaching behaviors. *New Directions for Teaching and Learning, no. 1*, 57-67. San Francisco: Jossey-Bass.

Erickson, G. R., & Erickson, B. L. (1979). Improving college teaching: An evaluation of a teaching consultation procedure. *Journal of Higher Education, 50,* 670-683.

Kerwin, M. A. (1985). The teaching improvement process. *The Journal of Staff, Program, and Organization Development, 3*(1), 10-11.

Povlacs, J. T. (1988). The Teaching Analysis Program and the role of the consultant. In K. G. Lewis & J. T. Povlacs (Eds.), *Face to face: A sourcebook of individual consultation techniques for faculty/instructional developers* (pp. 81-101). Stillwater, OK: New Forums Press.

Sorcinelli, M. D. (1977). A teaching consultation service for college instructors. *Teaching and Learning, 2,* 1-2.

Sorcinelli, M. D. (1982). Effect of a teaching consultation process on professional and personal development in faculty. *To Improve The Academy, 1*, 111-123.

Sorcinelli, M. D., & Cunningham. H. (1991). Developing teaching skills through individual consultation. *Nurse Educator, 16*(3), 7-11.

18. *Considerations in Setting Up a Peer Consultant Program*

Michael Kerwin

What is a peer consultant program? Morrison (1993) defines it as a structured program in which a faculty member—who may or may not be prepared through experience or education to be a consultant but who is recognized as having a consultant role—helps colleagues to analyze their teaching. In a peer consultant program, therefore, faculty with special preparation or skills are designated as "teaching consultants," but the primary responsibilities of these faculty are to teach, advise students, do research, and conduct community service activities rather than to consult with their colleagues. This paper describes considerations in setting up such a program. Although peer consultation is one of several approaches to instructional consultation, it shares many elements with other consultation programs; that is, the considerations in setting up a peer consultant program are similar to those one must consider in setting up other programs. I welcome comments from those with more experience than I in setting up different types of programs. I will begin by describing my own experience in instructional consultation.

Before I assumed the position of coordinator for faculty/staff and program development for the University of Kentucky Community College System in 1983, I had been a faculty member in a research university for five years and in a community college for eight years. Faculty development in both the research university and the community college had consisted of on-the-job training and attending workshops on teaching. On two or three occasions I had team-taught a course with a colleague. Most of the discussions in these situations, however, had focused on the content of the course; very seldom, if at all, did I engage in conversations with a colleague about the manner in which I was teaching. When I interviewed for my present position in December, 1982, I learned about a different type of faculty development program, a program that extended over the length of a semester, in which two faculty members would meet on a regular basis to discuss teaching. Although the program had been implemented in almost all of the University's fourteen community colleges in 1977, no one had been in the coordinator's position for over a year, and as a result, it was being offered on sporadic basis at only two or three colleges. As a faculty member, I saw this program as one in which I wanted to participate. I saw it as something that was missing at the colleges where I had taught. I saw the opportunity to expand this program to the faculty in a statewide system as a challenge. I also knew, when I accepted the coordinator's position, that I had the Chancellor's support to expand the program.

As I reflect upon the factors that caused me to want to expand this program, three stand out. First was my desire, as a faculty member, to engage in regular discussions about my teaching with one of my colleagues. I knew that other faculty members felt as I did and would appreciate the opportunity to do this. The second was the manner in which the program was conducted: data would be gathered about my teaching from interviews, observations, videotapes, and student questionnaires. In consultation with a colleague, I could determine the changes I would make in my teaching. I knew that other faculty members would like to see themselves from these perspectives and would also appreciate having control over what happened in the program. The third was my belief that the program would sell itself—any faculty who knew about it would want to implement it at his or her college. Implementation, I believed, would be easy.

More than ten years have passed since I accepted the challenge to expand this instructional consultation program to all of the colleges in the statewide system. All fourteen colleges currently offer the program; thirty-six faculty, representing almost every discipline offering a course in the system, function as teaching consultants. Over five hundred faculty have participated in the program, and those who have returned program evaluation forms (over seventy percent) rate their experience in the program as one of the most rewarding that they have had at the University. Moreover, a study conducted in 1988-89 (Rozeman and Kerwin, 1991) showed that a group of faculty who participated in the program received significantly more positive ratings from students as compared to a control group of faculty who did not take part in the program. Furthermore, the study showed that the changes that the faculty made in their teaching behavior as a result of participating in the program persisted into the semester following their participation.

In addition to the popularity of the program and the evidence of its effectiveness, the program has been conducted at a relatively low cost to the University. In 1992-93, a statewide program involving fourteen community colleges and affecting the teaching of over 100 faculty cost about $62,500. When one considers that each of these faculty teaches 200-300 students each year and that the changes they make in their teaching persist after their participation in the program, the relationship of costs to the benefit each student receives is very small.

Even though this program has proven itself to be low in cost, popular, and effective in a system of fourteen community colleges, implementation has not always been easy. Ten years of experience have taught me that it requires persistence, administrative support, faculty participation, coordination, and knowledge of program options—these are the fundamental considerations in the implementation process.

Persistence and Determination

In my opinion, the single most important factor in implementing a peer consultant program is the determination of an individual, usually a faculty member who coordinates or directs the college faculty development program, to do so. The Teaching Partners' Program at Ball State University began as a result of Linda Annis's determination to begin the program. Susan Kah's efforts established the Faculty Consultation Program at Miami-Dade Community College. The Teaching Consultation Program at Eastern Kentucky University began because Bill Jones was determined to implement it. Sandra Holmes' determination resulted in the implementation of a peer consultant program at the University of Wisconsin-Stevens Point. In each of these cases, a person who already had a full load of teaching, research, and administrative duties implemented the program because he or she was committed to it.

The first consideration in implementing an instructional consultation program, therefore, is that it will require more time and effort than maintaining the status quo.

Will the time and effort required to implement the program be rewarded? In terms of external rewards—money, prestige, and so on—probably not. Motivation to implement an instructional consultation program probably springs, as it did with me, from a desire to set up a process whereby faculty can engage in regular discussions about their teaching.

At the meeting of the American Educational Research Association, Mary Ann Shea, Jack Kelso, and Kristine Fitch (1993) presented a detailed case study of the interactions between a consultant and a faculty member at the University of Colorado. After hearing their presentation, I remember most the manner in which the consultant and the faculty member evaluated their experience. The consultant, an award-winning full professor, stated, "I am deeply appreciative of the benefits I obtained from this long term mentoring relationship." The faculty member stated, referring to the grade she got on her student evaluations, "I have never gotten C's again. I've progressed to higher and higher in the B range, with occasional A's, and the student comments tell me I'm being successful, at least in making the changes I've been trying to make." Comments like these are the rewards one must want to receive for setting up an instructional consultation program.

Administrative Support

Commitment must be accompanied, however, by support and authority from the administration (see Appendix). When I accepted the role of coordinating the teaching consultation program in the statewide system, I had the Chancellor's support to expand the program. I didn't realize how important this support was until many years later. In my position I did not have the authority to set up and enforce administrative policy or to allocate funds for computer support, supplies or travel. Such authority is vital to the implementation of a peer consultant program.

To illustrate the importance of having policy-setting support or authority, I will cite three examples. Although each could be classified separately as a consideration, all are policy issues that involve administrative decisions. The first addresses the concern of recognizing the consultation as a part of the consultant's workload.

In our program, faculty who function as consultants are released from one three-hour class to consult with two of their colleagues. This is a vital component of the program. Faculty, especially faculty who are regarded as outstanding teachers, have many demands placed upon their time. Oftentimes, they take on more than they should. Being a consultant in the teaching consultation program also demands a great deal of time: tasks include meeting with clients, doing research on teaching, observing classes, and preparing reports. In order to ensure that consultants have enough time to provide consultation services for their clients, I used the Chancellor's authority to set up and enforce an administrative policy that provides released time for consultants. Deans and division chairs often call me with compelling arguments detailing why they need a particular faculty member to be both a consultant and a person who teaches a full load. Without the Chancellor's support and the administrative policy, I could not protect consultants from such excessive demands on their time.

Another example illustrating the need for administrative support or authority pertains to the issue of consultant autonomy. In our system, consultants have the authority to chose the colleagues with whom they will consult. Sometimes, when a dean or a division chair gives a poor performance appraisal to a faculty member, he or she will recommend the program to the faculty member as a way to improve his or her student ratings. The consultant, however, has the authority to decide whether or not to accept this faculty member as a client. The consultant can usually evaluate the faculty member's motivation to change more effectively than the performance evaluator can, and this motivation to change is a crucial variable in determining what this client will actually do when he or she participates in the program.

The third example illustrating the need for administrative support is authority concerns the confidentiality of data. In our system, participation in the peer consultation program is voluntary and the data collected in the peer consultant program are confidential. Data are reviewed by the consultant and the faculty member during the program; when the faculty member completes the program, data are either destroyed or given to the faculty member. In addition, consultants are excused from participating in performance review or tenure deliberations regarding faculty with whom they have consulted. In this way, data collected during the program are not used in making tenure, promotion, or retention decisions. Faculty who participate in the program do so without being threatened by evaluative use of data collected.

In addition to being able to establish administrative policies regarding the program, the implementer of the peer consultation program must be able to allocate funds or obtain services vital to program operation. Computer support is one example of a support service vital to the operation of many peer consultation programs. In most peer consultant programs, data about teaching behavior are gathered through multiple sources—interviews, observation, videotapes, and student feedback. Very often, stu-

dent feedback is gathered through the use of student questionnaires. In our program, the Teaching Analysis by Students (TABS) questionnaire is used. If student questionnaires like TABS are used, computer support is needed to summarize the data so that it can be interpreted. A faculty member using appropriate software could generate sophisticated summaries from hundreds of questionnaires; it is more likely, however, that the students will respond to the questions on scan sheets and these sheets will be scanned and summarized using programs in a computer service office. Having access to computer services, including assistance in writing and revising computer programs, is an element that one must consider before implementing a peer consultant program if student questionnaires are part of the program. Although student questionnaires are not a requirement, they provide data that are difficult to obtain through other means.

Likewise, if data are collected through videotaping, consultants must have access to videotaping equipment. Oftentimes, videotaping is done by an instructional services department, and funds must be available to provide for this service.

Faculty Participation

Faculty conduct peer consultant programs; without faculty participation, they will not exist. As I said earlier, one of the factors that caused me to want to expand the program was my belief that the program would sell itself to faculty. My belief has been amply confirmed. I have never heard any faculty member say that he or she disliked the concept or would not participate. What I do hear, however, is that the program is more oriented to junior faculty or that they are too busy to participate at this time. On the other hand, on every campus, faculty who learn about the program will volunteer to participate, and very often, these volunteers are senior faculty with reputations of being outstanding teachers and researchers. The key is getting information about the program to these people. One of the simplest and most effective strategies is to distribute a memorandum describing the program to all the faculty and asking for volunteers to attend a meeting to learn more. Susan Kah used this approach on the Medical Center Campus of Miami-Dade Community College; the faculty who attended became the nucleus of the consulting group. Another strategy, which was used by Bill Jones at Eastern Kentucky University, is to invite selected faculty who have been recognized as outstanding teachers to participate in the program at its outset. Although this may be a more Machiavellian approach, it does give immediate credibility to the program.

Coordination

Each of the preceding elements implies that program coordination is an important element in its implementation. Someone introduces the program to the faculty, establishes program policies, arranges for administrative support, and implements a pilot program. This may or may not be the program coordinator. The program coordinator maintains the program. Maintenance requires several considerations: preparing additional faculty to function as consultants, providing professional development opportunities to consultants, answering questions about the program, providing continued program support, and conducting program evaluations. In fact, program implementers should consider setting up an evaluation plan as a part of the implementation plan. Since this is a faculty-owned and operated program, the program coordinator may be a senior faculty member who knows how to order materials that consultants need or to answer questions that the administration may ask about the program. Possibly, a team project structure, like that described by Total Quality Management advocates, could be used to coordinate the program. In this case, consultants would meet as a team to solve group problems. At any rate, the manner in which the program will be coordinated is an important consideration in the implementation process.

Knowledge of Program Options

The goal of all peer consultant programs is to develop an organizational culture in which inquiry into one's teaching is a common and valued practice. Various paths lead towards this goal, and the program that works at one college or university may have different features than the one that works at another. Successful program implementation requires knowing the organizational culture and being able to adapt the program to that culture. If faculty who function as consultants cannot receive released time,

for example, in what ways can their work be recognized? Can student perceptions of teaching be obtained in ways other than using student questionnaires? Knowledge of program options, which can be gained from reading other chapters of this book, and the ability to determine which of these options best fits into the organizational culture are two important factors that facilitate setting up a peer consultant program.

Conclusion

Although I know of no recipe for guaranteeing the successful implementation of a peer consultant program, I have identified and described several key ingredients that one must consider in the implementation process. Administrative support, faculty participation, and coordination are crucial. Knowledge of program options and being able to determine which of these options best fits into the organizational culture is helpful. Having a plan for evaluation built into the implementation plan pays dividends. Most important, however, is the determination and persistence of one or more key figures to develop a richer environment for student learning.

References

Morrison, D. E. (1993, April). *Exploring the practice of instructional consultation through a topology of programs.* Paper presented at the annual meeting of the American Educational Research Association, Atlanta.

Rozeman, J. E., & Kerwin, M. A. (1991). Evaluating the effectiveness of a teaching consultation program on changing student ratings of teaching behaviors. *The Journal of Staff, Program, and Organization Development, 9,* 223-230.

Shea, M. A., Kelso, J., & Fitch, K. (1993, April). *You're boring us silly back here.* Paper presented at the annual meeting of the American Education Research Association, Atlanta.

Appendix

Setting Up A Peer Consultant Program

Summary of Considerations

Preliminary Considerations

- establishing administrative policies for released time, confidentiality of data, and consultant autonomy
- establishing administrative support for supplies, collecting and analyzing data, travel, computer resources, and consultant remuneration
- involving key faculty in program development
- establishing a procedure for identifying consultants
- identifying program options
- setting up an implementation schedule

Implementation Considerations

- providing mechanisms to recruit faculty as clients
- preparing faculty to be consultants
- providing for program coordination
- conducting the program on a pilot basis
- providing mechanism for consultant feedback and program evaluation

Maintenance Considerations

- recruiting faculty as clients
- providing for consultant development
- providing for program revision and refining
- preparing other faculty to be consultants

Part Three:

The Context of Instructional Consultation

*I*nstructional consultation does not occur in a vacuum. Part Three examines the milieu in which instructional consultation transpires and the variables that affect it—from the broad trends in higher education to the individual differences in faculty clients to the skill level and developmental stage of the consultant. This part should be of special interest to experienced consultants who have mastered the basic practice and protocols of consultation, and who have become aware of larger issues surrounding their consultation.

Chapters 19 through 23 examine factors external to the instructional consultant that may affect consultation. In Chapter 19, Claxton situates instructional consultation by providing a succinct history of higher education. He defines some of the major issues—accountability, funding, and curricular change—and some significant shifts in thinking—about how knowledge is constructed and about how scholarship is defined—that are influencing higher education today. In Chapter 20, Morrison identifies seven themes around local campus variables that can affect consultation. She posits that these themes must be discussed by groups when planning a new or expanding an existing instructional consultation service: identifying clients' needs, which are related to their career stages; selecting a consultation program appropriate for a specific campus; selecting specific consultation activities; selecting and training those who will serve as consultants; interfacing with summative evaluation efforts; providing support for the program; and communicating with the campus community. Shea, in Chapter 21, describes thirteen types of faculty and teaching assistants who seek instructional consultation: those who receive mediocre student ratings, those who face a retention, tenure, or promotion decision; those who are competent but wish professional affirmation; those who are in search of the formula for good teaching; those who wish an in-depth analysis of their teaching; and so forth. Shea cites ways

for consultants to work successfully with these different types, and notes the effect that their motives and their expectations exert upon the consultation process. In Chapter 22, Spann and McCrimmon outline major demographic shifts and how those shifts are reflected in the characteristics of modern college students—in race, ethnicity, age, and gender. Spann and McCrimmon suggest a shift in thinking for teachers, away from thinking of themselves as teachers of a discipline and toward thinking of themselves as developers of students. In Chapter 23, Bauer examines the physical and social aspects of four learning environments: large lecture classes, laboratory classes, activity classes, and tutorial classes. She then analyzes the major learning and teaching issues of each environment and offers implications of each for instructional consultation.

Chapters 24 through 26 focus on factors unique to an individual consultant that may affect consultation. In Chapter 24, Border posits a typology of four consultation styles—supporter, facilitator, collector, and evaluator—and invites readers to assess their own style. (The editors invite readers to compare these styles to the approaches described by Brinko in Chapter 1.) In Chapter 25, Tiberius, Tipping, and Smith adapt a theoretical model of development in expertise to instructional consultation. They describe each of the five stages of development—novice, advanced beginner, competent, proficient, expert—and discuss how the model helps instructional consultants understand the nature of their own expertise as well as how it informs the design of training programs. In Chapter 26, Way reflects upon his own experience as an instructional consultant, and how development in his personal life paralleled development in his professional life. He divides his own development into four stages—academic/empirical, experiential/exploratory, letting go/epistemological, and transcendental/integrative.

From reading these chapters, experienced consultants

will have acquired a deeper understanding of themselves and of the many external variables influencing the consultation process. It is our intention that this knowledge will lead them to reflect upon and more deeply analyze their consultation philosophy and practice.

19. *Higher Education in North America*

Charles Claxton

*F*rom the early years to today, U.S. higher education has experienced a steady evolution towards greater democratization and expanding access. Beginning with the establishment of Harvard College in 1636 in the Massachusetts Bay Colony, the colonial colleges served the sons of the wealthy, who received training in the law, theology, and medicine. Institutions provided for their students a classical curriculum consisting of logic, Greek, Hebrew, rhetoric, history, ethics politics, and divinity.

Early History

During the 18th and 19th centuries, institutions experienced increasing pressure to change. Because of its strictly classical curriculum and its elitist orientation with respect to admissions, higher education was to a large extent irrelevant to many citizens. The U.S. was a robust young nation whose emphasis was shifting rapidly from an agricultural economy to one based on industry. This change was spurred by advances in knowledge, particularly in technical areas such as engineering. The interests of students and their parents were around practical and commercial issues, reflecting changes in the society at large.

In 1833, Oberlin became the first college to admit women to a formerly all-male institution (Levine, 1978), and three years later, Wesleyan Female College was founded in Georgia. In 1849, Avery College for Blacks was established in Pennsylvania and in 1854 the American Missionary Society was created. By 1860, the society had begun six colleges for African-Americans.

The Land-Grant Act, passed by Congress in 1862, provided funds and land for institutions geared to the need for more practical skills and information. Further changes in the curriculum were spurred by the advent of the elective system, begun at Harvard in 1869.

Very substantial changes in student clientele came after the Second World War when congress passed the Selective Servicemen's Act commonly called the "GI Bill." Suddenly a surge of older persons enrolled, as veterans began matriculating in record numbers. Many institutions established evening courses to accommodate the veterans, and faculty often found themselves teaching students who were older than they were.

Further impetus for democratization came in 1948 when a commission established by President Truman argued that far more people could profit from higher education than were enrolling at the time. It recommended the establishment of two-year colleges as a national priority. The Truman Commission believed that these institutions should meet the educational needs of persons who lived in the immediate community. The Commission also suggested that the curriculum be broader in scope than simply a transfer track. These new "community colleges" should also offer "terminal," career oriented degree programs that would prepare persons for the local job market.

Early movement to racial integration of colleges and universities in the South occurred in the late 1940's and 1950's. In the 1960's the Civil Rights Movement had a profound effect on all of higher education as the nation sought to redress some of the problems caused by racial prejudice. The Johnson Administration's "War on Poverty" funneled money into programs to assist this effort. This national focus, coupled with the demographic wave of the baby boom youngsters born immediately after World War II, fueled a huge expansion of institutions.

Emphasis on access was made possible in the U.S. in part by its pluralistic tradition. Higher education is offered by both public and private institutions. About half the colleges and universities are private, and these account for about one-third of the enrollment. In contrast, this blend of public and private institutions is not present in Canada, where almost all are public. There are systems of two-year colleges in the provinces, and access to universities is controlled by uniform admissions' policies.

Recent Developments in the United States and Canada

More recent pressures reflect the continuing struggle by colleges and universities to meet the demands placed on them. By the end of the 1970's the demographic wave of the baby-boom generation had passed. There was substantial concern because institutions had over built despite projected enrollment declines. As a result, many institutions placed a strong emphasis on recruitment of non-traditional students, particularly adults. Some colleges and universities set up programs specifically designed for adult students. These often took the form of weekend programs, classes in the evening, or special programs for these older students. There was a great deal of interest in assessment of prior learning through the use of portfolios so that adults could receive academic credit for college level learning which they had acquired through work and life experience.

This emphasis on "non-traditional education" has not been embraced by most Canadian institutions. In the opinion of Michael Skolnik, professor of higher education at the Ontario Institute for Studies in Education, Canadian universities look with "shock, skepticism, and frequently scorn" on such developments as credit for prior learning, non-resident graduate programs, and universities without walls (Skolnik, 1990, p. 90).

In the U.S., substantial attention has been given to the recruitment of poorly prepared students, so much so that an increasing percentage of institutions in the country adopted either open—or near open—admissions policies. Community colleges were key players in this process. At the same time, many other institutions, including urban public universities and small private colleges, aggressively looked for ways to maintain their enrollment base.

One result was the increasing presence of developmental or remedial education programs, as institutions created programs specifically designed to help poorly prepared students succeed in college. Today more than 90 percent of colleges and universities provide either developmental courses or developmental programs.

The trend to enrolling poorly prepared students remains a controversial issue in the U.S., and in Canada many argue vigorously against such practices. Some Canadian observers believe that the U.S. "emphasizes equality of opportunity while Canada (with its more restrictive admissions policies and a curriculum that is more standard throughout the provinces) emphasizes equality of results" (Skolnik, 1990, p. 86).

Another force having substantial impact on higher education in the U.S. during the 1980's was increasing concern about the quality of elementary and secondary schools. Reports by major commissions were extremely critical of the public schools. In the late part of that decade and into the 1990's, major political figures, including state governors, pressed for substantial changes. Unlike the situation in previous eras, education became a central feature in the national political dialogue.

In time a number of important studies detailing the shortcomings of higher education were also published. The emerging reform movement in higher education attempts to address the following criticisms: (a) absence of integrated learning experiences for students, (b) lack of clarity about just what a college degree stood for, (c) teaching practices which encouraged passivity on the part of students, (d) a reward system for faculty which ensured that in many institutions teaching remained a stepchild, and (e) lack of articulation between high school and college.

Substantial attention was given to these reports in the professional literature. Further, many professional associations, including the American Association for Higher Education, have made these criticisms and what to do about them central themes of their national conferences and their publications.

Current Focus: Basic Skills and Accountability

Criticisms of public schools have centered on two areas: the inadequate job done by teacher preparation programs and the increasing realization that a high school diploma was not necessarily an indication that students possessed the basic skills needed in the work place or in college. Assessment of students as they entered college confirmed their poor preparation for higher education.

Concern about basic skills and accountability has been emphasized in higher education as well as in public schools. One important response is the call by regional accrediting associations for institutions to demonstrate not simply the resources they have (for example, the number of faculty with doctoral degrees, the extent of library holdings, and so on) but also the impact these resources have on students. How are students changed by attending college? At graduation, do they possess the skills and abilities needed for effective functioning in today's society?

Canada does not have institutional accreditation but there is increasing concern about accountability. In 1992, the Association of Universities and Colleges of Canada conducted a study of higher education and said universities should develop "performance measures clearly understood by the public or risk having government or others establish criteria for judging the performance of universities" (Lewington, 1992, p. A 33).

The need for stronger teacher preparation programs in U.S. colleges of education continues to be a problem in the opinion of many observers. One result of this concern has been the establishment of alliances between high schools and colleges. Two purposes are thereby served: (a) students can experience a smoother transition between the two institutions, and (b) teacher preparation can be improved through the joint efforts of professors of education and practicing teachers in the schools.

There is also increasing recognition that much of the teaching that goes on in higher education is done poorly. This is often true even in institutions that pride themselves on being teaching centered, for example, community colleges and some private residential institutions. Teaching typically has a low status as compared with research, particularly where institutions, in response to declining resources from traditional sources, increasingly turn to grant writing in the hopes of acquiring external funding.

Similar concerns have been voiced in Canada. The Association of Universities and Colleges of Canada has recommended that universities change faculty personnel policies to reward good teaching, require professors who are poor teachers to take remedial courses to improve their skills, and ensure that new faculty members receive training in teaching methods (Lewington, 1992, p. A 33).

An important force for improved teaching, one which also links to the emphasis on outcomes assessment, is classroom research (see Angelo & Cross, 1993). Here college faculty are encouraged to gather data on their students and their experience in the course. The strength of this formative approach to evaluation, often done in ways that are not bound by the conventional and strict demands of social science research, is its particularity. Data are gathered about specific students in a specific course, so that a faculty member can make changes in the design of the course in order to help students learn more effectively.

The "excellence movement" in American industry, spurred by business leaders' concern about global competition, is impacting the way administrators in higher education think about how their institutions go about their work. Thus there is at least a "mini-movement" underway that appears under the rubric of "total quality management" (TQM). Administrators and faculty are working together in many institutions to develop systematic processes that focus on student outcomes, financial effectiveness, and collaborative decision making.

Curricular Responses

Institutions in the U. S. have adopted several major curricular changes in recent years. They include the following:

- **Courses providing integrative learning experiences**. Often this has taken the form of capstone or senior seminars, in which students are asked to look back on what they have learned in their various courses and try to find patterns and connections.

- **Responses to demographic shifts in the population**. Multiculturalism has become, finally, a major issue in higher education as colleges seek to respond to the diversity of students in their institutions. Similarly, more and more institutions are establishing women's studies programs.

- **Serving technical as well as baccalaureate students**. Many "tech-prep" programs are being established as high schools and local two-year colleges collaborate on curriculum programs that provide an educational experience in the high school and the college that culminate in students being prepared to enter well paying jobs.

- **Freshman orientation courses**. Typically these are credit bearing courses which help students make the transition between high school and college. Attention is given to helping students become aware of the many services of the institution, orienting them to the expectations of college, working with them on study skills, and assisting them with career and academic planning.

Canadian institutions have developed many of these same curricular responses. One particular approach that is expanding rapidly is cooperative education programs in which students have alternating classroom and work terms. About 10 percent of the total undergraduate population (some 50,000 students) at about 85 universities and two year colleges now participate in such programs (McMurdy, 1991).

Knowing About Knowing

While issues of accountability, funding, and curricular change are central to the academic enterprise, an even deeper level of discourse gained prominence in the late 1980s and early 1990's. It is concerned with the evolving views of **scholarship** and **knowledge**.

An expanded version of scholarship has been proposed by Boyer (1990) and Rice (1991). In an attempt to move beyond the limiting debate of teaching versus research with which many institutions struggle, these authors have suggested that the definition of scholarship be expanded to include four different emphases: (a) the **production** of knowledge, where faculty collect empirical data and thereby generate new knowledge; (b) the **integration** of knowledge, where they integrate different strands of information and weave them into a meaningful whole; (c) the **application** of knowledge, where they assist practitioners in the field in actually using research; and (d) the **representation** of knowledge, or teaching, where faculty translate knowledge from the field into ways and forms that are accessible to students in the classroom.

Beyond this new paradigm of scholarship, the work of several other writers, particularly Parker Palmer (1987), have added significantly to higher education's understanding of knowledge. In commenting on the absence of community in the culture at large and in higher education, he argues that progress in dealing with this issue will come only when we move to the level of **epistemology**: How do we know what we know?

He believes that one's epistemology, that is, the avenue one takes to arrive at truth, is not something with unimportant consequences (Palmer, 1987). Rather, **a way of knowing** becomes **a way of being**. It fosters particular capacities of the self while leaving other important ones ignored or at least underdeveloped.

In his view, the dominant epistemology in higher education is "objectivism," a way of knowing that insists on holding the object of study at arm's length. As a result, students develop the capacities for detachment, skepticism and abstraction but do so at the expense of other vital capacities essential to a satisfying personal and professional life: connection, relationship, and community.

Palmer (1987) says there are other epistemologies that are more relational in nature, and they tend to be located around the edges of higher education. They exist primarily in women's studies, Native-American studies, and African-American studies.

He does not advocate that objectivist epistemology be set aside and replaced by relational knowing. Rather, he suggests that both need to be honored in higher education, as do Belenky, Clinchy, Goldberger, and Tarule (1986) in their discussion of separate and connected knowing. He believes that deliberate engagement of students in the tension between these two polar ways of knowing is required if true learning and development are to occur.

Palmer (1987) also attacks as myth the belief that the individual is the primary agent of knowing. Genuine learning is a communal process, as learners share with each other their individual perceptions and ideas on an issue. Each person adds to the insights of others, as the group itself engages in a corporate search for understanding.

Such a view flies in the face of many teaching-learning practices in higher education today, from the arrangement of chairs in a classroom to the dominance of lecture as the primary teaching technique.

Towards a Vision for the Future

The reconceptualization of knowledge sketched in this chapter resonates with the findings of many developmental theorists (see Belenky et al., 1986, Fowler, 1988, Kegan, 1982, and Perry, 1970). In their view, persons at earlier stages of cognitive development view knowledge as an entity—something that learners "get" from all-knowing teachers. In the higher stages, knowledge is not so much something that only outside authorities have but which they themselves are involved in creating.

Erik Erikson (see Bok, 1989, pp. 153-156) believes there is an analog between stages of development of individuals and the stages of the culture at large. As more persons move to higher levels of thinking in their individual lives, the culture itself undergoes a shift in consciousness. Fowler (1988) believes we are now moving beyond what Belenky et al. (1986) have called "procedural knowing," where the emphasis is on a hypothetico-deductive approach to understanding, with its orientation to rationality and linear thinking.

We are entering, he says, the stage of "constructivist knowing," where it is understood that all knowledge is provisional, that what we accept as truth today can (and will) be replaced as new data and understanding emerge. In this view, each of us is aware that we create knowledge and that the knower is part of the known: What we see is powerfully influenced by what we as knowers bring to the issue at hand. Truth is found through the integration of detached, objectivist knowing and more subjective, intuitive knowing. Fowler's (1988) predictions about a cultural shift in consciousness is thus consistent with the call by Palmer and Belenky et al. to honor the polar opposites of objectivist and relational knowing.

At the institutional level, this speculation may mean that our way of thinking can move beyond conventional logic. What would replace it are ways of thinking that embrace not only knowing through detachment and skepticism but also knowing through connection and intuition. Thus higher education may increasingly be able to move beyond "either-or" thinking (teaching *versus* research, faculty *versus* administration, quality *versus* access) to systems of thought characterized by "both-and."

There are at least some indications that this shift in thinking is already underway. For example, the Boyer and Rice expanded views of scholarship can help academicians break free of the teaching/research dichotomy and create a sound rationale for faculty in all areas of their work. Such a view honors a much greater range of talent than was previously the case. Total Quality Management may be a vehicle that helps college personnel move beyond the faculty/administration split and foster more collaborative work in achieving the mission of the institution.

These new ways of thinking could also lead to new metaphors and images that can guide the work of higher education. In the 21st century, our metaphors may be influenced less by linear thinking, hierarchical organizational, and production. Replacing them would be images drawn from such areas as biology and the environment.

For example, Fowler (1987) suggests that the central task of an administrative leader is to create an "ecology of giftedness," a work setting where the varied talents of all persons in the institution—students, faculty, staff, and so on—have the opportunity to grow. In contexts such as these, colleges and universities can increasingly move towards their true mission: helping students think at the level of complexity required for fruitful lives, celebrating excellence in teaching and in the creation of knowledge, and creating curricular programs worthy of the diversity of the student body and the culture at large.

References

Angelo, T. A., & Cross, K. P. (1993). *Classroom assessment techniques: A handbook for college teachers*. San Francisco: Jossey-Bass.

Belenky, M., Clinchy, B. M., Goldberger, N. B., & Tarule, J. M. (1986). *Women's ways of knowing: The development of self, voice, and mind*. New York: Basic Books.

Bok, S. (1989). *A strategy for peace: Human values and the threat of war*. New York: Pantheon Books.

Boyer, E. L. (1990). *Scholarship reconsidered*. Princeton, NJ: Carnegie Foundation for the Advancement of Teaching.

Fowler, J. W. (1987). *The role of the dean and the issue of vocation*. Keynote speech, Deans' Institute, Council of Independent Colleges, Hilton Head, SC.

Fowler, J. W. (1988). *Weaving the new creation*. San Francisco: Harper & Row, Publishers.

Kegan, R. (1982). *The evolving self: Problem and process in human development*. Cambridge: Harvard University Press.

Levine, A. L. (1978). *Handbook on the undergraduate curriculum*. San Francisco: Jossey-Bass.

Lewington, J. (1992, August 8). Canadian universities put new importance on efforts to improve teaching. *The Chronicle of Higher Education*, pp. A 34-A 35.

McMurdy, D. (1991, October 21). Classroom meets the boardroom. *Maclean's*, pp. 42-43.

Palmer, P. J. (1987). Community, conflict, and ways of knowing: Ways to deepen our educational agenda. *Change, 19*(5), 20-25.

Perry, W. G., Jr. (1970). *Forms of intellectual and ethical development in the college years: A scheme*. New York: Holt, Rinehart, and Winston.

Rice, R. E. (1991, Spring). The new American scholar: Scholarship and the purposes of the university. *Metropolitan Universities*, 7-18.

Skolnik, M. L. (1990). Lipset's *Continental Divide* and the ideological basis for differences in higher education between Canada and United States. *The Canadian Journal of Higher Education, 22*, 81-93.

20. *Local Variables that Affect Consultation*

Diane E. Morrison

My earlier chapter in this book (Chapter 12) identifies and describes six types of instructional consultation programs. The typology is based on a review of research on instructional consultation, a close reading of published program descriptions, and my own experience in faculty development since the late 1970s. I have recently completed a comparative study (Morrison, 1995) of eight instructional consultation programs that reflect a range of program types. Site visits were made to seventeen institutions in both Canada and the United States. These institutions represent a range of characteristics and include two and four-year colleges and universities. The discussion presented in this chapter is based on my analysis of one hundred and fifty-five interviews with faculty members, teaching assistants, and administrators at these institutions.

Many institutions that offer instructional consultation provide what I have identified as the *traditional* type of service offered to individuals by full or part-time faculty developers. There are also a number of peer-based models offered in colleges and universities across North America. These differ from the traditional approach in at least one of three ways: 1) faculty members or teaching assistants are provided with training to offer *peer consultant* services for their colleagues on a one to one basis; 2) two participants work together as *peer partners* within a structured program; or 3) faculty members or teaching assistants provide assistance to each other as participants within a *group-based* setting facilitated by a developer or by another faculty member or teaching assistant. Group-based workshops often include a micro-teaching component, with each person teaching one or more short lessons, and receiving verbal and/or written feedback from the other participants.

This chapter identifies seven themes that can serve as agenda items for planning group discussions about a new or expanded instructional consultation service. The planning group may be working at a campus level or on an inter-institutional basis. The seven themes are:

- identifying needs of prospective participants,
- selecting the types of programs,
- selecting instructional consultation activities,
- selecting and training individuals for consultative roles,
- interfacing with evaluation and other developmental activities,
- providing program support, and
- communicating with the campus community.

Identifying Needs of Prospective Participants

Review Demographic Information

Program planners should review readily available demographic information. Many institutions offer their instructional consultation services to any interested faculty member whether full-time or part-time, tenure track or contract position. A review of demographic information for all groups can be valuable, and can include such factors as age, length of service, and gender, with variations across departments noted. If you are planning to offer services to teaching assistants, a similar review can be made for them. Pay particular attention to any recent or anticipated *changes* in the profile of faculty members, teaching assistants, and students at your institution.

Discuss Needs Related to Academic Career Stages

The planning committee should discuss why people in different career stages may choose to participate in instructional consultation at their institution. Prospective participants face multiple roles, with teaching being only one part of the academic's professional identity and responsibilities. Institutional and departmental contexts differ in their emphasis on teaching, research, and service roles, and these role expectations often shift over the career span. The following questions may help focus your discussions about the needs and interests of prospective participants who are at different career stages.

How many new faculty members are at your institution? Are these individuals also new to teaching, or are they experienced teachers new only to teaching at your institution? Are they moving from a part-time or temporary contract to a full-time academic position? Will new faculty perceive instructional consultation as a way to help them become knowledgeable about the teaching/learning environment at the institution? Will they perceive the service as a source of assistance with tenure and promotion processes? Will they be interested in including the results in a teaching dossier or portfolio?

The reasons that experienced faculty members participate will likely differ somewhat from those of new faculty. There may also be greater variation in the reasons of experienced faculty. The following questions may help guide your discussions about how to best serve experienced faculty members. Are a number of experienced faculty members currently working on curricular and/or instructional changes such as the introduction of new general education requirements, an emphasis on collaborative learning strategies, or the testing of new approaches to address the learning needs of diverse student populations? Are there internal or external grants for curriculum development that might prompt participation by experienced faculty in a program that can provide feedback on curricular experiments? Has interest recently been expressed in the use of classroom assessment techniques? Are experienced faculty engaged in conversations about finding ways to revitalize teaching on the campus?

Think about Participants' Needs Not Just Their Stated Preferences

Think about what participants' actual needs may be; don't rely on their stated preferences for activities. Some faculty members or teaching assistants may not indicate that they are personally concerned about student evaluations of their teaching; yet this may be a real need that draws people to a program that includes analysis of feedback from students and colleagues.

You may decide to explore campus interest in instructional consultation activities. However, don't rely only on written surveys. Use additional inquiry approaches, such as interviews with faculty members, teaching assistants, department heads, and senior administrators. Ask about the difficulties that teaching personnel face at your insti-

tution. Review any readily available sources such as cross-campus summaries of student rating responses and self-study or accreditation reports. Also, remember that needs assessment of prospective participants should occur on a continuing basis.

Selecting the Types of Programs

Discuss Program and Institutional Types

As a planning group, you should discuss whether you want to offer a traditional program, a peer consultant program, a peer partner program, a group-based program, or some combination. One way to think about what program type to offer is to examine the kinds of services offered at colleges and universities similar to your own. Some current patterns are described below.

- *Traditional instructional consultation services* for faculty depend on the availability of one or more full or part-time faculty developers. Services offered by full-time faculty developers tend to be found at large institutions, primarily universities and two-year institutions in both Canada and the U.S. Some community colleges, liberal arts colleges, and universities have part-time faculty developers working either in a continuing or rotational position. However, not all faculty developers provide instructional consultation services.

- *Peer consultant programs* are in place for faculty at Canadian universities; however, there are relatively few such programs at universities in the United States. Peer consultant programs for faculty are also found at some two year institutions in both the United States and Canada. Little information was found on peer consultant programs at four-year colleges.

- *Student observer programs* appear to be offered at only a few institutions in the U.S., including liberal arts colleges and universities.

- *Peer partner programs* for faculty are relatively new, with only a few models in place. Those that are currently offered are found at some community colleges, liberal arts colleges, and universities in both the U.S. and Canada.

- *Group-based programs* for faculty are offered in both countries. However, examples are more prevalent at community colleges, liberal arts institutions, and comprehensive universities than at research universities.

- *Teaching assistant programs* exist in both countries, including traditional, peer consultant programs, and peer-led workshops. Peer partner programs are not likely to be offered for teaching assistants.

Considerable caution is needed in interpreting the association of institutional characteristics and program type. Although these patterns are descriptive of the current situation in the field, they are certainly not normative.

Discuss Responses of Participants at Different Career Stages

Institutional commitment to teaching and teaching improvement can affect whether instructional consultation is perceived as a worthwhile activity by faculty members and teaching assistants. My interviews suggest that academic career themes are also important factors to consider in planning for new or expanded instructional consultation services. Academics appear to be motivated to participate in intensive teaching improvement activities to address different issues. Teaching assistants say they value the opportunity to develop "survival" teaching skills and to better prepare themselves for entry into a faculty position upon graduation. Individuals in the early stages of their careers or new to an institution often say that the opportunity to participate in instructional consultation activities has helped them to become established as faculty members in their new institutional environment. They also report that these programs help prepare them for tenure review processes. These faculty members often appreciate working with someone in another discipline as it allows them to examine their teaching strengths and weaknesses outside of departmental evaluation processes.

Experienced faculty members participate in instructional consultation for a wide variety of reasons. Some are searching for new ideas to enrich, expand, and enliven their teaching; others have one or more specific concerns about their teaching that they hope to address through feedback from students and colleagues. Experienced faculty members report that they value the opportunity to be engaged in joint inquiry about teaching and learning with students and colleagues. Experienced faculty members who participate in group-based activities often comment on the value of rich conversations about teaching that they have with colleagues, not only from their own disciplines, but from other ones as well. They also appreciate the sense of being part of a larger collegial community through active learning experiences shared with other participants.

Discuss Participation Patterns for Different Career Situations

Regardless of institutional type, a planning group should discuss whether they are trying to serve the needs of particular groups (for example, teaching assistants, those new to teaching or to the institution, mid-career, and

senior faculty), or whether they want a program design that will appeal to and meet the needs of various groups of participants.

Some junior, mid-career, and senior faculty members choose to participate in any of the six program types depending on what program is available on a local basis. However, there appear to be patterns of participation in different program types related to the individual's academic career situation. These patterns seem to generally hold across different types of institutions.

Many teaching assistants in research universities and junior or new faculty members in a variety of institutional types are open to participating in traditional and peer consultant programs when these programs are offered. Although experienced faculty do engage in traditional and peer consultant models at a number of institutions, they seem less likely to participate in these models than faculty members who are new to teaching, or new to an institution. However, many experienced faculty members seem to be attracted to peer partner and group-based program models. Although junior faculty members who participate in peer partner programs are also enthusiastic about their experiences, some institutions target peer partner programs for experienced rather than for new faculty members.

Individuals across the career spectrum participate in group-based programs. However, some group programs are specifically designed for individuals at a particular career stage, such as training programs for teaching assistants and orientation programs for new faculty. Outside of these specialized cases, group activities work well for faculty members with a range of experience levels, especially when groups represent a variety of disciplines.

Programs for individuals are offered as locally based activities as they include feedback from students and observation of teaching in one's own class. However, group-based programs, including inter-institutional ones, are sometimes offered in a residential setting. Both new and experienced faculty members report a range of benefits from participation in these intensive, residential teaching enhancement programs. In-depth collegial conversations about learning, teaching, and one's own strengths and weaknesses as a teacher are often generated within these residential and inter-institutional environments.

Research and practice has shown that it is harder to design professional development programs that appeal to experienced faculty than it is to provide programs of interest and value for new faculty. Peer partner activities and group-based workshops appear to be two types of instructional consultation that are attractive and beneficial for many experienced faculty members. However, these two programs types are currently most commonly offered at teaching-oriented institutions; therefore, it is not clear whether experienced faculty members at research universities will participate in either peer partner or group-based activities if they are offered for them.

Baldwin's (1979) interview-based study with 106 male faculty members in several liberal arts colleges found that junior faculty sought assistance with their teaching. In contrast, senior faculty addressed their professional development needs in a more autonomous, independent fashion. My research with both men and women faculty suggests that women participate in instructional consultation, and particularly in peer-based programs, in greater proportion to their institutional representation. It is not clear whether these gender participation patterns are also related to such factors as career themes, age cohort, institutional type, and discipline.

Selecting Instructional Consultation Activities

Discuss Specific Information-Gathering Activities

Although the planning group may suggest guidelines for programs offered for individuals, final decisions about the exact nature and focus of the approaches used should rest with the participant and the person serving in the consultative role. It is recommended that information be gathered from both the students and the consultant or peer partner. Student information can be collected through rating instruments, open-ended survey questions, or interviews. The consultant or peer partner should observe the class on one or more occasion and also offer to videotape at least one class session.

In many group-based approaches, participants provide feedback for each other from the perspective of their experiences as learners in microteaching sessions. The feedback is usually provided in both written and verbal formats, with videotaping used to supplement the feedback process. Other workshop designs may include the interpretation of feedback collected from students or a review of video-tape excerpts from one's own course setting.

Discuss Program Comprehensiveness and Flexibility

Programs within each type can vary considerably in terms of comprehensiveness and flexibility. Programs for individuals that are more comprehensive are ones that include multiple sources of information, multiple data collection points, support during a skill enhancement phase following initial feedback, and commitment for an extended period of time, such as the duration of a course. Comprehensive programs for individuals are more likely to be found at teaching-oriented institutions than at research universities.

Flexibility in programs offered for individuals refers to the extent to which participants and consultants are able to modify the program structure, the program activities, and the nature and focus of the feedback sessions. In programs with high flexibility, the individual and the consultant have considerable latitude in deciding how the process will be adapted to meet the needs of the participant and also the context of the course selected for study. With traditional services offered by faculty developers for individuals, the consultative activities are often planned on a case-by-case basis. Traditional services tend to have high program flexibility and to vary considerably in terms of comprehensiveness. In contrast, peer consultant and peer partner programs for individuals tend to have moderate levels of flexibility as they often provide a fairly consistent set of activities for all participants. However, the way in which the activities are carried out will vary across participants. Also, the extent to which a program is comprehensive will depend on local design decisions.

Similar to the programs for individuals, group-based programs can range considerably in level of comprehensiveness. The workshop design may be high in terms of comprehensiveness, for example, a one week workshop with three microteaching occasions for each participant. Group-based programs may also be much less comprehensive; in some shorter models, each participant teaches and receives feedback on only one lesson. Group-based programs tend to have moderate levels of flexibility, with the basic workshop design offered for different groups. However, there is often considerable flexibility in the nature and focus of the microteaching sessions.

Selecting and Training Individuals for Consultative Roles

Design the Selection Process

The planning group should discuss the process for selecting people to serve in consultative roles, recognizing that the criteria used will vary considerably depending on the type of program offered.

With the traditional program type, it may be a case of

modifying or expanding the responsibilities of the person who is already serving as a faculty developer. In some cases, a faculty developer position may be created with instructional consultation as a central responsibility. Student observers are usually selected by a program coordinator, often on the basis of recommendations of individual faculty members. The program coordinator also proposes matches between students and faculty participants.

In peer partner programs, the participants often select their own partners; however, the program coordinator also proposes matches between people. Peer consultants and facilitators of peer-led workshops usually take on the consultative role either as an additional assignment or through release from other responsibilities. If a program includes release time or overload payment, the selection process may need to occur within existing administrative and personnel processes. Often the selection process is the responsibility of a committee or a program coordinator. For established programs, recruitment and selection decisions often rest primarily with current team members.

The planning group should discuss criteria for selecting peer consultants and facilitators. The criteria should be broad-based and inclusive, rather than restrictive. Many people successfully serve as peer consultants and facilitators within existing programs. These people come from a wide range of backgrounds, and they draw on a variety of strengths to carry out the consultative work. What is probably most important is that the individuals selected have credibility with their colleagues, are committed to their own development as teachers, and are comfortable with the personal nature of working with colleagues to improve teaching practice.

When expanding the initial team of peer consultants or facilitators, whether on a campus or inter-institutional basis, it is valuable to have a variety of teaching and consultative styles represented in the group. One approach is to strive for diversity of perspectives across the team. As with the patterns of participation in consultation activities, my initial findings suggest that women are interested in serving in these consultative roles in a greater proportion to their numbers in the academy than are men. It is not yet clear if these patterns are also related to career themes, age cohort, institutional type, or discipline. Whether the program is offered on a campus or inter-institutional basis, the selection criteria and process should be chosen to match the particular type of program selected and should be one that is perceived to fit the local situation.

Plan Training Activities

Individuals in faculty development positions often develop their instructional consultation skills through in-

dependent study, attendance at conference sessions, discussion with colleagues at other institutions, and by gathering feedback during and after their work with participants. However, peer consultants, facilitators, and some coordinators of peer partner programs are provided with structured training and developmental opportunities on a local or inter-institutional basis. Many peer consultants and facilitators expand their knowledge of teaching, learning, and consulting through individual study initiatives. They report that these professional development activities help them in their own teaching as well as in their consulting work with colleagues.

Student observers participate in training activities and also draw on their experiences as learners in a variety of contexts within the institution. Participants in peer partner programs generally do not have training in instructional consultation; however, they attend orientation sessions for the particular program offered at their institution. Peer partner coordinators may have specific training, or they may develop their skills through individual study.

It is not feasible in this chapter to discuss specific training and development activities. However, the peer consultant and peer-led workshop programs appear to have been a testing ground for training and development activities. Institutions interested in initiating new or expanded peer-based models can draw on the experiences of existing programs including several described elsewhere in this book.

Discuss Prescriptive and Collaborative Consultative Styles

Instructional consultation services involve the participant working with at least one other person who is in a consultative role. However, there are variations in the nature of the consultative relationship that can emerge between a participant and a consultant, between peer partners, and among participants and facilitators in group-based programs. As in other teaching and learning situations, consultants and facilitators have different philosophies about ways to be helpful and they have different consultative styles. Participants also differ in their expectations, goals, and learning styles. The consultative relationship will vary according to these particular preferences and styles.

In the traditional approach and in some peer consultant programs, particularly when services are offered for new teachers, the person in the consultative role may expect and/or be expected to provide expert or prescriptive advice about teaching. The person in the consultative role in peer partner programs and in some peer consultant programs may expect and/or be expected to engage in a mutual inquiry process with the participant and the students. Some programs may caution new facilitators or consultants not to provide very much specific "advice" about what the participant should do in the classroom. Rather, their role is often a collaborative one, helping the participant generate his or her own alternative teaching strategies for experimentation.

In group programs, the facilitator is in a group leadership role, helping all individuals participate fully in the process. The participants and the facilitators provide feedback on each teaching event, but from the perspective of learners in the lesson, not as experts in teaching and learning. Facilitators strive to ensure a balance of challenge and support while assisting participants develop their understanding of teaching and learning through collaborative inquiry.

Interfacing with Evaluation and Other Developmental Activities

Review Institutional Evaluation Processes

Instructional consultation services are part of a larger range of activities provided on a campus to enhance teaching and learning. The larger context includes the formal evaluation processes along with the campus climate concerning these evaluation procedures. It is generally recommended that instructional consultation services be voluntary; however, some institutions expect new faculty members or teaching assistants to participate in orientation programs that include microteaching activities. Instructional consultation is viewed as a confidential resource for faculty members or teaching assistants; it should not be used for contract renewal, promotion, or tenure decisions.

There are a number of questions, however, that the planning group should discuss concerning the specific interface of instructional consultation and evaluation. Although these two activities should be clearly separated at the institutional level, they are not as easily separated in the minds of the participants. For some faculty members or teaching assistants, formal evaluation processes may prompt participation in instructional consultation. Individuals may not be satisfied with their student evaluations, or may feel uncomfortable about some aspect of their teaching. Department heads sometimes encourage faculty members or teaching assistants to participate in a program; however, most consultants will not work with someone unless that person contacts them directly requesting their assistance.

Some consultants write a summary report that the participant can decide to use for personnel purposes. However, not all consultants will provide a written report as some wish to keep their work completely separate from evaluation. In some programs, the consultants or facilitators have developed a policy statement that they will provide a report for a participant, but they will not become involved with discussions related to personnel decisions.

It is also possible that effort directed towards one kind of activity can serve the other. For example, an individual may want to add his or her own questions to student rating forms used for personnel purposes. Institutions that encourage the use of teaching portfolios for promotion and tenure purposes should also support their use for the planning of developmental proposals.

Link to Other Professional Development Activities

The planning group should also discuss the appropriate interface between instructional consultation and other professional development activities. In some of the more comprehensive programs, the process includes a skill enhancement phase after an initial information gathering phase. However, there should also be ways for participants to expand their teaching repertoire after the consultation program is completed.

A review of issues surfaced by a number of participants may suggest themes for additional professional development activities. For example, at some institutions, participants have expressed interest in learning more about particular teaching approaches such as leading discussion groups and designing collaborative or active learning strategies. Campus wide activities can be initiated in response to these kinds of expressed interests. Participation in instructional consultation may also be linked with internal or external grants for curricular or instructional development projects or with the development of sabbatical leave proposals. Although the specific nature of the link between instructional consultation and other professional development activities will vary across institutions, continual attention should focus on ways to build bridges.

Providing Program Support

Determine Implementation Schedule

Instructional consultation programs usually serve only a small number of participants at any one time; therefore, an institution needs only a few interested people to begin a pilot project. External support to initiate a new service may involve assistance during a planning phase along with training for consultants and/or facilitators. Although not everyone agrees with an incremental approach to program implementation, sometimes institutional support becomes available only as a program establishes a successful track record. Regardless of the schedule set for program implementation, careful thought should be given to the question of how resources will be provided as the program expands.

Identify Program Support Needed Over Time

There are several areas that require attention for successful program implementation. One is the provision of institutional rewards for peer consultants, facilitators, program coordinators, or student observers. Institutions provide rewards in different ways such as release from other service responsibilities, payment for overload assignments, or provision of additional developmental opportunities. The more comprehensive programs for individuals may require course release, particularly at institutions where the consultants have high teaching loads. Institutions offering student observer programs usually pay the students through a work-study program. Personal statements recognizing the value of the work of the individuals in consultative roles is also important — from department heads and senior administrators as well as from colleagues.

Opportunities for initial training, formative evaluation, and ongoing development is extremely important. Orientation activities for program participants can also contribute to program success. Additional professional development opportunities should be available for participants wanting to enhance their skills as a result of participation in the process. This may be provided within the consultative process depending on the comprehensiveness of the program. In some cases, time release for participants to work on their teaching skills is also important. For example, some institutions provide lighter loads for new faculty members.

Administrative assistance is needed to provide: program advertising; coordination of matches between participants and consultants, or between peer partners; on-going communication support; secretarial assistance; and, of course, refreshments for group meetings! Computer assistance for tabulating student rating surveys, technical support for videotaping, and a budget for supplies and the acquisition of reference materials are also important.

Several programs in both Canada and the United States are offered on an inter-institutional basis, thereby providing a range of benefits for participating institutions. Activities can be sponsored on a consortia or network basis, enhancing the exchange of ideas for teaching improvement across institutions as well as allowing for sharing of project expenses. Inter-institutional groups plan training, development, and evaluative activities and provide support for those in consultative roles, particularly in peer-based programs.

Communicating with the Campus Community

Develop a Plan for Communicating with Potential Participants

Provide information about your program to members of the campus community on a regular basis, using a variety of approaches. Look for existing channels of communication that have been effective in disseminating other information on your campus. Be prepared to discuss the program at departmental and campus-wide meetings rather than relying solely on print communication. You can also describe the program in such group settings as new faculty orientation sessions and brown-bag lunch seminars.

Although you need to help different sectors of the campus community be aware of the existence of the program, do not "oversell" the program, especially at the beginning. You only need a few interested people to get started in this kind of professional development activity. Allow enough time to establish the program on a solid foundation, rather than expanding the program too rapidly. Many campuses report that their program has grown through "word of mouth," with those having a positive experience recommending the program to others.

Develop a Plan for Communicating with Administrators

Provide regular information about the instructional consultation services to mid-level and senior administrators, and to trustees if appropriate. Assist campus leaders to understand the nature of the intensive instructional consultation services being offered. Highlight that the program is not only focused on immediate skill enhancement; it also helps participants identify areas for ongoing development after initial participation is completed. Point out that the program can be of benefit for faculty and teaching assistants who are addressing various career themes as the program is designed to serve individual needs and interests. Ask administrators for their cooperation to ensure that the program is perceived as serving all faculty and is not seen as a remedial program.

At some institutions, and particularly at research universities, ongoing effort may be needed to help establish a culture that values teaching. Within any institution, it may also be necessary to help foster an organizational culture that values and rewards members of the institutional community who are engaged in *continuing* improvement of their teaching.

In Conclusion

This chapter provides an overview of seven themes that should be discussed by any group involved in planning a new or expanded instructional consultation service. My companion piece in this book, describing six types of instructional consultation programs, can serve as another resource for your discussions.

In conclusion, I want to highlight several points for the successful implementation of a new or modified instructional consultation program. Focus early on the possible needs and interests of participants you want to attract. Pay particular attention to academic career themes. Are you primarily interested in serving new faculty, faculty new to your institution, experienced faculty, teaching assistants, or some combination of these groups? Remember, not all new faculty are at the same stage in their professional careers, and that career paths often vary for men and women.

Review the types of programs available at other institutions. There may already be a full or part-time faculty developer who can provide services or who can support the development of a peer-based program for individuals. Or you may prefer one of the group-based models offered by a faculty developer, or by a team of colleagues trained to offer a particular program. Support group activities may appeal to some faculty members or teaching assistants at your campus.

Selection of those to serve in consultative roles is important; you must also provide initial training, formative evaluation, and ongoing development opportunities for these individuals. Participants and students benefit from orientation activities, especially ones that provide guidelines about giving and receiving feedback. Although a variety of information gathering activities can be used, the final decision about the specific activities should rest with the participant in collaboration with the person in the consultative role.

In the minds of others, instructional consultation may seem more like an evaluation process than a professional development activity. Therefore, be sure to keep instructional consultation clearly separated from evaluation processes. Conversely, look for ways that the instructional consultation program can complement other professional development activities offered.

Carefully discuss support needed for the program you plan to offer. When you initiate a new or expanded service, start small and be prepared to modify your approach on the basis of your experience in a pilot project. As the program grows, be sure you are able to provide adequate rewards and administrative support for the successful operation of an expanded service. Communicate with constituent groups on a regular basis about the progress and evolution of the program. Remember that you may need to focus institutional conversations on establishing an organizational culture that values both teaching and continuous improvement of teaching.

This book provides a range of approaches to instructional consultation that can be used either at a campus level or on an inter-institutional basis. Your planning group has to decide what approaches might work to meet the needs of participants addressing different challenges in their academic careers within your particular organizational context. The seven themes presented in this chapter can serve as agenda items to focus the discussions of a program planning group.

References

Baldwin, R. G. (1979). *The faculty career process—continuity and change: A study of college professors at five stages of the academic career.* (Unpublished doctoral dissertation, Center for the Study of Higher Education, University of Michigan.)

Morrison, D. E. (1995). Opening doors to better teaching: The role of the peer-based instructional consultation. (Doctoral dissertation, The Claremont Graduate School, 1995). *Dissertation Abstracts International, 56*(6), 2134A.

21. *Variability Among Faculty*

Mary Ann Shea

*P*ersonal consultation about teaching is the highest priority of the Faculty Teaching Excellence Program (FTEP) at the University of Colorado at Boulder. Individual consultation, which we consider the single most effective way for faculty to reflect on teaching and to establish change, has been a part of the Program since its inception in 1985.

Consultation Services at the University of Colorado at Boulder

The Program operates on the assumption that there are many ways to teach effectively. Our consultation services to faculty are voluntary, individual, and private, with the object being self-discovery and reflection through collaboration with an experienced Faculty Associate. We offer three forms of assistance: classroom observation, videotaping, and the administration to students of a 37-item survey of teaching behaviors. (See Appendix A and B.) The survey asks students to describe specific teaching behaviors that fall more or less discretely into four dimensions of good teaching: knowledge of content, dynamism and enthusiasm, rapport with students individually and as a group, and clarity and organization.

The various interventions that make up a consultation are of relatively brief duration. Typically, a faculty member will contact the Program during the course of a semester, will meet once or twice with a consultant, and then will return to the classroom to put into practice the ideas that emerged during talks with the consultant. We offer to work with the faculty member on a continuing basis, but requests for additional consultations and follow-up are infrequent. However, because most faculty are satisfied with meeting once or twice with our Faculty Associates, we are usually able to accommodate the occasional request for more extensive assistance. More frequently than long-term consultations, professors will request another consultation a year or so later. (Our guidelines for conducting consultations are summarized in Appendix C.)

The Program operates on the assumption that there are may ways to teach effectively. We emphasize to faculty that the purpose of discussing teaching is for them to become insightful about pedagogy and learning rather than for us to impose solutions and prescriptions. Our Associates are careful to respect the fine line between participating in and sharing collaboration, on the one hand, and telling a faculty member how to teach, on the other. Finally, central to our work is the concept that teaching well and proudly is a process rather than a product of a limited number of years. One continually refines pedagogy and praxis across one's lifetime in the professoriate.

Each fall we send our *Consultation Service to Faculty* brochure to all tenured and tenure-track faculty at CU. This brochure explains the goals and philosophy of the consultative process, describes the three types of assistance we offer, and contains a mail-in panel to be returned to the FTEP. Interested faculty respond either by sending in this panel or by calling us directly. Judging from the comments of faculty seeking our services, word of mouth also plays an important role in attracting clients.

We pass these requests along to our FTEP Faculty Associates, experienced faculty trained to function as consultants. Our Associates combine expertise, enthusiasm, and strong interpersonal skills. We recruit them not only for their general excellence in teaching and scholarship, but also for a specific pedagogic expertise in areas such as large course teaching; graduate seminar teaching; first semester, first year seminar teaching; teaching sophomore critical thinking courses in the core curriculum of the College of Arts and Sciences; integrating multicultural perspectives into a course design; teaching by Socratic method; teaching through collaborative learning in the sciences; and teaching courses heavily infused with writing. The Associates are assigned by the Director, who tries to match the faculty client's declared concerns to the consultants' strengths. The Director attempts to preclude pairing, for example, a junior faculty client with a senior Faculty Associate from the same department, who would likely be judging the assistant professor's dossier during a review. Our seven 1993-94 Faculty Associates, all associate or full professors, represent the following disciplines: biology, communication disorders and speech science, sociology, psychology, law, anthropology, and political science.

Faculty approach the consulting process with a variety of motives and expectations. Ideally, of course, they are receptive to change and willing to collaborate with a consultant to explore ways to change. In reality, some consultative relationships have limited potential for success from the start.

Theoretically, all of our clients volunteer; however, some who apply for the service do so because they have been told to seek assistance by their Department Chair or Dean. Pressures to improve teaching performance come from Chairs, from departmental or college requirements, or from a coming promotion or tenure review, from students, and from the university at large. Among those who have been coerced, some do not really want help; others are open to it provided that it is offered with great tact. Among the true volunteers, some are already successful but want to do even better; others are not doing well and want to improve. Finally, some faculty clients desire a collaborative relationship with a consultant, while others want more specific, prescriptive advice. The true volunteers are often relatively open-minded about adjusting their approaches to teaching or even making wholesale pedagogical changes. Some of the coerced are also receptive, but do not give up resistance easily because they cling to the notion that "I haven't done anything for the students to be upset about." Perhaps lurking behind this notion is the sentiment "I was taught this way. Why shouldn't that be good enough for these students?"

The faculty member's motivation already embodies expectations about the outcome. The rapport developed with the Faculty Associate may, however, lead to provocative discussion of attitudes, fears, and dilemmas that were not apparently part of the initial motivating attitude. As this rapport unmasks otherwise hidden issues, the shared meaning of what it means to teach becomes less unique and more an act that the professoriate has in common and that the professoriate may, as a result, investigate collegially. Just as good teaching takes off the mask of oneself rather than putting on a mask, good consultation develops and relies on the qualities of open mindedness. In a real sense neither the faculty client nor the consultant knows what to expect. For some wonderment to find its way into the conversation, the consultant must be willing to rely on intuition, or at least on excellent listening skills and a sense of the right time and place to negotiate feelings as well as intellectual engagement in teaching strategy. In a conversation about an exercise as intimate as teaching, the language of probing, at the least the question "Can you say more about that?" is very appropriate. After all, we cannot say why students respond to some teaching and teachers; we can only explore the question.

Figure 1: Parameters Affecting Consultations for Teaching

1. Length of professional career

new————————seeking tenure————————mid-career adjustment————————nearing retirement

2. Knowledge and awareness of pedagogy

little or none————————moderate, but seeking more————————advanced, looking for 1 or 2 tips

3. Motivation for seeking help through consultation

coerced by Chair, Dean————————driven by poor ratings————————fully voluntary

4. Expectations for assistance

formula for achieving————————in-depth analysis————————tips to respond to
teaching excellence   of teaching   specific challenges

5. Conditions surrounding the consultation

extreme emotional upset with————————insecurity prevails;————————confident, looking
blame placed on self, outside   discreet help sought   for affirmation of
life, students or administration   teaching prowess

These and other parameters affecting consultations for teaching are summarized in Figure 1.

Motivation and Expectation: Portraits of Faculty Members Served

Here are some of the more frequently encountered portraits among faculty arriving for consultations for teaching:

1. Many faculty come for consultations after having received mediocre ratings on *student evaluations*. These faculty tend to be emotionally and intellectually shattered by the students' refusal to judge them as good teachers. Some are also hostile and resentful of students' opinions. Broad as the University of Colorado mandated course evaluations are in scope, they still provide some indication of an area or areas of teaching performance that need attention. The key in consultative work is to discern where the faculty member's perceptions and students' perceptions are mismatched.

2. Faculty facing a retention, tenure, or promotion decision may well feel guilty for having waited too long to address teaching deficiencies. Assistant professors usually propose to argue that they are making an effort to strengthen their teaching practice, rather than claiming to be very good teachers already. Some may be eager to receive assistance but will never have enough time to put newly learned techniques into use before the decision is made; others may resent the university system as a whole. On the other hand, a *faculty member coming up for review* may seek endorsement at this juncture in his/her career that his/her teaching practice is solid. In this case the consultation may be quite fruitful, since the granting of tenure may well lessen the demands for research and give the assistant professor time to make use of new insights into teaching.

3. Confident and competent teachers seek professional *affirmation* of their ability and performance or ways to be even better. They are seeking validation of their good teaching from a reputable source. These professors often assist the effort of the Program by recommending our services to their colleagues, by becoming departmental boosters of teaching excellence, or by becoming workshop presenters or, eventually, Faculty Associates. In short, they become emissaries of the consultation service of the program. Meanwhile, their teaching is likely to continue improving.

4. *New faculty* who approach us want to begin their professional careers on the right foot. Bob Boice's re-

search has shown that those faculty whom he calls "quick starters"—those who become confident and comfortable teachers early in their careers—are more likely to seek help from faculty development programs in their first year than those who do not. He argues persuasively that the key to this success is that they concentrate on the process of teaching rather than the content.

5. Some faculty are in search of a *formula* for better teaching. Believing that the perfect teaching methodology has been codified, somewhere, by someone, with mathematical precision, they assume that if we could just show them this method, they too could become excellent teachers. Even if we are able to convince these faculty that teaching improvement is a never-ending process without any easy answers, they insist on didactic, authoritarian guidance. The task here is to turn the point of view around so the faculty member looks not to the consultant for answers but towards his or her own performance, philosophy, and approach to teaching.

6. Other faculty come to us requesting an in-depth *analysis* of their teaching. They believe that every aspect of their teaching must be examined. They may be enjoying moderate success but have little confidence as teachers because the discipline has not lent any assistance in pedagogy, in new research in the field, or in organization of the content. We can easily accommodate their wishes by administering our 37-item survey, describing our observations of their class, and giving them a videotape of the class. They can then go away and, presumably, work on improving their teaching on their own. We comply, realizing that this is not an ideal method, first, because an analysis of teaching can never be objective and external, and second, because the more important part of the consultation is generating incremental steps toward change. We expect, therefore, to conduct a follow-up consultation perhaps a year later.

7. One of the most commonly encountered characteristics is *mystification* concerning teaching. When faculty begin with a relatively blank slate, consultation can be quite fruitful. Yet because mystified faculty have such a limited conscious awareness of their own teaching behavior and the craft of teaching, the consultant may have to work carefully to construct a framework so that they can see teaching as an objectified and somewhat measurable act.

8. Other faculty come to us during a turbulent *transition* period in their personal lives that infringes on their academic, professional lives. They may be in the midst of divorce, death of a loved one, chronic illness, or unresolvable departmental conflicts. To assist them means being a good listener and then helping them to focus on teaching.

9. Some older but still vital professors *approaching retirement* come to us feeling out of step with "new" developments in teaching, although they retain an interest in good teaching process. It is always a joy to encounter faculty with a quarter century of teaching experience who are determined to stay current with pedagogical innovation.

10. We also see professors who would like to improve their teaching through a *discreet collaboration* away from departmental constraints and politics. They are unwilling to solicit advice from their colleagues for fear of future retaliation. Having made the initial commitment to seek outside help, however, these faculty can establish excellent collaborative relationships with our Faculty Associates.

11. A few faculty request *long-term* help rather than a one-time-only intervention. They recognize the potential or actual progress in teaching that results from asking for a consultation. These faculty are kindred spirits who think as we do in valuing teaching highly. Frequently, they are assistant professors who would like to be mentored in good teaching practice.

12. Some faculty come for consultation because they need assistance with a very *specific teaching problem* or assignment. For example, they may be teaching a very large course for the first time. Take, for example, the professor who is remarkably skilled in the graduate student seminar but not the undergraduate, first-semester freshman survey course. With a returning emphasis on the first-year student, many faculty members will be well served to "refresh" their teaching and their understanding of the cognitive development of students.

13. Those who come laden with some evidence of poor performance often also come tenaciously prepared to *blame someone for their failure.* Some blame their students entirely; others blame themselves entirely. Such professors do not view teaching and learning as reciprocal. In this instance the consultant may want to suggest some readings and arrange an opportunity to observe others' teaching.

In responding to these motives and expectations, our Faculty Associates must have ready and equally varied repertoire of assistance strategies and tactics, strengthened by the same interpersonal abilities that have made them exemplary teachers. Above all, they need to be tactful, discreet, sympathetic listeners. In addition, they have to be skilled in the subtle art of suggestion, so that each idea for teaching improvement seems to emanate from collaboration, not solely from the Faculty Associate. They must attend to the faculty client's stated expectations but be ready to welcome other insights that emerge from the collaboration.

Teaching consultants need to "see" the professor the way a good teacher "sees" students, that is, as a whole person rather than just as a teacher in a particular course or just as an expert in cell biology. Every teacher is a person with a range of concerns, predicaments, lifestyle issues, strongly held views and sentiments. This fact helps explain why Faculty Associates and faculty clients from vastly differing disciplines have successfully collaborated despite different ways of teaching, varying disciplinary epistemologies, and different learning strategies. By way of example, one of the Program's Associates is a professor of Environmental, Population and Organismic Biology who provided a consultation for a dance professor. It was a successful collaboration not solely because each was open to something new but also because each was profoundly human, each was a professor, each was dedicated to a craft, and each was aware and respectful of the different ways of knowing. In another pairing, because the faculty client was panicked by the thought of watching herself on video, the faculty consultant compassionately shared her own video. In a third case, a department chair teaching a sophomore-level science course had been unable to express exactly what was wrong from his perspective. After a viewing of the taped class hour (without interruption from the consultant, who was unable either to find points to discuss or to engage the faculty member in a discussion of pedagogy or praxis), the Professor turned off the tape and said, "I know exactly what I am doing wrong. I am teaching at way too high a cognitive level without telling the students how I got there. Now I know what to do." That insight, facilitated simply by the artifacts of the consultative process and not by collaboration per se, made him a different teacher. In a less happy case, a junior faculty member arrived at his fourth-year evaluation newly married, beginning a family and adopting his spouse's family too. He appeared passive, dispirited, and disconnected, what we would call a resistant and closed faculty client—and at the end of a difficult effort on our part, he asked (twice, in different ways) "Do you think I'm a good enough teacher to be promoted?" These were the most powerful questions he asked; he asked no questions about become a more satisfied or satisfying teacher.

Future Developments

We would like to develop the link between our Instructional Workshops on Teaching and Learning and the consultation service. We offer twenty-five workshops during an academic year, from *Promoting Discussion in*

Introductory Courses in the Sciences to *Evaluating Student Learning* to *Active Engagement in the Large Lecture Course* to *Provoking Critical Thought in the Classrooms: The Use of Socratic Method*. Our most popular workshop is *Performance in a Nutshell*, which focuses on body language and vocal tone. It concentrates on three principles of enhancing presentation skills and provides each participant with a seven-item checklist of techniques for using these principles. We find that this workshop whets faculty appetites for videotape consultations. We would also like to expand the Faculty Associate program; ideally, each department or school in the university should have its own Faculty Associate.

Appendix A

Instructions for Survey of Teaching Behaviors

Below is a list of statements about teaching. We would like your help in determining how well each statement describes the teaching you have received from your professor in this course (please exclude your recitation section). This survey is intended to help identify good teaching skills, but will not be used to evaluate your professor. We wish your responses to be anonymous, so do not write in your name or ID number on the answer sheet. All that we need are your responses to the statements, written in #2 pencil on the answer sheet. Please use an **A** to **E** scale, where **A** indicates that you think the statement is **very descriptive** of your professor's teaching, **C** is **somewhat descriptive**, and **E** is **not at all descriptive**. For example if you think that statement #11 "Is well prepared" is *less* than somewhat descriptive, but *not quite* not at all descriptive of your instructor, you would fill in the circle under **D** for response #11 on the answer sheet, as follows:

very descriptive		somewhat descriptive		not at all descriptive
A	B	C	D	E
○	○	○	○	○

Please leave blank any items that you are unsure of. When you are finished, please pass both the list of statements and your responses to the aisle, and we will collect them. Thanks for your help.

List of Descriptors

1. Discusses points of view other than his or her own.
2. Contrasts implications of theories.
3. Discusses recent developments in the field.
4. Gives references for more interesting and involved points.
5. Generalizes from examples and specific instances.
6. Uses examples and illustrations.
7. Is able to improvise in awkward situations.
8. Stresses general concepts and ideas.
9. Uses exams effectively for synthesis and understanding of course material.
10. Explains clearly.
11. Is well prepared.
12. Gives lectures that are easy to outline.
13. States objectives for each class session.
15. Identifies what she or he considers important.
16. Gives frequent and timely feedback.
17. Uses a variety of instructional media (for example, films, overhead).
18. Makes a few major points during a lecture rather than many.
19. Encourages class discussion.
20. Invites students to share their knowledge and experiences.
21. Invites criticism of his or her own ideas.
22. Knows if the class is understanding him/her or not.
23. Has students apply concepts to demonstrate understanding.
24. Knows when students are bored.
25. Has genuine interest in students.
27. Relates to students as individuals.
28. Is accessible to students as individuals.
29. Asks questions of students.
30. Has an interesting style of presentation.
31. Is enthusiastic about the subject.
32. Varies the speed and tone of voice.
33. Uses a range of gestures and movement.
34. Has interest in and concern for the quality of teaching.
35. Motivates students to do their best work.
36. Gives interesting and stimulating assignments.
37. Has a sense of humor.

Appendix B

The Three Stages of a Consultation:
Observation, Survey, and Videotape

Once a Faculty Associate has contacted the faculty member, the next step in the consultative process is a classroom observation. The observation and subsequent discussion give faculty an extra set of eyes, a disinterested yet experienced visitor who can hold the mirror up to them as teachers. The discussion with the observer provides faculty with an opportunity to discuss subjects that are usually not mentioned within the department: the theory and praxis of teaching.

We also suggest that faculty have our 37-item Survey of Good Teaching Characteristics administered to the class being observed. Based on earlier lists of teaching behaviors developed at Berkeley, this survey asks students to rate performance on a five-point Likert scale over a wide range of observable behaviors. Examples of descriptors include "Is accessible to students outside of class" and "Uses a range of gestures and movement." The survey is administered by the Associate in the last ten minutes of class time with students recording their responses on computer answer sheets. These sheets are coded by the university's Research and Information Office and returned to the FTEP. The Associate reviews the results of the survey with the faculty member, concentrating on items that were rated relatively high and low as well as those that show a greater than average standard deviation. After the discussion the faculty member retains a copy of the results.

Videotaping is the consultative intervention that arouses the most anxiety among faculty. Every year at least a couple of faculty specify that they do not want to be videotaped. After all, video is an unforgiving medium. However, the curiosity to see oneself on the screen is generally strong in the video age, and most faculty appear to benefit from the experience. Many faculty have already undergone a three-minute videotaping and critique as part of our popular Performance in a Nutshell workshop, which is presented by one of our theatre professors. Others have been taped here or at other institutions in the past and have become critical viewers of their own performance.

Used sympathetically, video is a powerful impetus for self-reflection and self-improvement. Harold Nicholson has said, "We are inclined to judge ourselves by our ideals, others by their acts." Video allows the performer to view his or her work impersonally, as others do, judging by acts rather than ideals. Once the ideal view and the actual view are disentangled, progress can be made toward improvement. Faculty are given the only copy of the videotape to take home with them.

Tools

      1. Consultation Service Brochure
      2. 37-Item Survey

Appendix C

Guidelines for Conducting a Consultation

1. Before meeting the professor:
   - prepare a preliminary plan of action
   - consider issues that might arise, given the discipline, class size, etc.

2. At the first meeting:
   - get the client to say why your help has been requested
   - assure the client that you are not a threat; avoid being seen as an authority figure
   - listen as much as possible without interfering
   - get the client to disclose areas of concern, nervousness; try to judge the depth of any anxiety
   - explain that to understand the situation more fully, you will have to collect data through observation, surveys, etc.
   - ask to see documents from a current course being taught: syllabus, text, homework assignments, tests
   - ask the instructor to elucidate his/her objectives in teaching the course

3. First observation of a class:
   - attend the class from the point of view of a student
   - take thorough notes during class, both of content and of instructor behavior
   - keep in mind the four categories of teaching characteristics—(1) knowledge of subject material, (2) rapport, (3) enthusiasm, (4) clarity and organization-and how they apply to the teacher and the class
   -

4. Meeting the client after observation:
   - try to say something positive about the client's teaching
   - be an active listener, thus increasing empathy and trust
   - be very slow to make recommendations, trying to get the client to suggest his/her own ways of improvement
   - concentrate on just one issue, one possible area to improve per meeting

5. Approaches to doing a videotape consultation:
   - give the client a remote control device so that he/she can stop the tape whenever something troubling occurs
   - get the client to suggest his/her own agendas for improvement.

List compiled with help of articles in *Face to Face*, K. G. Lewis and J. T. Povlacs, editors.

22. *Faculty Face Student Diversity*

Milton G. Spann, Jr. and Suella McCrimmon

Our purpose in this essay is to paint a picture of the increasing diversity in American Higher Education. Racial, ethnic and cultural differences are compounded by competing value system and lifestyle decisions. Conflict is inevitable as these differences rub up against a faculty far less diverse by background and education than those they teach. We write this essay against the backdrop of a largely eurocentric, middle aged, middle class, male dominated Caucasian faculty frightened by the increasing numbers of students from cultural, ethnic, and gender backgrounds unlike their own.

For those faculty willing to face the challenges and opportunities presented, we also offer a perspective on the students they are or soon will be teaching and some ideas we think useful in teaching a more diverse student body.

Historical Snapshot

It's September, 1770, the eve of the American Revolution; a rather distinguished looking gentleman sits at a simple desk reviewing correspondence from every college in America, all nine of them. He gets up from his desk, goes down the hall and knocks gently on the door marked "President." "Sir," he says, "I have exciting news. The Harvard Class of 1771 will shortly confer degrees on 63 exceptional men. And sir, this will be our largest class ever. In fact, we will graduate more students this year than all our sister colleges combined."

It's September, 1992. The American Council on Education reports (Ottinger, 1992) there are more than 3500 institutions ranging from small, two-year community colleges and four-year liberal arts colleges to gigantic state universities with over 60 thousand students. Combined, these institutions of higher learning enroll nearly 14.2 million students in programs of study ranging from an associate's degree in cosmetology to a Ph.D. in quantum physics. Approximately 750,000 faculty teach these students, almost 60 percent of whom are full-time, tenured or tenure-track faculty. The total amount of money expended by these institutions is approximately 158 billion dollars. Indeed, between 1770 and 1992, higher education has been dramatically transformed in size, structure, and complexity and these changes have often mirrored the changes in the larger society.

Characteristics of Modern College Students

Increasing Diversity

Like the society, the history of American higher education has been one of increasing diversity. Until the early 19th century, students and faculty were overwhelmingly Caucasian males from upper middle class Protestant families. As the country moved into the 19th century, land grant colleges and universities began to enroll men of less affluent backgrounds and some women. Colleges specifically for African-Americans and women did not emerge until after the Civil War. These colleges were important forerunners to the notion that higher education was appropriate to the needs of women and minorities.

Following the second World War, the G.I. Bill provided access to higher education for large numbers of men and a few women. However, it was not until the 1960s, some thirty years after the feminization of the college classroom, that the number and percentage of African-Americans increased significantly. Responding to the Civil Rights movement and the Higher Education Act of 1965, higher education opened its doors to a wider audience. Since this time, representation from all minority groups has increased. According to the American Council on Higher Education, between 1988 and 1990 total minority enrollment in U.S. colleges increased 10 percent. This increase outpaced total enrollment for all groups in higher education, which grew by only 5 percent. During this span Asian-American enrollment increased by 12 percent; Hispanic enrollment by 12 percent; African-American enrollment by 10 percent; and Native American enrollment by 11 percent.

Whether we like it or not, the diversification of our institutions will be a reality by the year 2000. Demographers now know the gender, socioeconomic level, race, and ethnic mix of our kindergartners. According to Harold Hodgkinson (1987) of the Institute for Educational Leadership, one third of our kindergartners are now minority students. In Texas and California there is a minority majority in the five-year-old population. This increase in the percentage of minority students is due to the decline in the birth rates of whites, not a major increase in minorities. A dramatic example of these changes has already occurred at the college level. For the first time, the University of California-Berkley's fall 1987 freshman class had a majority of minority students: 12 percent African-American, 17 percent Hispanic, 26 percent Asian, and 40 percent white (Farrell, 1988).

Racial and ethnic diversity is perhaps the greatest challenge facing higher education as it moves into the 21st century. Most campuses have begun to open the doors to African-Americans, Hispanics, Native Americans, and Asian-Americans but many of these students do not feel that they belong in academe. Academic difficulties combine with varying degrees of cultural alienation to diminish the satisfaction of many minority students. White students and faculty, raised in a still substantially segregated society, can experience discomfort and demonstrate insensitivity when interacting with minorities. The frequency with which minority students continue to report personal experiences of racism testifies to the challenges facing higher education today.

Richard Miller (1990) states that at least three kinds of barriers can deter greater faculty involvement in efforts to promote recruitment and retention of minority students; these are lack of knowledge, negative attitudes, and lack of rewards. Miller goes on to indicate that lack of knowledge about minorities and negative attitudes can include racial stereotypes that may lead faculty either to interact in a negative way with minorities or to avoid them altogether. Since faculty interaction with students is the primary deterrent to student satisfaction with an institution, especially for students lacking self confidence, such knowledge and attitudinal barriers need to be reduced where they exist. Campus efforts to promote access and success will accomplish little if minority students' interaction with faculty in and out of the classroom makes them feel unwanted or unimportant.

At many, if not most, four year institutions, the reward system emphasizes scholarship and research productivity. Although this emphasis varies widely, young faculty members generally know that added time spent on teaching and advising activities is unlikely to be rewarded, and, indeed they may be punished to the extent that tangible scholarship is reduced as a result of these activities. Scholarship that stymies or prevents the building of an inclusive community must be examined.

The successful inclusion of a viable minority presence in higher education is one of the most important challenges of the 1990s, according to Miller (1990). It will require a) the development, operation, evaluation, and subsequent modification of a comprehensive campus-wide plan for minority areas; b) active faculty involvement as participants and planners in campus minority activities and programs; c) changing the faculty reward system to recognize their meaningful participation in minority related activities; and d) collaboration of colleges and universities with elementary and secondary schools to recruit and prepare minority students for college.

Increasing Numbers of Adult Students

The College Board (Brickell, 1992) reported that seven million adults (25 years of age or older) are enrolled in college credit programs and that an estimated 10 million are participating in college noncredit programs. Over 50 percent of all graduate students are 30 years of age or older. In 1992-93, only 20 percent of the total college population was full-time, in residence, and under 22 years of age.

While modern college students are characterized by increasing social and ethnic diversity, they may also be characterized by their expectations of a college. The modern adult student (25 years or older) comes to class with a different set of expectations than the traditional age student (19-22 year old). These expectations can be organized into six categories:

Today's adult students are more self-directed. Many are working full or part time outside the home and many are full-time or part-time homemakers seeking a new challenge. As successful adults, they expect to be treated as adults and can be frustrated if spoon-fed with information that is designed for high school students. They usually have clear objectives for being in class and, if college faculty are going to be effective, they must find out what those objectives are.

To be effective with the more self-directed adult students, faculty need to understand the nature of self-directed learning. Self-directed learning is often thought of as a form of study in which learners have the primary responsibility for planning, carrying out, and evaluating their own learning experiences under the guidance of a faculty member or mentor sensitive to learners' interests. Negotiated learning contracts are one of the more successful approaches to self-directed learning.

Today's adult students are highly demanding as consumers. Not only are they in class for specific reasons, usually for gaining the knowledge and skills needed to get a job or upgrade their job skills. They are likely to be paying the entire cost and they want their money's worth. Most resent time being wasted on issues unrelated to the course of instruction. They may become hostile if they sense their money and their time are being wasted. Such hostility can usually be avoided if faculty will take the time to assess students' interests and needs and to modify the course of instruction to accommodate some of them.

Today's adult students very often come to the classroom with rich life experiences. They are more likely to be readers of books, magazines, and newspapers. If we treat them as empty vessels, we will insult them. We must not assume they have no awareness of the subject matter we are teaching. Because of their experiences and maturity, they generally like to share what they know. To be effective teachers of adults, we must find ways to tap into their knowledge and experience and utilize it to motivate them to achieve course objectives.

Today's adult students will demand that they be treated as adults. They expect to be addressed as peers and respected as mature individuals. They perceive themselves to be at least equal in status to their teachers and sometimes professionally superior. Teachers of mature adult students should be aware that adult students generally like a more informal collegial relationship with faculty as opposed to a more formal or traditional classroom atmosphere. A coffee pot and an informal "living room" atmosphere will go a long way toward establishing this environment.

Today's adult students will demand relevance and immediate application. The adult student usually brings to the classroom a strong need for the direct application of the information, skills, and so on to a particular situation of immediate importance to them. Faculty who take time to assess students' career and avocational interests and relate, where practicable, to these interests will usually capture what motivates the adult learner.

Today's adult students may demand a role in developing the learning activity. They will expect to be consulted on the usefulness and relevance of classroom activities and to be treated as partners in the learning process. In a partnership, all parties have a voice and an investment in the outcome. While maintaining the integrity of the course, faculty who show flexibility in the way course goals are achieved can usually satisfy the partnership needs of most adult learners. Where the learner has a particular interest that may not fall within the purview of the course, a specialized learning project or independent study may be offered. Some students will bring considerable knowledge and experience to a course of study.

Where possible, this background should be recognized and alternative objectives provided.

In summary, the characteristics of the modern adult student may demand a thorough review of a professor's teaching style and methodology. Reading from the old yellow notes will no longer satisfy most adult students. If faculty are willing to be flexible, open-minded and responsive to this increasingly important constituency in higher education, they may find it to be one of the most satisfying teaching experiences of their lives.

The Feminine Majority

The typical college campus of today is more than 50 percent female. Among the more selective colleges, the percentage of female enrollees is even higher and there is evidence to suggest that women will remain the majority cohort of college students in the future. Given this fact, we believe that college faculty must question the adequacy of teaching approaches based largely on male learning preferences. Why has it taken us so long to question the male paradigm? This is not surprising if we remember that higher education from the Greeks through the great English universities and into the Americas was a male-only privilege until well into the 19th century. When women entered academic life, differences from the male norm were simply assumed to be deficits. We have come a long way since the feminization of the classroom both in terms of our perception of the intellectual capacity of women and our knowledge of the learning preferences or learning styles of women.

Carol Pearson (1992), one of the more articulate spokespersons on diversity in the classroom, offers a common sense approach to dealing with gender differences. Rather than emphasizing the needs of one gender over another, she reminds us that regardless of gender, students learn in different ways and at different rates. She encourages teachers to learn to appreciate not only gender differences but racial, cultural, and ethnic differences as well. All appear to have an impact on learning style.

To meet the needs of an increasingly diverse population, Pearson encourages teachers to use a variety of teaching methods to reach students so that during the delivery of the course all students will have the experience of being taught in ways appropriate to their learning preference or style. While acknowledging that students may learn best in their preferred mode, she readily agrees that learning the same thing in more than one way reinforces learning. For example, when we teach using visual, auditory, and kinesthetic modes, all students learn more easily. When we provide experiences which tap the "feeling" and "thinking" modes of decision-making, we not only advantage students with those preferences, we also speak to the feeling and the thinking side of each student, thus creating a more complete learning experience for everyone.

The more faculty assume a single standard for how things should be taught, the more we reinforce absolutist and dualistic thinking. The more we foster this kind of thinking, the less well equipped students are to live effectively in the increasingly pluralistic work world of the 1990's and beyond.

Developing Students: A More Satisfying Role for Faculty

Since the late 1960's and early 1970's an impressive number of theories and models of student development have emerged. In fact, using a rather broad definition of theory, there are at least 20 theories or models available to guide our thinking on how students grow and develop.

Probably no other psychosocial theorist has had more influence on those seeking to understand the development of students than Arthur Chickering (1981; 1993). His seven vectors of student development are based on a exhaustive survey of the literature. Growth along the vectors is not seen as simply maturational unfolding, but as requiring constant stimulation from faculty, fellow students, and other aspects of the learning environment. Student development is therefore seen as planned rather than serendipitous. In reviewing these vectors, faculty should consider creative ways to foster their development in both classroom, mentoring and advising activities. Faculty who appropriately challenge and support students in their growth along these vectors are likely to create the climate necessary for growth toward maturity and responsibility.

Vector 1: Achieving Competence. Here the emphasis is on the development of the skills of intellectual and interpersonal competence and the confidence necessary to achieve successfully what one sets out to do.

Vector 2: Managing Emotions. Here Chickering would have us focus on helping the students wrestle with a variety of intense emotions, particularly the emotions involving sex and aggression. We would aid the student in making the transition from the more rigid reflexive controls imposed by parents and society toward a more thoughtfully considered set of internally adopted standards and controls.

Vector 3: Developing Autonomy. As the student's intellectual and interpersonal competencies develop, the student begins to disengage from the need for parental approval and reassurance. Relationships based on mutual respect and helpfulness are established as the student confronts the paradox of personal independence and interdependence. In recent years Chickering has given increased emphasis to the student's interdependence with family, community and society.

Vector 4: Establishing Identity. Establishing a solid yet dynamic sense of self is important throughout the life span. Establishing this strong sense of self particularly depends on the student's growth along the competency, emotional, and autonomy vectors. Development along these vectors is necessary to encourage change along the remaining vectors. It is particularly important for young men and women to clarify their conception of their physical characteristics and personal appearance along with appropriate value-driven sex roles and behaviors.

Vector 5: Freeing Interpersonal Relationships. As the student's personal identity is solidified, he/she gains increased ability to interact with others and becomes more tolerant and respectful of those of different backgrounds, habits, values, and appearances. Chickering believes that the growing cultural diversity within our society makes it ever more important that we help students develop a greater sense of tolerance and respect for all persons.

Vector 6: Developing Purpose. Expanding competencies, identity, and interpersonal relationships requires a sense of future direction and purpose. Growth along this vector requires the development of plans that integrate priorities in all areas of one's life from recreational and vocational interests to life-style choices.

Vector 7: Developing Integrity. Here the emphasis is on the clarification of a personally valid set of beliefs that are reasonably consistent and that provide some general guidelines for behavior. In the process of developing integrity, values are reviewed. Some are rejected and those found suitable to the emerging identity are retained, personalized, and internalized.

As Chickering sought to bring knowledge and practice closer together, he identified six major areas through which colleges could influence either negative or positive growth along the seven vectors. These areas of influence and their effects include:

- clarity and consistency of institutional policies and practices;
- creation of small manageable communities within the larger institutional setting so that real participation is perceived and realized;
- flexible curriculum that promotes a variety of instructional styles and modes, thereby increasing the level of active participation in the learning process;
- residence halls that consciously promote the development of community among persons of diverse backgrounds and interests;

- frequent and friendly contact with psychologically accessible adults in variety of settings;
- student culture and interest groups reflective of institutional values.

As teaching faculty, we have found it quite helpful to reflect on Chickering's vectors as we plan our course content and processes. Doing so has brought about modifications in our reading lists, assigned papers and class discussions. In addition, it has challenged us to reflect on classroom dynamics and our own behavior as teachers. We find ourselves challenged, even haunted, by the important role we play as educators. We believe Chickering's Vectors provide useful guidelines for creating and sustaining dynamic, value-driven classrooms. Let us share a story illustrative of our shift from content specialist alone to that of student development educator. While in a workshop on teaching, someone asked the question, "What do you teach?" One said, "I teach math," another, "I teach history," and so on. One person responded, "I teach students and I use my discipline as one of many tools to help students learn and grow." That was the beginning of a conscious decision to shift from content specialist alone to the role of student development educator, a role we believe is highly appropriate in today's college classroom.

Accommodating Diversity Through Collaboration and Teamwork

As we think about how to accommodate an increasingly diverse group of learners and the challenges of a multicultural campus and society, we believe that one of the more promising approaches is found in what is commonly referred to as collaborative or team learning. The essence of this approach is the placement of students on learning teams where the success of each student contributes to the success of the team. (Two team techniques are described in Appendix A.)

Collaborative learning has been found not only to increase motivation, but also self-esteem and peer support for academic success. William Whipple (1987), chair of the American Association of Higher Education's Collaborative Learning Action Community, offers a number of characteristics useful to faculty interested in more action-oriented approaches to learning:

Collaborative learning gets the teacher and the student actively involved in the educational process. Active learning was encouraged in the National Institute of Education's 1984 report and was considered by its writers as one of the seven key principles of effective practice in undergraduate education. When students work together on joint projects, participate in various learning communities, and help shape a course or curriculum, it is more difficult for them to remain detached from the process of inquiry that underlies education. As faculty actively involve themselves in the collaboration, their need for involvement is met and they become energized by the interactions that take place among student and between students and faculty.

Collaboration bridges the gap between faculty and students. At the turn of the century, the typical college student was a 14 or 15 year old male and faculty were responsible, *in loco parentis*, for all aspects of his education, including character development. An authoritarian model may have been more appropriate in that day and under those circumstances. Today, it may not produce the desired results. Too often it produces alienated rather than energized learners. In higher education today, where increasingly larger number of mature adults (+25) are matriculating, a rigid authoritarian structure with the faculty as the sole source of knowledge may be an impediment to learning. In collaborative models it becomes apparent that the faculty is not the sole possessor of knowledge. As the students engage in responsible dialogue with each other and with the teacher, knowledge emerges from the members of this group and students are frequently empowered by it.

Collaboration creates a sense of community. Cooperation rather than competition becomes the intent—everyone helping everyone learn. While competition has its place, it may not be in the classroom. In today's world cooperation and teamwork in the workplace and in the community may not only foster life enhancing values (e.g. respect for diversity), but results in greater productivity and greater satisfaction. An analogy to family life may be helpful in making our point. An effective family does not dissolve the individuality of its members, but provides a base of support on which the uniqueness of its members can stand. Successful collaboration means that knowledge is created, not transferred. The "empty vessel" theory of education is far less effective in its application than we might think. Socrates knew better. Learning-how-to-learn skills and attitudes may be more useful than knowing all the answers to the latest version of Trivial Pursuit. Collaborative learning, when properly executed, encourages students to see their task as that of making knowledge for themselves and their lives. In this model, teachers are encouraged to view as a part of their craft the creation of situations leading to the development of new knowledge and a recognition that the knowledge of the group is greater than any one of its members. For example, a collaborative situation involving five persons results in six distinct knowledges represented—those of each member and that of the group as a collective entity. The latter is not antagonistic to the former; rather, it is complementary, providing a richer soil in which ideas can take root.

As faculty we see the opportunity that collaborative learning provides us as we attempt to involve and teach persons from diverse backgrounds. For example, we can imagine the richness of understanding and insight gained by comparing and contrasting patterns of effective communications within our respective family groups with those necessary to effectively communicate within our classroom groups. We could also explore how knowledge of each other's in-group communications might build understanding and trust between us. Applying the principles of collaborative learning offers some exciting alternatives that could be overlooked in a traditional didactic mode of instruction.

Conclusions

Will a largely middle-aged middle-class entrepreneurial faculty meet the challenges of an increasingly diverse student body? Will an overwhelmingly traditional faculty incorporate teaching modes suitable to racial, ethnic, and gender differences? Will the senior faculty at colleges and universities retreat into their academic disciplines and then wring their hands over the loss of the good old days when students looked and thought and learned in the same ways they did? Will students rebel and refuse to attend classes taught by faculty who are unwilling to learn about the backgrounds and interests of students who come from places and circumstances unfamiliar to them? If we faculty are unwilling, who will teach the citizens how to live in a pluralistic society? Who will teach them to be citizens of the world? Who will help them make the transition?

References

Brickell, H. M. (1992). *Adults in classrooms.* New York: College Entrance Examination Board. New York.

Chickering, A. W. & Associates. (1981). *The modern American college: Responding to the new realities of diverse students and a changing society.* San Francisco: Jossey-Bass.

Chickering, A.W., & Reisser, L. (1993). *Education and identity* (2nd ed.). San Francisco: Jossey-Bass.

Farrell, C. S. (1988, January 27). Stung by racial incidents and charges of indifferences: Berkeley trying to become a model integrated university. *The Chronicle of Higher Education,* A36.

Hodgkinson, H. (1987, April). Today's curriculum. *National Association of Student Support Personnel Bulletin,* pp. 2-7.

Miller, R. I. (1990). *Major American higher education issues and challenges in the 1990s.* London: Jessica Kingsley.

Ottinger, C. A. (Ed.) (1992). *Higher education today: Facts in brief.* Washington DC: American Council on Education.

Pearson, C. S. (Winter, 1992). Women as learners: Diversity and educational quality. *Journal of Developmental Education, 16*(2), 2-10.

Whipple, W. R. (1987). Collaborative learning: Recognizing it when we see it. *AAHE Bulletin, 40*(2), 3-7

Appendix
Team Techniques

Research on team learning conducted by Robert Slavin through the Johns Hopkins Team Learning Project resulted in the manual, Using Student Team Learning. In the manual, three extensively researched team learning techniques are presented along with detailed instructions on how to use them in the classroom. For details, write to the project c/o the Center for Social Organization of Schools, the Johns Hopkins University, Baltimore, Maryland 21218. Here is a brief description of the team techniques as described in the manual by Slavin. Adaptations for adult learners may be required.

Jigsaw. The Jigsaw Method was first investigated as a way to increase students' liking of others in integrated classes, but later research found it to have positive effects in other areas as well. In the Jigsaw, students are assigned to six-member teams. Academic material is broken down into as many parts as there are students on each team. For example, a biography might be broken into early life, first accomplishments, major setbacks and so on. Members of the different teams who have the same section form "expert groups" and study together. Each then returns to his or her team and teaches the section to the team. Often, the students take a quiz on the entire set of material. The only way students can do well on this quiz is to pay close attention to their teammates' sections, so students are motivated to support and show interest in each others' work. In Jigsaw II, a modification of the Jigsaw method, each student reads all of the material, but focuses on a particular topic. Students discuss their topics in the "expert groups," and then teach them to their teams.

Teams-Game-Tournaments. Teams-Games-Tournaments (TGT) is the best researched of the classroom techniques that use teams. In TGT, students are assigned to four or five member learning teams. Each week, the teacher introduces new material in a lecture or discussion. The teams then study worksheets on the material together, and at the end of the week, team members compete in "tournaments" with members of other teams to add points to their team scores. In the tournaments, students compete on skill-exercise games with others who are comparable in past academic performance. This equal competition makes it possible for every student to have a good chance of contributing a maximum number of points to his or her team. A weekly newsletter, prepared by the teacher, recognizes successful teams and students who have contributed outstandingly to their team scores. The excitement and motivation generated by TGT is enormous. Teachers using this method have reported that students who were never particularly interested in school were coming in after class to get materials to take home to study, asking for special help, and becoming actice in class discussions.

Student Teams-Achievement Divisions. Student Teams-Achievement Divisions (STAD) is a simple team technique in which students work in four or five member teams, and then take individual quizzes to make points for their team. Each student's score is compared to that of other students of similar past performance, so that in STAD, as in TGT, students of all ability levels have a good chance of earning maximum points for their teams. Thus, STAD is like TGT, except that it substitutes individual quizzes for the TGT game tournament.

23. *Effects of Classroom Environments*

Gabriele Bauer

For the purposes of this chapter, the term classroom environment reflects both the physical aspects of the classroom (for example, room size, arrangement of furniture) and the social aspects (for example, the students, the students' relationships to each other, and the instructor's interaction with the students). The chapter examines the classroom setting within the context of the instructor cultivating an environment for learning. The teaching environment constitutes only one dimension of the instructional context; other dimensions associated with learning and teaching are the course content, the organization of the course, the instructor's teaching style, and the nature of the curriculum. This environment can be teacher-oriented (for example, lecture), student-oriented (for example, independent study), interaction-oriented (for example, seminar), or experience-oriented (for example, laboratory setting).

Each of these four instructional settings brings forth different kinds of issues for us to address as consultants. For instance, whereas an observer in a music conducting class might focus on how the instructor models conducting behaviors (that is, skill-oriented focus), an observer in a computer lab might concentrate on how the instructor responds to students' questions (that is, interactive problem-solving focus). For the purposes of this chapter, I have tried to isolate those consulting issues that are most pertinent to a specific classroom environment. Nevertheless, given the complexity and dynamic nature of instruction, the same issues may also surface in other instructional settings.

The goal of this chapter is twofold: (1) to introduce instructional consultants to issues that arise when working with clients (that is, instructors and teaching assistants) who teach in large lecture classes, laboratory classes, activity classes, and tutorial classes; and (2) to offer instructional consultants strategies to respond to these instructional settings. In short, the chapter examines the implications of various teaching environments for the consultant and frames suggestions within the overall goal of active student learning and a collaborative, data-based approach to consulting (Nyquist & Wulff, 1988). Readers are invited to recall the classroom settings reflected in their institutions and how the issues addressed here apply to the needs of their clients. Questions, consultation tools, and resources are provided to facilitate practical applications.

The Initial Consultation

The initial personal contact with the client is crucial to establish a collaborative consulting relationship. As consultants, we need to acknowledge that clients bring with them certain beliefs about teaching and perceptions of their instructional skills, and we should view the initial consultation as a first opportunity for us to learn about these beliefs and perceptions. During our first meeting with the instructor we gather data about various dimensions of the instructor's teaching context. One such dimension is the classroom environment. We then use these data to determine what kinds of consultation approaches might best respond to the client's needs. For example, we might suggest to the instructor to observe her/his presentation skills or provide a videotaped account of the instructor's use of questioning.

I find that the kinds of questions the instructor and I discuss in the initial consultation phase directly influence our shared understanding of a given classroom environment. The following list of questions is structured along elements of the physical environment, the social environment, and the goal of active student learning. These questions are intended to help both the client and the consultant diagnose the classroom environment and to encourage the client to reflect upon the teaching environment.

Physical Environment

- What is the classroom setting like?
- Is there anything distinctive about the instructional setting that might influence student learning?
- Is the classroom large or small?
- How is the teaching space designed and arranged?
- What kinds of media are available?

- Is there adequate space to allow for interactive learning activities?
- Does the classroom setting pose challenges for the implementation of instructional activities?
- Are the chairs bolted to the floor or movable?

Social Environment

- What are the students' personal and academic backgrounds?
- Are they freshmen or seniors? Are they majors or non-majors? Are they transfer students?
- What is the instructor's background?
- What does the instructor bring to the course?
- How does the instructor perceive her/his role? As content expert? As facilitator? As mentor?
- What kind of classroom atmosphere will help students meet the proposed learning objectives?
- Is the classroom environment collaborative? Is it individualized?

Active Student Learning

- What are the learning objectives?
- What class activities have been planned to meet the students' learning goals?
- How are learning activities sequenced?
- What does the instructor expect the students to be doing in class?
- What does the instructor expect students to be able to do as a result of the course?
- What kinds of skills does the course focus on? Acquisition of factual knowledge? Acquisition of physical skills?

Any of these questions regarding the classroom environment can be used to help identify the nature and progress of an instructional consultation. I find that my interpersonal communication skills and listening skills are crucial in establishing a collaborative consulting relationship with the client, especially during this initial phase.

The following section describes four classroom environments (that is, large lecture classes, laboratory classes, activity classes, and one-to-one instruction) and raises some instructional concerns related to these settings. In addition, responses to these instructional concerns are offered, and implications for selecting consultation services are discussed. In an effort to address multiple consultation services (for example, videotaping, classroom observation, formative midterm student feedback), these services are distributed among the four classroom environments. For instance, videotaping is mentioned in the laboratory class setting but may also apply to the other three classroom environments.

Large Lecture Classes

This discussion refers to classes with over 75 students and small discussion sections taught by teaching assistants.

Most large classes serve as an introduction to further work in a specific discipline. Their main function may be described as helping first and second year students acquire basic knowledge in a field. The lecture format can be an effective way to present facts, to show relationships, to provide emphasis, and to develop ideas and concepts. Lecture formats seem to be most common at large research institutions, and in courses in the humanities, social sciences, physical sciences, and engineering. Discussion sections, also referred to as quiz sections, are linked to these large lecture classes and taught by teaching assistants (TAs). These classes are smaller in size (that is, about 30 students) and thus give students opportunities to interact more actively or in a different way with the course material. TAs are largely responsible for clarifying, reviewing, highlighting, and elaborating material introduced in the lecture class.

Major Issues

To help an instructor identify questions or areas of concern about her/his teaching of a large class, I often begin by asking open-ended questions such as, "What area(s) of your large lecture instruction would you like feedback on?" or "What area(s) of your large lecture instruction do you have questions about?" One frequent answer to these questions centers on the nature of classroom interaction. As one instructor stated, "When I look at my 200 students, all I see are blank faces. It's hard for me to read them. I cannot tell whether they are interested in the subject or whether they have difficulties with it since they don't ask me any questions. When I try to get their feedback and ask a question, I don't get a response. What can I do?" For this instructor both the large physical space of the classroom and the large number of students seem to project an impersonal atmosphere that is not conducive to interactive classroom activities.

A second frequently mentioned issue addresses the link between the lecture class and the discussion sections—how the instructor and the TAs work together in a course. Most often this link is perceived unfavorably by both the students and the TAs. Some common student statements are, "How does what we're doing in the section relate to the lecture?" and "Why do we have to attend the section in addition to the lecture?" TAs' concerns are reflected in statements such as, "I'm not sure what my role in the discussion section is" and "I have no clear sense as to what the students should be able to do at the end of a class session."

Implications for Consultation Services

The selection of a consultation approach most often occurs during the initial consultation. The initial meeting marks the beginning of the data collection process and the beginning of helping the client better understand her/his teaching, the students, and the classroom setting. Depending on an instructor's focus or interest, a variety of consultation services are appropriate for the large lecture class. For instance, to respond to a client's concern about student participation in the large class I may start with a class visit to get a descriptive account of teaching behaviors, patterns, and classroom dynamics. I try to attend the lecture several times and sit in various parts of the room to get a sense of the students in the class, their learning, and overall classroom factors, such as noise level, use of media, level of student attentiveness, and student note taking skills. In general, I have found classroom observations in large classes to cause little anxiety for the client because I blend in with the student crowd.

In the observation debrief I frequently take on the role of a student in the class. This role helps personalize the learning environment and provides the client with a sense of how a student may perceive a particular lecture presentation. For example, I might say, "As a student in your class, I found it difficult to follow the slides that explained how oysters were grown commercially. From where I was sitting, I couldn't read the writing on the slides and the pictures were blurry. I also had trouble taking notes."

Another way to integrate the student perspective into the discussion about teaching is to gather improvement-oriented student feedback at midterm. For example, an instructor asked me to collect student feedback in the large lecture about how the course was going and what she could do differently to enhance student learning. The instructor was particularly interested in the students' perceptions of the lecture, but she realized that their learning experience in the sections filtered into their learning in the lecture. Based on the client's concerns, we employed small group instructional diagnosis, designing a feedback form that included a question about the section link. A copy of the feedback form and an outline of the feedback gathering process appear in Appendix A and B.

In order to gain a comprehensive picture of the relationship between the large lecture class and the discussion sections, I find it imperative to attend both the lecture and the sections. These observations help me understand how the instructor thinks about the content and how s/he conceptualizes the link between the two instructional settings. For instance, one instructor made the link explicit when he integrated examples from the section in his lecture and introduced a project that was to be continued in the section. Course materials, such as syllabus and assignments, provide another avenue for insight.

I have experienced the most effective consulting at times when both the instructor and the TAs participated in the consultation process, and we gathered data from a variety of sources (for example, student midterm feedback, TA perspective, instructor perspective, observations of lecture and sections). These data allowed us to create a more complete and thus richer description of the actual teaching and learning processes. To enhance the instructional effectiveness of the entire course we asked some of the following questions: What kind of learning do we want the students to experience in the course? How do the large lecture and the individual sections contribute to this learning experience? How do the lecture and the sections complement each other in terms of classroom activities, class materials, and content? How can we solidify and unify the students' understanding of the content?

Laboratory Classes

Laboratory classes are typically associated with the physical sciences, engineering, and computer science, but they also are a part of language courses and writing skills instruction. Laboratory settings tend to be student-centered as they require students' active participation in structured learning experiences. The purpose of the lab classes varies depending upon the academic discipline, the level of the course, and the students' academic backgrounds, but the main function is to link theoretical with technical or practical considerations.

For example, in the sciences (for example, chemistry, physics, geology) three instructional goals can be identified: (1) to sharpen analytical skills (for example, to design, conduct, and observe experiments); (2) to get concrete learning experiences (for example, to observe capillary action); and (3) to acquire lab techniques (for example, to perform a dissection). Students have the opportunity to become actively involved in a given discipline as the instructional setting allows for greater interaction among students and instructors. The laboratory instructor circulates among the students to answer questions and to help with difficulties in performing experiments, and generally to introduce students to the ways in which scientists think about or approach a problem.

Major Issues

Laboratory instructors frequently have asked how to help students solve problems and think critically. One client shared this instructional problem with me: "While the students are working independently on their experiments, I try to monitor their progress by circulating around the room. As I stop at each student's desk and see how that person is doing, I find that either the students are doing fine and have no questions about the experiment or they are struggling with the pure mechanics of the experiment. How can I ensure that the students can set up the experiment correctly, and how can I engage them in talking about the experiment itself?"

The instructor's questions about the laboratory setting reflected issues of classroom management and teacher-student interaction. The instructor and I approached answers to these questions by investigating the following aspects of laboratory instruction: instructor preparation (What can the instructor do to anticipate students' potential difficulties with an experiment?), instructor role (How would the instructor describe her/his role in the lab? Is it to respond to students questions? Is it to initiate student questions that reflect their thinking about the experiment?), student learning tasks (What are the students doing in the lab? What kinds of skills do the students need to complete these tasks?), student-to-student interaction (How is the students' experiential learning enhanced when working with other students?), and integration of instructional media (How can we use the overhead to highlight critical aspects of the experiment?).

Laboratory instructors often express surprise that two lab sections do not proceed identically. Several variables of dynamic classroom interaction account for the differences, such as student prior knowledge and student learning styles. Another surprise for instructors is when students in their labs obtain inexplicable results after an experiment. Novel situations in the classroom present valuable opportunities for the instructor to identify pedagogical issues. These issues may be related to the set up of an experiment, the explanation of an experiment, or student approaches to problem-solving. In addition, the occurrence of such novel situations helps clients anticipate potential trouble spots and, with the help of consultations, select approaches to classroom management to respond to them effectively.

Implications for Consultation Services

The physical setting of the lab creates multiple challenges for the consultant, especially when conducting a classroom observation. Room sizes vary. Several labs occasionally share the same room. Experimental equipment needs to be set up carefully. Student movement in the room must be accommodated. Safety procedures must be observed. To prepare for these challenges I gather this kind of information about the teaching environment, and I plan the most appropriate observation procedure with the client. For example, an instructor in an upper division lab in food science wanted to get feedback on her interactions with the students. During a discussion of the classroom setting we decided to conduct a series of observations in which I focused on two pairs of students for each observation and kept a verbatim record of their interactions with the instructor. Since this kind of observation was rather obtrusive, the instructor introduced me and the purpose of the observations to the students. These systematic observations identified specific communication patterns for the instructor. She learned that she spent more time talking about the food samples with majors than with non-majors.

Similar issues need to be considered when we use videorecording as a consultation tool.

Some of these considerations are:

- What issues motivate the videotaping? What does the client want to see on the tape? Is the focus on the instructor, on the students, on the classroom interaction?
- What instructional activities occur in the class?
- Does the physical classroom setting lend itself to videotaping? What are possible constraints? How might these constraints be circumvented?
- What are logistical issues to remember? Who may be assisting me with the taping? Do I use a stationary camera or a camcorder? Does the microphone pick up both the instructor and the students?
- How is the tape ultimately going to be used? For an individual consultation? For departmental TA training activities? As part of the general TA orientation? What are ramifications of potential uses for obtaining participant consent?

Frequently instructors seek insights into whether the students are finding the lab course worthwhile. One way to learn about the students' experiences and perceptions is to conduct a formative student interview (for example, Small Group Instructional Diagnosis) at midterm. The Small Group Instructional Diagnosis is a process that uses class interviews with students to generally improve class instruction and enhance student learning. Consequently, as a consultant, I work directly with the instructor and the students in the class. On a given day, I meet with the students and, in the absence of the instructor, obtain the student feedback data. In small groups the students respond to the following questions: What helps you learn in this class? What recommendations for change do you have? How could these changes be made? Following the group work, I ask students to report to the entire class and make sure I clearly understand the information being reported. I then share the information with the instructor and help her/him develop a teaching improvement process responsive to the student data (see Appendix A and B and Chapter 15).

In gathering the student feedback I have found it critical to know the specific terminology for concepts, equipment, and supplies used in a specific laboratory setting. In preparation for the midterm interview of a computer science lab setting, I asked the client what specific terminology was important to know. She mentioned that the students might talk about types of computer packages (for example, generic package, package day set), computer procedures (for example, generic swamp), test programs, as well as types of libraries. When I was gathering the student feedback in class, a group of students indicated that they found the generic swamp confusing. Because the lab instructor had mentioned the term to me before, I was able to probe and help students articulate the cause of their confusion.

Activity Classes

Activity classes have traditionally been associated with professional schools and a variety of disciplines such as art, dance, drama, music, physical education, foreign languages, archeology, biology, geology, forestry and fisheries. These instructional environments are distinctive because they combine an emphasis on specific skills with knowledge and hands-on-practice. The experience-based activities and assignments in the classes (for example, field trips, role-plays, simulations, community service learning) add a creative learning twist to the traditional classroom setting. Field trips most commonly take students to a specific site and expose them to learning experiences not available in lecture presentations, seminars or lab exercises. Field trips are uniquely linked to specific courses and their objectives and can vary from a visit to a manufacturing plant for airplanes to a week-long trip on a sailing vessel to chart the migration of salmon.

Another variant of the field trip is the community service learning component in a course. For instance, the Carlson Leadership and Public Service Office at the University of Washington assists instructors who want to integrate academic study with public service. Such courses offer students opportunities to apply what they have learned in a course to the mission of community service agencies and to experience first hand what it is like to be an active member of society. One instructor who teaches a course on the geography of Latin America asks students to volunteer at an organization that serves Latin American people or to work with an organization for low income people who experience challenges that parallel those in Latin America. The students volunteer for 2-3 hours per week and reflect upon that experience in oral and written reports.

Major Issues

A foreign language class is a unique learning environment insofar as the method for teaching a particular language largely determines the nature of the classroom environment. For example, instructors in one department may speak only the target language with the students during class as well as during office hours. Instructors in another department may use primarily the target language but also refer to the students' first language when explaining grammatical structures or introducing assignments. Instructors in this setting often wonder how much English they should use in their instruction and whether they should translate for the students. Other instructional concerns center on the students' ability to communicate effectively in a given language. The students know the syntax and vocabulary of the target language, but they cannot use this knowledge to communicate effectively in the target language.

Instructors of other types of activity classes often express concern about students' skill levels, the practice of skills and their assessment. Specifically, clients talk to me about how to model specific skills, how to provide students with constructive feedback on these skills, how to monitor students' progress and how to evaluate students' performance in accordance with specific course goals. In one consultation case, a music instructor was concerned about how to make the course more student-centered. He wanted to help students improve their conducting skills by observing each other's performance and make these observations an integral part of the overall evaluation. He identified the specific skills of effective conducting such as hand movements and incorporated them in a handout that guided students through the observations.

Implications for Consultation Services

The consultation issues raised in foreign language classes demonstrate the challenge presented when we consult with clients from disciplines outside our area of expertise. As consultants we may not understand the language that is taught and spoken in class. This difficulty cannot as easily be overcome as the use of jargon could in the computer class mentioned earlier. The question remains: What skills and resources do we as consultants need to draw on when working with instructors in foreign language environments?

Students and instructors in these disciplines are crucial resources for us. As we establish relationships with them, we gain a deeper understanding of the language teaching context. This knowledge of the context proves essential in helping us select and provide appropriate consultation services. We can establish such discipline-based links in a variety of forms: ongoing conversations with members of a given discipline, familiarity with print and video resources in activity classroom environments, conducting classroom observations, and networking with other instructional consultants.

A first year instructor asked me how she could learn more about how French classes were taught on campus prior to her own teaching of French. I suggested she approach two of her colleagues in her department and ask them whether she could observe their classes periodically and talk to them about the observations afterward. In her observations she noticed that French was used exclusively in the classroom and that the students were practicing the language in group activities and role-playing exercises. When she talked to her colleagues about her observations, she learned that the classroom activities had been planned carefully to decrease student anxiety and to create an interactive learning environment. These activities helped the client discover different teaching approaches and familiarized her with the students' needs and concerns pertinent to language learning. When the client started to teach her own class, she in turn invited colleagues to observe her teaching and to share their responses. This example illustrates that both consultants and clients benefit from drawing upon person and print resources in their respective disciplines.

Instructors often ask me to observe their classes to get feedback on how the course objectives relate to the actual classroom activities. Some students learned how to form the past tense of regular verbs in German, for example. The instructor wanted students to practice the past tense by talking to another person about their spring break. After time spent working in pairs, students volunteered to role-play their dialogue in front of the class. The instructor wanted to know whether the dyads were an effective means by which to practice the past tense, and whether they prepared the students for the role-play.

To address the client's question, I used a diagnostic worksheet for the language classroom (Appendix C). Before the observation the instructor and I completed the

items on the worksheet that refer to linguistic objectives, communicative objectives, beliefs about the nature of language learning and the nature of teaching. During the observation I recorded the classroom activities and listened in as the pairs were preparing for the role-play. I integrated both data sources (that is, worksheet and observation) to help guide our discussion during the post-observation meeting. We discussed whether or not the dyad/roleplay allowed students to practice the past tense, whether or not the students worked effectively in the pairs, and whether or not they had the linguistic foundation to work on the tasks.

Instructors in activity classes often provide personal demonstrations and examples. Art instructors show students their own paintings and demonstrate specific techniques. Physical education instructors demonstrate how to shoot free throws and how to hold a tennis racket. Because of this focus on skills development, instructors are interested in whether or not they are effective in demonstrating desirable techniques, as well as how they correct students' mistakes and how they encourage student improvement.

I have found video technology effective in providing instructors with that kind of feedback, because it preserves an instructional event for subsequent viewing. Instructors can view the tape with the consultant, stop and pause to discuss a certain segment or replay the segment to look at particularly insightful teaching situations. A music instructor used video to focus on how she demonstrated particular conducting skills to the students, and how she corrected their performance. Viewing the videotaped instruction reassured the client of her effective skill demonstration. Regarding her feedback on student performance, the instructor noticed that she corrected almost every student error and deficiency but rarely pointed out improvement. The video alerted the client to the relationship between the nature of instructional feedback and student learning. She decided to monitor her feedback behaviors by identifying positive aspects of students' performance.

One-to-One Instruction

One-to-one instruction is probably the most personalized instructional environment because it provides opportunities for students and instructor to get to know each other outside the classroom. Office hours and tutorials supplement regular classroom instruction and offer students opportunities to explore the content in more detail. Office hours are made available on a regular basis, by appointment, or on a drop-in basis such as in clinical settings.

The independent study, another one-to-one setting,

promotes self-directed student learning. It introduces the student to research in a given discipline under the guidance of an instructor. The projects include an investigation of an assortment of themes, problems, issues, and questions, and incorporate relevant materials and resources into a presentation of results. For many undergraduate students this environment affects their career choice or their choice of an academic major because it most often serves as their first introduction to work in academia.

Major Issues

Many instructors are disappointed that only a small number of students take advantage of office hours. One instructor said, "I have scheduled my office hours at a time that fits most students' schedules, but only two students have come so far. I keep stressing the importance of office hours in class and encourage students to come and see me. I don't seem to get any response. What else can I do?" One client responded to this concern by requiring short writing assignments in her class that asked students to make an argument for a particular business choice. She scheduled certain office hour times for groups of students to discuss their arguments. Because the students came in groups, they got to know some of their peers, felt more comfortable about meeting with the instructor, and continued their interaction in class.

A second instructor concern relates to student perceptions of this instructional setting. Students who do come to office hours perceive them as a place to get answers to their questions. But quite often they might not know how to articulate their difficulties. This inability of students causes worry for instructors. Questions such as, "How can I help you? What would you like to discuss?" become difficult starting points for both parties and instructor questioning skills become more crucial. In such situations clients have found it helpful to start with questions that diagnose students' prior knowledge and to continue by engaging them in active problem solving rather than giving answers to questions. A student may start the office hour by saying, "I don't understand the limit of a function." The instructor may reply, "Let's go back to the term function. How can we define a function? Given that definition, how do we define the limit of a function? Let's look at an example."

Student anxiety also causes concern for instructors in independent studies. Instructors worry that the students are reluctant to ask for guidance for fear of being viewed as less competent. An instructor may wish to structure an independent study assignment such that it requires regularly scheduled meetings with the student.

Implications for Consultation Services

The intimate instructional setting of office hours places unique demands on the consultant. What kind of consultation approach may help collect appropriate data for the client? How can the client receive feedback about her instructional behaviors during office hours? Observations may be perceived as intrusive, and the observer's presence might impact the learning environment. An alternate approach is to have the instructor audiotape the instructional discourse during office hours. The consultant listens to the recording and transcribes the interaction or pieces of it, forming the basis for the instructional consultation. I do admit that the transcription can be fairly time-consuming; nevertheless, I have found it to be an extremely helpful consultation tool. Systematic audiotaping of office hour discourse allows both me and the client to describe patterns of communication and thought processes. In addition, we use the transcript to identify areas of instructional change and their impact upon student learning. Similarly, the instructor can use a journal to record thoughts and impressions at the end of each office hour.

In addition to the written account, the instructor can use a series of questions to reflect upon interactions with the students: What worked well for me in today's office hour? Why? Did it also work well for the student? What could I have done differently? Why? How would this change impact upon student learning? What questions still remain?

You might be working at an institution that does not offer a standardized student feedback form for the one-to-one classroom environment. I have selected items to refer to when helping instructors design such a feedback form (see Davis, 1988 for additional suggestions).

During office hours. . .

- the instructor seemed aware of my needs as a student;
- the instructor seemed concerned about whether I understood the material;
- the instructor knew me by name;
- the instructor presented different approaches to explain concepts;
- the instructor took time to clarify my questions;
- the instructor enhanced my understanding of the content; the instructor raised my interest in the subject matter;
- the instructor helped me become more competent in the subject area;
- the instructor gave me time to ask questions.

Summary of Instructional Consultation Skills

The examples interspersed throughout this chapter highlight the repertoire of consultant skills—feedback skills, questioning and discussion skills and perspective-taking skills—that contribute to a rewarding instructional consultation. Besides these skills, the following sets of skills seem to be most closely related to the four classroom settings.

Classroom Research Skills

As consultants, we draw upon and use classroom research skills throughout the entire consultation process with a client. We collect classroom data for an instructor when we conduct an initial interview, we look at quantitative student feedback, or we observe the actual teaching situation. We help the instructor to analyze the data when we identify categories, trends, or themes in the data. In large classes, instructor presentation of material may emerge as a theme. In small seminar classes, student involvement may appear as an instructional issue. We interpret the data when we provide suggestions or recommendations to the instructor. These suggestions may be based on the instructor's objectives or on the consultant's experience and knowledge of motivational theory. We translate the data when we convert the results into specific classroom behaviors or strategies for change. The instructor and the consultant may identify lack of student participation as an issue. The consultant may suggest the use of small groups to enhance student involvement, and the client may implement this pedagogical approach. Assisted by the consultant, the instructor is able to introduce a small-group activity to the students in the next class period. (See Nyquist & Wulff, 1988.)

Interpersonal Communication Skills

Although both client and consultant work with objective classroom data, teaching still remains a personal activity for the instructor. A consultant's listening skills, conflict-resolution skills, and positive nonverbal and verbal reinforcement skills are crucial to establish and maintain a relationship of trust and collaboration with the client. You may work with clients who are assigned to teach a given course in their department that is outside their area of academic training. You may need to listen, and be very supportive before you actually visit the client's classroom.

Knowledge and Utilization of Print and People Resources

This skill is crucial when we consult with clients from disciplines outside our area of expertise. Literature on instructional development, on teaching and learning, as well as that appearing in discipline-specific journals (for example, *Journal of College Science Teaching, Learning and the Law*) help us to match our consultation approaches with specific instructional situations and with clients' needs (see the end of the chapter for some suggested resources). Clients sometimes find it intimidating when a consultant confronts them with research findings. You might say, "One thing we know about student learning is that students tend to remember content better when they have opportunities in class to talk about it. How might we think about integrating this approach to student learning in your classroom?" Conversation with instructors, fellow consultants, and colleagues in the Professional and Organizational Development Network in Higher Education (POD) either in person, by phone, or via electronic mail is another method for consultants to learn about instructional settings, to share their experience and expertise, as well as to troubleshoot.

Implications for Ongoing Professional Development

How can we help novice consultants gain and practice these consultation skills? How can we diversify and refine our own repertoire of consultation skills? The chapter suggests two techniques: videotaped classroom examples and actual classroom visits.

Videotaped Classroom Examples

Viewing video examples of teaching in various classroom environments adds an element of authenticity to the training of consultants. Not only do these tapes introduce the consultants to teaching in a particular setting but they also are rich data sources for practicing consultation tools. A taped record of an anthropology lab session studying bones may be used in a session focusing on how to enhance a consultant's observation skills. We may gather data about the course through syllabi and other course materials, then proceed to view the tape and record our observations. We may then prepare for a consultation with the client and roleplay the actual consultation. See Appendix D for a worksheet I have used to record classroom interactions in various instructional settings and to trace elements of effective teaching across these settings.

Classroom Visits

Video captures the dynamics of classroom events. However, it limits the viewer's experience of that event and presents only what the camera sees. We may not see the students' reactions to an instructor's joke or whether all the students can see the replica of a human thigh bone on the table. Actual classroom visits permit more detailed experiences. They may be arranged by an experienced consultant who knows a client who wants to be observed. An experienced consultant may team up with a novice consultant to conduct this observation. Among the issues that consultants need to consider are: What to focus on during the observation, how to take notes, and what to do when the pace is too fast to follow. Such questions may be addressed in a consultant meeting where consultants share their notes, talk about their notetaking techniques, and report on the data they gathered in class. This activity also helps socialize new consultants into their roles and supports collegiality.

Summary

In this chapter I have addressed some of the major consultation issues that need to be considered when consulting with instructors who teach in a variety of classroom environments. The characteristics of four instructional settings are described, as well as the concerns about teaching that emerge in these settings. In addition, responses to these teaching concerns are offered and approaches for the consultant are provided. With examples, cases, and lists of questions, I have illustrated how we can employ various consultation methods to help an instructor describe, assess, and improve the classroom environment and its influence on student learning. Existing research does not adequately inform our instructional consulting. Experience does. I hope that the experiences I have shared may be of value to instructors on your campus.

References

Davis, B. G. (1988). *Sourcebook for evaluating teaching*. Berkeley, CA: Office of Educational Development.

Nyquist, J., & Wulff, D. (1988). Consultation using a research perspective. In E. Wadsworth (Ed.), *A handbook for new practitioners* (pp. 81-88). Stillwater, OK: New Forums Press.

Additional Readings

Brookfield, S. (1990). Lecturing creatively. In S. Brookfield, *The skillful teacher* (pp. 71-87). San Francisco: Jossey-Bass.

Cashin, W., & Clegg, V. (1993). Periodicals related to college teaching. *Idea Paper No. 28*. Kansas State University: Center for Faculty Evaluation and Development.

Christensen, C., Garvin, D., & Sweet, A. (Eds.). (1991). *Education for judgment: The artistry of discussion leadership*. Boston, MA: Harvard Business School Press.

Coles, R. (1989). Learning by doing through public service. *Change, 21*, 18-29.

Kirschner, P., & Meester, M. (1988). The laboratory in higher science education: Problems, premises and objectives. *Higher Education, 17*, 81-98.

Meyers, C., & Jones, T. (1993). *Promoting active learning*. San Francisco: Jossey-Bass.

Nunan, D. (1990). Action research in the language classroom. In J. Richards & D. Nunan (Eds.), *Second language teacher education*. New York: Cambridge University Press.

Pierleoni, R. (1988). Teaching in clinical settings. In E. Wadsworth (Ed.), *A handbook for new practitioners* (pp. 115-120). Stillwater, OK: New Forums Press.

Quigley, B., & Nyquist, J. (1992). Using video technology to provide feedback to students in performance courses. *Communication Education, 41*(3), 324-336.

Segerstrale, U. (1984). The multifaceted role of the section leader. In M. Gullette (Ed.), *The art and craft of teaching* (2nd ed.) (pp. 49-69). Cambridge, MA: Harvard University Press.

Weimer, M. (Ed.). (1987). Teaching large classes well. *New Directions for Teaching and Learning*, no. 32.

Appendix A

Small Groups Instructional Diagnosis
Course Name and Number
Date-Time

Number of Participants in Group_____

I. List the major strengths in this course. (What is the faculty doing that helps you learn the course or content?) Please explain briefly or give an example for each strength.

Strengths	Explanation/Example
1.	
2.	
3.	
4.	

II. List the changes that could be made in the course to assist you in learning the course content. Please explain how suggested changes could be made.

Changes	Ways to make changes
1.	
2.	
3.	
4.	

III. Other Comments:

In addition to other issues, please consider how the lecture and the quiz section fit together.

Center for Instructional Development & Research
109 Parrington Hall, DC-07
University of Washington
Seattle, WA 98195
(206) 543-6588
Reprinted with permission.

Appendix B

Small Group Instructional Diagnosis
(The SGID process has been adapted for the large lecture setting as follows.)

Gathering Feedback (10 minutes)

    Form groups of 5 to 6 students

    Choose a recorder to write down your group's responses

    Choose a spokesperson to represent your group in a discussion following small group work

    Discuss the questions on the feedback sheet

        Work for group consensus

        Be as specific as possible

        Include a consideration of how lecture and section fit together

Summarizing Feedback (20-25) minutes

    Spokesperson come to front of class to discuss feedback with interviewer (that is, consultant)

Follow Up

    Interviewer (consultant meets with instructor to review feedback report)

    Instructor acknowledges feedback to students

Appendix C

1. What are the linguistic goals of the lesson? List the lesson's linguistic objectives.

2. What are the functional/communicative goals of the lesson? List the lesson's functional/communicative objectives.

3. What are the major steps in the lesson?

4. What are the instructor's major beliefs about the nature of language?

5. What are the instructor's major beliefs about the nature of learning a language?

6. What are the instructor's major beliefs about language teaching?

7. What groupings of learners were used during the lesson? How much time was devoted to each instructional activity? (Distinguis among individual work, pair work, small group work and whole class activities.)

(Adapted from Nunan, 1990)

Reprinted with permission.

Appendix D

Worksheet to Record Classroom Interaction

Type of Classroom Settings: _____

Dimensions of Teaching Effectiveness	Teacher Activity	Student Activity	Questions/Issues
Stimulation			
Clarity			
Knowledge			
Organization			
Enthusiasm			
Other:			

24. *Identifying and Assessing Your Consultation Style*

Laura L. B. Border

Discussions of consultation style in the research literature tend to describe rather than analyze what consultants and clients are doing. Actually analyzing what consultants do during a consultation reveals several identifiable consultant behaviors. Consultants begin by creating a safe environment for the teacher to work in. Then, they listen to and observe the client. They give feedback and provide information. Finally, they give direction or guidance and help the teacher with a plan for improvement. During the consultation, clients adjust to the environment; talk, listen and observe; accept or dispute feedback from the consultant; choose to follow or reject the consultant's direction; and make a plan for improvement.

In this chapter, I focus on two aspects of consultant behavior: how consultants give feedback and how they guide or provide direction to their clients. I create a typology of four consultant styles and discuss the subsequent effects on the client. Consultants who are aware of these four broad areas can analyze their own personal style and choose to use elements from each quadrant when necessary and appropriate. In this way they can manage personal style in order to experience more productive interactions with clients and foster enduring teacher improvement.

Since the goal of a consultation is to improve the teacher's performance, feedback is an essential part of a consultation. The feedback that consultants give during a consultation usually falls along a continuum that goes from purely descriptive to ascriptive. Descriptive feedback tends to reflect the surface of what is happening. Ascriptive feedback reflects what is happening and also ascribes or attributes meaning to the teacher's behavior. Guidance or direction may be of a *laissez-faire* or a prescriptive type. The continua of descriptive to ascriptive feedback and *laissez-faire* to prescriptive guidance are used as axes that create four quadrants to describe consultant style. The four consultant styles created by the inter-

section of these axes are the Supporter, the Collector, the Evaluator, and the Facilitator as indicated in Figure 1.

Consultant Feedback Style

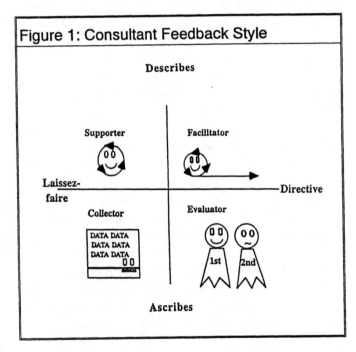

Figure 1: Consultant Feedback Style

The **vertical axis** represents a consultant feedback continuum that shows how the consultant provides feedback. The top of the axis represents pure descriptive feedback about teacher behaviors and about what is happening in the classroom. Descriptive feedback in this essay refers to feedback that mirrors what is happening in the classroom. For example, the teacher might say, "I was feeling pretty nervous," and the consultant might respond "You looked pretty nervous." The feedback is probably accurate. It is supportive in that it recognizes and reaffirms the teacher's perceptions. Supportive feedback is essential and creates a safe environment. This kind of descriptive feedback tends to be accepted by the teacher. However, if the consultant remains at the purely descriptive level of providing feedback, the consultation process leads to frustration for both the consultant and client, because no new perceptions are contributed.

The bottom of the axis represents feedback that ascribes or attributes meaning to teacher behaviors and what is happening in the classroom. Feedback that ascribes meaning to teacher behaviors attempts to go below the surface meaning. For example, if the teacher says "I was feeling nervous," the consultant might respond, "You looked nervous, were you feeling afraid (evaluated, unprepared, tired)?" By attributing meaning to the behavior, ascriptive feedback encourages the teacher to explore, examine, or defend the meaning of the behavior. Thus, the consultation process tends to provide information to both the consultant and the teacher.

The **horizontal axis** represents the direction that the consultant's feedback takes. From left to right the continuum goes from a *laissez-faire* avoidance of direction to a deliberate and directive form of intervention. A *laissez-faire* style consultant who chooses not to provide direction may create a supportive environment. However, the lack of guidance in the form of new information tends to create a feeling that neither the consultant or teacher know what to do to improve the teacher's performance.

Directive feedback is intended to guide the teacher toward improvement. When a consultant provides directive feedback, the teacher sees options or possibilities that go beyond what he or she may have been able to come up with alone. Directive feedback encompasses giving suggestions, providing solutions, presenting a bibliography, or modeling alternative teaching behaviors.

This paradigm allows us to isolate and delineate four common styles of consultation and to determine the extent of their usefulness. If we maintain the same axes and quadrants as in Figure 1, we can also postulate the teacher's response to the four consultant styles.

Teacher's Response To Consultant's Style

A further clarification of the typology demonstrates which aspects of each quadrant are useful and which are limited. In the upper left quadrant we find the consultant as **Supporter**. The axes portray the Supporter as a consultant who provides an atmosphere that is characterized by descriptive feedback, while at the same time avoiding direct intervention in the teacher's choice of behavior. The Supporter's style is identifiable by its circularity. If you watch a Supporter conduct a session, you quickly realize that although the consultation appears congenial and

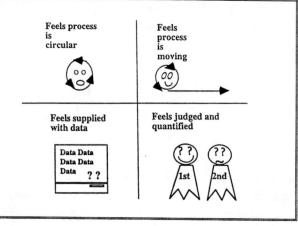

Figure 2: Teacher's Response to Consultant's Style

seems to be moving, the feedback process is in actuality circular.

Teacher: *I use the advance organizer to clarify my lecture.*

Supporter: *The advance organizer you wrote on the chalkboard before class began was clear.*

As a consultant, the Supporter tends to provide a safe environment. The client experiences a feeling of positive support. This experience is essential to the completion of a successful videotape consultation. However, if the Supporter remains at a purely descriptive and supportive level, the extent of his or her helpfulness is limited. The feedback that is provided to the client feels good, but leads nowhere because it tends to simply paraphrase what the client has expressed. The teacher learns nothing new about his/her teaching. The Supporter who doesn't know how to escape from the circle becomes frustrated. The skilled consultant who knows how to build a supportive environment, provide supportive feedback, and foster movement in the client avoids circular feedback.

In the lower left quadrant we find the consultant as **Collector**. The axes allow us to portray the Collector as an instructional consultant who collects and presents data to the teacher and attributes meaning to the data presented, while at the same time avoiding directive intervention in the teacher's plan for improvement.

Collector: *You wrote a helpful advance organizer on the chalkboard before class began. Three students in the back were chatting, didn't write it down, and didn't follow the lecture.*

Teacher: *Which three students do you mean? Everyone seemed to be following the lecture.*

With the Collector, the teacher is likely to feel as though classroom behavior is being watched, examined, and quantified. When data is presented to the teacher it may be perceived of only as the consultant's perception. The information may be seen as new, but if the process goes no further, integration of the data into the teacher's daily task is unlikely to take place. In the consultation process, the client may accept or reject the consultant's feedback, but in either case the client experiences the consultant as judging both the teacher's and student's classroom performance. The extent of the Collector's helpfulness is dependent upon the consultant's skill at giving feedback and on the teacher's receptivity to receiving that feedback. If the teacher has requested certain information, the teacher may be able to take the data and use it. If not, the Collector's data may be discarded.

In the lower right quadrant we see the consultant as **Evaluator**. The axes inform us that the Evaluator attributes meaning to the teacher's performance, while pointing the teacher in a prescribed direction for teacher improvement.

Evaluator: *I think the advance organizer you wrote on the chalkboard before class began was clear. It is a technique a lot of good teachers use. It is helpful to students. However, yours was too long. It would be better to limit it to three items rather than eight, so you and the students can focus on what is essential.*

Teacher: *Well, which ones did you think were not essential? I think they all are!*

An inexperienced Evaluator is likely to compare the teacher with an idealized "great teacher." One danger of this particular type of consultation is that the teacher is very likely to experience the Evaluator as a person who has the power to judge performance. If this occurs, the teacher is likely to fall into the trap of asking "Did I do a good job?" or is likely to become self-critical and think "Oh, no. You don't think I'm a good teacher, so I must not be."

In the upper right quadrant, the consultant is viewed as a **Facilitator**. The Facilitator acts as a change agent by describing teacher performance and providing guidance and direction for change.

Facilitator: *When you wrote the advance organizer on the chalkboard before class began, students began copying it down. They were still scrambling to get all eight points down when you began your introduction. Which of the eight points do you think/feel/believe are really essential? Would it be appropriate to reduce the number to three or four so students wouldn't have to scramble, yet could follow your lecture?*

Teacher: *I noticed they were copying it. That's why I get to class early. But I guess eight points is a bit much. I*

could really subsume 2 and 3 under number 1; 5 and 6 under 4, and combine 7 & 8 to create three main headings.

The Facilitator offers feedback that moves toward teacher improvement. In the most positive form, the Facilitator focuses on what the teacher has requested or on what is immediately observable in the classroom. The Facilitator provides support by focusing on what the teacher thinks, what the teacher wants to accomplish, and what the teacher plans to do to improve. The teacher experiences the consultation process as moving toward a directed outcome.

Usefulness of Style

The typology of consultant style described above allows us to identify and observe four different aspects of consultant style. The typology is not meant to be prescriptive, but rather to elucidate areas of consultation that we may not normally examine. Each of us needs to monitor which aspects we should be incorporating into a specific consultation session. Each of the quadrants can have a positive or negative valence. A holistic consultation with a teacher incorporates different combinations of the four quadrants. For example, it is essential that a consultant be supportive, but support is not enough even if it is warm and cozy. Support must be accompanied by appropriate feedback and direction.

Likewise, data alone is not sufficient, especially if the data was not requested or if the teacher doesn't know what to do with the data. A skilled consultant carefully considers the place for, the timing of, and the pertinence of data that is collected and limits feedback to data that will help the teacher move toward the desired goal for improvement.

Depending upon the consultant's view of consultation, evaluation may or may not belong in the consultation process. An experienced consultant is more likely to focus on a realistic view of the teacher's own work and what can be done to improve it. The goal of the consultation should be to encourage the teacher to judge his/her own performance and determine how he/she would like to improve it. Evaluation by an outside observer should be left to the teacher's supervisor.

And finally, it is obvious that change springs from a supportive environment, is built on solid data, is based on an assessment of important factors, and includes clear direction and a plan for improvement. The most effective consultation style is holistic in that it draws appropriately from all four quadrants. Successful consultants are always conscious of the appropriateness of their feedback and guidance with each teacher.

Assessing the Consultant's Style

You may be wondering which quadrants describe your style. This section details how to use consultant self-assessment or teacher assessment of the consultant to determine and evaluate one's own style. Two forms of self-assessment are helpful. The first is an immediate assessment of how the consultant experienced the consultation. This assessment can be done as soon as the consultation is over. It can help the consultant identify strengths and weaknesses, while also allowing him/her to identify and record personal questions and goals. An immediate self-assessment form is attached. (Appendix A)

The most effective method of doing a self-assessment of consultation style and performance is to videotape several consultation sessions and evaluate them according to the guidelines the consultant chooses. If we were to create an assessment form based on the consultant styles and assumptions described above, the consultant could then watch the videotape and chart his/her consultation behaviors, interactions, data supplied, and overall impression. (Appendix A can easily be adapted to use in reviewing videotapes.)

As always, we consultants can be kept honest by having our clients assess our performance. This assessment could be done just after the consultation or at a later date. The assessment could be written or oral. Questions would address the issues discussed above, but would have the added dimension of addressing what the teacher got out of the consultation and whether the consultation resulted in improved teacher performance. A sample teacher form for assessing consultant performance is attached as Appendix B.

Appendix A

Consultant's Name_____   Consultation with_____
                                                              Teacher's Name

Date_____

The Consultant's Self-Assessment Form

Please circle the number that indicates your performance level in your consultation with the teacher. If you circle (1), you demonstrated proficiency in this skill during the consultation. If you circle (2), you seemed hesitant to use this skill in the consultation. If you circle (3), you used the skill in the consultation, but felt a lack of skill in this area.

		Felt Proficient	Felt Hesitant	Felt lack of skill
1.	Rapport building	1	2	3
2.	Data collection	1	2	3
3.	Giving feedback	1	2	3
4.	Ability to follow teacher	1	2	3
5.	Skill at intervention	1	2	3
6.	Skill in helping teacher generate options/ possibilities	1	2	3

7. I feel I was most successful at _____
   _____

8. I feel the teacher made progress in _____
   _____

9. I would like to improve my consultation skills in _____
   _____

10. My goal as a consultant is to _____
    _____

Appendix B

Consultant's Name _____

Date _____(month/year)

Teacher's Anonymous Assessment of the Videotape Consultant's Performance

Please circle the number that indicates your videotape consultant's performance level. If you circle (1), he/she demonstrated proficiency in this skill during the consultation. If you circle (2), he/she seemed hesitant to use this skill in the consultation. If you circle (3), he/she used the skill in the consultation, but feel that he/she showed a lack of skill in this area. If you circle (4), this aspect of videotape consultation was not used in your consultation.

		Showed proficiency	Showed hesitancy	Showed lack of skill	Not applicable
1.	Rapport Building	1	2	3	4
2.	Data collection	1	2	3	4
3.	Presentation of Feedback	1	2	3	4
4.	Ability to follow teacher	1	2	3	4
5.	Skill at intervention	1	2	3	4
6.	Skill in helping teacher generate options/ possibilities	1	2	3	4

7. I feel/think my videotape consultant was most successful at

_____

_____

8. I feel/think the videotape consultant should work on

_____

_____

9. Because of the videotape consultant, I feel/think I made progress in

_____

_____

10. I would/would not (please cross out inappropriate response) like to go through another videotape consultation with this consultant, because

_____

_____

25. *Developmental Stages of an Educational Consultant: Theoretical Perspective*

Richard Tiberius, Jane Tipping, and Ronald Smith

*A*n understanding of stages of development can be extremely valuable to the process of developing expertise or of helping someone else develop expertise. Specifically, an understanding of the stages of our development can help us understand the nature of the problems we deal with as well as the process of acquiring the skills to deal with these problems. In this paper we use the Dreyfus and Dreyfus (1986) model of development of expertise to help us understand and design experiences that prepare educational consultants.

Educational Consultants Deal with Unstructured Problems

We must be more specific about the kind of problems that educational consultants face. Like nurses, physicians and managers, educational consultants are frequently confronted with unstructured problems. Unstructured problems are characterized by an unlimited number of facts, features, and situations whose relationship to one another is not clearly known. The skills necessary to address unstructured problems are different from the mathematical and logical skills required to solve structured problems such as traffic control, petroleum blending, or truck routing (Dreyfus & Dreyfus, 1986).

Skills in Unstructured Problem Areas Are Acquired by Experience

One of the central assumptions of the Dreyfus and Dreyfus (1986) model is that expertise in addressing unstructured problems is achieved only after considerable experience coping with real situations and problems. In contrast, long experience with concrete situations is not necessary when applying logical and mathematical skills to solve structured problems.

Skills in Unstructured Problem Areas Are Acquired in Stages

Another central assumption of the Dreyfus and Dreyfus (1986) model is that the skills of addressing unstructured problems are acquired in stages. They outline five stages in the development of the skills of the practitioner: novice, advanced beginner, competent, proficient, and expert (see Table 1).

The **novice** learns to recognize certain facts and features of a situation and to acquire rules to guide actions. These facts and features, as well as the rules, are "context free" in the sense that they are applied by the novice no matter what else is happening. The novice does not take context into consideration and does not exercise judgment. For example, the novice automobile driver learns to judge the proper distance to follow the car ahead by some rule such as "one car length for every ten miles per hour." The novice educational consultant is usually preoccupied with the facts and features of the consulting process without regard to the context. Novices often cling to checklists of things to do such as client interview, data collection, and so on. Novices rely on concrete rules such as "ten rules for the beginning consultant."

Advanced beginners learn more facts and features than novices. They also learn something new. After considerable experience coping with real situations they begin to recognize some of the "situational" features of their practice. Such situational elements are recognized, not from verbal descriptions, but by their perceived similarity to prior examples. The process is like recognizing the smell of coffee or the sound of a voice. However, the advanced beginner still does not make judgments. To stay with the automobile example, the advanced beginner uses road conditions, visibility and his or her own alertness (situational factors) as well as speed (a context-free factor) to determine the distance at which to follow the car in front. The advanced beginner is still tied to rules but is beginning to understand contingencies, rules applied to certain situations. For example, the consultant, recognizing that a teacher is unable to stimulate discussion, might search for some rule to apply to that situation. She or he has piled up enough cases in memory to recognize such common situations intuitively but still does not exercise judgment, does not sort or organize the situation. Advanced beginners are still attached to checklists, tips keyed to certain tasks, such as "getting discussion started," things to do in easily recognized situations.

Competence, according to Dreyfus and Dreyfus, is a coping strategy developed to manage the many context-free rules and situational cues that pile up and threaten to overwhelm the performer. In order to cope they must clarify the problem, organize the situation, and respond to only those factors that are relevant. This is the deliberate problem-solving phase of development. Competent practitioners do make judgments. They make conscious choices of goals and decisions after reflecting upon various alternatives. After a disaster or success, competent consultants will refer to a book or colleague in order to figure out what happened in an attempt to develop better contingency plans. The competent driver approaches the task with a goal or perspective. The goal helps to narrow choices and focus. For example a driver who is in a hurry might drive with less concern for passenger comfort, take more chances, choose more direct routes, pay attention to traffic conditions. Competent consultants look for a systematic approach to solving problems. They become bored or frustrated with "mere" checklists because they know that actions must be modified to fit each situation. However, they cannot yet respond to situations intuitively. They need to think through each step.

Proficient performers are at a transition stage between rational problem-solving and a more holistic proc-

Table 1: The Dreyfus and Dreyfus Model (1986)

Stages of Development	Basis for decisions	Method of Deciding	Driving a Car	Educational Consulting
Novice	Learns to identify specific and important facts and features of situations, independent of context.	Follows rules to determine action based on the features observed, regardless of what else is going on.	Stays a car length behind for every 10 mph.	Seeks and follows rules for preparing for interviews (the questions to ask, the forms to fill in). Relies on rules and lists, independent of what else might be happening in the situation.
Advanced Beginner	After considerable experience with real situations, learns to recognize features that are specific to the situation (i.e., not context free).	Follows more sophisticated rules including rules that are attached to situation specific features as well as to context free features.	More sensitive to road conditions and other situational factors.	Can recognize a poor climate, an uninspired lecture, confused students, and has specific suggestions for rules for teachers to follow in each situation.
Competent	As number of features becomes overwhelming, chooses a goal or plan, organized the situation and determines which features are to be considered important.	Although there is no rule for choosing the goal, after it is chosen, rules can be applied to the features that are relevant.	Uses a goal (e.g., to get to the hospital) to decide how fact to drive, which rules to bend.	Can choose goals which focus attention on those features related to those goals; e.g., organization, climate, participation, silence, etc. Then decides what to do by following the rules.
Proficient	As experience grows, whole situations come to be recognized, and patterns responded to effortlessly, creating an intuitive understanding and organization.	While problem situations are understood and recognized intuitively, decisions are still based on rules which are attached to the relevant facts and features of the situation.	Can sense when the care is going too fast for the conditions, then decides whether to brake or to just ease off the gas.	Because of experience can recognize whole situations as problematic (client is resisting, ready for a tougher challenge); then decides what to do based on analyzing the situation.
Expert	Intuitive understanding and organization of the situation.	Over time whole situations together with the strategies and responses that worked are connected, so decisions are made intuitively.	Just drives.	Intuitively recognizes a situation and responds skillfully and automatically using actions which have worked well in similar situations previously, without apparent thought.

ess. They recognize situations and make judgments holistically based on past experience but then seek strategies for dealing with these situations in a deliberate, problem-solving manner. Proficient performers experience their task from a specific perspective. This perspective causes certain features of the situation to become salient and others to fade into the background. Thus they recognize certain situations without deliberating consciously. They respond to patterns without decomposing them into component features, by a process of "holistic discrimination and association." They problem-solve or calculate only in the action phase. For example, proficient drivers, by some holistic process, may be able to recognize that they are driving too fast while approaching a curve on a rainy day. They then more deliberately decide what action to select of several possibilities — lift some pressure off the gas, release the gas foot, or step on the brake. Proficient consultants, by the same holistic process, may be able to recognize when a teacher is unable to stimulate discussion and then deliberately develop a plan to help the teacher.

Experts recognize situations and know what action to take without deliberating. They meet the needs of the situation the way most of us talk, walk, or converse socially, without making deliberative decisions. The experts are no more aware of using a skill than they are of using a part of their body when they are eating or walking naturally. Expert drivers become one with their car; they experience themselves as simply driving rather than as driving a car. Expert consultants find remedies popping into their heads without being aware of engaging in a problem-solving process.

According to Dreyfus and Dreyfus' theory of skill development, expertise is the highest level of skill that one can achieve in any problem area. The advantage of expertise lies in the speed and accuracy with which the expert can understand a situation and respond to it effectively. The process is intuitive, unconscious and instantaneous. But consultants will acquire this expertise only in the areas of their practice encountered most frequently.

An attempt to explain a complex theory in a brief article such as this runs the risk of raising more questions than it answers in the minds of the readers. (We recommend that you read chapter one in the Dreyfus' very readable book for a more detailed account.) We want to be sure that there is no confusion over at least the following two points: First, the theory does not claim that expertise is an unconscious process. The expert no doubt thinks and deliberates over problems, even problems in her or his field of expertise. What the theory claims is that the expert interprets the problem and thinks of solutions extremely rapidly, and as a result of some as yet unknown process,

which the authors variously calls "holistic discrimination and association" or "intuition." This process extracts wisdom from the cases directly, without building a heuristic. And the process happens without the deliberate effort of the expert. Of course, experts with professional responsibility and experience cannot put the problem aside after the intuitive flash. They must check out their thinking or reframe it in terms that can be communicated to others on their team, processes that require deliberation and problem-solving.

Second, it is important not to confuse the use of words like "holistic" and "intuitive," as used in the model, with the use of such words in theories of personality or learning style. The interesting question of the influence of personality type or learning style on cognitive development and vice versa is unfortunately not addressed by Dreyfus and Dreyfus. It is our guess that individual styles influence how a person develops cognitively but would not change the developmental progression from novice to expert as is outlined in the model. By intuition Dreyfus and Dreyfus (1986) do not mean wild guessing or supernatural inspiration. They define intuition as an ability to "respond to patterns without decomposing them into component features," a process of "holistic discrimination and association" (p. 28).

The Model Helps Us Understand the Nature of Our Expertise

Dreyfus and Dreyfus' (1986) model resolves a number of confusions about the practice of educational consulting. First, it helps us understand how educational consultants can effectively address such a broad range of problems. Although no one can be an expert in more than a few of the problem areas that general educational consultants encounter, consultants can be effective even outside of their areas of expertise. They accomplish this by problem-solving, a process which requires a lower level of development than expertise. Problem-solving strategies usually consist of some combination of the following steps: 1) clarification of the problem, 2) information gathering, 3) analysis and problem reformulation, 4) generation of likely remedies, 5) implementation and 6) evaluation of the success of the remedy. Consultants can function expertly in a few critical areas and competently as problem-solvers, with respect to the rest of the areas in which they get involved.

Second, the model can help us understand one of the peculiar characteristics of expertise, namely, that it is possessed without much awareness. We know how to do something without needing to think through the rules or explanations for it. A few years ago Donald Schön illustrated the tacit nature of expertise in an address to a large audience at the University of Toronto. While pretending to ride a bicycle, holding his hands out in front of him and lifting his knees alternately, he asked the audience how many of us knew how to ride a bicycle. Practically every hand went up. Then he asked us, "If your bicycle is falling to the right, which way do you turn the handle bars, to the right or to the left?" About one-third of the audience raised their hands to indicate the "right", one third to indicate "left", and another third was not sure. One of us (RGT) was among the "not sure" group although he had cycled to the lecture hall that very night, his bicycle helmet under his seat. Schön made the point that what we call practical knowledge — skill, or "know-how" — is often possessed without awareness.

The Model Helps Us Design Training Programs for Educational Consultants

In addition to clarifying the process by which expertise is developed, understanding the stages of development of expertise can assist in designing a program to teach educational consulting. The model states that development proceeds as a result of experiences. These stages of expertise can help us frame the questions that must be answered in designing a program based on experience (see Table 2): Are there learning experiences which would benefit persons in any stage of development? If there are, what are the major concerns or issues of individuals at each stage and what kind of learning experiences are therefore most appropriate for individuals at each stage

engaging in paper cases, simulations, real encounters? What is the role of conceptual learning and theory?

Dreyfus and Dreyfus do not distinguish between experiences in general and learning experiences, an important distinction to us as educators. A learning experience is one that is followed by *feedback* to the learner and the imposition of some alternative behavior. If learners receive no feedback, they will not know that a change is required and if they have no alternatives they will not be able to change even if they know one is required. We would like to restrict the meaning of the concept "experience." We would like to use it only to mean "learning experience."

While consulting in the department of emergency medicine, one of us (RGT) noticed that the chair of the department was pinning notes up on a cork board. They were follow-up summaries of what happened to the patients that were admitted to various wards of the hospital. The chair explained that emergency medicine is the only practice in the hospital in which the physicians are in danger of not improving because they do not see the consequences of their work. Other physicians receive the results of follow-up tests and examinations, after therapy, that enable them to assess the effect of treatment. Most educational consultants, like emergency physicians, rarely receive effective feedback. Consultants rely on information gleaned from casual interaction with their clients. Seldom is information systematically solicited from the clients, although a vast array of tools is available for doing so — rating scales, open-ended questionnaires, comment sheets, interviews, focus groups, and observation of client behavior.

And, feedback is only one of the components necessary to turn an experience into a learning experience. Feedback by itself is nothing but raw data that must be interpreted, reflected upon, reconciled with one's self

Table 2: Illustrations of the Issues or Concerns at each Stage of the Dreyfus and Dreyfus Model (1986)

Stages of Development	Major Issues/Concerns	What is Needed at Each Stage
Novice	How do I start? What should I look for? What is the first thing to do in an interview? What do I look for in the classroom? What do I do if the professor is nervous?	Check lists and flow charts that identify the sequence of events, important things to remember; e.g., make sure the camera works, that you have enough questionnaires. Illustrations of key concepts, opportunities to practice, someone to answer questions.
Advanced Beginner	When is a discussion off target? When is the class bored?	More practice in recognizing situations. More rules and lists.
Competent	How do I decide which area I should focus on?	Case studies which present complex situations and provide opportunities to assess problem identification.
Proficient	I can recognize the problem , but what strategy should I use?	Case studies and role plays, reflective practicums with more experienced consultants to discuss problem identification and solutions.

image, and so on in order to arrive at the kind of understanding that leads to positive change, to seeking and generating creative options (Schön, 1987).

In addition, the model reminds us that people at different stages will probably require different kinds of training. Novices and beginners have so little experience to draw on that they cannot function without some rules of practice. The rules and the check-lists may be rigid and awkward but they are necessary at an early stage.

Finally, the model suggests that education for consultants must include more than expertise in a few narrow areas. It must include a working knowledge of the various methods that are available for investigating educational problems, including methods of gathering information and of testing remedies. Consultants must be able to clarify a problem, gather information, analyze and reformulate the problem, generate likely remedies, implement the remedies, and evaluate their success.

References

Dreyfus, H. L., & Dreyfus, S. E. (1986). *Mind over machine: the power of human intuition and expertise in the era of the computer.* New York: The Free Press.

Schön, D. A. (1987). *Educating the reflective practitioner.* San Francisco: Jossey-Bass.

26. A Personal Account of the Development of One Consultant

David Way

*A*s an instructional consultant, a major focusing question for me has been how to use reflective thought, particularly self-reflective thought, in a constructive way. The work of Donald Schön (1983, 1987) has provided a useful framework for my efforts at finding answers to this question. This chapter includes some reflections on how I have developed professionally as an instructional consultant over the past 15 years. I have been guided by Schön's concepts of "reflection-on-action" and "reflection-in-action" in relating my professional experience and development. My professional development is, not surprisingly, directly related to my personal development.

A basic belief of mine is that my capacity to help an individual develop professionally is limited by my own experience and knowledge. This is not to say that I cannot be of assistance in areas or situations I have not experienced personally, my professional experience has yielded evidence that I can. What I mean is that if I have had a direct experience with the issue brought before me by a client, whether it has to do with my professional and academic development, or my personal growth, my ability to assist a client in coming to terms with that issue is enhanced. I consider my personal and professional growth and development as forming a curriculum of knowledge from which I draw to empathize with my clients and to know how to be of help to them. The nature of this curriculum, like all good curricula, is that it is continually changing in breadth and depth.

Over the past 15 years I have completed a doctorate in the field of education, specializing in curriculum and instruction. My professional experience began with designing and implementing instructional development programs for graduate and undergraduate teaching assistants within one department at a large research university. It has since grown to encompass the creation of a university-wide instructional development office consisting of a staff of six, serving both teaching assistants and faculty. During that time the transformation of my work and its theoretical orientation has reflected four distinguishable stages. The identification of these stages is a way I can explain my professional development. I do not mean to imply that all instructional development consultants must go through these same stages but I believe the stages reflect the epistemological shift that my work has followed. I also believe that the experiences which have led to these stages of growth are not unique and that many readers will find much to empathize with in this experiential account.

Some questions I have tried to answer in sharing these reflections include: What are my normative assumptions with regard to instructional consultation and how have they changed? What experiences have I had that have significantly influenced my values and beliefs? How have I responded to my learning experiences? What kind of growth do my responses reflect? How is this growth manifest in my relationships with my clients?

In general, my professional development has represented a gradual shift from seeking to comprehend instructional development from a single, general theory, to attempting to explicate teachers' personal theories of teaching and learning. To me, this represents a broadening of focus from a purely educational/pedagogical perspective, to a holistic view which honors the individual more. My experience in studying teaching has led to the understanding that no single theory can account for all the variables and complexity that make the act of teaching such a personal challenge intellectually, emotionally and spiritually.

In fact, it has been my understanding that good teaching involves the whole being of the teacher, which encompasses not just the intellect but the emotions and spiritual parts of a person. Such a full demand of an individual can only be understood on a personal level, thus my interest in helping my clients begin to identify their own personal theories of teaching and learning. When I began this work, however, my approach was much narrower and more simplistic.

Stage One: Academic/Empirical

My graduate training was undertaken in the latter 1970's and reflects the dominant research paradigms of positivism, behaviorism and, more specifically, process-product and classroom process studies. This training was the major factor that contributed to the first phase of my professional development—the Academic/Empirical Stage—which extended from 1977 through 1981. My graduate training culminated in a thesis which integrated counseling technique (Kagan, 1975, 1980) with educational theory (Gowin, 1981). Working heavily with videotape technology I learned that a very powerful way to help teachers become more conscious of their teaching was to use the videotape as a "recall stimulus" (Bloom, 1953). This meant going beyond what was on the videotape as a unit of analysis, to what the teacher could recall about his or her inner teaching experience, as those memories were stimulated by watching the videotape (within 24 hours of the teaching event).

This approach opened up all kinds of possible tangential areas of discussion, which some authors have referred to as the "cosmetic effect" (Allen & Ryan, 1969). The consultant's job, as I originally conceived it, was to help the client recall significant feelings and thoughts which were experienced in the act of teaching. Their significance was determined by the degree to which they had a positive or negative contribution to the explicit teaching evident on the tape. This "video recall" approach was an attempt to go beyond the behavioral interpretation of teaching and to recognize the influence that the client's thinking and feelings played in determining classroom processes and experiences.

In order to make sense out of the recall experience the consultant's role was to encourage the teacher, through general, open-ended leads, to recognize patterns in his or her teaching and to apply descriptive names to those patterns (Taylor-Way, 1981, 1988; Taylor-Way & Brinko, 1989). This naming of patterns was considered to be a conceptualizing process, where the teacher was learning to develop concepts of teaching through collaborative, empirical analysis with the consultant. The rationale was that if the teacher became more aware of recurring patterns inherent in teaching through naming them, it would influence the way he or she thought about teaching, thus video recall was intended as a cognitive intervention.

The problem with leaving it at the naming or conceptualizing stage is that concepts of teaching, like "warming up," "wait time," or "checking for understanding" are generic: they do not, in themselves, tell the teacher how to effectively deal with the situation at hand. This leads to the second role of the consultant, the "framing" role. Framing is where, through discussion with the client, the consultant helps the teacher frame principles of teaching around each identified concept so the teacher is left with a guide to action for each recurring pattern of teaching identified on the videotape. An example of a principle of teaching for wait time might be to count to one's self up to five while making eye contact, after asking a question, before saying anything additional. An example of a principle for checking for understanding might be to ask, "Who would like me to go over that again?" while maintaining eye contact and waiting a minimum of 5 seconds.

What I have retained out of this first stage of my development has been the use of the videotape recall methodology and the prominence of the conceptualizing and reframing aspects of the consultant's role. What has changed, however, are my epistemological beliefs. When I began instructional consultation I believed, without being particularly conscious of it, that knowledge gained for the teacher through this process was more absolute, generalizable and static than I have since come to realize it is. My "espoused" belief was that knowledge was constructed and ever-changing, whereas my "in use" practice reflected an inconsistency with that belief: there were general, universal laws of teaching that all good teachers must learn. I also found that using the video as a recall stimulus was not effective with all clients. A certain percentage of clients would have a much easier time using the videotape as a recall stimulus than others. Some people would never stop the tape to discuss it; others would have little to say when it was stopped. In those cases I would find myself doing a lot of the talking in the consultation session. I would always feel less effective under those circumstances because I felt I was taking the "ownership" of the outcome (and the focal point) of the session away from the teacher. After all, it is his or her teaching, not mine. If I give advice, I am not working from the teacher's frame of reference and my advice stands a good chance of not "taking."

What I have come to understand and reflect in my consultation practice is that knowledge is relative and constructed, and therefore very personal. This means that my job as a consultant, using videotape recall as a consultation tool, is not to help the teacher "discover" the underlying, general, universal principles of teaching all good teachers must learn to perfect, but to construct and articulate a personal framework or "theory" out of a careful analysis of his or her practice, which is further sharpened by a reflective evaluation and articulation of that practice. I did not, however, fully comprehend this idea until I had completed the next stage of my professional development.

Stage Two: Experiential/ Exploratory

The essence of the second developmental stage for me was making the abstract real: validating through experience and exploration what I had begun to understand intellectually. Stage two extended from 1981 through 1986. During that time I acquired a lot of experience which contributed to my learning about how teachers think and react to feedback on their teaching practice. I worked with literally hundreds of clients which allowed me to fine-tune, adapt and modify my skills as an instructional consultant using the videotape recall method. I became more flexible, and the act of carrying out a "recall session" with clients became kind of automatic. By automatic, I mean I became more comfortable with the process and my increased confidence lent me a sense of authority, which caused my clients to react more at ease and with confidence in the process.

A key factor in my learning during this and subsequent stages of development was continual formal reflection on my consultation practice. I did this through applying the same video recall method to my own consultation skills. I would get the permission of an occasional client who would permit me to videotape the consultation session and, either alone, or with a professional colleague, review the videotape.

During this stage I became more aware that a strict adherence to a true "recall" protocol was not necessary, and in the cases where the client found it difficult to actually use the videotape as a recall stimulus, it was a hindrance. Discussion centered more on the client's teaching, whether based on the videotaped record or not. Increasingly I began to focus on the discrepancies between what the client said he or she was trying to do in the classroom and the actual recorded account. This helped me stay closer to the client's intention and I gradually learned to share more control of the recall discussion with the client.

Whereas initially I had believed that it was most important to help the client integrate how his or her feelings and thoughts influenced teaching actions recorded on tape, I came to see the interrelationship between these three phenomena as reciprocal. It was no longer the case that feelings and/or thoughts always influenced action, but repeatedly acting differently could eventually change how a client felt or thought. This was a very powerful idea which helped some clients gain confidence in themselves. "Fake it until you make it." became part of my professional vocabulary. Often, upon first seeing themselves on the videotape, clients would make comments like, "I look more like a teacher than I thought!" or, "I was sweating bullets there but I don't appear to be very nervous at all."

Getting input from students about a client's teaching was always an important part of my consultation approach. Students can be very helpful in evaluating instruction and they provide a validating source for the conclusions reached between the client and consultant. When I began carrying out video recall sessions I routinely invited several students from the class to attend and provide input during the discussion of the videotape. By the second stage of my development I had abandoned this practice. The primary reason was the logistical problem of trying to schedule a session when four or five individuals' appointment calendars were involved, as opposed to two calendars. Also, not surprisingly, students frequently brought to the sessions their own covert agendas to review the course content one more time. It was not unusual to find the teacher responding to the students' requests to explain difficult points over again in the recall session. That in itself was good because they learned more and the teacher had a second chance to explain things. However, I was not always able to maximize the benefit to my client if 1) I was not very knowledgeable about the subject matter, or 2) the students got caught up in a deep and lengthy discussion.

During stage two, I began experimenting using mid-semester student diagnostic evaluations of instruction. I found this had several advantages. First it provided a more representative sample of the opinions of a client's students. Secondly, it focused more on instructional issues and less on content explication, which, for the most part, turned out to be for the better. In general it seemed a more efficient way of incorporating student input into the form of consultation I was providing faculty. It sometimes served to stimulate an interest in a client of discussing instructional issues with students outside the consultation process. More than one client, upon receiving his or her student evaluation scores, would discuss them openly in class with all students. Those that tried this found it to be both informative and liberating.

As time went on and my experience continued to accrue I gradually learned to let go of the need to base my consultations on video recall. Occasionally a client would feel uncomfortable being videotaped in class. Increasingly I found myself saying that if that was the case we could get by with me simply observing his or her class. The more I did this, the more I sensed I was evolving into a new stage of professional development.

Stage Three: Letting Go/Epistemological

Beginning around the fall of 1986 I found myself being strongly influenced, on a practical level, by the work of Donald Schön, specifically his books: *The Reflective Practitioner* (1983), *Educating the Reflective Practitioner* (1987), and the collection of essays on Schön's work by Grimmett and Erickson: *Reflection in Teacher Education* (1988). Schön's work had a liberating effect on me. It helped validate the discomfort and skepticism I had always felt regarding the prevalent trends in educational research and practice. In *The Reflective Practitioner*, Schön uses the terms "reflection-on-action" and "reflection-in-action" as key to the practice of a new "epistemology of practice." His basic premise is that in order to make significant and effective changes in our professional practice we need to honor a different way of producing knowledge about what we do. This involves taking the time necessary to reflect on our practice so we become more aware of why we do things the way we do, what doesn't work and why, and what may be more productive approaches. An example of this kind of metacognitive thinking includes monitoring student interest and comprehension "while in the act of teaching" and adjusting teaching practice accordingly on the spot. Another reflective approach to developing one's teaching involves using misconceptions to guide instruction. If I have spent enough time observing and reflecting on how my students' thinking prevents them from learning what I teach, I may gain some insight into how to be more effective as a teacher by explaining things in new ways.

One can read books which can influence the way we think about teaching but we learn how to do it and improve through trial-and-error practice, or doing what Fenstermacher (1986) describes as "conducting on-the-spot empirical experiments." The problem from the point of view of efficiently developing our teaching is that, for the most part, we make no records of these experiments, so our learning curve is dependent on our memory. If I am to trace the improvement of my teaching practice, a useful focal point is an analysis of the degree to which my practice is consistent with my thinking about teaching (my personal theory). Developing my personal theory is an epistemological issue as I discover and refine my knowledge about

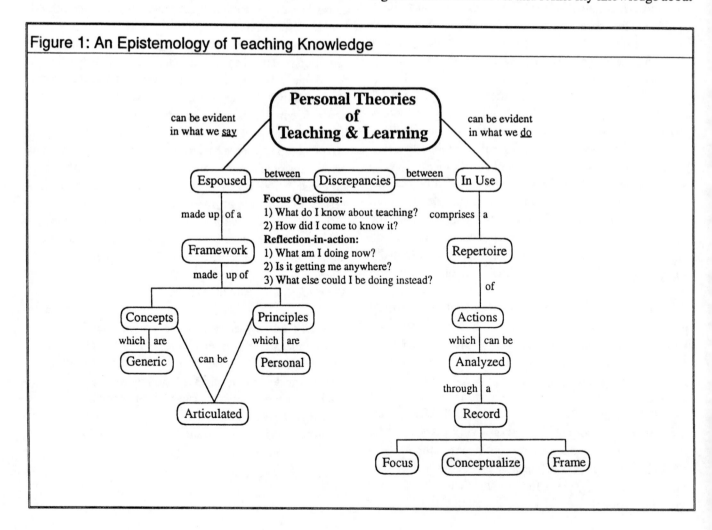

Figure 1: An Epistemology of Teaching Knowledge

teaching and learning. The basis of this epistemology lies in the interrelationship between what I say I do when I describe and explain my personal theory of teaching and learning, on the one hand, and what, in fact, I do in practice, on the other. That part of my theory which is evident in what I say I do and which I have reflected on enough to be able to articulate it is my "espoused theory" (Argyris & Schön, 1974). In contrast to my espoused theory is my "theory in use" which is what is evident in my behavior. The developmental question which is useful for me to continually reflect upon is, "To what degree is my espoused theory consistent with my theory in use?" or, more simply, "To what degree am I able to do, in practice, what I think and believe I should be doing?" Discrepancies between the two can lead me to further refine my thinking or my practice as the case may be. Figure 1 illustrates this epistemological perspective.

This diagram illustrates how our espoused theory is made up of a framework of concepts and principles which we use to think about teaching and which guide, in some ways, our theory in use. Reflecting on our actions taken helps us to integrate the two, so that we are more consistent, successful in achieving our intentions, and more knowledgeable about teaching practice in the sense that we can explain it to others and rationally justify our intentions. If we can articulate the knowledge that is evident in our actions, the implication is that our actions become more governed and justified by a coherent framework which is part of a personal theory.

Consultants can help their clients improve practice in a way which respects individual differences and personal style in teaching. While discussing their teaching with a consultant, clients are articulating their espoused theories and presenting an observational record of theories in use. If I am invited to reflect on my teaching actions by a consultant who has observed me and who asks me questions like, "What were you doing there? Was it effective? What alternative strategy might have been more productive?" I can begin to get used to reflecting on my teaching, which, in turn, may help me learn how to "reflect in action," as Schön calls it. I am able to reflect in action once I have articulated my personal theory to such a degree that my thinking and doing are consistent with each other. When I function on this level I am very efficient. My short-term memory is not cluttered by the necessity to think through every response and pay attention to every detail available to me. I can now use part of my short-term memory to monitor my performance by asking myself questions like, "What am I doing now? Is it getting me anywhere? What other principle do I know, or can I invent, which may be more productive?" In this way, through

reflection, I continually develop and refine my knowledge about teaching and learning which constitutes a personal theory I use to improve my practice.

Schön's work provided me with both a focal point (knowledge-in-action: "we know more than we can say") and a method (the client's reflection-in and on-action: "having a reflective conversation with the situation") to work productively with my clients. This newer framework honored the client's frame of reference more, helped me accept less control over the focus and substance of our discussion and clarified my role so I had less a sense of carrying out my own agenda in the consultation process and more a sense of helping the client become more aware of what tacit knowledge he or she was being governed by, both in planning for instruction, and in classroom performance.

Having said this, I don't mean to make it sound like I had a sudden awakening: that I had been very strict or manipulative in my consultation style up to that time. I had always recognized the issue of "ownership" right from the beginning of my professional practice and, as my counseling training had recommended, avoided adopting the role of consultant as advice-giver and evaluator. Even when clients would encourage me to play the role of judge ("Tell me what's good and bad, I can take it.") I would decline by explaining I knew there was a more productive role I could play.

By this stage of my professional development I had acquired a more thorough epistemology of teaching knowledge and its development, I was even more client-centered than I had been without compromising my own authority and knowledge base, and I was looking at a broader range of the client's teaching.

Gaea Leinhardt's (1983) work studying expert and novice teachers' knowledge processing and knowledge structures also strongly influenced the way I worked with clients. Others, like Schank and Abelson (1977), were suggesting that as teachers learned how to teach, the development of their practical knowledge formed an ever-increasing database which was stored in long term memory. The notion that expert teachers' short term memories were relatively free "due to the existence of a database of accumulated practical knowledge residing in long term memory" to process the immediate events of the classroom experience was both helpful and reinforcing in my consultation approach.

My work in helping teachers identify concepts of teaching based on an analysis of patterns in video recall sessions showed that not only could novice teachers conceptualize their teaching, but they could, in turn, use concepts of teaching to refine and add to a repertoire of principles to help deal with critical teaching issues which previously may have been perplexing to them. The articulation and clarification of this repertoire constituted, for me, the client's evolving personal theory of teaching and learning. Authors who are conducting research in this area (Ross, Cornett, & McCutcheon, 1992) have supported my notion that through the natural process of practicing teaching, the client is building a body of practical knowledge which can be heuristically and developmentally approached by the consultant as a personal theory of teaching and learning.

By this stage I had a very clear vision of my role of helping the client construct a framework of concepts and a repertoire of principles that would free up their working memory to be more efficient at processing the teaching experience such that it would more consistently lead to significant learning outcomes for his or her students. The following extract from a recall session serves as an example:

Consultant: *You've had several opportunities to take a look at yourself on videotape and reflect on your teaching. Where have you come?*

Client: *I just notice an ability to process a lot more in the classroom situation; to be able to respond to a lot of different things...it's like "This is what's happening. What does that mean? What have I done that works? Do that." or, "Is this a new situation that maybe I don't know how to react to too well now, but I'll think about it afterwards." I feel that I do that a lot more. Going about [acting on] the principle is like, "What's the situation? What do I do that can cause a positive result?" or "What am I doing that causes this? What things aren't I doing? What principle can I use?" Then I have to try it out to determine if that principle could be helpful in this situation. Does it really work?...There is value in labeling them so that you know, rather than it's just because you do it and you're lucky that it's good...You're really helping me to think a lot more than I realize while I'm doing it.*

Stage Four: Transcendental/Integrative

Beginning in late 1989, and continuing to the present time, my professional practice has evolved to a form which transcends all previous stages. I refer to it as transcendental and integrative because, by this time, I have had enough consultation experience to have come to the conclusion that I was limiting myself in consulting with clients as just teachers. I had to relate to them holistically, which meant as total human beings, going beyond their lives as teachers. The rationale for this is based on the recognition that clients' predispositions, both in terms of their teaching styles, and their ability to develop professionally through the consultation process, grew out of their life experiences, starting in childhood and extending through adulthood. I cannot be as effective working with a client's teaching if there exists some larger, more fundamental issue, like profound fear or anxiety, lack of self esteem, or underlying and unrecognized anger. In saying this I don't mean to imply that the consultant's role and requisite skills should be on the par with a psychotherapist. I simply mean that, to the degree that the consultant is experienced and confident in working with the client on a broader basis, he or she may be more effective in helping the client correct the most critical, fundamental problems with instructional practice.

Some examples will help make it clearer that I am not advocating the potentially dangerous practice of interfering in a client's personal problems without due professional consideration of my capacity to be of help, rather than having a damaging effect.

One client, a female graduate student, had given no strong outward signs (that I had detected) to indicate her extreme discomfort at the thought of going through the recall experience. Once we sat down in front of the video monitor to review her tape, she broke down in tears. The thought of re-experiencing what sounded to me like an extremely anxiety-laden and fearful episode was too much for her. I gave her some kleenex and reassured her we would not look at the tape. I found myself confronted with a person who described her inner daily experience as terrifying and I judged her emotional state to be out of my professional realm. My recourse was to do what I thought any considerate and responsible lay person might do under the circumstances: to calm her down, and reassure her. This case represents where I drew the line at my own experience, either in being able to empathize with her state, or with knowing how to address it within our professional relationship.

In contrast is another example of a female client experiencing extreme anxiety, but where my own personal experience was useful in effecting a constructive outcome. A graduate student who was taking a teaching seminar with me asked to talk to me about a personal matter that was extremely troublesome to her. She was contemplating transferring to another graduate school, but since she had already done so once before in her graduate experience, she was very concerned about whether she was making the right choice. In the course of our conversations (after she had canceled an appointment with a counselor at the institutional psychological services office) she went into detail about her personal and family life and how those experiences had contributed to her present state of anxiety.

Hearing her story I was able to empathize with her fear, confusion and lack of confidence. In the earlier days of my consulting I might have brushed these factors aside and approached her problem from a purely academic perspective. By revealing her story to me I knew she trusted me enough for us to work on a more fundamental level. By self-disclosing a bit of my own resonating experiences and describing retrospectively the way I have learned to deal with similar stressful situations, our mutual understanding contributed to her making, after spending several weeks in rational reflection, a decision she was comfortable with.

I suspect that all teachers or consultants have run into similar experiences and worked through them with the person concerned without compromising their professional expertise. The point is that as I have grown with professional experience, I find the nature of my relationships with clients has expanded to encompass a broader range of life's issues. My experiences in dealing with people on this level have lead me to believe that when I talk back to the client out of my own fear, anxiety, strength and integrity, I am more effective in being of help.

As a human activity, teaching is about relating to others. It encompasses both the intellect and the emotional self. When I begin talking about a holistic consultation approach I mean we are including what I will refer to as the spiritual self. In using the term "spiritual" I am not implying anything religious. For me, the spirit has to do with relationships: the individual's relationship with self, ways of relating to others, and to life in general, with all its surprises, complexity and confusion. If I have learned, as a consultant, to integrate my intellectual, emotional and spiritual selves, the "me" that my clients see and experience from their perspective is the same "me" that I am experiencing from my own personal perspective: what is on the outside is the same as what is on the inside. This is my sense of what personal integrity consists of. It is possible only if I strive to be as honest with myself as possible, and therefore requires that I am as honest with others as I am with myself. This level of functioning and relating carries with it a much more profound sense of responsibility. I must be able to accurately determine the degree to which my client can work on developing instruction if it means addressing more fundamental issues.

In actual practice, I have found myself relating to my clients on this level without consciously trying to. My way of relating to them reflects my way of relating to myself. Needless to say, I underwent some very profound experiences in my personal life, all of which are common enough that most readers could empathize with them. These experiences have lead to a stage of personal development where relating to my clients on a holistic level has become necessary and inevitable.

This stage of my development has been characterized by a gradual moving away from the strict protocol I had been used to with video recall. I have found that I can produce very satisfactory results working with clients if I base my consultation on classroom observation notes. I have also found I am more oriented toward the issue of instructional planning, as contrasted with limiting my discussions with clients to classroom performance. My consultation style more typically consists of twice as many consulting sessions per client: the first to review the client's teaching plan, the second to focus on classroom performance using either observation notes, or video recall, depending on the client's preference.

I find this approach to be more effective because I can catch major instructional problems before they occur in class by reviewing the client's planning for instruction. The focus is the same as it always has been: the integration of thinking, feeling and action.

My consultation, however, is now oriented more toward the client's thinking during the planning stage of instruction. In spite of the fact that I have always been oriented toward the analysis of the relationship between intent and action "where the major discrepancies exist," now in reviewing videotapes with clients we more frequently see and discuss instances where the client made a decision to modify his or her teaching plan on the fly. Processing decisions made spontaneously can help the client develop reflection-in-action skills, whereas helping the client analyze his or her instructional planning can help the client develop reflection-on-action skills. My consultation practice has now expanded to more consistently addressing a broader part of the client's experience with the teaching process. I say consistently because, of course, issues of planning have always come up in the video recall sessions. Now, however, the structure of my consultation has a whole segment devoted to the planning and instructional design skills of the client.

In this stage of professional functioning the curriculum of knowledge my consultation practice is based upon has grown to encompass and integrate the intellectual, emotional and spiritual aspects of human existence. I can be much more help to a person if I have had first-hand, personal experience with what I am trying to teach my client. My consultations are characterized by a much more complete and profound sense of being. Because of this I believe I am more effective, based on the feedback and unsolicited testimonials I get from my clients, from the significantly improved student ratings they receive, and from my own successive observations of their practice.

References

Allen, D. W., & Ryan, K. (1969). *Microteaching*. Reading, MA: Addison-Wesley.

Argyris, C., & Schön, D. (1974). *Theory in practice: Increasing professional effectiveness*. San Francisco: Jossey-Bass.

Bloom, B. S. (1953). Thought processes in lectures and discussions. *Journal of General Education, 7*(3), 160-169.

Fenstermacher, G. D. (1986). Philosophy of research on teaching: Three aspects. In M. C. Wittrock (Ed.), *Handbook of research on teaching* (3rd ed.). New York: Macmillan.

Gowin, D. B. (1981). *Educating*. Ithaca, NY: Cornell University Press.

Grimmet, P., & Erickson, G. (1988). *Reflection in teacher education*. New York: Teachers College Press.

Kagan, N. (1975). *Interpersonal process recall—a method of influencing human interaction*. East Lansing: Michigan State University, Department of Psychiatry.

Kagan, N. (1980). Influencing human interaction—eighteen years with IPR. In A.K. Hess, *Psychotherapy supervision: Theory, research and practice* (pp. 262-283). New York: John Wiley & Sons.

Leinhardt, G. (1983). Novice and expert knowledge of individual students' achievement. *Educational Psychologist, 18,* 165-179.

Ross, E. W., Cornett, J. W., & McCutcheon, G. (1992). *Teacher personal theorizing—connecting curriculum practice, theory and research*. Albany, NY: SUNY Press.

Schank, R., & Abelson, R. P. (1977). *Scripts plans, goals and understanding: An inquiry into human knowledge structures*. Hillsdale, NJ: Lawrence Erlbaum.

Schön, D. (1983). *The reflective practitioner: How professionals think in action*. New York: Basic Books.

Schön, D. (1987). *Educating the reflective practitioner*. San Fransisco: Jossey-Bass.

Taylor-Way, D. (1981). *Adaptation of interpersonal process recall and a theory of educating for the improvement of college teaching*. Paper presented at the annual meeting of the American Educational Research Association, Los Angeles.

Taylor-Way, D. (1988). Consultation with video: Memory management through stimulated recall. In K. G. Lewis & J.T. Povlacs (Eds.) *Face to face: a sourcebook of individual consultation techniques for faculty/instructional developers* (pp. 159-191). Stillwater, OK: New Forums Press.

Taylor-Way, D., & Brinko, K T. (1989). Using video recall for improving professional competency in instructional consultation. *To Improve the Academy, 8,* 141-156.

Part Four:

Evaluating Instructional Consultation

By far, Part Four was the most difficult section for which to recruit authors. Very few instructional consultants evaluate their programs and services. Because instructional consultation programs (like psychological counseling programs) demand strict confidentiality, the task of evaluation becomes more complicated than for other programs that serve faculty (for example, wellness programs).

We are pleased to include three chapters in this part. The first chapter provides an overview of the issues concerned with evaluating consultation. In Chapter 27, Erickson poses nine questions that can be used to design a program evaluation: What needs to be evaluated? why evaluate? for whom are we evaluating? whom should we consult? what should be the general design of the evaluation? for whom and when should we collect what kinds of data? how should we analyze, summarize, interpret, and report data? and to whom should the results be distributed?

Erickson also discusses the ethical issues involved in evaluating an instructional consultation program.

Chapters 28 and 29 present case studies of two programs that underwent evaluation. In Chapter 28, Erickson describes how the instructional consultation program has been evaluated at the University of Rhode Island using a combination of external evaluators and internal evaluation methods. In summary, he lists five lessons learned from the process. In contrast to Erickson's program which utilizes professional instructional consultants, Millis' program (Chapter 29) utilizes peer consultants. Millis received a three-year grant from the Fund for the Improvement of Post-Secondary Education (FIPSE) to evaluate her consultation program. In Chapter 29, she provides a brief description of the program followed by a detailed description of the evaluation design, methodology, and results. Like Erickson, Millis shares some lessons that she learned from implementing the evaluation process.

27. Issues in Evaluating Consultation

Glenn R. Erickson

*Y*ears ago, when we began our teaching consultation service, we asked every user to assess our competence and the value of the experience. A faculty senate oversight committee did annual evaluations which included an anonymous survey of clients. We hired external evaluators to interview and poll clients, and we even conducted a relatively large and systematic evaluation study of our own. We're convinced that our early willingness—even compulsion—to evaluate what we did, and to publicize the results, increased our credibility and helped establish the teaching consultation program at our university. We believe that it made us more competent and effective as consultants. We think that it demonstrated our willingness to monitor our performance in much the same way that we ask teachers to evaluate theirs. And we certainly liked hearing that most faculty thought we were doing a good job.

While we continue to evaluate every workshop, seminar, and new wrinkle added to our program, we have not kept up the routine evaluation of our consultation service. We decided that all of that study activity imposed too much on clients for too little new information of value to us or anyone else. Now, though, we're wondering if we haven't grown complacent and if we shouldn't go back and do some more checking, although perhaps in less intrusive ways. Moreover, the recent Marsh and Roche (1993) evaluation study has reminded us of how much fun and stimulating (and challenging) evaluation can be.

So we, too, are considering the issues I'm raising in this chapter: What's to be evaluated? Why evaluate? For whom? Who should we consult about criteria and appropriate data? What should be our general design? What data should be collected from whom and when? How should data be summarized, analyzed, and reported? Who should get the results? What are some of the ethical issues?

I won't have answers, because they depend upon situation, needs, and interests. But this chapter and the appended checklist may help sort out evaluation needs and options in preparation for necessary conversations with evaluators and statisticians.

What Needs to be Evaluated?

Possibilities include ourselves as consultants, the impact of our consultation service, elements of the consultation process (for example, initial interviews, our use of videotapes, data review and interpretation, negotiating change, and so on), the materials we use (student questionnaires, interview protocols, and so on), and things like our recruiting strategies and materials.

Why Evaluate?

For veteran consultants, the most likely answer is to check on the effectiveness of consultation and see how faculty assess its value. Beginning programs or consultants more likely need routine feedback in order to sharpen skills and sift through what does and does not work with various clients. We may also want to monitor consumer satisfaction over time, be certain that clients have opportunities to critique and make suggestions, model the commitment to evaluation and adjustment that we're asking of faculty, announce to the world our readiness to be held accountable, affirm for ourselves that what we're doing is appreciated, and use evaluation studies as a recruiting strategy. More evaluation, especially if it's well done, would no doubt contribute to the credibility of our profession as well.

For Whom Are We Evaluating?

Most often, I think, we're evaluating for ourselves as consultants who want to improve, to monitor our effectiveness, to be assured that we're doing a good job and are appreciated. We may also evaluate for a funding agency, decision makers in our institution, the staff of our program—any of whom may want to brag about the service or decide whether or not to continue their support.

Whom Should We Consult About Evaluation Criteria and Sources of Data?

Having decided what we want to evaluate, why, and for whom, we need to get down to deciding *how* we're going to do it. A good place to begin is by asking people whose opinions matter what they consider to be credible and appropriate criteria and sources of data. It won't do much good to demonstrate that faculty clients think that we're the greatest thing since tenure if the people who control our money won't settle for anything less than proof that our clients' students learn more after we've been consulted than before. And it would be foolish to limit our data collection to students if faculty satisfaction is what will make or break us.

Campus administrators, relevant faculty committees, and funding decision makers need to be consulted before we undertake program evaluations intended to demonstrate our importance to the academy. It's important, too, to talk to those who oppose the program for whatever reasons. Such conversations provide important opportunities to clarify for everyone what is essential (for example, that faculty users are delighted with the service), what is credible (for example, anonymous questionnaire data from clients and their students, not signed testimonials), and what is feasible (for example, evidence that students see positive changes in teaching performance after their teachers consult with us, but probably no direct evidence that students are learning more). We have been surprised to find that our standards of credibility and rigor have generally been more demanding than those of the decision influencers we've consulted.

Whatever our evaluation goals, we're likely to gain from consulting with clients, potential clients, and colleagues; looking over evaluations others have done (Marsh and Roche, 1993, is especially challenging and inspiring; Erickson and Erickson, 1979, is more down home); and referring to other books on program evaluation. I expect, too, that posting a request for ideas, suggestions, and examples on the POD listserv would turn up lots of help. The important thing is to come up with a credible, practical set of evaluation criteria and data sources—and we shouldn't forget to check back with those we've consulted after putting together our proposal.

What Should Be the General Design of the Evaluation?

Design has to do with the organization and structure of the evaluation. Should consultation users be compared to non-users? How should we decide who will get consultation and who won't? Do we want to be able to generalize our findings to other faculty? To other consultants? To other kinds of teaching problems? How many faculty clients do we need and how should they be recruited and selected if we want to have confidence in what we find? Should we collect our data early, mid, or late in the semester? From one semester to another? In general, how do we set up our evaluation to answer the questions as unambiguously as possible?

Design is probably not much of an issue if our interests are limited to keeping tabs on consumer satisfaction and being responsive to the reactions and suggestions of our clients. For that we can use periodic questionnaires or interviews without much concern about comparison groups, random samples, or the appropriateness of alternative tools of statistical analyses. If, however, we want to demonstrate that our teaching consultation has an impact on instruction, that it will likely have an impact on the teaching of most faculty who choose to use it, or that our funding ought to be tripled instead of halved so that more faculty can take advantage of our services, design is going to be important indeed. And if we're interested in establishing those kinds of things, we need to get together with experts on evaluation design and statistical or qualitative methods before we collect any data or even recruit faculty subjects. We need to do that whether we end up trying a quasi-experimental design with a control group, a simpler pre/postdesign without any comparison group, case studies, or catch-as-catch-can. Otherwise we run the risk of contaminating our evaluation in ways that will make the results meaningless or suspect.

On our campus, expertise on evaluation design is scattered. We've gotten help from Education, Psychology, Experimental Statistics, Sociology, Institutional Research, and the Academic Computer Center. Many grants require evaluation, so you might want to check and see who's being consulted locally about those evaluations. If you can't find anybody on your campus, the POD Network includes people who can help out.

From Whom and When Should We Collect What Kinds of Data?

Faculty clients, their students, the teaching consultant—all are likely sources of data for most of our evaluations. Department chairs, administrators, and potential faculty clients are others. Good ideas for questionnaires, interview protocols, observation systems, and such are readily available from other evaluation reports and POD-ers (another reason to get on the POD listserv). Trying out our data collection devices and attempting to make sense out of the results is critical before we commit ourselves to any general application. Bear in mind that the less structured the data (interviews, open-ended questionnaires, tapes, observations), the more difficult and ambiguous the analysis and interpretation.

How Should We Analyze, Summarize, Interpret, and Report Data?

For anything but the simplest data analyses and the most straightforward interpretations, we've always relied on evaluators and statisticians much more expert than ourselves. But for much of the evaluation we do, not much is needed beyond tallying responses, typing up written comments or interview notes, and writing summaries which identify apparent strengths and problems. We think that the simpler the better—but be very careful not to draw conclusions unwarranted by the data. We've learned, too, to remember as we write any report that it is likely to be read by a variety of audiences, mostly friendly, but some hostile and some easily offended.

To Whom Should the Results Be Distributed?

We've been very open with our results because we've wanted it generally known that we were evaluating what we did and because the findings were meant to be public. Full reports, written as if for publication in professional journals, were distributed to everyone directly involved in making decisions about our program and to anyone else who asked. We have included references to the results in subsequent recruiting and publicity materials. We have not prepared newsy summaries for more systematic publicity blitzes, but I think it would be good public relations to do so.

Ethical Issues

We need to consider a variety of ethical questions as we plan, conduct, and write up our evaluations. Examples include: What constitutes appropriate informed consent for faculty subjects and/or their students? Can we use data nominally collected for one purpose (anonymous written comments for feedback to consultants, for example) for other ends (as quotes to sell our services)? Should we offer anonymity and confidentiality to faculty and their students? If so, what are reasonable safeguards? How careful should we be to confine our conclusions to what's warranted by our evaluation design and the data we've collected? If we get mixed results, can we publicize the good and ignore or gloss over the bad? These are tough questions, but ones which are almost certain to come up when we begin to evaluate our services.

In Conclusion

I've suggested that we need to decide what, why, and for whom to evaluate; against what criteria our success should be assessed; what evaluation design makes the most sense; from whom and when we should collect what data; how the data should be analyzed, summarized, interpreted, and reported; and to whom our reports should be distributed. I've also noted some likely ethical issues.

I have not described in detail how to do all of those things, however, and evaluations can easily go awry. I know from experience that simple mistakes or oversights at the beginning can muddy things up in ways which are difficult to reverse without starting all over. That's why I emphasize the need to seek out people with experience and expertise to help plan and conduct our evaluations. Collaborating with them should make it easier for us to relax and enjoy the evaluation experience and feedback.

References

Erickson, G. R., & Erickson, B. L. (1979). Improving college teaching: An evaluation of a teaching consultation procedure. *Journal of Higher Education, 50,* 670-683.

Marsh, H. W., & Roche, L. (1993). The use of students' evaluations and an individually structured intervention to enhance university teaching effectiveness. *American Educational Research Journal, 30,* 217-251.

Appendix A

Issues in Evaluation: A Checklist

I. What's to be evaluated?
    ___Consultant(s)
    ___Consulting service
    ___Chunks of the consultation process
    ___Materials (e.g., questionnaires, handouts)
    ___Other

II. Why are we evaluating?
    ___To assess/demonstrate the effectiveness and value of the service
    ___Routine feedback for monitoring and improvement
    ___To give faculty a chance to critique and make suggestions
    ___To model our commitment to evaluation
    ___Other

III. For whom are we evaluating?
    ___Consultants
    ___Program
    ___Institution
    ___Funding agency
    ___Other

IV. Whom should we consult about evaluation criteria and sources of data?
    ___Decision makers
        ___campus administrators
        ___faculty advisory or monitoring committees
        ___program director
        ___external funding agency
        ___other
    ___Clients and potential clients
    ___Those who don't like us
    ___Colleagues, including PODers
    ___Publications
        ___other evaluation studies and reports
        ___handbooks on program evaluation
        ___this sourcebook
        ___other

V. What should be the general design of the evaluation?
    ___Consult experts

VI. From whom and when should we collect what kinds of data?
    ___Faculty clients
        ___questionnaires—retrospectively or along the way
        ___interviews by consultant or evaluator

    ___video or audio tapes

    ___classroom observation

    ___other

___Students—individually or collectively

    ___ratings or assessments of change in teaching performance

    ___evidence of learning—quiz or test scores,
      self-assessments, and so on

    ___interviews by consultant or evaluator

    ___other

___Consultant(s)

    ___self-assessments

    ___records, logs, notes, and so on

    ___other

VII. How should we summarize, analyze, and report data?

    ___Simple tabulations, frequency distributions,   narrative summaries

    ___Comparisons (with or without formal statistical tests)

      ___faculty users vs. non-users (control group?)

      ___over time (mid- to late-term; term to term; year to year)

      ___course to course or section to section

    ___Case study

    ___Formal evaluation report, with statistical analyses, tables, charts, and so on

    ___Consult evaluator, statistician, qualitative methodologist

VIII. To whom should the results be distributed?

    ___Consultant

    ___Students

    ___Program staff

    ___College community

    ___College administration

    ___Anyone interested

    ___Funding agency

    ___Others

IX. Ethical concerns

    ___Informed consent

    ___Confidentiality; anonymity

    ___Warranted conclusions

    ___Other

28. *Evaluating a Teaching Consultation Service*

Glenn R. Erickson

*L*ike many of the 1970's faculty development programs, ours was created with the help of a grant which paid a significant share of its costs for the first three years. While the program was not exactly imposed upon the faculty by an overzealous administration, as some claimed, neither had its creation followed the normal proposal and review process typical for new programs. When Bette LaSere Erickson and I were hired to establish the program, we therefore doubted that it would outlast the grant unless we were able to convince the various reviewing groups and their constituencies that we provided important services effectively.

Our strategy was to do lots of assessment and to be very public with all of the results of those evaluations. We hired external evaluators to conduct interviews, develop and administer questionnaires, and write reports; we helped an oversight committee of the faculty senate conduct its evaluations; and we designed and did evaluations of our own. I'll elaborate on each of those a little, then summarize a few of the lessons we think that we learned from the experience that may be useful to others.

The core of our program was a teaching consultation process which had originated at the UMass/Amherst's Clinic to Improve University Teaching (see Chapter 17) where we had worked before moving to Rhode Island. Our evaluations were intended to assess the value of that service for faculty who chose to use it, and to help decide whether or not the University should continue to support such a labor intensive (expensive) faculty development program.

Using Outside Evaluators

We used external evaluators the first couple of years because we didn't know much about how to do program evaluation, because we wanted to focus more on providing services than on evaluating them, because we thought outsiders would lend credibility to our evaluation efforts,

and, not least, because an external evaluation line had been written into the grant proposal. Our first year evaluator was someone with extensive experience in evaluating state and federally funded education programs but little knowledge of higher education. In the second year we turned to someone who had both faculty development and program evaluation experience. Although both wrote very favorable reports, the second was more helpful and it is his work to which I refer below.

He interviewed stakeholders (including us) about appropriate evaluation criteria, interviewed users of the consultation service, and developed assessment questionnaires which we distributed with instructions that they be returned to him (See Appendix A). His written report was based on his interviews, questionnaire responses, and a review of our records of work with clients. It was appended to our annual report and broadly distributed. He also met with various stakeholders to review his report and answer questions.

The outside evaluator was particularly useful in helping us decide on important assessment issues and credible evidence. He interviewed a variety of people, solicited their suggestions without making commitments ("What sort of evidence would convince you that the IDP is effective here at URI? What would you most like to know about the program? If the program were adequately fulfilling its mission, what would it be doing? What sort of effects would it have?"), then decided with us and a faculty senate monitoring committee on reasonable evaluation questions and types of data. He was able to help people differentiate between feasible and impractical criteria and types of data. (We were surprised, but probably shouldn't have been, to find that most people were less concerned about whether consultation had any impact on teaching or learning than they were about whether faculty found consultation an attractive option and a positive experience.) His interviews and questionnaires also turned up faculty reservations and suggestions which might have been difficult for them to present to us directly or for us to listen to without being defensive.

Working With a Faculty Review Committee

Our program is administratively located in academic affairs, but a faculty committee on teaching is our oversight and policy-making group. Their charge included submitting an annual report regarding the IDP to the Faculty Senate. They were also the first level of review for the decision about continuing the program beyond the grant period. There was reason, then, for them to know what we were doing and how it was being received, but not to know who was using our services.

The committee wrote their own questions for our faculty clients ("Why did you seek this individual help? To what extent do you feel the program has increased your effectiveness as a teacher? What suggestions do you have for improving the program?"). Along with a cover letter, we sent these questions to all of our consultation service users each year, asking them to return their anonymous answers to the committee. At the same time, we asked them to mail us an enclosed postcard with their name so that we would know to whom to send reminders. Virtually all responded, and the committee wrote their report on the basis of those returns.

The system worked well. It gave the committee a count of our clients without identifying them or their departments, and it allowed the committee to ask the questions which they thought were important. The results were reports to the Faculty Senate which they found credible and informative.

Doing Our Own Evaluations

We did additional evaluations to provide us with ongoing feedback about faculty client response to our consultation and to see whether students saw any improvement in our clients' teaching. For the first, we routinely asked clients to complete the anonymous, two-part, *Instructor Evaluation of Teaching Consultation Service*. (A sampling of items is attached as Appendix B.) We asked them to do Part I soon after the meeting in which we met to review data about their teaching and to decide upon goals for change. We requested Part II at the end of the semester. These surveys helped us monitor faculty reactions to the various elements of the consultation process and to our performance as consultants. We also wanted to demonstrate our commitment to the same sort of feedback that we were asking them to collect from students.

Our efforts to determine whether or not consultation resulted in changes in teaching which were apparent to students are described in detail in Erickson and Erickson (1979). I'll just skim over them here. We invited every teaching faculty member to take part in a study to evaluate the effectiveness of the consultation service and randomly divided the 31 volunteers into experimental and control groups. The experimental group faculty went through the entire consultation process, including mid- and late-semester self and student ratings of instruction. Control group faculty had mid- and late-semester self and student ratings of teaching as well, but did not see the results or meet for a consultation until the semester's end. Both self and student ratings of instructional improvement were more positive for experimental than for control group faculty. In a later study to control for the possibility that those differences were the result of different student expectations of change, we followed up 20 faculty from one to four semesters after their experience of the consultation service. Their current students completed the mid-semester ratings with the same instructions as had the earlier students. In most cases, the ratings were significantly more positive in the follow-up semester than they had been before consultation in the earlier term. We interpreted the results of those studies as indicating that the consultation process resulted in positive and persistent changes in teaching which were apparent to students.

Lessons Learned

We think that we learned a few things about evaluating consultation services that may be of use and interest to others. In no particular order:

1. An evaluation study can be a good recruiting tool. Asking for volunteers to help assess a program lets faculty get involved without having to own up to any teaching problems. After they've tried it, it's easier for them to discuss the experience with colleagues as well.

2. An early emphasis on evaluation can pay off for a long time. Our evaluations helped us make the transition from soft to hard money and to survive several subsequent budget crunches. We could argue that we had more evidence of effectiveness than most academic programs, new or old, and people involved in our evaluations became lasting and outspoken supporters.

3. Evaluation can be overdone. We asked our early clients to complete our feedback forms, to rate their own teaching effectiveness, to complete surveys and participate in interviews by external evaluators, to respond to a questionnaire from a Faculty Senate committee, and to collect student ratings twice during the semester. Although that became less of a problem as the pool of clients got larger, all of that evaluation seemed an imposition, especially once it became clear that the results were generally consistent and little that was new was turning up.

4. Outside evaluators can be very useful. Their expertise is certainly useful, but that can probably be had from someone on the home campus. The real value is having someone without a stake in the outcome doing interviews and summarizing what they hear for program personnel and for others who have an interest.

5. Decisions about continuing or cutting back support for consultation are less likely to turn on evidence that consultation really changes teaching or has a demonstrable impact on student learning than on the number of satisfied users. I think that evidence of positive changes in teaching and what and how much students learn is what we ought to be looking for because it's an implicit promise in what we do. Because even the best planned and managed evaluations are unlikely to yield unequivocable proof of such changes, we should be leery of promising proof we can't deliver—especially when it's not being demanded. Better, perhaps, we ought to concentrate on demonstrating that faculty stay happier and don't burn out as quickly when they have access to teaching consultation.

Our program might still be here, relatively intact, even if we had not invested as much effort, time, and money in evaluation during the early years. We doubt it. We're convinced that our stance of inviting accountability and our cooperation with others who were planning and conducting evaluations helped establish our credibility and the importance of the consultation service. We believe that all of the feedback made us better consultants as well.

Reference

Erickson, G. R., & Erickson, B. L. (1979). Improving college teaching: An evaluation of a teaching consultation procedure. *Journal of Higher Education, 50,* 670-683.

Appendix A
External Evaluator's Survey Questionnaire for Faculty

1. Looking back to your consultation experience, how helpful was it overall?
   Not helpful at all   1   2   3   4   5   Extremely helpful

   What made you give the program as high a rating as you did?

   What kept you from rating it higher?

2. What, if anything, are you doing differently in your teaching this year as a result of your participation?

   If you have not made any significant changes, please check the appropriate reason below:
   ____ Consultation was inappropriate for my needs.
   ____ Consultation reaffirmed current practices.
   ____ I need more time to consider the consultation before I act on it.
   ____ Other (please specify)

3. Have you recommended this program to colleagues?   YES   NO
   (If yes) How many? _____

4. Has the IDP had an impact in any way upon the teaching practices of your department or school as a whole? If so, please specify.

5. How can the IDP staff be most useful to this University?

6. If the decision were made to discontinue the IDP, what would your reaction be?

7. What else needs to be known about this program?

Appendix B
Instructor Evaluation of Teaching Consultation Service

We would like to know your reactions to the teaching consultation service and to your consultant. Your feedback is important to us and should help us become more effective. Please complete the questionnaire and return it to us as soon as possible in the attached envelope. Your responses will be anonymous, but please discuss with your consultant any issues raised by the survey.

Part I: [completed after data review meeting]

SA A ? D SD	1. By the end of our initial interview, the consultation service's goals were clear to me.
SA A ? D SD	2. The procedures used within the IDP's consultation service were clearly explained to me.
SA A ? D SD	3. Procedures and instruments for collecting data about my teaching were made clear to me.
SA A ? D SD	4. During the initial interview, I was able to clarify my personal objectives in working with the IDP.
SA A ? D SD	5. The initial interview gave me a clear idea of how much of my time and my class's time would be required by the IDP's data collection procedures.
SA A ? D SD	6. My consultant answered all of my questions satisfactorily.
SA A ? D SD	7. All in all, I think the initial interview was well worth my time and effort.
SA A ? D SD	8. The potential value of each type of data (observation, videotape, student rating, self-assessment) was clear to me.
SA A ? D SD	9. The consultant's observation and videotaping of my class was not disruptive or otherwise poorly handled.
SA A ? D SD	10. I was happy with the way the administration of the student rating of my teaching was handled.
SA A ? D SD	11. Generally, I believe that the data collected was sufficiently comprehensive to provide the basis for making decisions about my significant teaching strengths and weaknesses.
SA A ? D SD	12. The computer printout of the student ratings was clear and an adequate display of the data.
SA A ? D SD	13. I found the opportunity to preview the videotape and student ratings by myself useful.
SA A ? D SD	14. The consultant appeared to be well prepared for our data review session.
SA A ? D SD	15. The consultant did a good job of presenting and explaining the data about my teaching.
SA A ? D SD	16. In spite of the consultant's help, I was overwhelmed by the amount and/or variety of data which was made available to me.
SA A ? D SD	17. We were able to identify significant teaching strengths that were indicated by the data.

					18.	The consultant and I agreed on significant teaching problems which were substantiated by the data.
SA	A	?	D	SD		

					19.	The consultant and I agreed on some practical and potentially worthwhile teaching improvement strategies for me to try.
SA	A	?	D	SD		

					20.	So far, I am pleased with the consultant's work with me.
SA	A	?	D	SD		

Part II: [completed at the end of the semester]

SA A ? D SD   21. I was impressed by the consultant's ability to suggest potentially useful improvement strategies.

SA A ? D SD   22. The consultant was sensitive to my personal style, responsibilities, and specific teaching difficulties when suggesting possible improvement strategies.

SA A ? D SD   23. I felt I shared the responsibility for designing improvement strategies.

SA A ? D SD   24. The consultant was receptive and supportive of my suggestions as we planned improvement strategies.

SA A ? D SD   25. The consultant spent enough time helping me plan improvement strategies.

SA A ? D SD   26. The consultant gave me plenty of support as I tried improvement strategies.

SA A ? D SD   27. The consultant and I were able to develop good procedures for assessing the success of the improvement strategies which I tried.

SA A ? D SD   28. I believe that the improvement strategies which I tried helped me improve my teaching.

SA A ? D SD   29. I thought that efforts to collect data about changes in my teaching performance were adequately comprehensive.

SA A ? D SD   30. The data provided me with convincing evidence about whether or not my teaching performance had improved.

SA A ? D SD   31. Overall, I found the consulatation service useful and worth my time and effort.

SA A ? D SD   32. I would recommend the teaching consultation service to my colleagues.

29. *Evaluating a Consultation Program for Part-time Adjunct Faculty*

Barbara J. Millis

"Affirming! I believe validation, growth, and community are the three principle positives," declared an enthusiastic respondent to a 1988 survey conducted to determine the effectiveness of University of Maryland University College's Peer Classroom Consultation Program. Another part-time faculty member wrote in a 1990 letter to the dean of Undergraduate Programs:

> The Peer Visit Program provides faculty with a mechanism to receive feedback in a constructive non-threatening way. Evaluations are invariably thoughtful, supportive and specific. Everyone likes to know how they are doing and this program offers that opportunity. Comments . . . from [my] two evaluations . . . have been very helpful in making me a better instructor. In addition, as a visitor I have been able to observe a variety of teaching styles and approaches which have improved my class presentations. I believe that every instructor desires to conduct their classes in the most effective manner possible. The Peer Visit Program is a tool that can be used to achieve that goal.

Qualitative feedback such as this and much positive anecdotal evidence convinced us about the importance of pursuing a three-year quantitative study of our program: of peer classroom consultations focused by classroom visits conducted over two semesters by adjunct lecturers. Fortunately, the Fund for the Improvement of Post-Secondary Education agreed with us, and we conducted a long-term classical experimental/control group study. These research efforts were also supported by a grant from the Maryland Assessment Research Center.

This article describes the University of Maryland University College's Peer Consultation Program, which has been replicated in whole or in part at a number of other institutions; discusses the FIPSE study augmented by MARC funds and the possible directions for further research; and then suggests some of the pitfalls and promises inherent in the evaluation and assessment of instructional consultation programs with the hope that successors will profit from our experience.

The Institutional Context

One of the eleven campuses of the University of Maryland System, University of Maryland University College (UMUC) has been an independent, self-supporting institution since 1970. Priding itself on its teaching mission and its responsiveness to adult learners, UMUC staffs the vast majority of its undergraduate classes—seven to eight hundred courses a semester throughout the state of Maryland, including military installations—with well-qualified adjunct instructors.

These instructors tend to be intrinsically motivated, highly committed, academically credentialed working professionals. A majority of them are individuals characterized by Martin Wachs (1993) as "practitioner-faculty," reflective professionals functioning in the real world of work who can "pass along to the next generation their special skills, their insights, the nuances of their craft" (p. 8). Because they consider teaching an avocation, they generally welcome the support UMUC offers to help them meet the demanding challenges of a student population composed primarily of working adults. Due in part to a flexible admissions policy and a welcoming climate, UMUC's student population is refreshingly diverse: 51 percent of the students are female, 29 percent are minorities.

UMUC adjunct faculty recognize that such student populations require new responses in the classroom. Di-

Note: The author gratefully acknowledges the contributions of Laurie Richlin in processing the final data and of Barbara Kaplan in shaping the narrative in the methodology section and reworking the tables.

29. Evaluating a Consultation Program for Part-time Adjunct Faculty / 245

verse teaching approaches which emphasize "the flexibility of a college instructor's teaching repertoire, and his or her readiness to draw on a range of teaching styles for a variety of ends" (Adams, 1992, p. 15) are essential. Thus, virtually all instructors, beginning with a mandatory three-hour New Faculty Orientation, participate in a wide variety of faculty development opportunities, including general and discipline-specific faculty meetings; a workshop series; faculty newsletters; a teaching portfolio initiative; awards for teaching excellence; and teaching-related travel grants. The highlight of these opportunities is our extensive Peer Visit Program, one of the few systematic classroom consultation programs for part-time faculty in the nation.

A History of the Peer Consultation Program

Initiated in 1985, the Peer Visit Program, as it has historically been called at UMUC, sends an experienced, trained visitor into the classroom of instructors new to UMUC (about 180 a year) and instructors nominated for the Excellence in Teaching Award (about 65 a year). The program is designed not only to strengthen teaching, but also to give part-time lecturers a sense of "connection" with the institution. It has also proved to be a significant public relations tool because students see with each visit that UMUC is committed to their learning. Originally only a single visit occurred, but thanks to the three-year grant initiated in 1990 from the Fund to Improve Postsecondary Education and subsequent UMUC funding, follow-up visits now take place the following semester, resulting in a more meaningful long-term consultation process.

UMUC's Peer Visit Program has consistently and smoothly met the needs of faculty, students, and the institution. It is more fully described in Millis (1994). Several factors have contributed to its success:

(a) Faculty, from the day they are recruited, learn of the program as a collegial, supportive means of putting them in touch with an experienced UMUC instructor who will help them reflect on teaching successes and enhancements;

(b) The program has always received full backing, including financial support, from the highest administrative levels;

(c) A full-time administrator, the Faculty Development Coordinator, carefully orchestrates the process using peer visit preference forms completed by the visitors, the faculty data-base, and a special scheduling software program that matches available visitors to the faculty needing visits and generates scheduling letters with detailed infor-

mation for both parties. With an exemplary teaching background and a Ph.D. in history with a related science background, the coordinator also provides credible auxiliary consultation to faculty wishing to receive further teaching insights.

(d) The faculty-to-faculty contacts are carefully focused through a 32-page Peer Visit Packet containing an overview of the program, self-assessment instruments for the faculty member being visited, and guidelines for the visitor regarding constructive interpersonal and pedagogical exchanges;

(e) The observations are systematic, consisting of a three-tier process. During the pre-observation period, the faculty members go over the syllabi together and discuss the broad course goals and immediate classroom plans and activities. After being introduced to the students, who are informed in advance of the nature and purpose of the visit, the visitor observes the class for one to two hours. During the post-observation discussion, the visitor provides teaching-related feedback, reinforcing positive practices and encouraging substantive changes in areas where teaching could be strengthened.

(f) A faculty-developed classroom observation instrument prompts concrete, focused narrative (Appendix A). This written review, which complements the oral feedback, is sent to the faculty member with a cover letter from the Faculty Development Coordinator encouraging these "practitioner-faculty"—even those with excellent teaching reviews—to follow the dictum that instructors, like their students, are life-long learners.

(g) The peer visitors are selected for their exemplary teaching records and interpersonal skills. They are fully trained through annual workshops and carefully supported by personal contact and feedback on their reviews;

(h) The program is constantly being assessed and refined, primarily through faculty input. For example, each August when we offer a training workshop for the new peer visitors, we ask veteran consultants to participate and to share ideas for program improvement. Furthermore, we conducted informal, but comprehensive qualitative studies in 1986, 1988, and 1993.

An on-going consultation process is extremely complex with many, many variables affecting the outcomes—personalities and commitment of the two parties, nature and motivation of the students, the discipline, institutional pressures and priorities, and so on. Boice (1992), in fact, commented that any type of mentoring "often occurs in a gradual, unsystematic fashion, making it hard to study (p. 51)." Despite this knowledge, we set out with confidence and funding support to determine the efficacy of our two-semester peer consultations.

Evaluation, Design and Results

Objectives

The objectives of the evaluation project were: (a) To assess the extent that peer classroom observations affect student ratings of instruction; (b) To link any changes we identified with student learning outcomes. Our working hypothesis was that consultation with experienced teachers helps faculty improve teaching effectiveness.

Design and Implementation

The original research design, formulated by an outside consultant and UMUC experts from both faculty and administrative ranks, relied on a typical experimental/control group format. We knew from the onset that the experimental group of part-time adjunct faculty would be composed of two bipolar groups: (1) faculty new to UMUC, but not necessarily new to teaching (only 22.2% have never taught before, according to 162 respondents at our mandatory New Faculty Orientations); and (2) faculty nominated for the Excellence in Teaching Award. We expected the latter group to show less teaching improvement as a result of the two visits simply because they were already near the top of the "teaching curve." We carefully tagged these individuals and, in fact, included only five of them in the final research study. Faculty in the experimental group received peer consultations, focused on classroom visits, both fall and spring semesters, while control faculty did not. Selection of faculty for the control group was based on a course-by-course match. If an instructor teaching an English 101 course was included in the experimental group, then we identified another instructor teaching a 101 course as a control group member. If no exact match was possible, then we selected a course within the discipline which seemed a close match. Fortunately for the study, we used "overkill" on the control group and always included far more classes than in the experimental group.

Both groups contained men and women; a comparatively diverse range of disciplines was represented in each group. For the instructors undergoing consultation (the experimental group), we attempted to schedule the same peer visitor to observe classes both semesters. In order to insure a genuine consultation experience, the peer visit reports were discussed with the instructors after each classroom observation.

Results

We obtained student evaluation results for both experimental and control groups each of the three years. Not all instructors submitted both evaluation instruments, the locally developed CRIS and the nationally-normed IDEA, as requested, primarily due to their reluctance to use class time to administer two separate evaluation forms. In response to this problem, we altered our design to include data from instructors who turned in either (as well as both) CRIS and IDEA forms for the two semesters.

Our final sample size was also limited by the fact that—as often happens in programs using adjunct lecturers—some instructors in the experimental group were not scheduled to teach or had courses canceled the following semester. Further, we often found it difficult to schedule the same peer visitor for both the fall and spring semesters, because of the consultant's own unavailability. This latter fact serendipitously allowed us to measure the impact of having a single peer visitor versus two different visitors.

The total number of viable participants in the three-year study included 40 peer visitors (instructional consultants); 49 instructors in the experimental group; and 74 instructors in the control group.

In this chapter, we report data for eight scores on the two student evaluation forms. The eight items, chosen specifically because they reflect student perceptions of learning, included three CRIS scores and five IDEA scores. These are:

(1) "Pedagogical" aggregate (CRIS)
(2) "Rapport" aggregate (CRIS)
(3) "Overall" aggregate (CRIS)
(4) "Good Teaching" subgroup (IDEA)
(5) "Learning Outcomes" subgroup (IDEA)
(6) "Overall Evaluation" score (IDEA)
(7) "Would Like Instructor Again" score (IDEA)
(8) "Improved Attitude Toward Field" score (IDEA)

Because we were interested in net change between the first and second semester of the project, we subtracted the scores from the first semester from those of the second to show a positive difference for those who improved and a negative one for those whose scores decreased. We compared the changes in the eight items for participants in the experimental and control groups as a whole, by participants' sex, and whether participants in the experimental group had the same or a different visitor for the second semester.

The report of our external evaluator concluded that (a) the experimental group changed in a positive direction in all eight categories and the control group changed in a negative direction in five categories, (b) women showed greater positive change than men, especially those who had the same peer consultant for both classroom observations, and (c) results were not correlated with the participants' department, with holding a terminal degree, or with full-time teaching status.

Discussion

Despite Herculean efforts, we did not achieve startling statistical breakthroughs with this long-term quantitative study. Nevertheless, the findings suggest that UMUC's Peer Classroom Visitation Consulting Program results in improved instructor performance and enhanced perceptions of students about the quality of their education.

Because of the complexity of instructional consultations, it may be that a qualitative approach is more useful than quantitative approaches that unsuccessfully attempt to control for extraneous variables. For example, a Faculty Development TQM committee composed of a broad range of UMUC staff including administrators, faculty, and clerical support staff spent eighteen months focusing on UMUC's Peer Consultation Program. In addition to making several recommendations for continuous improvement, such as the inclusion of a one-page teaching-oriented biography of the visitor with the scheduling letter, they conducted two informally constructed but in-depth surveys. There were 73 responses to the survey which included both instructors who had served as peer consultants and instructors whose classes had been visited. An astonishing 83 percent agreed or strongly agreed that the program positively affects teaching behavior through improvement and reinforcement of effective teaching practices and that it provides opportunities for mutual learning experiences. Such informal assessments can certainly supplement and augment the more formal quantitative studies. Virtually all researchers advocate multiple measures of program efficacy.

Therefore, we plan to continue the study, adding a qualitative component. We hope to discover, for example, those variables that make for a positive visit (one resulting in significant improvements on the two instruments) and those that have less impact. The role that gender plays in the visits may be an interesting avenue of pursuit. We are also interested in the impact the visits might have on the visitors themselves and on the validity of our UMUC-developed CRIS instrument vis-a-vis the nationally normed IDEA instrument. It might be useful, also, to look carefully at the fifteen supplementary questions added to the IDEA instrument to determine what actually is going on in UMUC classrooms, at least as students perceive the activities.

Some Final Thoughts

These final thoughts are intended to serve as cautionary advice for anyone undertaking the assessment of an instructional consultation program. They are not intended as definitive guidelines: we hope merely to focus thinking and generate discussion.

Don't underestimate the complexity of the problem. Anyone attempting to assess the effects of instructional consultation should consider, as we have, the value of using both quantitative and qualitative measures. Furthermore, the number of variables involved is almost infinite, as suggested earlier. Many variables will not even become apparent until the project is well-launched. For example, because our return rate for the CRIS and IDEA instruments was not as high as expected in either the experimental or control group, we began to question as the data came in whether those who take class time to have students complete two assessment instruments a semester, were already instructors predisposed to reflect on and improve their teaching. Many other factors could also have affected the study, such as instructors' prior teaching experience or the location of the participating classes (on or off-campus: if off-campus, at a business site, teaching center, or military installation). Controlling for all such variables is virtually impossible. Furthermore, Eison (private conversation, January 5, 1994) cautions that it is hard to tease out precise impacts, particularly with short-term interventions.

Don't neglect the people side of any assessment project. It is easy to get caught up in the grandeur of pure design and theoretical research and then to overlook the practical implementation. Cooper (1993) cautions about this critical aspect, which includes 'people skills': "It is essential that the assessment procedures be spelled out to participants and agreed to, from the onset. Clear time lines for doing assessment must be identified and adhered to.... Most people are defensive about being assessed. It is critical that you create a 'safe' environment for faculty to function." (n.p). We sent advance notice to all faculty about the evaluation, urging their participation; emphasized its importance at faculty meetings; and included a positive letter with the IDEA instruments. Still, we received less compliance than we had hoped for, no doubt because of a number of tangled human factors.

Put a great deal of thought into the up-front evaluation design. Everyone advocates this practice and most of us go happily into research projects confident that we have covered all the quantitative bases. There is a common saying in the world of publications that there is never enough time to do it right the first time, but there is always enough time to do it again right, meaning that if we rush through production, we will face glaring errors that necessitate redesigning or simply reproofreading a particular piece. With research—as with some publications—"retakes" are not possible. As the Total Quality Management gurus exhort, we must usually "get it right the first time." We can't, for example, reassemble students in classes who did not complete our assessment instruments. In this study, we picked our control group randomly, based on faculty who were teaching the same or similar courses to those in the experimental group. In retrospect, however, this selection process was not ideal, because in the control group we included a number of faculty who were themselves peer visitors, a form of intervention in itself, or who were full-time faculty, not a viable comparison with the adjuncts we typically included in the experimental group.

Build into the assessment project, if possible, a component that evaluates the implementation. Cooper (1993) states that such a component should "ensure that the things that are supposed to go on in the intervention classroom are actually going on. If the intervention is not faithfully implemented, it may not be reasonable to expect changes in student and faculty performances." (n.p.). For example, we provided explicit training in conducting peer classroom observations and providing effective, concrete feedback during annual workshops. We also reinforced these practices through the 32-page Peer Visit Packet. Each classroom observation report was also carefully reviewed and summarized before being forwarded to the instructor undergoing the instructional consultation procedure. Nonetheless, we cannot be certain that each observation followed the prescribed format of a pre-observation discussion, a professionally conducted in-class observation, and a meaningful post-visit conference to offer constructive feedback. From discussions with all faculty involved, it is clear that some peer consultants spent far more time and effort on the entire process than did others. Likewise, those being visited invested varying degrees of effort and reflection in the process. Thus, it is difficult to know—and certainly impossible to quantify—the exact nature of the full instructional consultation.

Expect glitches and learn to roll quickly with the punches. Our FIPSE project ran into a number of unforeseen problems. We did not realize, for instance, that our anticipated sample size would be rapidly decimated by lecturers who did not teach a second term: adjuncts, even those in a stable institution accustomed to their use, often have other obligations; the new faculty used in our study may be the last to be offered classes; and classes at off-campus sites are sometimes canceled because of low enrollments. To counter this problem, after our first-year experience, we alerted the assistant deans and program managers who staff classes of the need to provide—if at all possible—a two-semester experience for the new faculty beginning in the fall semester. They complied whenever possible, increasing our sample size the second and third years. When we realized that it was not always possible to schedule the same peer consultant for a second classroom observation, we reacted quickly by sending the new visitor all relevant paperwork, including the original peer classroom observation form completed by the original visitor and any instruments such as a teaching self-assessment form or a teaching action plan (TAP) completed by the instructor undergoing the instructional consultation. Our hope was that the second visitor could thus build on the feedback given by the initial consultant. Furthermore, when we got to the data analysis stage, we realized that we had a unique opportunity to discover if having two different visitors had a measurable effect on teaching enhancement and perceived student learning outcomes.

If you plan an ambitious project and don't have the time or the professional expertise (background in research design, knowledge of statistics, and so on) then hire competent consultants, preferably from the start, who are in tune with your project, institution, and goals.

We made a mistake in hiring our first consultant, a man with impeccable credentials, who did not, unfortunately provide the kind of research design the project warranted, identify a viable software package to capture and analyze the data, or offer the long-term investment in this project we had anticipated. Later, we wisely tapped our own faculty expertise by establishing an ad hoc faculty/administrative Evaluation Committee which helped us modify the original research design predicated on determining student learning outcomes based on retention and success in subsequent classes. We found these original suppositions untenable because of a fluctuating (drop in, drop out) adult student population hit by a recession. Our final consultant—the "number cruncher"—came on board too late to modify the research design and had to work creatively with the data we had already captured.

Don't despair as assessment/evaluation projects take their ups and downs. A key lesson for us was to "keep the faith"—keep the project going, keep gathering data as planned—despite short-term set-backs and long-term reservations about our final success.

What we accomplished, however flawed, was worth doing because no one else had ever attempted such an ambitious study. What we learned reinforced our own commitment to the value of peer consultations focused on classroom observations and should provide encouragement to others contemplating similar projects.

Perhaps more importantly, the conclusion that peer classroom observations and consultations do positively affect teaching and learning outcomes is a significant one if only because the Peer Visit Program at UMUC is an extremely economical, faculty-driven model, one which could be replicated on virtually any campus with large numbers of adjunct faculty. Furthermore, as indicated earlier, the program's benefits go far beyond teaching and learning measures: faculty and student morale and commitment to the institution are also positively affected.

The study we conducted can be used as a blueprint for similar studies, ones which can now build on our experience. The Fund for the Improvement of Postsecondary Education has always encouraged innovative experimentation. As they are quick to note, the lessons learned from such efforts often can be as valuable as definitive studies which close the door on future research. In the meanwhile, we are pleased that the Peer Visit Program does have positive results; we celebrate a TQM, can-do approach; and we remain encouraged by Nietzsche's reminder that "Truth has never yet hung on the rim of an absolute."

References

Adams, M. (1992). Cultural inclusion in the American college classroom. *New Directions for Teaching and Learning*, no. 49, 5-17. San Francisco: Jossey-Bass.

Boice, R. (1992). Lessons learned about mentoring. In M. D. Sorcinelli & A. E. Austin (Eds.), *Developing new and junior faculty*. New Directions for Teaching and Learning, no. 50, 51-61. San Francisco: Jossey Bass.

Cooper, J. (1993). *Some thoughts on assessing faculty training programs.* Unpublished paper circulated at 1993 FIPSE Project Director's Meeting.

Millis, B. (1994). Forging the ties that bind: Peer mentoring part-time faculty. *New Directions for Teaching and Learning*, no. 57, 73-80. San Francisco: Jossey-Bass.

Wachs, M. (1993). The case for practitioner-faculty. *AAHE Bulletin, 46*(3), 8-10.

Appendix A

University College Undergraduate Programs Classroom Visit
(Condensed Version)

Faculty Member:_____ Course & Section: _____

Date: _____ Length of Visit:_____ Place: _____

Visitor:_____

Number of Students Present:_____

Classroom: Note any inadequate aspects of the classroom (size, temperature, acoustics, lighting, etc.)

Instruction: Comment on the presentation of the material: points to be covered and their relevance to class session, knowledge of subject matter, organization of lecture, explanation of terms and concepts.

Instructor/Student Rapport: Comment on student involvement and interaction with the instructor: opportunities for students to ask questions, answers to questions, guidance of class discussion, openness to suggestions and ideas.

Style of Presentation: Comment on gestures, physical movement, pitch and tone of voice, eye contact with students, use of resources such as blackboard, audio-visual media, handouts and other materials, demonstrations, student presentations and group activities and the integration of various elements of the class session.

Syllabus: Comment on the syllabus and other written materials provided by the instructor. (Please refer to the University College Syllabus Construction Handbook.)

General Comments: What part of the class seemed particularly to enhance the learning process? What specific suggestions can you give for improving this particular class?

Part Five:

Training Instructional Consultants

*P*art Five, the final section of the sourcebook, focuses on structured, systematic training programs for instructional consultation practitioners. We begin this part with a theoretical overview of some concepts that are—or should be—prominent in training programs, then move to descriptions of established training programs in a variety of institution types. This part should be especially helpful to experienced consultants who are designing training programs for novice consultants or who are seeking professional development for themselves.

In Chapter 30, Smith highlights three theories that can shape how instructional consultants reflect upon their own practice. Arygris and Schön's notion of theory-in-use vs. espoused theory helps consultants uncover discrepancies between what they say they do and what they actually do. Senge's notion of mental models focuses on assumptions that consultants have about clients, teaching, and the consultation process. Kennedy's perspectives on expertise provide a framework for evaluating how we acquire consulting skills.

Chapters 31 and 32 contain descriptions of instructional consultation training programs in community colleges. In Chapter 31, Searle and Cook describe a state-wide training program for community college faculty who become peer consultants for each other on unionized campuses that have no formal faculty development programs. This training involves three one-day workshops and a stipend over the course of a calendar year. In Chapter 32, Kerwin and Rhoads describe another state-wide training program for community college faculty. In contrast to Searle and Cook's program, these consultations extend over one semester and utilize faculty recognized for their excellence in teaching as consultants. Kerwin and Rhoads' training involves extensive data collection, followed by a one-day workshop in which the primary activity is sharing and discussing videotape clips of clients' teaching.

Chapters 33 through 36 focus on training programs in research-oriented universities. In Chapter 33, Black and Gates describe a workshop for training experienced teach-ing assistants to work with new teaching assistants as peer consultants. This three-hour, instructor-centered workshop is facilitated by two professional instructional development staff. In Chapter 34, Nyquist and Wulff describe a two-week intensive seminar that involves new as well as experienced instructional consultants who are discipline-based staff in a faculty development center. As follow-up to the seminar, each new consultant has a supervisor, staff notebooks and videotapes, team meetings, think tank meetings, colloquia, and opportunities for co-consulting with another instructional consultant. In Chapter 35, Marincovich describes a one-day workshop to train teaching assistants as instructional consultants in three data collection techniques: classroom observation, videotaping, and Student Small Group Evaluation. This workshop is notable in that it is inexpensive in terms of time and resources, yet it is successful. A long-term evaluation of the consultants who underwent training showed that they felt they received the training that they needed to perform the duties of an instructional consultant; that the experience benefited them professionally as teachers; and that they remained active in teaching improvement activities after they graduated and went on to other colleges and universities as junior faculty.

While the training programs in Chapters 33 through 35 focus on training new consultants, the training program in Chapter 36 addresses an effort to develop the skills of experienced consultants. In Chapter 36, Hofer, Black, and Acitelli describe their six-week plan for staff development that included preparatory readings and analysis of their consultation as captured by videotape in each of the stages of the consultation process. In addition to skill development, the outcomes of the experience included the development of a common language for professional discussion, an increased empathy for clients, and a greater sense of being part of a team.

In the final chapter of this part, Chapter 37, Millis offers two case studies that can be used in training either new or experienced instructional consultants: "The Case of the Disgruntled Philosophy Professor" and "The Case of the Crammed Chemistry Course." However, rather than using the traditional case method that requires considerable expertise, Millis suggests using the cases with collaborative learning techniques, a method with which she has found success when training department chairs, volunteer classroom observers, and peer partners.

From studying this part of the sourcebook, experienced consultants will have expanded their theoretical and practical perspectives about how to train novices for the task of instructional consultation. In addition, experienced consultants will have gained new insight on how to reflect upon and improve their own practice as they endeavor to enhance their own professional development.

30. Instructional Consultants as Reflective Practitioners

Ronald Smith

In higher education the practice of teaching, as well as the practice of instructional consultation (that is, of helping others to improve their teaching), is most often learned through a process of trial and error. Since there are so very few programs to train people to become teachers in their disciplines, and even fewer programs to train instructional consultants, perhaps the only way to learn is from experience on the job. However, this approach is often painful; the tests come first, the lessons later. This approach of "learning by doing" has a long history. Some people (including many of those involved in formal professional training programs) argue that it is the only way to really learn; others argue that being able to do something is the only real test that you know it.

In this chapter, I want to reflect on the practice of instructional consultation in terms of our learning from our own experiences and in terms of helping faculty to learn from theirs. The starting point for this examination will be the work of Donald Schön (1983, 1987) on the "reflective practitioner" and his work with Chris Argyris on "theories of action" (Argyris and Schön, 1974). I will also consider how our personal metaphors, or mental models as Senge (1990) might call them, as well as our conceptions of expertise (Kennedy, 1987) can influence both our practice and our reflections about it. These ideas will be elaborated and then connected both to the development of instructional consultants, and to faculty members' development as teachers.

Reflection-in-Action

Donald Schön, in his 1983 book *The Reflective Practitioner: How professionals think-in-action*, provides the basis for his epistemology of practice; that is, how we come to the knowledge that is so evident in our daily actions. As he describes it, we go along acting effectively, demonstrating our knowledge through our skillful action, often without much conscious attention, until we encoun-

ter a problem, a puzzle, a surprise, or as he sometimes calls it, a "mess." Our usually skillful actions do not produce the responses we expect. It is then that we begin to "**reflect-in-action**," going into his cycle of **framing**, or naming, the problem we have to solve; **making moves**, or taking action, to solve the problem we have named; **listening** to the "talk back" from the situation which results from our actions; and then **deciding** on the basis of these consequences if we have solved the problem we have set for ourselves. If it is not solved, we can either try some new actions to solve it, or **re-frame** the situation and set a different problem to be solved.

This description of practice, of problem solving in the context of action, is presented as an alternative to the more traditional view of professional practice as the application of theories to solve problems (which Schön has called "technical rationality"). In those indeterminate situations so common to the practice of instructional consultation and teaching which are characterized by ambiguity, uncertainty, uniqueness, and value conflicts, reflection-in-action highlights the difficulty, as well as the artistry, involved in choosing or naming the problem to be solved (which itself is certainly not a technical task). Schön argues that in educating or training practitioners we need to provide reflective practicums where professionals can discover, discuss, and examine how they think-in-action; that is, how they set the problems to be solved, how they act to solve these problems, and how they come to learn about the adequacy of their problem frames and their action strategies.

These concepts relate to our work as instructional consultants in three ways. First, reflection-in-action provides the basis of a model for consultants to use in working with their faculty clients. Consultants can help faculty members and TAs to become reflective practitioners, to examine how they were thinking and acting in those situations in their teaching that didn't turn out the way they expected. Second, reflecting on practice provides a model for helping consultants to improve their own work through self-directed learning efforts; for example, after some training they could learn to write and analyze case studies about their own practice. Third, the reflective practicum provides a model for developing programs to help consultants to improve their skills; for example, new and experienced consultants could come together to share their cases and learn from each other.

Reflecting <u>on</u> Reflection-<u>in</u>-Action

Both consultants and teachers need to reflect <u>on</u> their practice to discover how they were reflecting-<u>in</u>-action. Schön not only provides a description of what practitioners do; that is, how we think and act in the action situation; he also provides a framework within which to analyze our actions in order to learn from them. What is the focus of this analysis? One suggestion comes from his work with Chris Argyris. In *Theory in Practice: Increasing Professional Effectiveness* (1974) they suggest that we design our actions in order to achieve our intentions and that we have theories about how to design our actions in order to be effective in achieving those intentions. These "theories-of-action" are our personal theories of effective behavior. For example, we have theories about giving effective feedback, about handling resistance in faculty, and so on. Thus, one goal in reflecting on how I was acting in a particular situation is to identify my theory-of-action in that situation, what rule I was following.

Since no one would intentionally design their actions to be ineffective, we need to discover (become aware of) how we were thinking in that situation in order to act as we did. We need to give ourselves reason, how we were thinking for our actions to make sense to us. We also need to identify any counterproductive features in the ways we reason and act. It is somewhat surprising that this is usually much more difficult than it may seem because the rules we actually follow in designing our actions (our theories-in-use) are often different from the rules we say we use (our espoused theories).

Let me illustrate these ideas with a brief example. Consider the problem of trying to encourage a reluctant professor to experiment with a new approach to responding to student questions. You might say or espouse that your theory of encouragement was to be supportive and say positive things. By examining what you actually said in the situation ("I've seen you handle situations like this in other classes. You shouldn't worry, I'm sure you can handle this one.") it can be discovered whether you did say words which could be interpreted as positive and

supportive. From this you could also discover other features of your actual theory of encouragement. When you believe a professor is reluctant to follow your suggestion, you assume that your assessment is correct and that he/she needs encouragement. When you assume a professor needs encouragement, you say that you have more confidence in them than they seem to have in themselves. It is not clear how telling a reluctant person to try something, or how telling a person who is worried not to worry, would be either supportive, positive, or encouraging. Thus, it is possible to discover from reflecting on your practice whether or not your actions match your espoused theory. (Instead of being positive and supportive, are you presumptuous and controlling?) You can then decide if you need to modify your actions (to be more consistent with your espoused theory of encouragement), or to modify your theory.

Reflection on Practice as Problem Solving

Improving our practice by examining how we think in action is a form of problem solving. This approach has been described in general by Argyris and Schön and has been applied to teaching and faculty development (Smith, 1983; Smith & Schwartz, 1986, 1988, 1990). At its core is the writing and analysis of "case studies" about a difficult situation in one's professional practice. The reflective practitioner, the case author, is invited to write up a description of a difficult episode in their practice of teaching or consulting, one where they were not satisfied with the outcome, or one which they anticipate they would have difficulty handling. Appendix A provides the detailed guidelines. The case write-up includes: a description of the problem; the strategies they used; the barriers they encountered; as well as a piece of dialogue, including what was said and thoughts and feelings which were not communicated, that reflects the difficulty in the situation. The case study provides a rich description of an actual episode of a person's professional practice from which to infer their theories-in-use, to identify counterproductive features in the way they reason and act in difficult situations in their practice, and to invent new ways of thinking and acting.

It is helpful, if not necessary, to have some standards or criteria to use in assessing the effectiveness of our problem solving and in identifying the counterproductive features of our thinking-in-action. Let me suggest some criteria for effective problem solving: 1) Is the problem solved? 2) Does the problem stay solved? and 3) Have the relationships been so harmed that we will not be able to work well together in the future?

These seem reasonable, but how are they to be achieved? Argyris and Schön have suggested what might be required for these criteria to be achieved and for problem solving to be effective. Professionals must behave in ways which are consistent with 1) the generation of valid information about the situation at hand; 2) the promotion of free and informed choices about the actions to be taken; and 3) the creation of an internal commitment to monitor the outcomes of the decisions taken. The generation of valid information requires what Argyris has called "productive reasoning." Professionals must use "hard data" (that is, descriptions of reality which are easily accepted as valid by people with contradictory views); they must make their premises explicit; they must make their inferences explicit; and finally, they must publicly test their conclusions (Argyris 1985, p. 262).

Most professionals accept these criteria as necessary and valid, we take them for granted and assume that they inform our practice. One goal in reflecting on our practice, in analyzing our case studies, is to identify our ineffective problem solving, our counterproductive behavior and our unproductive reasoning. More specifically, to answer such questions as: Have I made judgments, attributions, or evaluations about the other person which are not illustrated or tested? Are my actions based on the assumption that these judgments are true? Do I advocate my position without inviting inquiry or discussion? Am I withholding important and relevant information? If the answer to any of these questions is yes, then the consequences for my effectiveness as a problem solver is clear. Not only might I be acting on inaccurate information, perhaps trying to solve the wrong problem; but I could also be creating counterproductive interpersonal dynamics. The misunderstanding, miscommunication, and mistrust which is generated will not only limit my problem-solving effectiveness (that is, I will be solving the wrong problem); but they will also limit my learning about my effectiveness (that is, important areas will remain undiscussed and perhaps undiscussable).

Thus, in reflecting on our practice in order to evaluate it, in order to learn from it and to become more effective, we need to identify the theories-of-action we were using, and then assess the extent to which they are consistent with the criteria for effective problem solving described above. At a fairly abstract level, this could mean making attributions or evaluation about a client; that is, he's fragile, she doesn't really care, she's more interested in protecting herself than in helping the student, he can't handle direct feedback, and so on; and then acting as if these judgments

were true. This way of acting has several obvious, at least to me, counterproductive consequences: I may be wrong and not discover it for awhile, if ever; my actions may become self-fulfilling and create the very situation I "feared"; there will be misunderstanding, mistrust, and probably little learning and change. See Appendix B for suggestions about analyzing your own case.

Metaphors, Mental Models, and Personal Paradigms

What models or theories inform our practice as consultants (or as teachers)? Each of us has our own personal theories-of-action about how to give constructive feedback, about how to encourage another, about how to deal with conflict, and so on. If we go beyond this micro-level of theorizing about our practice, we can also identify larger or more macro-level frameworks, a sort of grand theory about what our role as instructional consultants and professors should be. These larger frames might be thought of as mental models, metaphors or personal paradigms for action. Their effect is to position us for action, they determine what is important to attend to as well as what can be ignored, what data matter, what questions can and cannot be asked, and so on In reflecting on our practice this is another level of analysis that is important to consider. For example:

Do we see ourselves as **clinicians**, coming in to treat someone who is lacking some vital ingredient, and our job is to diagnose and treat, until the person is well enough to function on their own?

Do we see ourselves as **bankers**, making deposits to their store of knowledge, skill, and so on?

Do we see ourselves as **gardeners**, sowing seeds, and cultivating them in a supportive environment?

Do we see ourselves as **midwives**, helping clients give birth to their innate knowledge and skill?

Do we see ourselves as **travel agents**, helping clients reach whatever destination they would like, by providing a variety of routes and alternative means of transportation?

I know I certainly haven't exhausted the list of possibilities. Each of these images emphasizes different aspects of our role, highlighting our theories of change, our beliefs about learners, and so on. I think this avenue is potentially very important in reflecting on our practice, because in helping to identify our personal paradigms and frames, those core ideas which inform our practice, we also come to discover how we evaluate our accomplishments.

In reflecting on our practice we need to become aware of the theories of consulting or teaching that inform our professional practice. It is also important to consider the extent to which we discuss these with our clients, our colleagues, and our students. For example, if we believe that it important for the other person to discover his/her own solutions to problems, do we discuss this directly by describing how we will be behaving in our interaction? We will rarely answer questions or give our judgments directly (when asked for our advice or an evaluation). We would prefer that the other person come to their own conclusions with the assistance of our helpful questioning. If we have not made our theory of being helpful explicit to the other person, we may be experienced by them as being evasive, or even patronizing, as trying to leading them to our conclusions.

We have considered the examination of our professional practice from the point of view of how we reason and act in the specific situation, and from the general metaphors or models that might influence our general strategies. We now turn to a consideration of some views of what expert performance should look like.

Models of Expertise

What does it mean to be an expert, an expert in a discipline, an expert teacher, an expert consultant? What is the expertise of teaching or the expertise of instructional consulting? How does it come to be acquired? Our answers to these questions will have a significant impact on our practice. They will determine what we do in our efforts to learn to teach or to consult, as well as how we might design programs to help others acquire these skills. Dreyfus and Dreyfus have developed a five-stage model of the movement from novice to expert which is described in Chapter 25. Mary Kennedy in her 1987 article, "Inexact sciences: Professional education and the development of expertise," has articulated four different models of expertise, including their assumptions, critiques, purpose and methods of instruction, exemplars, and transition experiences. It is described in some detail in Appendix C.

Expertise **as technical skills** is derived from the specific tasks professionals must perform. Competency-based teacher education is an example of this approach. What are the specific skills an instructional consultant should have? (for example, observation skills? feedback skills? operating video-equipment?)

Expertise **as the application of theory or general principles** reflects our desire, if not our practice, to be able "to treat particular cases as examples of categories about which something is known" (Kennedy, 1987, p. 137). This approach is best reflected in medical and engineering education where students regularly take two or three years of basic sciences before they move on to their clinical or

design studies. What are the theories or general principles of instructional consultation or good teaching? (for example, principles of systematic instructional design? adult learning principles? principles of good practice or of active learning?)

Expertise **as critical analysis** "prescribes a paradigm for examining and interpreting situations" (Kennedy, 1987, p. 143) and is most clearly reflected in law schools where students learn to think like lawyers through the use of case studies. There are approaches to teaching that have almost acquired the status of paradigms; for example, the case approach as the sole method in some business schools, or PBL in some medical schools. Are there paradigms for instructional consulting? (for example, the Rogerian approach? the clinic approach?)

Expertise **as deliberate action** assumes that professionals must be "capable of deliberation about, and critical examination of, their own actions and the consequences of those actions" (Kennedy, 1987, p. 148). While no field has adopted this definition as the guiding principle for education, Schön (1987) provides illustrations from such areas as architecture, town planning, psychotherapy, and management. This chapter has illustrated how this approach might work in instructional consulting.

These models provide a template for examining our practice and our development as practitioners. How do we think about our own work as consultants? What is the expertise we are trying to demonstrate and develop? And what is the nature of the expertise of teaching that we hope the professors we work with will acquire? These models would also have implications for faculty members in their efforts to help their own students come to acquire the expertise of their individual disciplines.

This chapter has provided the model of the reflective practitioner as a framework for instructional consultants to consider in working with their faculty clients, to use in the on-going development of their own expertise, and as a model for educating consultants. I hope the illustrations have been clear enough to suggest what might be involved in becoming a reflective practitioner. The most critical factor in determining success as a reflective practitioner may be the way we frame competence and what it means to make an error. If we are always making mistakes then we are not competent. If we expect never to make a mistake, then we will probably never do anything. Our competence will be determined by what we do when we make a mistake. Are errors seen as learning opportunities and to what extent do we behave in ways which will increase our effectiveness at learning about our effectiveness?

My idea of a productive work environment is one in

which we regularly discuss with our colleagues the most difficult cases in our practice in order to learn to be more effective. This is in stark contrast with the more typical work setting where we routinely hide our most difficult cases in order to be seen as competent. Our challenge as professionals is to create learning organizations in our work settings. The list of references provides further reading to help in this endeavor.

References

Argyris, C. (1985). *Strategy, change, and defensive routines*. Marshfield, MA: Pitman.

Argyris, C., & Schön, D. (1974). *Theory in practice: Increasing professional effectiveness*. San Francisco: Jossey-Bass.

Kennedy, M (1987). Inexact sciences: Professional education and the development of expertise. *Review of Research in Education, 14*, 133-167.

Schön, D. (1983). *The reflective practitioner: How professionals think in action*. New York: Basic Books.

Schön, D. (1987). *Educating the reflective practitioner*. San Francisco: Jossey-Bass.

Senge, P. M. (1990). *The fifth discipline: The art and practice of the learning organization*. New York: Doubleday.

Smith, R. A. (1983). A theory of action perspective on faculty development. *To Improve The Academy, 2*, 47-58.

Smith, R. A., & Schwartz, F. (1986). A theory of effectiveness: Faculty development case studies. *Journal of Staff, Program, and Organization Development, 4*(1), 3-8.

Smith, R. A., & Schwartz, F. (1988). Improving teaching by reflecting on practice. *To Improve the Academy, 7*, 63-84.

Smith, R. A., & Schwartz, F. (1990). Teaching in action: Criteria for effective practice. *Teaching Excellence*. Winter Spring.

Appendix A

Instructions for Writing a Case

1. Pick a difficult problem that is important to you. Briefly state the problem and how you understand it.

2. Briefly describe the strategies that you have used to try to solve the problem.

3. Describe any barriers.

4. Please provide a piece of conversation that describes a time when you've come face to face with the problem. Take a piece of paper and divide it in half. On the right hand side, write down what you and the others actually said or did in the situation. On the left hand side of the page, write down any thoughts and feelings you might have had but did not say (see below).

   It is important that you remember the exact words that you and the others used in the conversation. Your best recollection will be fine. It is important, though, to write an actual dialogue, as if out of a play. Below is an example of the case format:

What I thought or felt but did not say	What I and other(s) actually said
Thoughts/feelings I had but but did not say	Me: (What you said.)
	Other: (What he or she said.)
	Me: (What you said.)

5. Briefly state what, if anything, puzzles you or stands out for you as you think back on the encounter.

Adapted from Argyris & Schön, 1974.

Appendix B

Suggestions for Analyzing Your Own Case

Do not worry about how accurately you recall the incident, or how well you plan the future dialogue. If our theory is correct, you cannot write down anything except what is consistent with your theory-in-use.

Now put the case away for at least a week. When you reread it, analyze it as if you were trying to help a friend. Here are some of the questions that you can ask about the dialogue.

- Do the sentences indicate advocating a position in order to be in control and to win and not lose? Or is the advocacy of the position combined with encouraging the other person to inquire? Is there an easy-in or forthright strategy? How aware is the writer of the possible interpretations by the receiver?

- Are the evaluations or attributions made with or without illustrations? Are they tested publicly or do they go untested?

- What kind of information is on the left-hand side of the paper (thoughts and feelings)? Does it contain information that would better enable the other person to understand your intentions? If so, what prevented you from communicating this information?

- If the feelings and thoughts in the left-hand column would predictably upset others, what change would be necessary so that they could be effectively communicated?

More important, why does the writer think and feel about other people in ways that are not directly communicable? Sure, it may be that they are S.O.B.s. But it may also be that the writer is unknowingly creating self-fulfilling and self-sealing processes.

The next step would be to try to redesign some part of the dialogue, especially the sentences with which you find it difficult to deal.

- read the sentence(s) several times and write down the (culturally acceptable) meaning that you infer (rung 2 on the ladder of inference).

- Write down the meaning that you would impose on the cultural meaning (rung 3).

- Invent a possible solution to deal with such meanings.

- Write an actual conversation that produces the invention you just made.

Feel free to make all the changes you wish during the exercise. Every change is a sign of learning and another opportunity for practice. This is not a win/lose competitive situation with yourself or with others.

Again, put your written work away, this time for at least a day, before re-reading it. If you prefer not to wait for the week, or the day, show your efforts to someone else. It is best to do this with persons who are also interested in learning about themselves, and who might reciprocate by showing you a case they had written in this format. The set is then one in which both of you are learning.

From: Argyris, C. The Executive Mind and Double-Loop Learning. *Organizational Dynamics*, Autumn 1982, p.16. Reprinted with permission.

Appendix C

Perspectives on Expertise

Experitse as Technical Skill	Expertise as the Application of Theory or General Principles
Based on: the specific tasks professionals must perform.	**Based on:** the general principles and theory that enable practitioners to treat particular cases as examples or categories about which something is known.
Assumptions: •the constituent skills can be identified; •the skills can be transmitted to prospective practioners; •The skills can be appropriately drawn upon in practice.	**Assumptions:** •Theories and general principles can be applied to particular situations. •practitioners can recognize particular cases as examples of general principles; •they can adjust predictions derived from general principles to accommodate the special features of a particular case; •they can blend the variety of potentially relevant principles to form an integrated body of knowledge that can be applied to specific cases; •learn the principles and theories (first) in school and then learn the skills on the job.
Critique: •segments practice into observable behaviors which fails to consider the wholeness of professional practice and misses the intentionality of practice; •overlooks the judgment and reasoning that determine whether or when to apply particular skills.	**Critique:** • real cases do not present themselves as examples of general principles; inhibits professional judgment by requiring practitioners to attend only to the particular variables mentioned in the principle; •does not provide rules of thumb regarding how to apply unidimensional principles to multidimensional situations; •does not provide rules for selecting among different principles which are in conflict; •and not all relevant principles derive from science, consider experience and social norms.
Purpose of instruction: to teach the skills of professional practice.	**Purpose of instruction:** to teach theories, principles, and their application.
Methods of instruction: micro-teaching of specific skills: by presenting theory, by modelling, by providing opportunity for practice with feedback, and by coaching for application.	**Methods of instruction:** in practice-relevant principles need to consider: (1) the relationship between the general and the specific (e.g., basic and clinical studies done simultaneously), and (2) the integration of principles from different discplines (e.g., organize courses around body organs or specific health problems).
Exemplar: Teacher education	**Exemplar:** Medical education, engineering education.
Transition experience: laboratory	**Transition experience:** Clinical experience or internship

Adapted from Kennedy, 1987.

Expertise as Critical Analysis	Expertise as Deliberate Action
Based on: the paradigm for examining and interpreting situations which are unique to the profession, e.g., thinking like a lawyer.	**Based on:** the interactive relationship between analysis and action, such that each influences the other.
Assumptions: •the major task of professionals is to analyze situations; •general principles provide the vehicle for interpreeting cases.	**Assumptions:** •analysis is not independent of action; •experiences can only contribute to expertise if practitioners can learn from it; successful deliberate action requires: * a body of experience on which to draw, * the ability to conduct mental experiments, * the ability to critically evaluate the outcomes, * the ability to revise one's definition of the situation, if not satisfied, and * a highly developed sense of purpose.
Critique: •a lack of attention to codified knowledge; e.g., the task of lawyering; •fails to assure that students acquire knowledge of the general principles; •emphasizes process over content, leaving students unsure of what they have learned, or if so, what; •produces students able to analyze cases, but unable to make decisions - to act on the cases; •narrows the scope of analysis; e.g., sound legal judgment entails consideration of social, organizational, economic, and political issues, as well as legal issues.	**Critique:** •the criteria for evaluating the effectiveness of action are: - the action solved the problem as defined, - the actor liked what happened, - the action made the situation more coherent, - the solution was congruent with fundamental values and theories. •these criteria are ambiguous and continually evolve in the light of new experiences, •since the criteria are discovered in the process of action, it is difficult for independent observers to assess the appropriateness of professional decisions.
Purpose of instruction: to transform students into people who routinely apply the paradigm of professional reasoning to new situations.	**Purpose of instruction:** to transform students into people capable of learning from experience by deliberation about, and critical examination of, their actions and the consequences of the actions.
Methods of instruction: students are active thinkers who presented with difficult case studies for which there are no "answers." •cases provide the material for analytic discussion; •faculty use question and answer format; •students learn to read material reconstructively, as something to be taken apart and put back together.	**Methods of instruction:** must entail both analysis and action. Students must: (1) deliberate to define problems and solutions, (2) act on their deliberations, and (3) evaluate their actions in light of their original formulations of goals and problems. Thus, students must be full participants, not merely spectators, analysts, or advisors. The situations must be multifaceted, and yet to be resolved. Their action is not purely analytic, but instead is motivated by the need to define the problem and to find a solution. And the environment must enable the teacher to deliberate along with students as students are working and deliberating, for that is when they are most ready to learn. Teachers help students with their skills as well as their reasoning.
Exemplars: Legal education, and some business schools.	**Exemplar:** See Schön's Educating the Reflective Practitioner. Jossey-Bass (1987).
Transition experience: not necessary, immersion	**Transition experience:** prior to or concurrent with courses

Adapted from Kennedy, 1987.

31. *Training New Consultants in the Connecticut Community-Technical College System*

Bill Searle and Patricia A. Cook

"The best professional development I have done in 25 years of teaching. . ." "I loved doing this." "When can I do it again?" "This program shows that with some tools and time to think and talk, ordinary teachers like my partner and I can really do a lot."

It would be great to write that we knew our peer teaching consultation process would produce reviews such as these when we designed it. Great, but untrue. Several years ago the statewide board for our Center for Teaching charged a committee of six faculty members with the task of creating a viable teaching consultation program. The committee worked under the following constraints:

- Must involve 12 colleges
- No campus has a director of faculty development
- Little chance of getting any full or part-time faculty development professionals in the future
- No history of faculty development efforts
- Most experienced faculty members did not stay current with developments in teaching/learning
- Normal faculty work load is four courses per semester, plus the equivalent of a course's work in college/community service
- A maximum of $30,000 available to cover all annual expenses
- Little chance of increasing the budget in the future
- Minimal administrative support on campuses
- Union contract covering all faculty members

The committee responded by suggesting that we adapt the "New Jersey faculty mentoring model" to our situation (see Chapter 14). Each year we train twelve pairs of faculty as peer teaching consultants—one pair from each college. These "Teaching Partners" work with each other and report their findings to no one else.

A key to our success is that faculty administer the project, conduct all workshops, and provide assistance to each other. Our faculty know that the people running the program teach the same students as they do, day and night. We face the same problems as our participants. An additional benefit has been solid support from the strong faculty union.

Objectives

Our fundamental belief is that people change most effectively when they believe they are controlling the change. (For an outline of our beliefs about change see Appendix A.) Thus, it is critical to us that experienced faculty work together as peers, not in a mentor-type relationship.

Building the collective knowledge of our faculty about learning and teaching, and promoting dialogue about teaching are additional objectives. As our Teaching Partners gain success with new ideas and techniques, we need them to spread their ideas. We expect that these faculty will become campus activists for other teaching and learning projects.

While we are explicit that there is not one best method of teaching, we do want to promote active learning strategies in our classrooms. Breaking the lecture-and-listen structure is important.

Finally, our Teaching Partners must receive all the benefits of a teaching consultation program!

How Do We Attract Faculty Members?

"Faculty will be too scared to sit in on each other's classes." "You'll never get enough volunteers." "You have to recruit the right faculty or the project will fail."

Ah, the advice that we got! Guess what? We have

many problems, but they are not the ones we were warned about. Faculty who trust one another enjoy both sitting in on each other's classes and talking about teaching. We have plenty of volunteers. Also, we have not found it critical to recruit the 'right' faculty. It helps that there is no connection between Teaching Partners and faculty evaluations or other personnel decisions. Academic administrators do not participate in the program except to provide support.

The local faculty committee that runs the Center for Teaching on each campus does most of the recruiting, reviews applicants, and recommends faculty for the project. Having a faculty committee make the recommendation reminds everyone that it is faculty who run the project. It also establishes a positive tone, attracting average and excellent teachers—not people being "sent by the administration" for remediation. Lastly, it generates additional dialogue about our project on campuses.

In academe in the 1990's, however, nothing is simple. A "contract" (Appendix B) makes certain everyone knows the basic requirements of the project.

What about someone passing their "problem faculty" to us? (We know this would never happen on your campus!) The Chair of the local faculty committee also represents the college on the statewide Center for Teaching Steering Committee, which reviews problems with all projects quarterly. Faculties who send us their "problems" know that they will hear about them.

Why did we say that recruiting the "right faculty" was not critical? Nearly everyone rates their Teaching Partner experience as highly rewarding. Since we let faculty select their own partners, we have no guidelines requiring people to be from different departments or institutions. The process works well for average and excellent teachers.

Since we limit participation to 24 faculty members per year, on many campuses it is a privilege to be selected.

When Does This Project Happen?

New Teaching Partners begin in January and work together for a calendar year. Odd. Do we not know that the academic calendar begins in September and ends in June? Everything must follow it.

This is a rule in higher education.

Evaluate our reasoning yourself. New Teaching Partners must participate in a full-day workshop before starting. They need time to read pre-workshop materials. They need time to discuss how they will work together. Care to speculate about the chances of all this happening during the end of August?

Another benefit of the January-to-December approach is that many Teaching Partners report that they talk over the summer when they have more time to think. Several teams have added visitations to summer classes. Because we use regular faculty as consultants to each other, every extra conversation they have, every article on teaching and learning that they have time to read, every chance they have to write out an idea is precious.

What Does This Project Cost?

Each Teaching Partner receives a $1,000 stipend—$500 after one semester and $500 at the end of the project. Through a unique partnership, the faculty union supplies half the stipend money. This makes it clear that the union leadership strongly endorses this approach to professional development.

Our faculty teach four courses per semester, with committee and college work comprising the equivalent of a fifth course. Some college administrations show support by granting participants partial credit toward their "other work" for being a Teaching Partner. This represents an indirect cost of the project.

The total cost for all three workshops is $1200. Since presenters are unpaid, excellent food consumes most of the money.

The Project Coordinator is a faculty member, with a one course release per semester. Direct costs are pay for two adjunct faculty to cover her classes.

Total cost for the entire project is just under $30,000 per year.

Training the Teaching Partners

Very few of our faculty have completed courses in teaching or teaching development programs. Thus, the learning/teaching content we supply in our project is virtually the only content we can rely on. This pressures us to cram information into the workshops.

Participants attend three, day-long workshops. The first occurs just before the spring semester, the second is in April, and the final workshop occurs the following November.

Prior to the first workshop, we send out "homework." As we gain experience, we send out more information. People read it because we tell them that they have a choice—study the material and identify questions they have, or risk having us lecture on it at the workshop. It works. Many even boast that they truly enjoy the readings!

What do we mail out? First, since we are dealing with new people each year, we provide basic information about the project. Second, we try to orient participants to the peer consultation process by sending out material on teaching styles, teaching philosophies, and issues in teaching. The quarterly papers sent to members by the POD Network, citations from *The Teaching Professor* (Magna Publications) and *College Teaching*, and articles written by our own faculty all furnish grist for our paper mill.

Someday, we hope to send out material written entirely by our own people. Remember our objectives? We want faculty to reflect on teaching and learning. We want to build a culture that cherishes teaching and learning. We want faculty to realize how much they can learn from each other. Accomplishing this requires our faculty to write about their experiences with their students.

The First Workshop

Icebreakers. Since this workshop mixes people from different campuses, we structure it both to help them get acquainted and to provide the basic information necessary for effective consultation. Thus, we start with ice breaking exercises. (A good source is *Icebreakers: A Sourcebook of Games, Exercises, and Simulations*, Ken Jones, Pfeiffer & Co., San Diego, CA.)

Describing the project. After the icebreakers, we discuss the Teaching Partners project, addressing exactly what we expect of participants. There is nothing quite like telling faculty about something they have to do to get them to ask questions! They get involved immediately.

Our teaching consultation process rests on a triangle consisting of classroom observations, gathering student feedback, and engaging in constructive dialogue about teaching improvement. The content of our consultation training reflects this.

Training in classroom observation. We assume that our faculty have no training in classroom observation. Most have neither sat in on a colleague's class nor had anyone but an evaluator visit one of their own classes. We acknowledge that it is not easy either being observed or doing observations; consequently, we structure this portion of the workshop to deal with both technique and emotions.

We need a classroom observation technique that faculty can learn quickly, practice easily, and feel comfortable with almost immediately. Therefore, we present our variation of "scriptwriting" - writing non-valuative notes on everything that is happening, paying the most attention to student actions and reactions.

Although we teach the basics in five minutes, an advantage of teaching scriptwriting is that we can add thoughts later. For example, during subsequent discussions or during the second or third workshop we can point out that it may be useful to add a time log in the margin, or to keep track of student participation by sex, age, or seating in the classroom. As faculty gain experience, we add sophistication to the technique.

After the initial presentation, participants take notes on a live mini-class, presented by a past Teaching Partner. They then share observations with each other. Frequently these discussions yield insights into differences in perception, teaching styles, and in what is considered important. Thus partners begin the process of conversing about teaching—as they are developing observation skills.

At this point, an experienced classroom observer (and former Teaching Partner) describes what she wrote down about the sample class as a comparison for our new classroom observers. We examine why the experienced observer wrote down certain points and provide tips that make the technique more useful.

Of course, the most difficult aspect of observation is keeping judgments and evaluations out of the class notes. We try to model non-judgmental statements in the way we write our own classroom observations and in the way we answer questions (and challenges) throughout the workshop. We stress that there is no list of "shoulds" that is perfect for all situations.

Keeping a teaching journal. From observation we move to reflection by encouraging maintenance of a teaching journal. While not critical to teaching consultation efforts, our approach emphasizes that a teaching journal forms the basis for our long term goal of developing "reflective practitioners." A former Teaching Partner who uses journals in her own courses orients participants to practical ways to organize their thoughts. By supplying the journals and having participants write in them during this first workshop, we jump-start the process.

We also know that faculty resist taking the time to keep a journal. We emphasize that journals help us keep track of teaching ideas, innovations, and classroom assessment results.

Gathering student feedback. Since we strongly encourage faculty to interview students from each other's classes, two former Teaching Partners conduct a student interview role play. After the role play, we hand out sample questions they can adapt to their needs. During the discussion, we also present different models of working with students, and common problems. Finally, we emphasize that many past Teaching Partners believe students gave them the most useful information—something that new participants find hard to believe. Many students enjoy being part of a program that concentrates on teaching improvement.

To accommodate participants who want a different

approach to classroom observation, we hand out a copy of *How Am I Teaching?* from Magna Publications. The book contains numerous student-colleague-self feedback instruments.

Constructive dialogue between partners. Finally, the best classroom observation notes, the best student interviews, the best ideas about improvement are worth nothing if the personal interaction between partners is inadequate. Trust is the most important component to success in our teaching consultation program.

It is difficult for faculty to provide feedback to a colleague. Unlike many professionals in business, we do not regularly have the opportunity to provide formal or informal constructive criticism to colleagues (nor do we have experience receiving such constructive criticism). Initially, it surprised us how few people were interested in even discussing how to give constructive criticism. Now, we know we must approach the subject gently.

Our project starts with an advantage. Almost all partners choose each other—meaning there is already friendship and trust between them. The emotional ties exist. The practical skills often do not.

A role play exercise is the heart of our approach to promoting constructive discussions between partners. A former Teaching Partner (the "observer") provides feedback to the mini-lesson presenter—feedback laden with subtle judgments and evaluations. Some fairly obvious body language rounds out the scene.

After the role play exercise, our new consultants identify particularly effective and ineffective things that the observer said and did. They jot down their own observations for several minutes, then discuss their points in a small group for a few minutes.

After the small group discussions, we open discussion to the full group. During that exchange, someone invariably mentions how judgmental the observer was. We seize the opportunity to review how often the observer slipped in the "shoulds," "don't you finds," "research shows," "it-is-good-practice-tos," and "buts" that people employ when making subtle judgments.

We encourage clarity about beliefs and reiterate how our beliefs affect what each of us does and says. We illustrate how our values influence the conduct of our workshops. For example, since we believe that people benefit most from being actively involved in their learning, we sit in small groups. Groups regularly have brief, intensive discussions about issues, then present key ideas to the full gathering. We gather feedback regularly. Lectures are minimal.

Follow-up, Follow-up?

Clearly, the information we furnish during the first workshop is more than anyone can absorb. Nevertheless, we send more material in the next few months. What goes out is less significant than maintaining regular contact with everyone.

We want participants to have the resources to successfully complete their Teaching Partners project and to involve them in informal consultations after their year as a Teaching Partner. Sending a variety of material (such as *The Teaching Professor*, *College Teaching*, *The National Teaching and Learning Forum*, and articles by Linc. Fisch in *The Journal of Staff, Program, and Organization Development*) exposes faculty to the sources we refer to for ideas.

The Second Workshop

Given the nature of our peer consultants, a mid-semester workshop is crucial. Once they actually do peer consultation, many issues and thoughts surface that were not clear before the actual work. This workshop gives everyone a chance to discuss problems and successes.

This is also a time to refine some skills. Kolb's active learning model emphasizes the importance of doing, and ties "doing" with "thinking about doing." We demonstrate active learning concepts while conducting a mini-workshop on Kolb's learning styles. The particular learning model we use is not important. What is important is introducing the idea that people learn in different ways.

Reinforcing prior learning about gathering and using feedback from students and each other, and sharing nonjudgmental comments, are other major components of this workshop. Reflecting on what they are practicing, remembering tips, and reinforcing skills is critical with peer consultants.

Faculty talk for a living. We use this skill to draw everyone further into a community of people working toward similar goals. It seems important that people not feel alone, not feel as though everything depends on them. Participants share what worked for them and what did not. They come up with a great variety of suggestions on how to deal with behavior problems in the classroom, diversity issues, and learning style differences.

The Third Workshop

Our third and final workshop is a recent addition. It is an experiment we have added to the past two Teaching Partner cycles because participants said they needed something to provide a sense of closure. They were right.

Since this workshop concentrates on closing the circle on the teaching consultation process, we emphasize participant-led discussions. There is a dual focus. First, we discuss their experiences as peer consultants. Second, we ask them to provide feedback about the project and the workshops. We ask the questions; they provide the answers. Comments and questions flow.

Finally, since we also want to build a cadre of people interested in learning and teaching, we provide information about additional teaching improvement ideas. Classroom assessment gets discussed, and we bring in copies of Angelo and Cross' book (*Classroom Assessment Techniques*, 2nd edition, Jossey-Bass, 1993). Creating teaching portfolios is also an important topic. (We like *The Teaching Portfolio*, American Association for Higher Education.) These "teasers" will, hopefully, tempt participants into additional projects.

Significantly, this year's participants have already asked for a mini-workshop on teaching to a diverse student body. Something must be working. We may not have to think up the "teasers" ourselves anymore.

Physical Arrangement of Training Sessions

We train in college classrooms, but not just because they are free! This is where we work, the focus of the project. Regular teachers. Regular classrooms. Regular problems with heating and lighting. Ideally, we would use a classroom with circular tables and chairs to help break open another college teaching paradigm.

How About Alternatives?

We have in mind several alternatives to the project as we described it above.

Initial workshop. We plan to experiment by doing more on classroom assessment. We are reviewing whether to start with the "Teaching Goals Inventory" from the Angelo and Cross book.

After focusing on teaching goals for a specific class, partners gain common ground by seeing specific classroom assessment techniques. This material, coupled with classroom observations and student feedback interviews,

might furnish a fuller picture of what is happening in the class.

Second workshop. We have experimented with doing a "learning styles" mini-workshop for participants. It was well received. We are exploring conducting an extensive workshop on learning styles in the future. This might give participants something new to address during the second semester of their work together. Another alternative would be to do a Myers-Briggs workshop, with the same goal as above.

Compensation. Releasing faculty from one course for participating is ideal. Colleges where faculty normally teach a five-course load should definitely release faculty from a course and pay a stipend. Doing a teaching consultation correctly takes enormous amounts of time.

Training length. For projects where more funding is available for workshops, a two-day residential workshop held prior to beginning a teaching consultation project is preferable. More time for demonstrations, discussion, and practice with classroom observation and giving and receiving feedback will definitely improve the quality of a peer consultation project.

Presenters. Our workshop presenters are former Teaching Partners, something we will not change. This provides past Teaching Partners an opportunity for additional learning, since we all learn best that which we teach others. Ideally, however, experienced Teaching Partners could attend advanced workshops on subjects such as instructional goal setting, classroom assessment/research, classroom observations, or learning styles. Now, we rely on their professional interest to learn on their own so they can more effectively help others.

Ideas?

What we do today is based upon what others did in the past, what has worked for us, and what we have experimented with. Since we cannot try something that has not occurred to us, we would love to have you contact us with ideas, critiques, or suggestions. We firmly believe excellence in teaching happens because of constant improvement.

Appendix A

Beliefs About Change

When we start to do something new, we are open to a variety of ways to do it. However, we quickly learn some behaviors that work reasonably well for us. These behaviors become habits, and we internalize them. Without consciously thinking, we keep doing the habits, ingraining the behavior deeper and deeper. The deeper the habit is ingrained, the harder it is to change. Most significant teaching habits are deeply ingrained. While there is nothing inherently negative about habits, some are ineffective.

The first step to improve our teaching is, therefore, to learn something about what our habits are. A non-threatening environment is best, so that our defenses are as much at rest as possible.

The next step to improve our teaching is to learn about alternate behaviors. Again, the best environment for this is a non-threatening one.

Step three means trying out different behaviors to see what works for us. There must be strong support for this, and virtually no chance for retaliation. Otherwise, we will quickly revert to whatever habits got us this far in our careers.

The fourth step involves making our new behaviors habits, while internalizing the need to continually examine them. In the fourth step, the danger is that we will become complacent and allow this new habit to become something we do without thinking, because anything we do without thinking is probably going to become a weakness someday.

Biases About Change

- People change when they decide to change, not when someone else thinks they should change. Forcing someone to change when they do not want to either requires great effort to succeed, or fails. Failure is about as likely as success.

- People work hardest and smartest for something they think that they control. This seems particularly true for college faculty.

- Most people want to improve what they do. College faculty are no different.

- For jobs that require much thinking, analysis, and independent work, the best forces for change are an individual's co-workers. For faculty, this means that specific, focused discussions between people who respect each other often produce change.

- People cannot work on changing more than one or two things at a time, unless what they are changing is quite minor.

- The best feedback for someone is clear, close to the event when an action occurred, specific to what the individual thinks is important (which may, of course, be influenced by what a person's supervisor and colleagues think important) and able to be discussed with someone else. The "someone else" must be a respected person—respected either as an expert in the field or as a conscientious friend.

- The best way to make a changed behavior "stick" is to show how the change is working as it is being done—through feedback and discussions with a respected "other."

- Changing habits formed over a considerable period of time requires sustained, consistent support over a considerable period of time.
- Being a master teacher means observing yourself teach as you are doing it. Doing this allows the master teacher to think about ways of doing the job better.

- Teaching faculty how to develop their own methods of evaluation and ways to get meaningful feedback produces the greatest change over the longest period of time. Change becomes a constant-internally generated and natural process, rather than a force imposed from the outside.

- Changes based on forces applied from the outside must:
    a. Be constantly reinforced, because if there is a letup, change will stop,
    b. Degrade over time, because all "new projects" suffer from a degradation in enthusiasm, since the people forcing the change (supervisors in most systems) get tired and burned out with continually forcing,
    c. Produce a reaction from the weakest of the people being forced, pushing the supervisors to spend an inordinate amount of time with them,
    d. Produce an increase in bureaucratization, because the weakest people will challenge holes in the system, compelling others to continually make new policies and procedures to fill the holes,
    e. Absorb the best people in an activity that takes their time without benefits that they can see, producing cynicism.

- Any activity continued over a long time must benefit someone, in some way. The more significant the activity is, the more people it must benefit. [Read the word "benefit" loosely here. It may not be obvious what the "benefit" is—it may be merely a benefit because something is simple, or not important enough to put the extra effort into changing.] So, who benefits from the current system, and why, are important considerations in developing any change because these people will, covertly or overtly, resist the change.

- People resist changes they do not control when the change produces more work.

- People resist evaluation and pressure to change from someone they do not consider better at what they do than they are. They particularly resist when they consider the other person to be not as good as they are.

Appendix B

Teaching Partners Project
A Project of the Connecticut Center for Teaching

<u>Notice of Commitment</u>

I, _____, hereby agree to participate as a Teaching Partner/Discipline Teaching Partner for the calendar year _____. My colleague in the partnership is _____. I agree to fulfill the following obligations.

1. I understand that this involvement requires a regular schedule of class visitations over the course of two semesters. Two possible formats for this schedule are:

    1) One semester I will observe my colleague's class weekly. The other semester I will be observed weekly.

    2) Each semester we will alternate classroom visits weekly. One week I am an observer and the following week I am observed.

2. I will schedule regular conferences with my Teaching Partner during these two semesters to discuss classroom dynamics, teaching goals, student concerns, and any project that impacts on teaching effectiveness; i. e., overviews, textbook selection, test design, etc.

3. I agree to maintain a journal recording my experience of the Teaching Partners' process. I will use this personal journal to prepare two reports . . . one at the end of each semester.

4. I will submit two end-of-the-semester reports to the Coordinator of the Teaching Partners' Project.

5. Over the course of the two semesters, I agree to schedule formal conferences with students selected from my Teaching Partner's class to receive student perspectives.

6. I will attend three workshops, on January _____, April _____, and November _____.

7. I will be eligible for a stipend of $1,000.00.

_____	_____	_____	_____
Teaching Partner	Date	Dean of Acadmic Affairs	Date
		Participating School	
_____	_____	_____	_____
Teaching Partner	Date	President	Date
Coordinator		Participating School	

32. *Training New Consultants in the Kentucky Community College System: The Teaching Consultants' Workshop*

Michael Kerwin and Judy Rhoads

*L*enze and Menges (1993) have documented that professional development materials and activities are needed for novice teaching consultants. The geographical isolation of consultants who are the only people with this role on small, rural campuses exacerbates this need. In addition, the consultant may be a full-time faculty member who receives a teaching load reduction in order to provide consultation services at the college; what little time this person has for professional development is often taken by research and other discipline-oriented activities. This article describes a professional development activity that has enabled consultants who conduct a peer-type consultation program in a statewide community college system to develop and refine their consultation skills and knowledge. The purpose of the article is to provide a model that other statewide systems, consortia, or professional development organizations could adopt to provide professional development opportunities to teaching consultants. We believe that veteran consultants who provide consulting services from centralized offices on larger, more urban campuses could also benefit from the model.

The activity described in this article is called The Teaching Consultants' Workshop. This workshop provides a structured opportunity for teaching consultants to discuss client cases with their colleagues. Consultants who have participated in the workshop state that it enhances their ability to help their clients make changes in their teaching.

Institution and Program Contexts

The Teaching Consultants' Workshop has been a key component in the Teaching Consultation Program (TCP) offered in the University of Kentucky Community College System (UKCCS) since 1977. Knowing how the workshop functions as a professional development activity for teaching consultants in UKCCS will help the reader to understand how the workshop could function in other contexts.

UKCCS consists of fourteen community colleges headed by a Chancellor who is directly responsible to the President of the University of Kentucky. Although the Chancellor's Office is located on the Lexington Campus of the University, the fourteen community colleges are geographically dispersed throughout the Commonwealth. These colleges range from rural institutions in eastern and western Kentucky enrolling slightly more than 1000 students each semester to a multi-campus college in Louisville enrolling more than 11,000 students each semester. Over four hundred miles of highway, some of it narrow, winding, and mountainous, separate the colleges on the eastern edge of the Commonwealth from those on the western edge.

Teaching consultants, who are located on each of the fourteen community college campuses in the System, offer TCP to the faculty at that college. TCP is modeled after the program developed by the University of Massachusetts in the early 1970's and described by Bergquist and Phillips in Volume 2 of *A Handbook for Faculty Development* (1977) and in Chapter 17 of this book. The program provides for client confidentiality, voluntary participation, and independence from performance review and requires sixteen weeks to complete. Unlike the University of Massachusetts program, however, full time faculty members serve as teaching consultants. These faculty, who have been previously recognized by their colleagues as outstanding teachers, volunteer to serve as teaching consultants and attend a workshop to prepare them to serve in this role. Teaching consultants work with two or three faculty each semester and are released from one three-hour class to do so. In the 1993 spring semester, twenty-seven teaching consultants worked with forty-two faculty clients on fourteen UKCCS campuses.

Using the University of Massachusetts model, UKCCS teaching consultants follow a set of procedures designed to help faculty recognize and consciously develop instructional behaviors most appropriate for themselves and their students. The key stages in this process are initial interview, data collection, data review and analysis, planning and implementing changes, and evaluation. Data collection, which begins with the initial interview, includes classroom observation, videotaping, and gathering student perceptions of instructional behavior through the Teaching Analysis By Students (TABS) questionnaire. The data collection phase leads into the data review and analysis phase, which occurs during the sixth week of the semester. The phase of planning and implementing changes begins in the seventh week of the semester and continues until the evaluation phase begins in the twelfth week.

The Teaching Consultants' Workshop

In the sixth week of each semester, teaching consultants in the UKCCS Teaching Consultation Program are invited to participate in a one-day workshop designed to help them become more effective as consultants. Because these consultants are at campuses in different locations in the Commonwealth, the workshop begins at 1 PM on Thursday, includes an overnight stay at the workshop site, and concludes at noon on Friday. The morning of the first day and the afternoon of the second day are set aside, therefore, to enable consultants to travel from their campuses to the workshop site and return.

The coordinator of the Teaching Consultation Program schedules the workshop at the conclusion of the data collection phase of the program and at the beginning of the data analysis and review phase. By this time, consultants have observed their clients as they teach, videotaped a classroom session, and administered the TABS to the clients' students. Because most of the colleges do not have the computer resources to process the student questionnaires, the consultants have sent the student questionnaires to the program coordinator who has prepared two sets of computer printouts summarizing these results. The coordinator distributes these printouts to the consultants at the

beginning of the workshop. The major part of The Teaching Consultants' Workshop consists of a series of twenty-five minute sessions in which consultants "present" their clients to the other teaching consultants participating in the workshop. The presentations follow a prescribed pattern. The consultants begin their presentations with a four or five-minute introduction of the client, show a ten-minute videotape of the client teaching in a classroom situation, and ask the other consultants to comment on the client's teaching behavior and to suggest changes that the faculty member might want to make in his or her teaching behavior. (See the workshop schedule in Appendix A.)

To enable all consultants to present their clients in a five-hour block of time (three hours on the first afternoon; two hours on the second morning), the workshop coordinator schedules concurrent sessions for each twenty-five minute session. From 2:30 PM to 2:55 PM, for example, four different teaching consultants may be presenting their clients to four different groups. The workshop coordinator also schedules these sessions so that the clients being presented, for example, may be teaching nursing, English literature, criminal justice, and biology. This structure enables consultants who have a particular discipline to attend all of the sessions presenting clients from that discipline.

Benefits for the Consultant

Consultants attending the Teaching Consultant Workshop, therefore, present one or two client case studies to the other consultants attending the workshop. They also attend eight or nine other case study presentations. Presenting and attending these sessions provides for an intensive interchange of ideas and expertise among the consultants. Over a five-year period, a consultant may have worked with ten different clients and have attended eighty to ninety workshop presentations. The impact of this experience, involving a large number of case studies and interacting with eighteen to twenty consultants, benefits the consultant in at least five ways.

First, preparation of the case for presentation at the workshop is a growth experience for both the consultant and the client. Preparation requires both to focus directly on pertinent data (interview, videotape, observation, notes, and class materials) and to make collaborative decisions about the strengths and weaknesses of the client. Although the student data and feedback from other consultants is not available at this time, preparation for the workshop results in the client and the consultant synthesizing the data and focusing on a particular direction for the case. Many times this is a turning point in the development of a case. Consultants develop their problem-solving, analytical and synthesis, and decision-making skills when they prepare for the workshop.

Second, by interacting with the other consultants at the workshop, consultants learn new ways of working with their clients and new classroom techniques. Consultants who attend the workshop come from fourteen different colleges, have from one to twenty years of consulting experience, and represent a diversity of academic backgrounds and expertise. They are often considered to be the best instructors on their campuses—in fact, this is one of the reasons that faculty on their campuses volunteer to participate in the program, i.e., the chance to discuss teaching on a regular basis with one of the best instructors on campus. The range of innovative ideas generated from such a diverse group is obviously broad. Many consultants report a changed perspective in the case as they listen to the suggestions from other consultants.

Third, the workshop benefits the consultants by expanding their resource network. Consultants frequently leave the workshop with new resources in their hands or a list of consultants who will mail promised materials. One example is the sharing of syllabi from a specific discipline for a consultant who wanted to help her client rework class requirements. Consultants frequently share discipline specific resources such as books, videos, handouts and student questionnaires. Consultants also develop an informal network of other consultants. They frequently call one another to discuss a problem or to look for solutions and strategies in working with a client. The networking developed through the teaching consultant workshop is an invaluable resource for consultants.

Fourth, participating in the workshop motivates consultants not only to assist their clients in becoming more effective teachers, but also to improve their own classroom performance. Asked to comment on the benefits of the workshop, consultants reported that the interchange of general and discipline-specific strategies that they learn there are personalized for their own use. Specific comments include the following:

- I use more of a variety of teaching techniques (flip charts, overhead projectors). I am more aware of remembering to use closure techniques and opening techniques.
- I've tried to implement most of the ideas I've learned, especially regarding moving around in the classroom asking thought-provoking questions and summarizing.
- I've become more aware of the importance of emphasizing course objectives throughout the semester, rather than doing so only at the beginning of the

semester. I've learned to use more writing as part of my classroom strategies.
- I always return to my classroom with renewed enthusiasm for my teaching. I also pick up ideas for student involvement or presentation of materials which I incorporate into the classroom activities.
- Sharing my ideas has helped me in teaching my classes. I always see that I can do more.
- My confidence as a teacher and consultant has increased, and even my philosophy of teaching has changed.
- The workshop gives me a broad focus, both as a teacher and as a consultant. It stimulates me to rethink my strategies and not fall back into my own natural patterns. The workshop continues to reinforce my personal conviction about the value of student involvement and a personal commitment to promoting this value.

In fact, many long-term consultants leave the workshop making commitments to apply techniques and strategies they already know. Sometimes they say "knowing and doing are two different things." As a result of interacting with other consultants, they go back with renewed energy to apply strategies to situations that they have known for years.

Finally, by continually improving their own teaching, consultants become not only more effective teachers, but also role models on their campuses. Consequently, the workshop benefits the consultant in another way. It helps consultants enjoy what they do and continue in the consultant role. A number of consultants across the state have been consulting for ten or more years.

Implementation Factors

Instructional consultation programs differ in at least three ways: (1) in the relationship of the consultant to the person being consulted (Morrison, 1993), (2) in the manner in which data are collected, and (3) in the length of the consultation process. Although the workshop can be adapted to different types of programs, implementers must consider four factors: (1) the manner in which data are collected, (2) client confidentiality, (3) the scheduling of the workshop, and (4) the use of technology to conduct the workshop.

Data Collection by Videotaping

Because the videotaped segment of the client's teaching is such an important part of the presentation session, we believe the Teaching Consultant Workshop model would best serve to stimulate collaboration among consultants in programs where data are collecte through videotaping. Examples of such programs included the Lilly Teaching Fellows Program at the University of Massachusetts at Amherst (Sorcinelli et al., 1992), the Teaching Analysis Program at the University of Nebraska at Lincoln (Povlacs, 1988), and the Teaching Partners Program at Ball State University (Annis, 1989).

Client Confidentiality

By showing a videotape of the client teaching, consultants reveal the identity of their clients to the other consultants, which may seem to compromise the confidentiality of the program. Because this is such a vital component of the program, however, consultants explain this use of the videotape to their clients in the initial interview phase of the program. Clients agree to this use of the videotape by signing a contract and release form before they begin the data collection phase. Their signature indicates that they agree that their "pictures or likenesses and recordings of their voice in the production of a videotape may be used at workshops for teaching improvement."

Prior to the videotaping session, the teaching consultant or the client has also informed the students in the class being videotaped that they may be videotaped. Students are given the opportunity to be excused, without penalty, from that session if they object to being videotaped. The teaching consultants or the clients notify students in writing using a one-page announcement that they circulate to students early in the semester.

Scheduling the Workshop

Although interaction between the teaching consultant and the faculty member extends throughout a sixteen-week period in the UKCCS program, this interaction follows the phases identified by Brinko as being characteristic of the consultation process. Brinko conceptualized the consultation process as having four phases: initial contact, conference, information collection, and information review and planning session. Brinko's (see Chapter 1) description of these phases indicates that the initial phase in the UKCCS program corresponds to the initial contact and conference phases; the data collection phase to the information collection phase; and the phases of planning and implementing changes and evaluation to the information review and planning session. It is our view that a consultants' workshop modeled after the UKCCS workshop would benefit consultants most at the end of the information collection phase or at the beginning of the information review and planning session phase. In cases in which the interaction between the consultant and the client has ended, however, the consultant could present the videotape as a case study; even if the consultation has proceeded into the information review and planning session phase, consultants could receive helpful insights from other consultants.

Using Technology to Conduct the Workshop

The Teaching Consultants' Workshop is an especially useful model when workshops can be delivered via satellite or interactive video to multiple receiving sites. Consultants who are employed at small colleges in rural areas could benefit from interactivity with their colleagues. Using satellite technology, a consultant could send a brief introduction and an edited ten-minute segment, to the transmitting site. Consultants at the transmitting site could react to the videotape, as could others at remote sites who could communicate via telephone to all receivers during the workshop.

Conclusion

The Teaching Consultants' Workshop provides a means for increasing collaboration among instructional consultants, enhancing their ability to help their clients make changes in their teaching, reinvigorating consultants' interest in teaching, and building community among them. Key components are using videotape as part of the information collection process and providing for client permission to use the videotape at the workshop.

References

Annis, L. F. (1989). Partners in teaching improvement. *The Journal of Staff, Program, & Organization Development, 7*, 7-13.

Bergquist, W. H., & Phillips, S. R. (1977). *A handbook for faculty development*, Volume 2. Washington, DC: The Council for The Advancement of Small Colleges.

Lenze, L. F., & Menges, R. J. (1993). Materials for training instructional consultants. Presentation at the 1993 annual meeting of the American Educational Research Association, Atlanta.

Morrison, D. E. (1993). *Exploring the practice of instructional consultation through a topology of programs.* Paper presented at the American Educational Research Association Annual Meeting. Atlanta, April 15, 1993.

Povlacs, J. T. (1988). The teaching analysis program and the role of the consultant. In K. G. Lewis & J. T. Povlacs (Eds.), *Face to face: A sourcebook of individual consultation techniques for faculty/instructional developers* (pp. 137-157). Stillwater, OK: New Forums Press.

Sorcinelli, M. D., List, K., & Hill, D. (1992). Mentoring junior faculty: Some models. *Educational Forum 3*, 57-68.

Appendix A

TEACHING CONSULTANTS' WORKSHOP
February 20-21
Museum of the American Quilter's Society
Paducah, Kentucky
Revised Agenda

February 20

1:00	Welcome and Introductions Mike Kerwin	Classroom A
1:10	TABS Analysis by Consultants	Classrooms A, C, D
2:30	Presentation of Clients Each consultant will have a maximum of 30 minutes to present his or her client. The presentation begins with a five-minute analysis of the client's strengths and weaknesses as revealed by data, includes a ten-minute videotape presentation, and concludes with a fifteen-minute discussion of teaching strategies. The schedule of presentations is shown below.	
2:30-3:00	Concurrent Session #1 1. 2. 3. 4.	Classroom A Classroom C Classroom D Conference Room
3:05-3:35	Concurrent Session #2 1. 2. 3. 4.	Classroom A Classroom C Classroom D Conference Room
3:40-3:55	Break	
3:55-4:25	Concurrent Session #3 1. 2. 3. 4.	Classroom A Classroom C Classroom D Conference Room
4:30-5:00	Concurrent Session #4 1. 2. 3. 4.	Classroom A Classroom C Classroom D Conference Room
5:05-5:35	Concurrent Session #5 1. 2. 3. 4.	Classroom A Classroom C Classroom D Conference Room
7:30	Dinner	Ninth Street House

February 21

8:05	Presentation of Clients (Continued)	
8:05-8:35	Concurrent Session #6	
	1.	Classroom A
	2.	Classroom B
	3.	Classroom C
	4.	Classroom D
8:40-9:10	Concurrent Session #7	
	1.	Classroom A
	2.	Classroom B
	3.	Classroom C
	4.	Classroom D
9:15-9:45	Concurrent Session #8	
	1.	Classroom A
	2.	Classroom B
	3.	Classroom C
	4.	Classroom D
9:50-10:20	Concurrent Session #9	
	1.	Classroom A
	2.	Classroom B
	3.	Classroom C
	4.	Classroom D
10:25-10:55	Concurrent Session #10	
	1.	Classroom A
	2.	Classroom B

11:00   General Session   Classroom A
    1.   Final Evaluation by Client Report
    2.   Pilot Projects at Ashland, Henderson, and
          Hopkinsville - update
    3.   1992 May Workshop - Madisonville, Louisville,
          Lexington
    4.   Bright Idea Presentations
    5.   Brochure Orders for Fall Semester
    6.   1992 Fall Workshop, Hazel Green, October 1-2
    7.   1993 Spring Workshop, February 18-19, a
          college site
    8.   1993 Fall Workshop, a retreat site?
    9.   1994 Spring Workshop, Henderson
    10.   Evaluation

12:00   Adjournment

33. Training TA's as Consultants at the University of Michigan: Workshop for Peer Mentors

Beverly Black and Bronwen Gates

*T*his workshop was developed at the University of Michigan for training mentors to provide support and encouragement to new teaching assistants within the Department of History. These were upper-level graduate students who had been recommended as excellent teachers. One of their duties was to observe new TAs' classes and give feedback to the TA. This type of relationship often produces anxiety for both the mentor and the new TA: the mentor because he or she is often unsure of what to look for and how to give feedback, the new TA, who may not yet be comfortable in class, because he or she is often afraid of being judged. Variations of the workshop have been used in a number of training programs to train consultants in this method of observing classes and giving feedback to both TAs and faculty members.

The workshop is for the mentors (or consultants) and is designed to help them learn a method of consultation that respects and validates the instructor's (TA's) knowledge about teaching and learning while at the same time extending his or her vision of effective teaching. This instructor-centered method acknowledges that there are many approaches to effective teaching. The emphasis is to help instructors clarify their goals as teachers, reflect on their own teaching, and gain a clearer picture of what is happening in their classroom, both from their perspective and from the student's point of view. The method validates what instructors do that helps them reach their goals and also encourages them to identify areas they might change to more fully reach those goals.

This workshop is designed for people who do not have a lot of time for a lengthy training session. It takes three to four hours depending on whether some of the steps are repeated. Two facilitators are necessary to carry out the activities.

Outline of Workshop

Icebreaker (10 Minutes)

An icebreaker is important since the workshop requires that all participants feel comfortable about taking risks, especially in the role-playing exercises that help them develop their interpersonal skills. We use simple icebreakers, such as having each person introduce and tell a little about themselves. We sometimes have everyone pair up, learn names, departments and one interesting fact about the other person, after which they introduce each other to the group. If it is a large workshop we have them get acquainted with four or five other participants in small groups. These simple icebreakers allow the participants to get to know each other and develop a feeling for who else is in the workshop. It also creates a little hubbub at the beginning of the workshop which tends to relax everyone.

Writing and Posting Goals (15 Minutes)

Participants spend two minutes individually reflecting on and writing down some of their goals as mentors. Each person shares these with the group and the goals are posted. Participants tend to come up with a range of goals including helping the new TAs become comfortable in the role of a TA, help them develop confidence, be a role model, and so on. This activity helps participants expand their vision of what a mentor can do. This also leads to a discussion of how observing and giving feedback to the new TAs can help mentors reach some of their goals. (If time is short, this portion can be cut.)

Presentation (10 Minutes)

One of the presenters outlines the goals for an instructor-centered approach for observing and giving feedback and briefly describes the method. (These goals often turn out to be a subset of the overall goals developed by the mentors.) The presenter gives an outline of the workshop.

Recording Classroom Data (15 Minutes)

Participants view and discuss a portion of the videotape "Observing Teaching" that demonstrates how to record descriptive data while observing an actual class. (The commercial videotapes that are used in the workshop are listed at the end of this article along with where to obtain them.) This method has the observer writing, in as much detail as possible, everything that happens in the classroom: how the room is set up, what students do as they enter, the seating arrangement, how the instructor starts the class, what questions are asked, who answers them, and so on. The goal is to record in an objective and descriptive way as complete a picture as possible of what actually happens in the classroom.

Practice (15-30 Minutes)

Participants practice recording descriptive data while viewing a five-minute segment of a videotape of a TA teaching a class. (The five-minute segments of actual classroom scenes that we use in this workshop are selected from videotapes of TAs at the University of Michigan that have been taped by a staff member at the Center for Research on Learning and Teaching. The TAs have given written permission for the tapes to be used for educational purposes.) Several participants share their writing with the group followed by a discussion of the differences in the observations. It is often hard for participants to leave out judgments, so for comparison it is important to have one sample that is "objective." (Leaders of the workshop should do this exercise ahead of time so they can share what they have written if it is needed to demonstrate objectivity.) This exercise helps participants to be better observers. It is always amazing to everyone to see the differences in what people observe and record. If there is time, this segment can be repeated with another tape. In our experience the second time produces much more complete and accurate records.

Giving Feedback (10 Minutes)

Everyone writes for about five minutes about what kind of feedback they might give to the TA on the short segment of teaching for which they recorded data. This gives them a chance to think about what might be important to emphasize. This activity can be enhanced if there is time for everyone to share their writing with at least one other person.

Modeling a Feedback Session (10-15 Minutes)

Based on the same five-minute segment of teaching, the workshop facilitators roleplay a feedback session. One facilitator plays the part of the *TA* observed in the videotape and the other plays the *Mentor*. During the roleplay session the *Mentor* uses non directive feedback strategies which include the skills of active listening and connected knowing, to help the *TA* reflect on his or her teaching: reflect on what is happening in the classroom from the student's point of view, clarify teaching goals, and devise strategies for reaching these goals. The goal for the *Mentor* is to listen to the *TA* and to try and understand the *TA's* thinking about teaching—why the *TA* does what he/she does. (This is an example of active listening. Belenky et al., 1986, discussed this process under the rubric of connected knowing.) The mentor works collaboratively with the *TA* to interpret the classroom data: What is the *TA* doing that helps reach his/her goals? What gets in the way of reaching the goals? The *TA* is encouraged to think of alternative strategies to reach his or her goals. (These are all examples of non-directive feedback.) Others adapting this model might be interested in having two roleplays modeled—one with an agreeable TA, one with a defensive; or one with an experienced TA and one with an inexperienced. By modeling more than one response, facilitators demonstrate that their consultation style is not static and carved in stone but rather changes depnding upon the client's needs, experience, personality, and so on. (When the authors have done this workshop, although we have always used the same tape, the *TA* is played differently each time—with a different personality—so the exercise does not get routine for the *Mentor*. In debriefing this activity, we often discuss the variations with the participants.)

Discussion of Feedback Session (15-20 Minutes)

The facilitator who played the TA leads a critique of the feedback session. This session tends to be lively with many questions and comments from the participants. The facilitator who played *Mentor* shares the notes she took during the observation and the methods she used to prepare for the feedback session, including the development of possible focus points and questions prior to the meeting. Since the questions never match what was asked during the roleplay they tend to trigger a discussion about the fact that each feedback session will go differently and different questions will be asked depending on the needs of the instructor. The nuances of non-directive feedback sessions are discussed, including how the consultant can incorporate his or her observations and thoughts into the feedback session, while still keeping it instructor centered. Within this discussion most of the important aspects of giving feedback come up including giving accurate data, focusing on only two or three issues, and sandwiching negative information in between positive. We also talk about the need to provide feedback as soon as possible after the observation, setting a friendly atmosphere and helping the TA develop "next steps."

Discussion of Questioning (10 Minutes)

A discussion about different types of questions and their role in a feedback session tends to flow naturally from the questions used in the roleplay of the feedback session. The types of questions discussed are questions that, based on descriptive data, help the TA reflect on his/her teaching (for example, "I noticed you asked a lot of questions that required very short answers—what is your rationale for doing that?" "The student in the far corner asked and answered a lot of questions, is this a usual pattern? What are your thoughts on him?") We also view and discuss a segment of the videotape "Observing Teaching" that demonstrates open- and closed-ended questions.

Roleplay (20 Minutes)

Participants roleplay a feedback session in groups of three. They each have a role: the mentor, the observer, the TA. While viewing another five-minute segment of a videotape of a different class, the *Mentors* and the *Observers* record objective data and the *TAs* get into the roleplay by deciding what their goals might be for the class and how the class was planned. After viewing the videotape the *Mentors* spend three to five minutes planning a feedback session and the *TAs* continue to get themslves into the role of the instructor on the tape. In each small group the *Mentor* and the *TA* roleplay a feedback session while the *Observer* takes objective notes. This activity is lively and less threatening than having two people volunteer to do a roleplay in front of the larger group. It also gives everyone a role to play and gives each person a chance to practice his or her mentor role.

Feedback to the Mentor (10 Minutes)

After the roleplay, members of each trio reflect on the roleplay and share with each other what they learned and what they felt. Everyone is given questions to address in the small group (see Appendix A). The *Mentor* will tell what was learned and any feelings that came up during the session. The *TA* will talk about what the *Mentor* did that was helpful and things that didn't work as well and the *Observer* will talk about his/her observations.

Discussion in the Large Group (10 Minutes)

The small groups are asked to share with the larger group strategies that the *Mentor* used that were particularly effective and anything that they learned through doing the exercise. Participants tend to have a lot to say in this session. It is useful to have them describe how the *TA* was played in their groups and what the *Mentor* did in response. It is amazing how many different TAs can be played from the same five-minute segment of a classroom. Within this discussion the important aspects of giving feedback are again emphasized.

More Practice (30-35 Minutes per Practice)

The last three steps are repeated two more times until everyone gets a chance to play each role and give and get feedback. When we have had limited time or a small number of participants we have tried the roleplay in pairs (a TA and a Mentor) which required only two practice roleplays. If you have time, groups of three work best. An observer often sees things that the two doing the roleplay do not and feedback to the *Mentor* tends to be richer.

Discussion of the Process (15 Minutes)

In the large group, the whole process is discussed with participants asking questions and raising concerns. Participants are encouraged to re-examine the goals they wrote at the beginning of the workshop and make any adjustments. The workshop ends with each person telling what he or she learned by participating in the workshop. These last two activities help everyone see some real changes in the attitudes and skills that participants brought into the workshop.

Discussion of Results

We have had very positive experiences with this workshop and participants have rated it highly. Participants in the workshop often comment that it will certainly help them be better mentors and also that they learned many things that will help them with their own teaching.

We'd like to share one particularly gratifying memory

that affirms for us the value of this approach. During one workshop, a particularly outspoken student indicated that he felt he already knew everything he needed to know about observing classes and giving feedback to the TA. We asked that he play along with us and try it out before he made judgments but he continued to make small remarks throughout the workshop that indicated that he wasn't going to bother with all this stuff. When he role-played the *Mentor* he was extremely directive, telling the TA what he thought went well and what needed to be changed and he was very defensive when anyone gave suggestions. But as a *TA* his *Mentor* was particularly adept at listening and getting him to talk about his teaching and his goals and she did a marvelous job of collaboratively developing a plan for more fully reaching his goals. When he shared with the larger group how it felt to him he was totally won over. He said he felt respected and energized and could see that someone could come away from a feedback session like that feeling more confident and

excited about his/her own teaching. He had made the discovery that it is preferable to discover your own strengths and weaknesses than to be told of them by someone else.

This, to us, is the beauty and power of this method of observation training. The feedback to the instructor is truly formative and when done effectively both consultant and instructor feel energized by the exchange.

References

Belenky, M. F., Clinchy, B. M., Goldberger, N. R., & Tarule, J. M. (1986). *Women's ways of knowing.* New York: Basic Books.

Clinical supervision lesson #2: Communicating effectively [Videotape]. (Undated) Bloomington, IN: Agency for Instructional Technology.

Observing teaching [Videotape]. From the series "Strategies on College Teaching." (Undated) Bloomington, Indiana: Indiana University Audio Visual Center.

Appendix A

Questions for Reflection After Roleplay

Please reflect on the roleplay and share with each other what you learned and how you felt. Also address some of the following questions:

Mentor (consultant)

What did you learn from this session?

Were you happy with the way your meeting went with the TA? Did it go as planned?

What were your goals for the session?

If you could do it over again, what would you do?

TA

How did the session go for you?

Did the consultant do anything that helped put you at ease? What?

Did you feel that the consultant was really listening to what you had to say?

Did the consultant help you reflect on your own teaching? How?

Did you come away from the session with actions you could take to be more effective?

Observer

What did you see the mentor do that seemed effective?

How did the consultant help the TA feel at ease?

How did the consultant help the TA clarify his/her goals?

How, in your perception, did the TA respond to the feedback?

34. Professional Development for Consultants at the University of Washington's Center for Instructional Development and Research

Jody D. Nyquist and Donald H. Wulff

*A*s national attention has focused on improving teaching in higher education, programs to assist faculty have emerged in ever-increasing numbers in institutions across the country. Whether these programs are organized and staffed by faculty committees or organized within campus centers, a key role seems to be played by instructional consultants. Many universities and colleges now have professionals who meet one-on-one with instructors—faculty and teaching assistants—and work closely with administrators and departments to provide consulting services designed to enhance the overall quality of teaching and learning across all disciplines on the campuses.

The roles of these instructional consultants require that they demonstrate specific skills and understandings to be effective with their clients. This chapter describes how one instructional development center, the Center for Instructional Development and Research (CIDR) at the University of Washington (UW), assists consultants to develop the needed skills. We have found that this assistance works best when we: 1) identify the skills, background, and expertise that we believe must be represented among the consulting staff; 2) provide an intensive professional development seminar for both new and continuing staff; 3) provide structured, ongoing professional development opportunities throughout the year; and 4) monitor our consultants' and clients' satisfaction with the consultants' work.

What Skills, Background, and Expertise Should Instructional Consultants Working At CIDR Demonstrate?

Instructional consultants at CIDR are either Instructional Development Specialists—Ph.D.s and M.A.s with instructional expertise in specific disciplines—or Staff Consultants—graduate students who also have teaching experience, instructional expertise, and background in specific disciplines but who are still in the process of completing their dissertations and hold half time, temporary appointments, typically for at least two years. The Instructional Development Specialists have teaching experience and background in the theory and practice of instruction at the college/university level in one of four areas: mathematics and/or sciences, arts and/or humanities, social sciences, or the professional studies of law, business, medicine, or education. In addition, the consultants usually have specific skills in the use of a particular instructional strategy such as small groups, videotape, instructional technology, or writing, or in working with specific groups such as the International Teaching Assistants, or they are particularly skilled in a specific research methodology. It is crucial to the work of the Center that each of these areas of expertise be covered in some way by at least one member of the staff.

Staff Consultants are selected from various departments on campus because they have interests in instructional issues in their disciplines and because they are interested in consulting with others, not only in a specific discipline but also across a wider range of disciplines. The staff consultant role provides them with specialized experience that broadens their understanding of instruction in their own and related disciplines and, according to their testimony, enables them to become more effective teachers when they assume faculty positions at other universities.

Whether they are Instructional Development Specialists or Staff Consultants, CIDR consultants, like most instructional consultants, need all of the following:

- *Understanding of the institutional culture.* Particularly if they are from other campuses or have been deeply-rooted in the perspective of a specific department, CIDR consultants need to understand the culture of the University of Washington and the diversity that exists across departments, instructors, and students.

- *A discipline-specific perspective.* The consulting approach used to achieve the Center's mission is designed to recognize the variation in the ways different disciplines are taught and to tailor services to needs within specific departments.

- *Ability to function as instructional researchers.* Because of the emphasis on research at this institution and in the Center, the consultants must be data-driven problem-solvers who are challenged by instructional issues. They must be prepared to approach instructional consulting using a research perspective because we describe our consultants as "classroom researchers in other peoples' classrooms," where their responsibility is to collect, analyze, interpret, and translate data for instructors so that the instructors can make informed decisions about their teaching (Nyquist & Wulff, 1988).

- *Interest and skill in working collaboratively.* Because Center staff are divided into work teams and because many projects and papers are developed by groups rather than individuals, consultants must demonstrate the ability to function as effective collaborators.

- *Broad repertoire of instructional development tools.* Consultants have to be prepared with a variety of tools (classroom observation, SGID, video-critique, and so on) to assist in instructional development, curriculum development, evaluation of teaching, and program evaluation and with the theoretical and research bases for the use of such tools.

- *Ability to translate classroom research into specific strategies for change.* Consultants must be able to sit down with teaching assistants as well as full profes-

sors to assist them to make a difference in what happens in their classrooms and in other student/instructor interactions. They also must be prepared to act as catalysts, confederates, advocates, resources, and partners in whatever instructional challenges the instructor faces.

- *Broad repertoire of instructional methods and communication strategies to use with clients.* Because the teaching process in different disciplines represents varying instructional styles and diverse students, consultants need a broad repertoire of strategies that they can use both for interacting with the instructors and for suggesting specific instructional approaches.

- *Resources.* Consultants must be able to identify and use the variety of resources available to them, some of which are offered through other units on campus and many of which can be found within the print, video, and human resources of the Center.

We attempt to help instructional consultants develop this range of professional competencies both through an initial preparation and through ongoing professional development activities.

What Kind of Initial Preparation for the Role of Instructional Consultant is Provided by CIDR?

As initial preparation for consulting at CIDR, we close the Center's doors to clients during the last two weeks of June each year and provide a structured, in-service, intensive seminar for the staff. This seminar is one of the most important events in the life of the Center, and all staff are expected to attend. It is designed with goals that address the needs of the particular group of consultants each year.

Seminar Goals

Among the goals for 1993 were the following:

- To enhance understanding of the overall philosophy and operation of the Center for Instructional Development and Research;
- To enhance understanding of the roles, interdependence, and overall organization of various CIDR staff;
- To expand individual and collective CIDR staff repertoires for responding to clients;
- To enhance understanding of diversity issues in the classroom and in the CIDR work place;
- To identify print, video, and human resources for use in the consulting process;

- To identify approaches to and results from instructional research at CIDR;
- To enable participants to establish a personal agenda for professional development.

The goals have been continually refined as the program has evolved since its inception in 1986. In the last few years, for instance, the goals have been modified to address the needs of returning staff, to emphasize the interdependence among staff with various job responsibilities, and to incorporate even more fully the information and strategies necessary to address the diversity of needs both within the CIDR staff and within the university community. The goals provide the focus for the content of the two-week intensive seminar.

Seminar Content

The content of the seminar emphasizes collaborative relationships, the CIDR philosophy, the CIDR service process, the consulting framework, and instructional consulting tools (see Appendix A for a sample schedule of topics).

Collaborative relationships. The seminar begins with an activity designed to introduce staff to each other and to increase awareness of staff backgrounds. Although the activity has varied from year to year, it usually requires staff to find out about special information or expertise of other staff members (see example in Appendix B). The activity is designed to reinforce the notion that internal communication is essential to the operations of the Center. To further the importance of collaborative efforts, we develop a brief biographical sketch of each staff member, including information on background and special areas of expertise.

CIDR philosophy. Next, the focus of the seminar moves to the history and philosophy of CIDR and the role of the Center in the University. Before this session, consultants are asked to read (or review) and be prepared to discuss materials about the mission and organizational structure of the university, about the place of the Center within the institutional mission, and about the specific Center philosophy within the context of the University (Nyquist, 1986; Wulff, Nyquist, & Abbott, 1991; University of Washington, 1989).

Consultants plunge into activities in which they apply their understanding of the Center philosophy as improvement-based, free, confidential, and client-oriented for faculty, administrators, and TAs. Consultants work in groups to analyze samples of letters (that they will later need to compose themselves) that either reflect or violate parts of the CIDR mission and philosophy. The samples are either copies of actual letters (with names removed) that pre-

vious consultants have written or fabrications designed specifically for this activity (see examples in Appendix C). The groups report the results of their analyses both as a way for new consultants to begin to apply the basic philosophy of the Center and as an opportunity for more experienced consultants to raise questions about nuances in the application of the philosophy in an ever-changing institutional culture.

CIDR service process. After consultants have had experience working with the philosophy of the Center, they are provided with a brief overview of the CIDR service process, including the basic stages of initial client request, consultant's preparation for response, call for appointment, review of materials for initial consultation, consultation, and follow-up (see Appendix D).

With this brief background, each new consultant is then given a case describing a client request that a support staff member or some other member of the staff has received. Each new consultant then has at his/her disposal any resources within the Center to determine how best to proceed through the steps of the service process. New consultants have several hours to consult with experienced staff, refer to departmental and confidential files, and to use print and video resources, all in an effort to propose a way to follow the stages of the service process with their imaginary clients. With the help of the workshop leaders and experienced staff, new consultants are able to take initial steps in proposing how they might proceed with the cases. In addition, however, the exercise reinforces the importance of using the Center's resources in the consultation process and creates the need to know the basic information in the remaining portions of the seminar.

Consulting framework. Once consultants have the need to know more about the consulting process, they are provided with the specific consulting framework that is used at CIDR (see Appendix E). To create the need to know more about how to collect, analyze, interpret, and translate data in the instructional process, we provide new consultants with a case study that contains several different sources of data, including information from an initial interview, student ratings, an SGID, and an observation. In this instance, all consultants focus on the same case. They then meet with experienced consultants to determine how they might use the consulting framework while working with a client. What typically becomes clear in this session is that the consultants need a more complete understanding of the various tools and resources available to them. Thus, much of the rest of the two-week seminar is devoted to providing information and developing the skills related to some of the tools and resources most commonly used in the consulting process.

Instructional consulting tools. Approximately one day of the two-week seminar is devoted to each of the major tools that consultants might use in their work. Experienced staff with particular expertise design the day-long sessions focused on such consulting tools as student ratings, videotaping (video critiques and micro teaching), observation in classrooms, SGID's, and workshops. Facilitators design the sessions to present information, model the use of specific tools, provide opportunities for new consultants to develop strategies through practice, and identify resources to use in the consulting process.

Additional resources. Near the middle of the second week of the seminar, we provide additional information about communication within and outside of the Center. Again, we structure activities to reinforce the notion that there are many different resources available. During this part of the schedule, special programs and specific experienced consultants within the Center are identified as important resources that consultants can use as they work with instructors. Typically, for example, the writing specialist facilitates a session on helping faculty use writing as a teaching/learning strategy; instructional computer specialists present a session to clarify possible uses of computers in instruction; specialists consulting with International Teaching Assistants explain their program; and all staff members involved in programmatic research talk about their projects and ways that the projects inform their practice. In addition, the entire support staff, including student assistants, present a session in which they clarify their roles in the Center and explain how they serve as resources for consultants.

Seminar Activities and Approaches

We use a number of different approaches in the seminar. In addition to lecturing, role-playing, analyzing cases, observing, videotaping, and working in small groups, we ask experienced consultants to be instructors, create mentoring teams, schedule social activities, and assist consultants to develop agendas for professional development.

Experienced consultants as instructors. Experienced CIDR consultants participate in the seminar by providing input into the content and the design of the program and by serving as instructors and models. They use their expertise to add important information and unique perspectives. In addition, as they teach, they gain confidence in their own knowledge and skills and simultaneously model a variety of approaches and strategies for new staff to consider. Typically, teams of consultants select the areas that they would most like to teach and then work together in advance of the seminar to design their sessions.

CIDR mentors. An important part of that two-week period is the mentoring process established to assist new consultants. Each year experienced consultants participate in a mentoring team (usually 3 people) that works closely with a new consultant during the seminar (see Appendix F). Before the seminar, we provide the mentors, led by a team facilitator, with instructions about their roles in the seminar; and they fulfill their responsibility by helping the new consultants during case study activities, taking the new consultants to lunch to discuss interests and concerns, and offering to be available during breaks and off-times to present additional explanations, answer questions, or provide moral support. In addition, the mentors monitor the progress of new consultants and participate in a "Seminar Staff Meeting" at the end of each day of the seminar to provide insights that will help the facilitators for the next day's sessions anticipate how best to adapt to the new consultants' most pressing needs and concerns.

Seminar social activities. A special part of the socialization process during the two-week seminar is the opportunity for staff to meet in less formal settings outside the context of CIDR. On the Friday evening of the first week of the seminar, all staff and their families are invited to a picnic hosted by the experienced staff. On the Friday of the second week of the seminar, CIDR hosts a luncheon for all staff, including student assistants, at the University's Faculty Club. Both events provide opportunities for staff to get to know each other on an informal basis outside their professional roles.

Agendas for professional development. Another important activity of the introductory seminar is creating what we have called "Individual Agendas for Professional Development." These agendas are developed by individual consultants throughout the seminar. At the beginning, each consultant is provided with a sheet on which he/she lists the information and skills that he/she thinks has been mastered and the information and skills still needed (see Appendix G). During the seminar the agendas provide a specific way for consultants to track what they are learning and determine what individual gaps still exist. From time to time during the seminar, some gaps can be addressed, particularly in meetings with mentoring teams. By the end of the seminar, the consultants use the agendas to assess their development during the two-week session and set their goals for future learning in the area of instructional development.

What Ongoing Professional Development Activities Are Helpful for Instructional Consultants?

Shortly after the two-week seminar, each consultant meets with a supervisor to discuss areas from the two weeks that have been mastered and areas that still need to be addressed. The consultant and supervisor then discuss ways in which each need can be met in an ongoing program of professional development. The discussion focuses specifically on how the need will be met and when it has to be met, in order for the consultant to do his/her job. In this way, we obtain a sense of what needs can be fulfilled by having consultants work individually, what needs can be met by having consultants with similar needs work in small groups, and what outstanding needs still exist for the entire staff. Beyond this follow-up, however, there are other mechanisms in place to assist all staff with ongoing professional development, including, staff notebooks/videotapes, team meetings, opportunities for "co-consulting," think tank meetings, colloquia, a research-in progress forum, and individual meetings with supervisors.

Staff notebooks/videotapes. Two major resources for all consultants during ongoing professional development are the staff notebooks that are developed during the two-week period of the seminar and videotapes of each seminar session. The notebooks are compilations of all materials developed by facilitators for use in their sessions during the seminar and typically include workshop outlines, cases, exercises, summaries, lists of references, and actual print resources. The two-volume set of materials is particularly useful as a resource in addressing consulting issues that arise throughout the year. In addition, during the seminar, all sessions are videotaped so that the videotapes are available for consultants to use in conjunction with the notebooks. The notebooks and videotapes are essential for staff training in those infrequent instances when an individual joins CIDR without having gone through the intensive seminar.

Team meetings. Applying Total Quality Management principles, we have recently flattened the hierarchy in CIDR and formed teams to serve clusters of departments. The structure provides a way to enhance communication among consultants who work with the same or similar departments and provides opportunities for more comprehensive services for individual instructors and departments. Within the team concept, consultants work in one of four consulting teams that serve groups of depart-

ments roughly organized into: 1) the sciences, math, and engineering; 2) the humanities; 3) the social sciences, and 4) the professional schools (see Appendix H). The teams consist of three to four consultants who bring a variety of levels of experience and expertise to their assigned departments. The teams, led by an experienced team facilitator, meet on a regular basis to discuss client requests and distribute work load. In addition, they assist each other in problem solving and in providing resources. Through the team meetings, staff learn from each other, and the new staff in particular have additional opportunities to observe more experienced consultants in the process of solving instructional puzzles and preparing for the consulting process. In some instances, when teams consult other teams for additional expertise or resources, the consultants also learn from members of other teams.

Co-consulting. Although the team structure provides opportunities for sharing information or resources among consultants, there are specific occasions when clients require the expertise of more than one consultant. These situations, when two or more consultants work simultaneously with one client, have created for the consultants what we have termed "co-consulting" relationships. Although resources prohibit assigning two consultants to the same client on a regular basis, in some cases the co-consulting relationship is necessary to provide the best range of services. For example, the client who wants help with instructional uses of computers and use of writing as a teaching/learning tool may engage two consultants. At various stages of the process, the two consultants work together to determine how best to use the resources to meet the needs of the client. Such instances provide additional opportunities for professional development as consultants are exposed to the thinking and style of other consultants with different backgrounds and expertise.

Think tank meetings. Another approach to the ongoing professional development of staff at CIDR is provided through "think tank" meetings in which all consulting staff meet together. Every two weeks, all consultants convene in this forum to discuss a particular issue that a consultant or group of consultants is trying to address. It may be an issue such as how to design a particular workshop, how to refine the use of a particular tool or instrument, or how to work with a particularly challenging client case. During this meeting, which is facilitated by the individual(s) requesting the input, staff consultants share ideas, hear others' thoughts about important instructional issues, and learn from each other.

Colloquia series. Often, when a significant number of the consultants express interest in learning more about a particular topic that draws from outside resources, we arrange for colloquia with presenters from other organizations or in other roles on campus. Thus, the consultants' professional development is enhanced by hearing presentations, for instance, from someone in the Ombudsman's Office for Sexual Harassment or the Office of Minority Affairs. For example, when consultants had increasing need for more detailed information on legal precedents related to student misconduct, we arranged a colloquium in which a vice provost and legal representative for the University conducted a session on legal precedents related to problematic instructor-student interactions. Such colloquia, then, arise from consultants' ongoing needs and provide information that keep consultants abreast of the most current information and resources. In cases in which visiting scholars are working in the Center, they, too, provide colloquia on topics related to their special areas of expertise.

Research-in-progress. Another source of professional development for CIDR consultants is the forum on research-in-progress. Once a month during the academic year, informal luncheon meetings are held so that consultants can talk about their research projects. During this time consultants briefly explain their research, identify issues with which they are struggling, and seek input from other consulting staff. Such sessions provide opportunities for all consultants not only to be apprised of the work of their colleagues but also to hear research ideas, discuss varying research methodologies, and learn more about issues that are being addressed through instructional research.

In summary, professional development for consultants at CIDR begins with the intensive seminar that orients consultants and begins to provide them with the important tools and resources that they need in their work. The ongoing elements of the program consist of individual activities, group activities, and all-consultant meetings in which the consultants strive to develop their professional skills. Both the initial seminar and the ongoing program are then assessed to determine the impact and to establish future directions for professional development of the consultants.

How Can We Continuously Monitor the Professional Development of Instructional Consultants?

A comprehensive program of professional development for consultants can be informed by a variety of sources about the impact of the training. At CIDR, we gather feedback from the consultants themselves, from the clients with whom the consultants work, and from supervisors of the consultants.

Consultant Feedback

The most direct way we obtain feedback about the program is to seek input directly from the consultants at different stages of the process. For instance, immediately after the seminar, we seek feedback by administering a questionnaire. Typically, we design the instrument to determine which sessions were most useful and which goals were most fully achieved in the initial part of the professional development program (see Appendix I).

During ongoing professional development activities, we ask consultants to identify areas for additional training as they progress. For example, we use bi-weekly meetings as opportunities for consultants to obtain additional information or skills that will help them in their development. When consultants feel the need for additional information or skills, in consulting with clients about a newly-instituted student ratings system, for example, the consultants can request a meeting devoted to such a topic. We provide the appropriate workshop session as a part of ongoing professional development. Such opportunities are particularly important when priorities are changing in our institution and the kinds of requests to which consultants must be responsive contain elements of contingency.

Finally, consultants' input is included near the end of the professional development program for one year as plans are beginning for the next year's program. Because consultants' perceptions of the usefulness of various components of the program can change over time, we obtain perceptions after one year of professional development. Although it is certainly possible to obtain this information in the form of a questionnaire, we prefer at CIDR to obtain the feedback at a group meeting in which consultants are asked to think back and identify those portions of the training that were most useful, those areas that were not particularly useful, and the needs that were not adequately addressed in the professional development program. This feedback is then incorporated as part of the design for subsequent professional development programs.

Client Feedback

Another source for input about the way consultants are prepared is the client. We acquire such input from the follow-up as part of the consulting process, a formal assessment conducted by the director of CIDR, or unsolicited feedback that clients provide.

As part of the consulting process, consultants

prepared to follow-up individually with their clients, certainly to determine how the consulting assistance is working, but also to obtain any input that will help them improve the quality of service they provide. A short phone call, an e-mail message, or a note provide additional contact through which consultants gather insights about how satisfied each client is. Such follow-up often elicits comments that cause consultants to be reflective about their work and to return to staff meetings where they can address issues related to a particular tool or approach that they have tried with a client.

Another source of input, and certainly an essential one in our program, is the formal client feedback about the quality of service. For each consulting service, a letter is sent from the director to individual clients requesting feedback once service(s) has been completed. These letters are accompanied by a brief questionnaire designed to obtain feedback on the specific service (see Appendix J). Items about the appropriateness of the service, how well the service was implemented, and how well the consultant followed up are designed to produce formative feedback for the consultants. In addition, open-ended questions on the questionnaire elicit responses that assist consultants and supervisors in assessing the quality of the consultants' work and specific areas of professional development that still need to be addressed.

Sometimes, although far less frequently, unanticipated feedback also provides a way to think about how consultants can best be prepared for their work. In some cases, clients may call administrators of the Center or send unsolicited letters to praise consultants' work or request additional services. Sometimes in meetings or other settings on campus, consultants or Center administrators overhear helpful feedback about the consulting services. Such feedback provides formative data to reinforce or suggest future directions for professional development programs for consultants.

Feedback from Other Staff

Feedback from other staff is also useful in monitoring the quality of consultant work and determining directions for future training. An obvious source of such input is supervisors. As supervisors and consultants work together in ongoing performance evaluation and in relationships designed to develop strategies, supervisors obtain a sense of each consultant's needs. As those needs are analyzed across consultants, supervisors develop their own perceptions of the kinds of review and additional training that would be helpful for consultants. An additional source of insights is the facilitator of each team. The team facilitators, as the more experienced consultants, offer insights about areas that they perceive are being handled well by consultants and areas for which they think there is need for additional professional development.

In short, at CIDR we attempt to tap a variety of sources of input, both to assess the quality of services consultants provide and to identify future directions for ongoing professional development for the consultants. Additionally, we have learned that needs identified from various sources must be carefully documented so they can be considered in the design and implementation of future professional development programs. Documentation is particularly important because our program attempts to meet the needs of both new and experienced consultants and, thus, varies from year-to-year.

Conclusion

The program of professional development at CIDR, with its intensive seminar and ongoing activities, is one case example of efforts to prepare instructional consultants for their roles. We recognize, of course, that there are many possible ways to approach the task of professional development, and this chapter represents one attempt that is continually evolving to meet the changing needs of instructional consultants in a university community. Perhaps some portion of the program discussed in this chapter—consultant competencies, the intensive seminar, the ongoing professional development activities, or the assessment of the program's effectiveness—will inspire additional reflection about the importance of preparing consultants for their roles in specific post secondary institutions. Clearly, when consultants are well prepared and feel that they are being provided with appropriate professional development, everyone benefits, including the instructors, the students, other consulting staff, supervisors, and the consultants themselves.

References

Nyquist, J. D. (1986). CIDR: A small service firm within a research university. *To Improve the Academy, 5,* 66-83.

Nyquist, J. D., & Wulff, D. H. (1988). Consultation using a research perspective. In E. C. Wadsworh (Ed.), *A handbook for new practitioners* (pp. 81-88). Stillwater, OK: New Forums Press.

University of Washington. (1989). University organization chart, C 00.2. *University of Washington Operations Manual* (pp. 1-7). Seattle, WA: Author.

Wulff, D. H., Nyquist, J. D., & Abbott, R. D. (1991). Developing a TA training program that reflects the culture of the institution. In J. D. Nyquist, R. D. Abbott, D. H. Wulff, & J. Sprague (Eds.), *Preparing the professoriate of tomorrow to teach* (pp. 113-122). Dubuque, IA: Kendall/Hunt.

Appendix A

Monday, June 17, 1991

9:00	Opening Session
10:15	Break
10:45	History/Philosophy of CIDR, Role of CIDR in the university--Jody, Don (Small Groups with Sample Documents)
12:15	Lunch (with Mentors?)
1:45	Overview of CIDR Serivce Process--Don
2:30	Case Study of Initial Contact (Mentors available)
4:00	Discussion of Initial Contact Cases
4:30	Announcements (Article Assignment)
4:45	Seminar Staff Meeting

Tuesday, June 18, 1991

8:30	Overview of Consulting Process--Jody, Don
9:15	Distribution of Case Study (Group Application of Consulting Model)
12:00	Lunch Break
1:00	Synthesis of Concerns Raised By Case Study--Ken, Jody, Don
2:00	Overview of Training Framework--Don
2:15	Mentor Meeting on the Consulting Relationship
4:00	Announcements
4:10	Seminar Staff Meeting

Wednesday, June 19, 1991

8:30	Introduction to SGID Process Ken, Mike, and Bob P.
9:00	Model SGID
9:30	Discussion of Data Analysis and Interpretation
10:00	Break
10:30	Analysis and Interpretation of SGID Data (In Groups to Prepare Report)
12:00	Lunch
1:30	Discussion of SGID Feedback Reports
2:00	Feedback to Don and Jody
3:15	Practice of SGID Introductions (Small Groups)
4:00	Announcements (Article Assignment for Student Ratings)
4:10	Seminar Staff Meeting

Thursday, June 20, 1991

8:30	Introduction to Videotaping--Brooke, Kati, Karen
9:15	Videocritique Case Study
10:00	Break
10:30	Videocritique--Model and Practice
12:00	Lunch
1:30	Microteaching Case Study
2:00	Team Practice
3:30	Discussion of Principles
4:00	Announcements
4:10	Seminar Staff Meetings

Friday, June 21, 1991

8:30	Various Uses of Student Ratings--Bob, Gabriele, Don
9:30	Information on IAS Printouts
10:30	Break
11:00	Role-Play of Student Ratings Consultation
12:00	Lunch
1:00	Case Study of Student Ratings Data
2:15	Discussion and Practice of Case Study
3:15	Announcements
3:30	Seminar Staff Meeting
4:00	Close Office--Volleyball and Picnic at Jody's

Monday, June 24, 1991

9:00	Workshops--Working with Departments--Ken, Mark, Gabriele, Debby
10:15	Break
10:45	Workshop Design--Roleplay
12:00	Lunch
1:00	Workshop Design--Practice in Small Groups
2:30	Workshop Design--Presentation of Format and Feedback
3:30	Principles of Workshop Design
4:15	Announcements
4:25	Seminar Staff MeetingTuesday, June 25, 1991

Tuesday, June 25, 1991

8:30	Observation as Part of the Research Model--Lisa, Margy, Mark
9:00	Principles of Conducting Observations
9:45	Break
10:15	Case Studies of Observation Process
12:00	Lunch and Observations of UW Undergraduate Courses
2:00	Debriefing of Observations: Data Analysis
2:45	Translation of Observational Data--Roleplay
3:30	Summary--Role of Observation in Data Collection
3:45	Announcements
4:00	Seminar Staff Meeting

Wednesday, June 26, 1991

8:30	Internal and External Communication at CIDR--Jody, Bob, Don
10:00	Break
10:30	Support Services--Brenda, Madelle, Kent, Nina
12:30	Lunch
2:00	Writing as a Teaching/Learning Strategy--Debby
3:30	Announcements
3:40	Seminar Staff Meeting

Thursday, June 27, 1991

8:30	Use of Computers in Instruction--Bob, Eric, Randy (Room 124)
10:00	Break
10:30	ITA Program--Mark, Gabriele, Karen, Margy
12:00	Lunch
1:30	Research at CIDR--Bob
3:00	Announcements
3:10	Seminar Staff Meeting

Friday, June 28, 1991

8:30	CIDR Working Styles--Jody
10:00	Break
10:30	Synthesis/Learning Agenda--Jody, Don, Bob
11:30	CIDR Lunch at Faculty Club

Reprinted with permission.

Appendix B

Introductory Exercise--CIDR Staff

This activity should allow us to find out some interesting facts about our colleagues. You have two tasks to complete: 1) Obtain signatures to match each statements, and 2) Sign for statement that fit you. Please do not announce which statement fits you. Only sign when asked specifically if the statement fits you and it true. See if you can complete this list.

1. "The most consuming part of my job is writing letters." _____

2. "I send 40-50 QuickMail messages a week." _____

3. "My most time consuming job is keeping papers filed and organized." _____

4. "My most unusual consultation was when Prof. X asked me for my opinion on the _____

    book "Cultural Literacy.""

5. "The most stressful parts of my job are meetings." _____

6. "My most important trip was to San Francisco." _____

7. "My puzzle deals with how the biennium budget process works." _____

8. "I really wish I knew how to manage the complexity of so much information." _____

9. "My most important trip took me to Philadelphia." _____

10. "My most unusual consultation dealt with a client trying to talk with me about whether _____

    she should marry her long-distance boyfriend."

11. "Going to China helps me in my job." _____

12. "I use the telephone approximately 3 times an hour." _____

13. "My most consuming task is preparing for meetings with clients." _____

14. "Something I do that some others do not is take care of my plants." _____

15. "I have been at CIDR longer than the directors." _____

16. "My most important trip is 45th and I5." _____

17. "I've been a staff member for 12 years." _____

18. "I've backpacked in the High Sierras." _____

19. "The most stressful parts of my job are the interruptions." _____

20. "I've spent a week at the Hopi village of Shongopovi." _____

21. "The most difficult part of my job is keeping track of all the achievements and _____

    activities of CIDR staff."

22. "My most unusual consultation was being asked out on a date by a client who _____

    would not take no for an answer."

23. "My most important trip was to Japan." _____

24. "My most unique client request: "Can you do 23 SGIDs next week?"" _____

25. "I like youth work." _____

26. "I'm teaching summer school." _____

27. "I've become very interested in children." _____

28. "I know where the articles go that are routed in CIDR." _____

29. "I'm the newest member of CIDR." _____

30. "I've just moved." _____

Reprinted with permission.

Appendix C

Given the operational philosophy of CIDR, examine the attached documents and sort them into two groups.

Group A

Those documents which reflect the philosophy as you understand it. Be able to defend your decisions and explain how you could determine that the document represents the Center appropriately.

Group B

Those documents which do not reflect the CIDR philosophy. Take these documents and either

1. explain why this service or approach would be inappropriate in view of the Centers operational philosophy, or

2. revise the language and approach of the document so that it will represent the philosophy of the Center. Again, be prepared to explain and defend your decisions.

We will work in small groups until _____. Please select someone to be the spokesperson for your group. The other members of the group are to act as "coaches" to supply the explanations for the groups decision making.

Center for Instructional Development & Research
109 Parrington Hall, DC-07
University of Washington
Seattle, WA 98195(206) 543-6588

Reprinted with permission.

Sample C   **University of Washington**

May 30, 1992

TO: Professor _____
          Finance and Business Economics, DJ-10

FROM: XXXXXXXXXX
          Staff Consultant, CIDR

RE: TA Training

(handwritten: Great!)

    I enjoyed meeting with you to discuss TA training possibilities for the TAs in Finance and Business Economics. I hope the session was helpful in generating possible approaches for use in your orientation and in your ongoing training program.

    As I mentioned in the session, I would be happy to meet with departmental and school representatives in the School of Business if you decide such a meeting would be helpful to coordinate your departmental training with training for the entire school. I will be on staff throughout the summer to assist with plans for TA training.

    I look forward to working with you and your TA training program. You can call me at 3-6588 to let me know how I can best assist you in the next stages of your planning.

Sample B   **University of Washington**

May 22, 1992

TO: Professor XXX
          Department, KL-22

FROM: XXXXXXXXXX
          Assistant Director, CIDR

RE: Forwarding Materials

    After our telephone conversation of 5/16/92, I checked our files to find that we do have copies of the summaries of the SGIDs that were conducted for you in Winter, 1990, and Spring 1991. I will forward copies of the SGID feedback for those two quarters to your department chair. Then, you and the chair can make the decisions about how best to use the information to enhance your teaching.

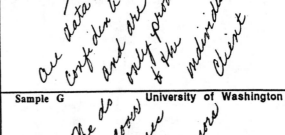

(handwritten: All data are confidential and are only provided to the individual client)

Sample E   **University of Washington**

(handwritten across top: We do not deal with other than instructional issues)

February 27, 1992

TO: Professor XXXXXX
          Department of XXXXXXXXX, VV-12

FROM: XXXXXXXXXX
          Assistant Director, CIDR, DC-07

RE: Request for Materials on Colleague/Peer Review

    In response to our telephone conversation on 2/26/92, I am sending the following information to assist you in your efforts to be promoted to associate professor.

    1. A booklet entitled *Evaluating Teaching: Purposes, Methods, and Policies*,

    2. A chapter on using evaluation results for purposes of promotion and tenure (by Miller);

    3. Miscellaneous handouts we have developed for workshops we have presented on achieving tenure.

    I would be happy to meet with you if you need additional information. In the meantime, good luck with your efforts. I will look forward to hearing from you if I can provide additional assistance as you go through this process.

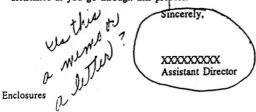

(handwritten: Is this a memo or a letter?)

                     Sincerely,

                     XXXXXXXXX
                     Assistant Director

Enclosures

Sample G   **University of Washington**

(handwritten across top: We do not cover classes for professors)

March 12, 1992

TO: Prof. UUUUUUUUU
          Department of JJJJJJJJJJ, YU-77

FROM: MEMEMEMEME
          Video Specialist, CIDR, DC-09

RE: Videotaping of Students

    Please consider this letter confirmation that I have scheduled videotaping of your final lecture for your Geography 153 class. You and I will meet in Room 207 Parrington Hall, on Friday, March 15, at 9:30 for the actual videotaping of your presentation. Since you will be out of town for the final class of the quarter, it will be important that the students have the following information:

    1. The class will meet in Room 207, Parrington Hall, at their regularly scheduled class time on Thursday, march 21, to view the videotape.

    2. I will meet the class in Room 207 and be sure they are prepared for playback of the videotape.

    3. There will be no alternative viewing times so students who are absent will not get the inforamtion from your final lecture.

    As we discussed, you can have a copy of the videotape if you decide you would like one. Otherwise, we will erase it and return it to our pool of tapes.

    Let me know if you have any questions about these details. Otherwise, I will proceed with the arrangements as described.

    I am happy to provide these services to enhance the quality of education at UW. Have a good trip, and I will look forward to hearing from you upon your return.

Appendix D

Steps in Handling Inquiries and Referrals

I. Client Request
   A. Contacts CIDR
      1. Telephone call, service request
      2. Memo asking for service
      3. Cold calls (try for a return call, if necessary)
      4. Drop-In
   B. Is referred in-house
      1. Chair interview request from Jody
      2. CIDR initiated contact--TA Training letters, etc.
      3. Staff referral

II. Consultant Preparation for Response
   A. Search department files
   B. Search confidential files
   C. Check with Administrative Assistant
   D. Follow up on any previous contacts with CIDR staff

III. Consultant Call for Appointment
   A. Have a prepared schedule of questions
   B. Establish credibility
      1. "In cases like this..."
      2. One tip/gift

IV. Consultant Review of Materials for Consultation
   A. Review relevant models or frameworks
   B. Consult relevant print materials or media

V. Consultation--A Research Process
   A. Collect data
   B. Analyze data
   C. Interpret data
   D. Translate data into a set of recommendations
      (These steps will be examined thoroughly later.)

VI. Consultant Follow-Up
   A. Log the contact--advising others
   B. Determine next contact--telephone, memo, service provided
   C. Evaluate service
   D. Respond to referring agent, if appropriate

VII. Go to second concern or goal and begin process with II and work through again. Continue until individual or department work is completed.

Reprinted with permission.

Appendix E

Consultation: A Research Process

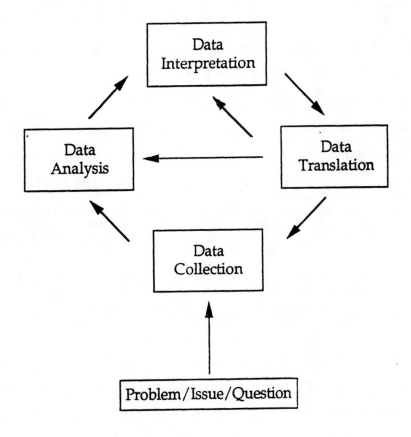

Appendix F

Mentoring Memo

June 11, 1991

TO: 1991 Mentors for Staff Development Seminar

FROM: Don and Jody

RE: Mentoring

The mentoring program designed to assist with the socialization of new staff has been very successful in the past training seminars. This year we will continue the practice with mentoring teams (and one person designated as lead mentor) to assist new staff during the training process. In order to assist you with the mentoring roles, we have compiled the following information for the 1991 staff development seminar.

Among the major goals of the mentoring program are the following:

- To help the new staff feel welcome and comfortable by keeping in contact with them throughout the seminar;
- To clarify roles of the new staff by discussing and answering questions about your typical activities and responsibilities;
- To help new staff understand the consulting process by discussing cases and giving specific examples of procedures, strategies, etc.
- To assist new staff in beginning/continuing to develop profiles of the departments (or contexts) in which they will be working;
- To meet with and discuss with new staff during the "working sessions" of the training when they have been asked to go off and work on an issue, case, assignment, approach, etc.
- To assist new staff with the development of their workshops during ongoing training by providing relevant information and resources.

Feel free to meet with new staff members whenever it is appropriate or necessary to obtain a pulse on their progress and assist them in digesting the information. We will, from time to time, and particularly during the staff seminar meetings at the end of each day, be asking you for any feedback you may be receiving from new consultants about the workload, level of interest, intensity, etc. The scheduled meeting times we have provided for mentoring are as follows:

Monday, June 17--We thought you might want to arrange to meet during the lunch time of the first day to establish rapport and get started.

Monday, June 17 (2:30-4:00)--Be able to assist new staff with information about their cases for the initial contact.

Tuesday, June 18 (9:00-12:00)--Work, as needed, with new staff on their case study of the consulting process.

Tuesday, June 18--We have provided time from 2:00 to 4:00 P.M. for mentors to meet with new staff about consulting. Perhaps during this time you can use cases to help new staff think about the kinds of situations they will encounter and the kinds of procedures they will be using, as a way of preparing them for the focus on specific tools in the forthcoming sessions.

We hope, however, that each team of mentors will also be able to work closely with new staff as they prepare workshops for presentation during ongoing training. The list of new consultants and mentoring teams is attached. Good luck and thanks for all your help.

Appendix G

Consultant's Development Plan

Individual Agenda	Ways to Address Items on Individual Agenda
Skills, training, information, assistance I still need to do my job well include. . .	The ways I could accomplish/obtain the skills, training or information on my agenda might be to. . .
1.	1.
2.	2.
3.	3.
4.	4.
5.	5.
6.	6.
7.	7.
8.	8.
9.	9.
10.	10.
11.	11.
12.	12.
13.	13.
14.	14.
15.	15.
16.	16.

Reprinted with permission.

Appendix H

Consultant Teams

Team A (TEAM MEMBERS 1, 2, 3, 4)

Aeronautics & Astronautics
Applied Mathematics
Astronomy
Atmospheric Sciences
Biochemistry
Biophysics
Biostatistics
Botany
Center for Quantitative Science
Chemical Engineering
Chemistry
Civil Engineering
Computer Science
Electrical Engineering
Engineering
Environmental Studies

Fisheries
Forestry
Genetics
Geology
Industrial Engineering
Life Sciences
Materials Science & Engineering
Mathematics, Applied Mathematics
Mechanical Engineering
Microbiology
Oceanography
Physics
Speech and Hearing Sciences
Statistics
Technical Communication
Zoology

Team B (TEAM MEMBERS 5, 6, 7)

#5 GROUP

Anthropology
Economics
General Studies
Political Science

#6 GROUP

Education
Psychology
Sociology
Speech Communication

#7 GROUP

Aerospace Studies
Afro-American Studies
Art
Art History
Asian-American Studies
Chicano Studies
Geography
Military Science

Team C (TEAM MEMBERS 8, 9, 10, 11)

Architecture
Classics
Comparative Literature
Drama
English
English as a Second Language

History
International Studies
Language Learning Center
Languages (all)
Linguistics
Music
Philosophy
Women Studies

Team D (TEAM MEMBERS 12, 13)

#12 GROUP

Business Administration
Dentistry
Medicine
Physiology
School of Communications

#13 GROUP

GSPA
Health Sciences
Law
Nursing
Pharmacy
Social Work

Reprinted with permission.

Appendix I

Evaluation: CIDR Professional Development Seminar

Circle the number which most accurately represents your response to each of the items.

Section I.

Overall, how valuable was the Staff Development Seminar for you?

Not Valuable   1   2   3   4   5   Very Valuable

How valuable was the process of working with a group to design training activities for a full day on one specific tool?

Not Valuable   1   2   3   4   5   Very Valuable

Section II.

For each of the following, rate how valuable you felt the session was. (You may need to review the schedule, the handouts, and your notes.)

6/17 - History/Philosophy of CIDR and Role of the Center in the University

Not Valuable   1   2   3   4   5   Very Valuable

6/17 - Overview of CIDR Service Process

Not Valuable   1   2   3   4   5   Very Valuable

6/17 - Case Study of Initial Contact (Individual work in files to follow-up on initial contact)

Not Valuable   1   2   3   4   5   Very Valuable

6/18 - Overview of Consulting Process, Discussion of Article

Not Valuable   1   2   3   4   5   Very Valuable

6/18 - Case Study--Group Application of Consulting with a Research Perspective

Not Valuable   1   2   3   4   5   Very Valuable

6/18- Mentor Meeting on the Consulting Relationship

Not Valuable   1   2   3   4   5   Very Valuable

6/19 - Introduction to SGID Process

Not Valuable   1   2   3   4   5   Very Valuable

The above format continues for all major sessions of the seminar.

Section III.

1. For each of the following, identify your response. Briefly explain your responses.

I felt free to participate in the discussions when I wanted to.

Strongly Disagree 1   2   3   4   5   Strongly Agree

When we had discussions, they stayed reasonably close to the targeted objectives.

Strongly Disagree 1   2   3   4   5   Strongly Agree

My own questions about my role were answered sufficiently.

Strongly Disagree 1   2   3   4   5   Strongly Agree

2. How well do you think the Staff Development Seminar achieved its objectives? They were:

   ° To develop an understanding of the overall philosophy and operation of the Center
   ° To develop understanding of the roles of various Center staff
   ° To provide opportunities for Center for Instructional Development and Research staff to practice skills needed in their roles at the Center
   ° To expand Staff repertoires for responding to clients
   ° To identify resources for use in the consulting process
   ° To enable participants to establish a personal agenda to be accomplished during the summer.

3. What was the "best" part of the Staff Seminar for you?

4. What do you feel could have been handled more effectively in the Seminar? What recommendations for change do you have? (Use the back of this sheet for extra space.)

Reprinted with permission.

Appendix J

Evaluation by Client

«DATA eval ltr mrg file93»

University of Washington

January 5, 1994

«Title» «First» «Last»
«Dept»
«Mail»

Dear «Title» «Last»:

As with most service operations, we are very interested in knowing how satisfied you are with the services provided you during Autumn Quarter 1993 by the Center for Instructional Development and Research. Could you please take a few minutes to fill out this form, simply fold it in thirds, tape or staple it shut, and place it in campus mail? Thank you in advance for your cooperation.

Sincerely,

Jody D. Nyquist
Director

JDN/mq
Enclosure

SMALL GROUP INSTRUCTIONAL DIAGNOSIS (SGID)

CIDR Staff: «CIDR Staff»   Name of Client: «Client»

SGID Administered: «Date»   Department: «Dept»

1. Small Group Instructional Diagnosis (SGID) process was adequately explained.

strongly disagree	disagree	agree	strongly agree
1	2	3	4

2. SGID was an appropriate service to meet my instructional needs.

strongly disagree	disagree	agree	strongly agree
1	2	3	4

3. Center Staff persons were effective in implementing the SGID process.

strongly disagree	disagree	agree	strongly agree
1	2	3	4

4. Center Staff person(s) reported results to me in a clear, concise, useful form.

strongly disagree	disagree	agree	strongly agree
1	2	3	4

5. Overall, I feel the service was valuable.

strongly disagree	disagree	agree	strongly agree
1	2	3	4

6. I would recommend use of Center services for colleagues in my department who wish to work on the improvement of teaching. (Please comment on your response.)   Yes   No

ADDITIONAL COMMENTS:

RECOMMENDATIONS TO CENTER STAFF:

Reprinted with permission.

34. Professional Development for Consultants / 303

35. *Training New Consultants at Stanford: The TA Consultants Program*

Michele Marincovich

Since 1975 the Center for Teaching and Learning (CTL) has offered teaching support services on the Stanford campus, initially only to teaching assistants but, after a 1979 request from the Faculty Senate, to faculty and lecturers as well. Individual teaching consultation, in association with videotaping, small group evaluation, or classroom observation, has been one of the major and most popular of these services. In order to offer consultation on any scale, I have developed at CTL a paraprofessional staff of TA consultants who do the vast majority of the consultative work with teaching assistants. This chapter describes how these paraprofessional consultants are trained, shares materials used in the training, and highlights some of the results.

The TA Consultants Program: An Overview

The TA consultants program arose out of a simple dilemma. In 1979, CTL had one professional staff member, myself, to provide teaching support services to a potential faculty population of approximately 1,000 and a TA population almost as large. As on any campus, only a fraction of the members of either of these groups requested individual help in any one year but it still seemed unwise to promote videotaping, classroom observation, or other important means of teaching evaluation and improvement without being able to provide sufficient one-on-one follow-up. Different solutions to this lack of staff were possible—to train groups of faculty and TAs within departments to work as peer consulting teams, to press for the budget to hire more staff (not as impossible then as it would be now but still an uphill battle), or to concentrate on teaching support activities with a group rather than an individual focus. For various reasons, I chose to formalize the system of TA volunteers who had been informally doing work for CTL, put them through organized training, and use them to provide personal consultation services.

The program had another inspiration. In late 1978, I had attended a POD preconference workshop on the teaching improvement methods of the University of Massachusetts Clinic to Improve University Teaching. Although the Clinic itself did not survive as an entity, I was impressed with the Clinic's materials, especially with its six-step approach to teaching consultation through: 1) an initial interview with a client, 2) the collection of data, 3) the analysis of data, also called "localization," 4) improvement strategy contracting 5) a second round of data collection to see if the improvement strategies were working (perhaps followed by still other rounds), and 6) wrap-up and evaluation. I felt that I had a model not only for my own work with faculty but a model for the training of potential TA consultants.

Hence as 1978 was ending, I recruited a dozen potential TA consultants to go through an initial, experimental training program. Ten of the twelve were themselves TAs, all with highly successful teaching records, and two were lecturers, again with illustrious reputations for their teaching effectiveness. A few of these potential consultants I had already known and worked with; an invitation to participate in this new program had been sufficient to secure their commitment. The rest of the participants were recommended by the few faculty departmental TA training coordinators that then existed at Stanford. In subsequent workshops, realizing that it would be a way to strengthen ties with the departments, I came to rely exclusively on consultant nominations from department chairs.

The Training

The first year's training program consisted of 10 hours

spread over four weekly meetings and followed the Clinic model very closely. It became almost immediately apparent, however, that modifications would be necessary to make the training fully appropriate to the Stanford situation. I discovered, for example, that this first class of consultants objected to the underlying medical model in the Clinic approach and its terminology. For them, the medical model implied that those who were seeking teaching consultation considered their current teaching poor or ailing (just as, until the recent wellness movement in medicine, those seeing a doctor generally did so because they had a medical problem). Instead, these future consultants felt that all teachers, even the highly successful, should reflect on and seek to enhance their instruction. To do so should not imply any problem but just a strong commitment to excellence. They—and I—also came to feel that the six Clinic steps were too time-consuming and too cumbersome for the 10 week Stanford quarter. At that time, TAs often taught only one quarter per year and perhaps only one or two times during their graduate career. We needed a more condensed and efficient approach when our window of opportunity was open for so little time.

Thus began a process of modifying the training workshop, gathering feedback, and doing more fine-tuning that has occurred each of the fourteen times that the training has been offered. Rather than going through this process year by year, however, I describe how the workshop is currently structured and comment as needed on the "why's" of various features. I also note that although I have conducted each of the fourteen workshops, Mark Gonnerman, CTL's coordinator of TA training, played a considerable role in recent years.

First, since we have learned that the workshop goes much more smoothly if participants have already met and gotten to know each other somewhat, we get them together for lunch about two weeks before the training. At the lunch, consultants interview the person next to them (a classic ice-breaking exercise), explore his or her teaching background and interests, and look for something memorable about the person—whether this is an unusual hobby, experience, or teaching challenge—to mention as part of the introductions. As a group, we also talk about the role of teaching and TAs at Stanford and elsewhere in higher education. During the last few years especially, I have been able to highlight the increasing importance of a successful teaching record, even at research universities, though this is still truer of some fields (English, History) than in others (Physics, Chemistry).

When the training workshop starts, we keep introductions very brief. (This is important since we try to do the training on one day, a Saturday shortly after the academic year starts, rather than over several meetings. Single-day training has considerably simplified the problem of scheduling). The participants are asked to identify themselves and their department and to say one thing they'd like to get out of the training. I follow this up with my three goals as the workshop leader: to give participants a model for teaching consultation and the confidence to use it successfully; to help participants develop a richer conceptualization of teaching that will help them as teachers and consultants; and to make them part of a network of people on campus committed to teaching. I then briefly provide the ground rules of the workshop, stressing the confidentiality of discussions and analyses of people's teaching, and the need for them to participate fully in the six hours of workshop that follow. I also explain that the only way such a brief period of training can work is that it basically takes their informal knowledge of teaching and interpersonal relations and formalizes the most important aspects of it. If participants had not already built up impressive and effective teaching records and not been selected for their interpersonal skills, then training of this duration would be hopelessly inadequate.

The heart of the workshop then commences with a dyad exercise. I ask the participants in their pairs to condense into as few categories as possible their notion of the components of effective teaching. They are given ten minutes to do this, and each pair is then asked to report its conclusions to the whole group. I write the responses on the board, trying—whenever appropriate—to point out when groups have said essentially the same thing in slightly different words. We then compare the group's responses to three handouts, two from Seldin (1980, pages 9 and 11 [p. 11 is Appendix A]) and one from Miller (1974, pages 32-33), summarizing research on the characteristics of effective teaching. Invariably, the group has come up with categories quite similar to those found in the research. Thus, the first exercise builds participants' confidence and gets them to think more analytically about what we mean by effective teaching.

From here it's a natural segue into CTL's teaching observation form (Appendix B). Like the training itself, this form has evolved over the years—with lots of input from consultants and clients—into its present manifestation. But the roots of its major categories still derive from the analyses of Seldin (1980) and Hildebrand, Wilson, and Dienst (1971), though the organization and terminology are slightly different. For one thing, we divide the form as a whole into style and content factors, with much of what Hildebrand would call "enthusiasm/dynamism" and Seldin "enthusiasm/stimulation" put under style factors. We did this when we realized that most of our users expected feedback on their style and initially seemed to worry most about such things as eye contact and gestures. Separating these out allowed us to deal with them and yet move on to more substantive elements.

I go over the observation form carefully, explaining that the consultants do not have to use it in every case and should never treat it simply as a checklist. But since a standardized appraisal form has been recommended to enhance the reliability of colleague observation (Seldin, 1980), we provide one to guide and help structure what the consultants look for and record. I also explain that instead of coming up with scores or grades in each category, observers are encouraged to make helpful comments. On the line beside the "Introduction" category, for example, a consultant might write, "Try a longer, more detailed preview." Their attention is also turned to the back of the form, where in collaboration with the client they will eventually summarize the results of a consultation in three categories—"Aspects to Maintain," "Targets for Change," and "Methods for Improvement." I'll return to this part of the form when I discuss the last steps in a consultation.

With the groundwork laid in the initial hour by the discussion of effective teaching and the CTL observation form, the training then focuses on a consultation model organized around three stages: 1) initial contact, 2) collection and analysis of data/preparation for feedback, and 3) feedback and exchange. (These stages are a condensation and simplification of the six-part Clinic model, telescoped to fit into the more harried pace of a quarter system.) The model can be applied whether the consultation is built around a videotape, a classroom observation, a student small group evaluation, a particular issue chosen by the client, or—ideally—a combination of all of these.

Initial Contact

The first stage of the consultation process is the initial contact. If a teaching consultation is to be successful, the consultant and client must establish a relationship of trust and rapport, ideally from their first meeting. They must also have a shared sense of their goals for the consultation and for the client's teaching. It is especially crucial that the consultant and client establish this process as a joint one; the consultant is not there to pass judgment or decide whether or not the teacher is "good." The consultant is there to help the client become more reflective, more observant, more aware of his or her teaching options and assumptions.

The participants get two more handouts at this stage: the first is a list of questions that would typically be asked during the initial contact phase of a consultation (see Chapter 4 for further discussion); the second details characteristics of effective listening, a hallmark of good consultation but especially of a successful initial contact (Appendix C). To drive the effective listening handout home, participants are asked if there's anything not on the list that others in the past have done for them to make them feel listened to. Participants are generally unable to add any new categories although they think of plenty of personal examples to illustrate the handout's existing categories.

I next have the participants watch about ten minutes of an initial contact interview on videotape. I did the tape over ten years ago with a real client who had subsequently become one of CTL's teaching consultants. The taped interview was staged, then, though it was as faithful as the two of us could make it to what we recalled of our actual initial contact.

Participants are asked at this point to practice an initial interview through a role play with the person sitting next to them. (If they already know the person next to them well, they are asked to pick somebody else.) They take turns being the client and the consultant in an initial contact interview lasting about seven minutes for each person. As the pairs get into their roles, I circulate around the room, listening to the interactions and using this as a chance to get to know more about each consultant. (Because the din gets quite loud, it is important to have a large room with moveable chairs and plenty of room to spread out.) Actually getting into the consultation process energizes the group and generally allows us to complete the morning part of the workshop without taking a formal break.

When the time for the role play is over, I let each member of the pair give the other a minute or two of feedback. I then ask the group as a whole to talk about what went well and what was difficult. Generally, participants say that the hardest part is making the initial contact seem friendly and informal and yet getting certain questions and information taken care of. They begin to see the advantages, indeed the necessity, of actually practicing the process beforehand and having a strategy for the initial time together.

Collecting and Analyzing Data/Preparing for Feedback

We next move into the second stage of the consultation model—data collection and preparation for feedback. (In our consultation work, most feedback is built around the analysis of a videotape, the observation of an actual class, or—only occasionally in the case of TAs—the analysis of class materials like the syllabus, exams, or homework. Since TAs rarely have responsibility for the design of a course, such things as the syllabus or exams are generally less relevant.) To prepare the workshop participants for the first step of data collection, I show them 10 minute segments from several different kinds of classes and ask them to record their observations. I urge them to do the observations once without CTL's observation form and the other times with it. Most find that the observation form does indeed help structure their observations without straitjacketing them. After each taped segment, observations are shared first in pairs and then as a whole group. Although participants' comments tend to be of high quality from the beginning, their skills sharpen as they hear each other's observations and view several different types of classes and teaching approaches. Participants are reminded to concentrate on what they saw, to emphasize behaviors and the raw data rather than judgments.

Once participants have practiced observing for a while, they move into the analysis of their observations and their preparation for giving feedback to the client. Although these stages are broken down for training, they often occur more or less simultaneously in an actual consultation. As a consultant and a client watch a videotape, for example, one or the other will often comment on a particularly good or bad moment. The teacher may ask if a certain question worked and, if it didn't, why it didn't, and what he or she should have done differently. With our consultants, however, especially when they are new, we want them to emphasize raising questions and helping teachers to think through their approach, not telling them that this or that was good or bad. Consultants are generally relieved that they don't have to pass judgment, but they also usually find that the critic's role is hard to forego. They have been rewarded for years for finding the flaws in things, not for working collaboratively to improve a process. They find it awkward to keep their analysis tentative and to work in concert with the client during feedback.

The whole process of analysis of the data, moreover, seems to me more analogous to the interpretation of a poem or of an historical event rather than to data analysis as it would be carried out in the social sciences. So, like the teacher of literature or of history, I cover this stage more by examples and practice than by the presentation of a rigorous methodology. We go back to the same data that we had taken on previous videotapes and together practice their interpretation. There are sometimes disagreements but as we explore the basis of the disagreements, we

usually find that it is more a matter of assumptions or philosophy than of accurate observation. This is a caution again to consultants about the nature of their role.

As a last step in this stage, consultants are exposed to some rule-of-thumb guidelines for preparing to give feedback to the client. I generally advise consultants to find at least two or three aspects of the client's teaching that are already strong and to begin with positive comments about these. If the consultant feels that certain questions or issues need to be raised about other aspects of the client's teaching, I advise that these be kept to a relatively small number, say three to five things, since clients rarely seem to respond to a whole checklist of deficiencies. I also recommend that the consultant choose for discussion one or two aspects of the teacher's approach that could be changed easily and would have some immediately positive impact. Since it is often crucial during this stage that the consultant be ready to suggest improvement strategies to the client, we have prepared a list of possible issues and appropriate strategies for improvement (Appendix D). I go over these and encourage consultants to add their own ideas.

Feedback and Exchange

Next the participants move into what they tell me is the most difficult part of the workshop—and I agree. I show them a videotaped segment of an actual teacher, give them some real background on the teacher—including the goals for the class and concerns about it—and then ask them to practice a feedback to the teacher of what they observed and how they analyzed it. They are supposed to do this collaboratively, drawing the teacher and her own observations out and resisting telling the teacher if she is good or bad and why. Part of the difficulty is that this is done as a role play, with the participants taking turns playing the teacher and yet not knowing just how the teacher would have really reacted during the feedback. I am especially careful to circulate among the different pairs during this stage since consultants' styles are really beginning to emerge at this point.

As part of this assignment, each of the consultants—in collaboration with the person role-playing the teacher—is asked to use the observation form, front and back, as they would in a real consultation and then turn it in, signed, to me. It is the back that becomes especially crucial since this summary of "Aspects to Maintain," "Targets for Improvement," and "Suggestions for Change" ideally provides a sense of closure for a particular consultation encounter and represents a concrete action plan for the client. When I later look over these forms, they indicate to me the consultants' readiness for and sophistication in their consulting work.

Student Small Group Evaluation (SSGE)

Participants have now covered the most important aspects of the consultation process and practiced each step in it. Another handout summarizes for them the administrative logistics of video-feedback in particular, since this is their most common task.

With only a half hour or so to go, one essential task is left to accomplish in the workshop—to show the participants how to do a Student Small Group Evaluation. Since CTL gets up to 75 SSGE requests a year from TAs, we especially need the teaching consultants to be trained in doing these.

Student Small Group Evaluation is a form of mid-course feedback from students originally developed by Joe Clark at the University of Washington (see Chapter 15) and adapted for use at Stanford following its introduction in 1980. At the teacher's invitation, a teaching consultant goes into a classroom twenty minutes before the end of the class (twenty minutes at the beginning is also possible, but less desirable); divides the students into small groups, generally of four to six; and asks the students in those groups to answer three questions—what they like about the class thus far, what needs improvement, and how the improvement could be carried out. We have found that SSGEs yield very helpful and specific data on students' perceptions of how a course is going. This is so especially if the course or instructor is new or if the instructor is eager to improve his or her teaching evaluations but data from the university-mandated student evaluations aren't rich enough. (Stanford's official university-wide student evaluation form asks only six questions, all at a high level of generalization, about the course and the instructor.)

At the workshop, consultants are trained by having the technique briefly explained and then demonstrated on them as if they were in a class in which the SSGE were being done. Participants seem to pick the procedure up with little difficulty. The more challenging part is to cover some of the things that can go wrong in an SSGE, such as some students leaving as soon as the process is announced or taking too long to answer the questions. Since the major problems that occur are few and well known, however, we manage to cover these in a relatively brief amount of time. We also go over how to make the evaluation maximally beneficial to the instructor by meeting with him or her afterward (as soon afterward as possible). In a sense, we are rehearsing many of the principles of successful con-

sulting that were covered earlier in the day. It is especially important to be prepared to help the teacher brainstorm responses to what students see as improvements needed in the class. Appendix D is pertinent here. Equally, we stress the importance of talking to the teacher about what to say to the students at the first class meeting after the evaluation. Ideally, the teacher not only acknowledges the students' feedback but, if at all possible, responds positively to one or two things the students recommended.

We then give each consultant a disk formatted to facilitate the write-up of an SSGE. We also give them several different examples of real write-ups of past SSGEs, with all identifying information deleted. (One of these is reproduced as Appendix E). They also receive two handouts reminding them of the steps of an SSGE as they are to do it in the classroom and as our office handles it administratively. If we had more time in the workshop, we would have them role play a feedback session for an SSGE, but we've never found this possible. Fortunately, consultants seem to pick up a solid overview of the process but do sometimes call us just before their first SSGE to make sure that they have all the steps correctly in mind. Most later report that they enjoy the SSGE follow-up meetings more than any other kind of consultation, even a videofeedback.

Evaluation

Our closing exercise is to ask the participants to fill out a workshop evaluation which, they will recognize, has been structured along the lines of an SSGE (Appendix F). Since we encourage participants to fill these out on the spot, we have had close to a 100 percent response rate. Workshop participants may also take the evaluations seriously because during the workshop I refer to changes I have made in the training as a result of comments from previous participants. Certainly the amount and kind of structure that characterize the workshop and that have drawn significant positive comment in the evaluations are a result of helpful comments over the years. For example, a significant improvement in the 1993 workshop came in response to comments in 1992 that the final role play was too artificial.

To evaluate the program along yet another dimension, in 1989 we decided to do a survey of all current and former consultants to get an idea of how they perceived the program's impact on them and CTL's TA users. (See Appendix G for a copy of the survey.) By then about one hundred people, mainly graduate students, but including a few undergraduate TAs and several lecturers, had participated in the program. We had an excellent response rate of 70 percent.

The results of the survey have been written up elsewhere (Marincovich & Gordon, 1991) but I will summarize the most relevant findings here. Perhaps the most important is that the consultants felt their knowledge and their confidence and expertise about teaching improved as a result of their participation in the program. Although they had been recruited to help others, they felt they had received genuine professional benefits themselves; over half mentioned, for example, that being a consultant had been helpful on the academic job market. Of the consultants who had not stayed in academia, the majority (five out of nine, admittedly very small numbers) felt they had benefited. Other significant results were that consultants had not felt either the training program or their consulting duties were too time-consuming (in spite of the very modest, one-time honorarium they had received for their time—$75 in the early years and $100 subsequently); on the other hand, they felt that if budget and time permitted, CTL should increase its interactions with departments, something we subsequently undertook. Finally, we were gratified to learn that many consultants (30) were staying active in teaching improvement activities as they graduated and moved on to other campuses.

Overall, the results of the survey were so positive that no comprehensive changes in the program or its consultant training component seemed indicated. If anything, we felt that we could start asking more time from consultants for CTL's TA work and in the years since the survey have done that successfully. We also use the results at our initial, get-acquainted lunch meeting with prospective consultants to discuss the kind of benefits that previous consultants have reported as a result of the program.

Finally, to check on whether the consultants are doing an effective job as a result of their training, at the end of every quarter we invite everyone who has used our videotape consultation service to fill out an evaluation of their experience (Appendix H). These evaluations have generally been very positive but have not come in at a high response rate. This is still an unresolved problem.

Conclusion

I am enthusiastic about the advantages of a TA consultants program for a teaching and learning center, its clients, and its consultants. At Stanford, the program has proven an inexpensive and well received way to increase our staff and make individualized services available to many more potential clients. I hope that by discussing our consultant training approach in some detail, providing

copies of many of the handouts, and discussing our consultant survey results, more offices will tap the energy of potential graduate student consultants and provide them with this important professional training opportunity. I also hope that colleagues will send me comments and feedback on our training approach and materials.

I note in closing that this consultant training workshop has also proven a useful way to help train new professional staff at CTL. So far, three of CTL's incoming associate directors and its two coordinators of TA training have taken the workshops. Not only is this an efficient use of my time as director, but it has also enriched the training workshops for the new consultants.

References

Hildebrand, M., Wilson, R. C., & Dienst, E. R. (1971). *Evaluating university teaching.* Berkeley: University of California, Center for Research and Development in Higher Education.

Marincovich, M., & Gordon, H. (1991). A program of peer consultation: The consultants' experience. In J. D. Nyquist, R. D. Abbott, D. H. Wulff, & J. Sprague (Eds.), *Preparing the professoriate of tomorrow to teach: Selected readings in TA training* (pp. 175-183). Dubuque, Iowa: Kendall/Hunt Publishing Co.

Miller, R. I. (1974). *Developing programs for faculty evaluation.* San Francisco: Jossey-Bass.

Seldin, P. (1980). *Successful faculty evaluation programs: A practical guide to improve faculty performance and promotion/tenure decisions.* Crugers, NY: Coventry Press.

Additional Readings

Brinko, K. T. (1990). Instructional consultation with feedback in higher education. *Journal of Higher Education, 61,* 65-83.

Brinko K. T., Habel, J., & Pendleton-Parker, B. (1987). Formative feedback from peers. In N. V. Chism (Ed.), *Institutional responsibilities and responses in the employment and education of teaching assistants: Readings from a national conference* (pp. 193-207). Columbus, OH: Center for Teaching Excellence, The Ohio State University.

Fisher, M. (1980). A TA/TA consultation program: The unanticipated benefits. *Contributed Papers, Sixth International Conference on Improving University Teaching* (pp. 55-61). Lausanne, Switzerland.

Hruska, L. (1979). Training peers as teaching consultants. *Contributed Papers, Fifth International Conference on Improving University Teaching* (Vol. 1, pp. 262-263). London, England.

Lewis, K. G., & Povlacs, J. T. (Eds.). (1988). *Face to face: A sourcebook of individual consultation techniques for faculty/instructional developers.* Stillwater, OK: New Forums Press.

Puccio, P. (1987). TAs Help TAs: Peer counseling and mentoring. In N. V. Chism (Ed.), *Institutional responsibilities and responses in the employment and education of teaching assistants: Readings from a national conference* (pp. 219-223). Columbus, OH: Center for Teaching Excellence, The Ohio State University.

Stelzner, S. L. (1987). Peer training in a teaching improvement program for TAs. In N. V. Chism (Ed.), *Institutional responsibilities and responses in the employment and education of teaching assistants: Readings from a national conference* (pp. 208-214). Columbus, OH: Center for Teaching Excellence, The Ohio State University.

Appendix A

Apparent similarities of dimensions found in
16 factor analyses of instructor ratings

Dimensions	Organization/ Clarity	Enthusiasm/ Stimulation	Instructor Knowledge	Groups Organizational Skill
Studies Isaacson et al. (1964)	Structure	Skill		Rapport
Solomon Rosenberg, and Bezdik (1964)	Clarity, expressiveness vs. obscurity, vagueness	Energy vs. lethargy		Lecturing vs. encouragement of student participation
Solomon (1966)	Precision/ organization vs. informality, obscurity: Difficulty of presentation vs. clarity	Energy, facility of communication vs. lethargy, vaguness	Control. factual emphasis vs. permisiveness	Warmth, approval vs. coldness: Learning vs. encouragement of broad, expressiveness student participation
Deshpande, Webb, and Marks (1970)	Cognitive merit	Stimulation		Affective merit
Turner (1970)	Pentrating, clear, focused	Exciting, humorous, stimulating	Prepared, probing, demanding	Approachable, warm, cheerful
Hildebrand, Wilson, and Dienst (1971)	Organization/ clarity	Dynamism/ enthusiasm	Analytic/synthetic approach	Instructor/ group interaction
Frey (1973)	Organization/ clarity	Teacher's presentation		Teacher accessibilty
McKeachie and Lin (1973)	Structure	Skill		Group Interaction
Blazek (1974)	Instructor clarity	Instructor knowledge/ enthusiasm	Instructor knowledge/ enthusiasm	Instructor openness
Pohlman (1975)	Organized in presenting material	Increases student's appreciation of the subject matter		
Rugg and Norris (1975)	Structure and Guidance	Stimulating teaching	Subject matter expertise: Research methods expertise	Interpersonal rapport, respect for students

* Peter Seldin, Successful Faculty Evaluation Programs: A Practical Guide to Improve Faculty Performance and Promotion/Tenure Decisions. Copyright 1980 Coventry Press. Reprinted with permission of the publisher.

Appendix B (Side 1)

Teacher: _____ Class: _____ Date: _____ Consultant: _____

Aspects the teacher particularly asked you to observe: _____

STYLE FACTORS

Eye Contact _____

Non-verbal gestures: appropriateness, variety (note distracting gestures) _____

Enthusiasm/affect/humor _____

Poise _____

Speech speed/wait time after questions _____

Voice quality (volume/ inflection/modulation) _____

Spontaneity (easy mobility; ability to deviate from notes) _____

Pacing _____

Use of audiovisual aids/ blackboard _____

CONTENT FACTORS

Motivation:

Answers "so what?" question _____

Arouses interest (through drama, paradox, devil's advocate, etc.) _____

Connects material with students' previous knowledge or experience _____

Interaction with group:

Uses student names if appropriate _____

Looks for students' reactions and difficulties _____

Varies level/types of questions _____

Accepts or invites criticism _____

Establishes conditions for student participation _____

Organization/Clarity:

Introduction (Telling the students what you're going to tell them) _____

Major/minor points distinguished _____

Transitions clearly marked _____

Mini-summaries periodically given _____

Varieties of explanation _____

Repetition as needed _____

Use of diagrams, graphs, etc. _____

Use of examples, analogies, models _____

Concise, concrete language _____

Conclusion (Telling them what you've told them) _____

Conceptual Framework:

Organizes material conceptually _____

Makes assumptions clear _____

Explores implications of theories _____

NOTES:
1. What did the teacher hope to accomplish in this class?

2. How did s/he hope to accomplish it?

3. Evidence of his/her success:

Reprinted with permission.

Appendix B (Side 2)

ASPECTS TO MAINTAIN

1.

2.

3.

4.

5.

TARGETS FOR CHANGE

1.

2.

3.

4.

5.

METHODS FOR IMPROVEMENT

1.

2.

3.

4.

5.

Appendix C

CHARACTERISTICS OF EFFECTIVE LISTENING*

Ineffective		Effective

Non-Verbal Behavior

Listener looks bored, uninterested, or judgmental; avoids eye contact; displays distracting mannersims (doodles, plays with a paper clip, etc.)

Listener maintains positive posture; avoids distracting mannerisms; keeps attention focused on speaker; maintains eye contact; nods and smiles when appropriate

Focus of Attention

Listener shifts focus of attention to himself; "When something like that happened to me, I . . . "

Listener keeps focus of her comments on the speaker; "When that happened what did you do?"

Acceptance

Listener fails to accept speaker's ideas and feelings; "I think it would have been better to . . . "

Listener accepts ideas and feelings; "That's an interesting idea; can you say more about it?

Empathy

Listener fails to empathize; "I don't see why you felt that . . . "

Listener empathizes; "So when that happened, you felt angry."

Probing

Listener fails to probe into an area, to follow up on an idea or feeling

Listener probes in a helpful way (but does not cross examine); "Could you tell me more about that? Why did you feel that way? listener follows up; "A few minutes ago you said that . . . "

Paraphrasing

Listener fails to check the accuracy of communication by restating in his own words important statements made by the speaker

Listener paraphrases to guarantee that she has understood correctly and to assure speaker that this is so

Summarizing

Listener fails to summarize

Listener summarizes the progress of the conversation from time to time

Advice

Listener narrows the range of alternatives by suggesting one "correct" course of action

Listener broadens the range of ideas by suggesting (or asking the speaker for) a number of alternatives

* William H. Bergquist and Steven R. Phillips, *A Handbook for Faculty Development*, Volume 2. Washington, D.C.: Council for the Advancement of Small Colleges, 1977, p. 207.

Permission granted by the Council of Independent Colleges formerly Council for the Advancement of Small Colleges (CASC).

Appendix D

Suggestions on Improvement Strategies

Problem
- Appears disorganized
- Does not distinguish major from minor points
- Lacks introduction or has too brief an introduction
- No summary or conclusion

Resources and Strategies
- Ask to see person's lecture or discussion notes and check their structure.
- Are they well-organized? Did they allow for foreshadowing, repetition, review, and periodic summary?
- Show your own notes on the person' class and where you had trouble following.
- Suggest Craig and Winograd videotapes on how to lecture.
- Ask about the purpose for the lecture or class and how it was implemented.
- See if they are organizing material around information instead of concepts or themes.

Problem
- Appears nervous or lacking in confidence, this may show itself in poor eye contact or ineffective body language.

Resources and Strategies
- See if the person does indeed feel discomfort, and, if so, find out why.
- Reassure him that almost all teachers feel some nervousness and that this isn't all bad because it can lend energy to a situation.
- Tell him that he has to learn to control certain behaviors; those that will put students ill at ease.
- Ask him to practice eye contact and more assertive body language with you.
- Recommend strategies for stress reduction, meditation or confidence building, such as practice in front of a videocamera or mirror.

Problem
- Unresponsive class; lackluster discussion

Resources and Strategies
- keep close watch on the instructor's questions. Are they open-ended, "discussable?" If not, show her a list of her questions and go over why they aren't working.
- Check how the instructor responds to students' questions: Does she encourage response, build on students' answers?
- Are students prepared? If not, why?
- Does the instructor exert too much control? Not enough?
- Has she found exciting themes to build the discussion around?
- Recommend Halliburton and Bernstein videotapes on discussion and the Hill handout.

Problem
- Poor pacing: too fast, too slow, or too much time on housekeeping

Resources and Strategies
- It will often be hard to judge pacing without student input, but sometimes it is so poor that it will be obvious.

- Time various parts of the presentation—especially the time spent on administrative details. Ask if that seems to be the best use of time.
- Brainstorm other ways to handle time-consuming details: lists, handouts, etc.
- If pace is too fast, discuss the number of concepts (generall three to five) students can handle in 50 minutes.

Problem
- Accent or other language difficulties

Resources and Strategies
- Suggest she use the blackboard, hand-outs, or overhead to help the students follow.
- If the problem is very severe, suggest she check with Linguistics/EFS for some coursework or individual tutoring.

Problem
- Weak voice, too many "uhs" or pauses, talks too fast.

Resources and Strategies
- If he really wants to work on a weak voice or other problems, ask CTL to contact the Drama Department to arrange private tutoring.
- For "uhs," suggest he work with a tape recorder, monitoring himself every five minutes or so.
- If he talks too slow or pauses too often, ask him to talk as if they had only 5 minutes to say 10 minutes worth of material. If that pace proves right, have him continue to use it.
- If he talks too fast, help him decide the right speed and have him practice it on tape.

Problem
- Awkward gestures—especially of the hands

Resources and Strategies
- Have her talk informally to you, using her hands as she normally would. If she uses them well, suggest she keep these movements. If not, show her what you or others do or suggest a podium, etc.

Appendix E

Student Small Group Evaluation of Anthropology
Name, Teaching Assistant
Tuesday, April 30, 199X at 2:45 PM

The student small group method of teaching evaluation has been in use at Stanford since the spring of 1980. It is a procedure initiated by the instructor and done in his or her absence during approximately 20 minutes of a class period. During this time, a consultant from the Stanford Center for Teaching and Learning interviews the students regarding the following three questions:

1. What the students like about the class.
2. What the students feel needs improvement.
3. How to carry out the change (unless obvious).

If the class is very small, the students are interviewed as a whole; if large, the students are divided into groups of three to six. For this evaluation, the class of ten students was broken into two groups.

This method has been found to yield very specific and useful information from students. The results of the evaluation are discussed with the instructor in a private session afterward, and the evaluator and the instructor consider what changes in the class, if any, seem appropriate.

The results of the evaluation are as follows:

1) What students like about the class:

Group 1:
- No final. The course emphasizes papers and discussion, which are a more productive concentration.
- Work is well-distributed over the quarter.
- The seminar format is comfortable and elicits good discussion.
- Reading other people's summaries helps to clarify ideas.
- Films are good.
- Instructor is excellent.

Group 2:
- Instructor mediates discussion very well. He's extremely attentive to students and takes care to follow up on their views.
- Instructor is flexible.
- The variety of subjects is stimulating and interesting.
- The small size and the seminar format are good.
- Writing the summaries makes us read more closely.

2) What needs improvement:

Group 1:
- Notes might benefit from being focused, especially on the major texts.
- Some reserve readings are difficult to get.
- Instructor can sometimes be almost too considerate—he could assert himself more to give direction to discussion.

Group 2:
- Some reserve readings are hard to get—only on 2-hour reserve.
- Books for the class are extremely expensive.
- Discussions sometimes are redundant.

3) How to carry out the improvements (unless obvious):

Group 1:   •   Instructor can be more confident in determining the direction of the class.
                  •   It would be useful to have more concrete guidelines for the project assignment—perhaps a list of suggested topics.

Group 2:   •   On Tuesdays, the instructor might lecture a little on the background of the
                  •   authors and the readings.
                  •   Course might include more contemporary works.
                  •   Have an earlier deadline for choosing a topic for the term papers—that way people will have time to clarify the assignment.

Comment: Though it did not emerge specifically in the points presented by the individual groups, the general discussion made clear that the students are very satisfied with the class and the performance of the instructor. Several people said that this was their favorite class, and everyone agreed that the instructor was exemplary in his respect for students and his interest in providing help.

    Evaluator:

    Teaching Consultant

Appendix F

Evaluation for the Teaching Consultants Workshop
October 16, 1993

1. Please list up to three strengths of the workshop:

2. Please list up to three weaknesses:

3. Suggestions for improvement:

4. Other comments?

Thank you so much for your participation and ideas!

Reprinted with permission.

Appendix G

TA Consultant Survey
Center for Teaching and Learning

Your answers on this survey are completely confidential. In most cases you need only check a box or circle a number, so it should go fairly quickly. We are hoping you can return the survey in the envelope provided by June 9th. Thank you in advance for your help.

SECTION I:

How you got involved with the program and the nature of your involvement

- How important were each of the following in your decision to join the TA consultants program?

	not important		somewhat important		very important
helping with other TAs	1	2	3	4	5
it was an honor to be asked	1	2	3	4	5
sounded interesting	1	2	3	4	5
learning more about teachng	1	2	3	4	5
enjoyment of teaching	1	2	3	4	5
meet grad students outside my department	1	2	3	4	5
the honorarium	1	2	3	4	5
wanted to be part of CTL's work	1	2	3	4	5
other_____	1	2	3	4	5

- What CTL activities did you participate in as a consultant?
  - [ ] TA orientation planning
  - [ ] TA orientation workshop leader
  - [ ] videotape consulting
  - [ ] student small group evaluations
  - [ ] departmental activity (orientation, workshop, etc.)
  - [ ] other_____

- Looking back, how involved were you in the program?

uninvolved			moderately involved			very involved
1	2	3	4	5	6	7

- How important were each of the following in making the program worthwhile for you?

	not important		somewhat important		very important
interesting activites	1	2	3	4	5
helping other TAs	1	2	3	4	5
learning about teaching	1	2	3	4	5
improving teaching at Stanford	1	2	3	4	5
Interacting with other consultants	1	2	3	4	5
other_____	1	2	3	4	5

Appendix G (cont'd)

- How involved were you in these other teaching-related activities as a graduate student?

	uninvolved		somewhat involved		very involved
departmental activities	1	2	3	4	5
tutoring	1	2	3	4	5
informal get-togethers with other TAs	1	2	3	4	5
conversations with faculty about teaching	1	2	3	4	5
other_____	1	2	3	4	5

- How did your involvement in the program influence your subsequent career?

	decreased			no effect			increased or supported
likelihood of seeking out speaking or teaching opportunities	1	2	3	4	5	6	7
likelihood in teaching	1	2	3	4	5	6	7
likelihood of seeking out faculty development or teaching improvement activities	1	2	3	4	5	6	7
likelihood of discussing teaching with my colleagues	1	2	3	4	5	6	7
confidence as a teacher or speaker	1	2	3	4	5	6	7
other_____	1	2	3	4	5	6	7

- If you are in an academic institution, have you sought ways to contribute to teaching or faculty development on your campus? Please explain briefly.

_____
_____
_____

- If you are in business or industry, has the consultant experience been an advantage to you in that context? Please explain briefly.

_____
_____
_____

- What might we have done to increase your participation in the program?
   [] I could not have done any more than I did!
   [] phone me more often to ask me to do things
   [] planned greater variety of teaching-related activities
   [] arranged more social get togethers
   [] paid me more
   [] other _____

35. Training New Consultants at Stanford: The TA Consultants Program / 321

SECTION II

Impact of the program on your graduate years and beyond

• How did your participation as a consultant affect each of the following

decreased			no effect			increased or supported

confidence as a teacher

1	2	3	4	5	6	7

interpersonal skills

1	2	3	4	5	6	7

teaching successes

1	2	3	4	5	6	7

contact with new colleagues from other dept.'s

1	2	3	4	5	6	7

motivation as a teacher

1	2	3	4	5	6	7

concern for teaching in general

1	2	3	4	5	6	7

organization of your teaching

1	2	3	4	5	6	7

ability to deal with students

1	2	3	4	5	6	7

knowledge of teaching approaches and techniques

1	2	3	4	5	6	7

motivation to continue development of my teaching skills

1	2	3	4	5	6	7

knowledge of how to improve my teaching

1	2	3	4	5	6	7

other _____

1	2	3	4	5	6	7

• What was the most important aspect or memory of the program for you?

_____
_____
_____
_____

• If you have been on the academic job market, how helpful was your ecperience as a TA consultant in the following ways?

	no help		some help		a great deal of help
evidence of teaching ability	1	2	3	4	5
evidence of interpersonal skills	1	2	3	4	5
evidence of university service	1	2	3	4	5
other_____	1	2	3	4	5

• What awards or recognition, if any, have you received for teaching since the consultants' program?

Date

1. _____ _____

2. _____ _____

3. _____ _____

4. _____ _____

CTL Consultant Survey

SECTION III

Evaluation of the program

• How much of a contribution did the program make to the TAs on the campus in the following areas?

	none		some		a great deal
greater information on teaching	1	2	3	4	5
training opportunities	1	2	3	4	5
support for the teaching roles	1	2	3	4	5
one-on-one assistance	1	2	3	4	5
teaching evaluation services	1	2	3	4	5
other _____	1	2	3	4	5

• How much of your time did the consultants program take?

too little			just right			too much
1	2	3	4	5	6	7

• How adequate was the amount of training you received as a consultant?

too little			just right			too much
1	2	3	4	5	6	7

• Budget and staff constraints aside, how important would each of the following be to improving the TA consultants program?

	not important		somewhat important		very important
do more publicity	1	2	3	4	5
organize more events	1	2	3	4	5
have consultants from every department	1	2	3	4	5
work more intensively with departments	1	2	3	4	5
expect more from consultants	1	2	3	4	5
produce more handouts or other materials	1	2	3	4	5
other_____	1	2	3	4	5

CTL Consultant Survey

SECTION IV:

Some information about you to help us understand the information you have already given

- In which of the following was the main emphasis of your graduate work?
    1 [ ] Humanities
    2 [ ] Social science
    3 [ ] Science/Engineering
    4 [ ] Other _____

- Which of the following best represents your current employment situation?
    1 [ ] teaching in a college or university
    2 [ ] in business, industry, or government
    3 [ ] self-employed
    4 [ ] continuing your education
    5 [ ] seeking employment, or temporarily out of the job market
    6 [ ] other _____

- Which of the following best represents your orientation toward teaching?
    1 [ ] currently using my teaching skills in academia or business
    2 [ ] anticipate using my teaching skills in the future
    3 [ ] not using, or anticipating the use of, my teaching skills

- What year did you first join the CTL program?   19___

- How many years were you a consultant with CTL?
    1 [ ] one year
    2 [ ] two years
    3 [ ] three years
    4 [ ] more than three years

Thanks again for your time!

CTL Consultant Survey

Appendix H

Videotaping Evaluation Form

1. How did you hear about the videotaping service?
    __ CTL brochure __ TA Orientation __ Department
    __ Friend __ Professor __ Other (please explain)

2. How was your request handled? Promptly? Courteously? Please comment:

3. Did the taping itself go smoothly? Unobtrusively? Please comment:

4. Did a consultant view the tape with you? Yes __ No __
    Name of consultant: _____

5. Did the consultant provide helpful comments?

6. What was the most beneficial part of this service for you?

7. Would you recommend any changes:

8. Other comments:

Please return to: Center for Teaching and Learning, 110 Sweet Hall, Stanford, CA 94305 or
ID Mail: MC 3087. Thank you for your time and ideas.

Reprinted with permission.

36. *Reflecting on Practice: Observing Ourselves Consulting*

Barbara Hofer, Beverly Black and Linda Acitelli

We who work in development programs for teaching assistants and faculty bring varying professional vocabularies and attitudes about teaching effectiveness drawn from our own disciplines. In our roles as instructors and workshop facilitators we are observed by our peers only occasionally; in our individual consultations, seldom. We provide consultation and training for others, but we may also benefit from such services ourselves.

Interested in reflecting more on our practice as consultants, five staff members at the University of Michigan's Center for Research on Learning and Teaching (CRLT) developed a series of activities designed to improve our skills in providing individual services to teaching assistants and faculty. This process enabled us to articulate and refine what we mean by a "client-centered" approach and strengthened our professional relationships with one another and our sense of ourselves as a team. It was also important to us to directly experience what we expect our clients to do: to be videotaped while teaching and to receive feedback about our performance.

At CRLT we offer a variety of workshops for faculty members and TAs, several of which include micro-teaching sessions. In these sessions, participants take turns teaching a concept from their field to a group of peers. One of our staff members then facilitates a critique, using multiple sources of feedback: the reflections of the instructor, excerpts from the videotape, the impressions of the learner, and the comments of the staff facilitator. In addition to offering workshops, CRLT staff members also consult with individual TAs and faculty members about teaching issues. These consultations may include a meeting to discuss class planning and to tailor an observation of a class to an instructor's needs, a visit to the class (often with video camera), and a consultation afterwards, again using multiple sources of feedback. We wanted to experience, analyze, and improve upon each of these roles. The intent of this article is to describe how we went about

developing a process to create intentional reflection on our individual practice.

With the encouragement and guidance of Arye Perlberg, a visiting scholar at CRLT from Technion-Israel Institute of Technology and an expert in the areas of micro-teaching and clinical supervision (see Perlberg, 1983), we designed a staff development module for five of our staff members during the spring of 1989. These staff members included the coordinator of the TA workshops, the coordinator of departmental TA training, the coordinator of the international TA training program, the coordinator of the instructional workshop program for faculty, and the coordinator of instructional video services for both the TA and faculty development areas.

Dr. Perlberg recommended readings for the group: chapters from *Clinical Supervision* by Goldhammer (1969) and from *Techniques in the Clinical Supervision of Teachers* by Acheson and Gall (1987). These readings on clinical supervision enabled us to develop a common language and to conceptualize a theory and structure for the process we utilize. Because we prefer a less hierarchical, more peer-oriented relationship with our clients, we prefer to call ourselves consultants rather than "clinical supervisors." Briefly, the stages of the consultation process (or "clinical supervision") are as follows:

Stage one: Pre-observation conference. The consultant and instructor meet to discuss the purpose of the observation, the instructor's objectives for the class that will be observed, and any particular concerns of the instructor.

Stage two: Observation. The consultant observes a class, recording as comprehensively as possible (and perhaps videotaping), so that the observation can be discussed fully with the instructor.

Stage three: Analysis and strategy. The consultant

The authors wish to acknowedge the contributions of Arye Perlberg, who was an inspirational teacher and mentor during this process, and to CRLT colleagues William E. Moore and Judy Goings, who also participated in the activities described in this article.

reviews the observational data and prepares for the consultation.

Stage four: Consultation conference. The consultant and instructor meet to review the class observed.

Stage five: Post-conference analysis. The consultant's work is examined, generally by other professionals, in much the same manner that the instructor's work is reviewed.

Our plan for the staff development module was to experience these stages in sequence as a group, with each of us taking turns in the various roles: instructor, consultant, and peer reviewer in the post-conference analysis. We decided that each of us in our instructor roles would prepare a 15-minute interactive lesson, meet with a consultant for a pre-observation conference, teach the lesson to the class (all of us), and then meet for a consultation conference. In our consultant roles we would move through each of the stages above, working with a partner, and then as peer reviewers we would all participate in a group post-conference analysis for each staff member. We decided to videotape the pre-observation conference, the teaching sessions, and the supervision conferences. We drew names in order to pair off so that each of us would serve as a consultant to another person in the group, and then scheduled the necessary paired conferences, teaching sessions and group meetings over the next few weeks. The module was designed to span about six weeks, beginning with the distribution of readings, and required an average of about six hours per week for each person. (See Appendix A for an outline of the schedule.)

Stage One: Pre-observation Conference

The general purpose of the pre-observation conference is to plan and guide the observation. The consultant encourages the instructor to offer background about the class and the goals of the lesson to be observed. In addition, the instructor may seek the consultant's assistance in planning the lesson or may ask for feedback on particular components of the plan. The instructor may also identify a particular focus for the consultant's observation.

In our staff training we videotaped the pre-observation conferences with a stationary camera. In the following excerpt, the instructor has described his plans to present a portion of a workshop he regularly conducts for faculty; he has decided to introduce new activities and wants to try them out with this group.

Instructor: *So, that's what I'm planning. Now, during the presentation, as an observer out there . . . what I'd like you to look at is, one, the clarity.   Do people understand*

. . . what's going on? And, two, I'd say, my presentation style.

Consultant: *Can you be more specific?*

Instructor: *Ok, how am I doing? (laughter) What can you do to help me in terms of a more natural presentation style as opposed to what I call an "official-hat-on" presentation. So, the speaking style. (pause, instructor nods) Third, am I still talking too much? How can the information that I think is important, the ideas, the concepts—how can I do a better job of conveying that precisely and to the point and not saying too much, not overtalking. Those are the concerns, the pitfalls, what I need to look out for. The other would be, as a participant, being asked to do these sorts of things, some feedback in terms of how you feel about that. Does it feel suitable, does it feel appropriate, does it feel natural? Do you experience these sorts of exercises as appropriate?*

This excerpt illustrates the type of conversation that often precedes a classroom observation and which helps to focus the observation toward the instructor's needs. Generally those who request an observation know what they would like observed most closely. The consultant can assist the process of self-reflection and the willingness of the instructor to share this aloud by being non-judgmental, affirming, sincere, and supportive. The building of trust and rapport is key at this stage for moving on to successful observations and supervision.

Stage Two: Observation

Each staff member was expected to teach a 15-minute class. We had agreed that we could present something we were preparing for another audience or a topic we thought would be of general interest to the group. We also agreed that the material should be presented in an interactive format, rather than as a lecture, since we were each interested in improving our skills in this area. Examples of our classes included a portion of an upcoming workshop on questioning, a presentation on assertiveness training, and a lesson on pattern and design. These classes were scheduled on two different days, two lessons in one session and three in another, and were videotaped by an additional staff member. During the 15-minute classes, the consultant for each instructor took notes, recording the observations as he or she chose, based on examples from our reading and on our own practices.

Immediately following each person's presentation, the group provided feedback on the teaching, since this was the only opportunity we would have as a group to comment on each other's teaching, rather than on the consultation process. We facilitated these feedback sessions the way we do our micro-teaching workshops, with the instructor speaking first and making his or her own comments and then soliciting feedback from others. Unlike our workshop sessions, we did not take time to look at the videotapes here, since the real focus of our module was the consultation process.

Stage Three: Analysis and Strategy

As soon as possible after these 15-minute lessons, we resumed our consulting roles and individually studied the videotapes of our client's teaching and the notes we had made during the observation. Although Dr. Perlberg had recommended that we try to do our analysis by thinking aloud and either videotaping or audiotaping our process, we declined, although we now concede the merits of having access to this material. Examining how each of us actually prepares for the consultation conference, how we sift the data we have collected to determine what is worth sharing with the instructor, and, equally importantly, how we plan the process of sharing it, would be valuable information. Because we each espouse a commitment to non-directive, client-centered consultations, these independent planning sessions could be most insightful for shedding light on how each of us envisions the process of translating our own observations.

Stage Four: Consultation Conference

Within a day or two following the presentation, each instructor met with his or her consultant for the consultation conference. These sessions were conducted as we regularly do: the instructor and consultant met in a conference room at the Center, seated at a table with the VCR in front of them, the remote control in the hands of the instructor, and the TV a few feet away so that it is convenient but does not dominate once discussion is underway. Again, these meetings were recorded with a stationary camera.

The consultant often begins by asking the instructor some version of "Would you like to start by looking at the tape or would you like to talk about anything in particular first?" Some of us preferred to begin with the tape, others to review the class orally or to reiterate what they wanted to look for before the tape was turned on. The instructor was encouraged to stop the tape at any point, while the consultant could do the same.

Here is an excerpt about half an hour into a conference

with a staff member who is also an artist and art teacher. In her micro-teaching session she had conducted a paired exercise which had been planned as a lesson in design and pattern, but the class discussion focused instead on group process. The instructor and consultant have just stopped the videotape during the class discussion and begin to talk about what they have seen on the tape:

Consultant: *How did you feel about how you moderated from there? We all were doing a lot of talking and you were our moderator and a lot of rich stuff came out.*

Instructor: *I felt very comfortable. When I was in that role I felt very comfortable. And like I told you, I had that insight later about how fascinated I am by group process and that it has always been a dilemma for me, focusing on the art, or on the process. You just brought it home to me with your comment. I don't know how I appeared, but I was very interested to know what the process was like for each person and for each team.*

Consultant: *And we basically talked about that and not about the design at all . . . not how we moved to putting the design on paper.*

Instructor: *I think it was pointed out that if we had worked individually that might have been more the focus.*

Consultant: *But how we worked as teams became the focus. Is that where you wanted it to go?*

Instructor: *I didn't know that I wanted it to go that way. But now, looking back on it, yes (smiles), that is where I wanted it to go. That's what I wanted, yes. (Pause, laughs) Because I didn't care that much how you got your design information. Or maybe I would have structured it —I wasn't sure about the team idea when we talked about it beforehand, but you encouraged me and since I really wanted to try it . . . perhaps if, I don't know, if we had worked individually I think we would have talked about design — no! maybe we wouldn't have, maybe I would have picked out a way to ask people about the process. (laughs)*

Consultant: *Because that may be what you're really interested in.*

Instructor: *Because it just occurred to me - I could figure out a way to get to the process that way too and I bet I would have! (Laughter)*

As this excerpt illustrates, these sessions, in addition to providing material about ourselves as consultants for later analysis by the group, enabled us to experience the perspective of the instructor receiving consultation. Moments such as this, when realizations about one's own agendas in teaching were brought out, also gave us the opportunity to appreciate the value of the consultation process.

Stage Five: Post-Conference Analysis

Our final sessions were the post-conference analyses, planned for two half-day meetings in order to give adequate attention to each person. We individually prepared for this part of the process by reviewing the videotaped material of our roles as consultants and selecting portions for discussion by the group. This meant looking at the tapes of the pre-observation conference and the supervision conference, and possibly again reviewing the tape of the instructor teaching, if that also seemed helpful in reconstructing how the supervision and observation had proceeded. During the post-conference analysis with the group, we each played the portions of the tapes we had selected and solicited feedback on our consultation.

Although our consulting with one another had been generally satisfactory, we each selected more problematic or awkward moments for review by the group. For example, the staff member who had served as a consultant to the assertiveness training instructor found himself less than pleased with how he had intervened in her planning process and, in viewing the videotape, realized how he might have missed her non-verbal cues of detachment and disagreement. While we laughed with one another at the irony of this happening over a lesson with the content of "assertiveness training," we also talked through what could have happened here instead, how to listen to a client's needs, how it feels to have someone else's agenda forced, how to share ideas cooperatively, how to read non-verbal cues. With both the videotape and the client herself present, the issues could be examined with vivid, multi-dimensional recall.

The staff member who had consulted with the art instructor showed the section of the videotape transcribed above (in "Stage 4: Consultation Conference"), and the moments following it, when the consultant asked a prepared question from her notes. The videotape shows the client moving from a relaxed open posture to a fidgeting pose with eyes averted, and following a long silence, saying: "I don't think I understand. Could you repeat that question?" The mood had shifted from intimate peer counseling to interrogation, to the dismay of both parties - and the earlier ambience was never recaptured. Sharing this portion of the tape with the group catalyzed discussion about the nuances of non-directive counseling and how to incorporate notes prepared during the analysis and strategy session. In viewing this same segment of the consultation conference again, we also discussed the content of the conference, and the issue of how this instructor's class had strayed from initially expressed goals.

Having now experienced both roles in the non-directive consultation process, we each felt that it was preferable to make a discovery about our own teaching rather than to receive pointed feedback from another. When we viewed successful moments of a consultant enabling an instructor to reach such discoveries on his or her own, we could see the elegance of the method, as well as the skills essential to its success. In observing ourselves consulting, we reaffirmed that we are each striving to be non-directive but not directionless, to find comfortable ways of sharing our own professional judgments in a manner that is client-centered and without manipulation, and to be genuine, involved, and spontaneous, rather than rehearsed and detached or operating too much from our notes and plans. This aspect of our counseling was the subject of some of our most fruitful discussions - and continues to be area of work and growth for us as individuals, within the supportive team we created through this training.

Conclusions

Although the training required time that we were all convinced we did not have, we were pleased with the outcomes — skill development, empathy with our clients, development of a common language for professional discussion with one another, and the sense of being part of a team. We now encourage each other's observations of our work, team teach more than in the past, go to one another to discuss concerns with our consultations, and call the group back together for rehearsals of upcoming presentations. We have also incorporated aspects of our training module into other programs we administer. We developed a three-session micro-teaching workshop on "Facilitating Active Learning" for TAs, and conduct a similar unit within the three-week intensive workshop for International TAs. Our trainings for other TA trainers, and our training of new consultants, resembles aspects of our own training as well.

The module could be replicated by staff of other large institutions with similar faculty development units, or by individuals from smaller colleges with fewer staff who could cooperatively plan training at a centrally located site. Faculty who supervise TAs in different departments within a university might work together on a similar training approach. Although we used these activities as a means of reflecting upon and improving our existing practice, this module could work well as training for new faculty development staff. We encourage others to explore the opportunities inherent in professional development conducted with peers.

Bibliography

Acheson, K. A., & Gall, M. D. (1987). *Techniques in the clinical supervision of teachers*. New York: Longman.

Goldhammer, R. (1969). *Clinical supervision*. New York: Holt, Rinehart and Winston.

Perlberg, A. (1983). When professors confront themselves: Towards a theoretical conceptualization of video self-confrontation in higher education. *Higher Education, 12*, 633-663.

Appendix A
Staff Development Module: The Consultant Process

Week one: Distributed relevant readings, scheduled meetings

Week two: Met to discuss readings, paired off as consultant/instructor dyads, scheduled all sessions.

Week three: Individuals chose topics and planned 15-minute interactive presentations.

Week four: **1. Preobservation conference**
        Met in pairs (videotaped)

Week five: **2. Observation**
        Entire group gathered to serve as the class members (videotaped); immediately afterwards, the instructor also received group feedback on teaching.

        3. Analysis and strategy
        Individual planning for the consultation conference; review of notees and videotape of class observed.

        4. Consultation conference
        Met in pairs (vidoetaped).

Week six: **5. Post-conference analysis**
        Each consultant showed pre-selected portions of videotapes for viewing and analysis with group.

37. Using Case Studies to Train Instructional Consultants

Barbara J. Millis

*T*he power of cases, like the power of "stories," has been well-documented. They bring immediacy and reality to potentially theoretical material. They stimulate in-depth collaborative problem-solving and thought-provoking, context-specific discussions. Perhaps best of all, they offer opportunities for active, experiential learning. In workshops, as Wilkerson and Boehrer (1992) note, "They can be used to introduce new educational concepts, provoke attitude change, provide practice in solving . . . problems, and stimulate the desire to acquire new skills" (p. 253).

Cases can be particularly effective in workshops designed to promote specific skills, such as providing effective feedback. In workshops for training instructional consultants, particularly consultants who must provide constructive feedback following a classroom observation, written case studies have proved to be effective, flexible catalysts for learning. For almost two years, I have used two paired case studies—carefully modified—in a variety of training settings (research institutions, community colleges, continuing education units) with varied audiences (department chairs, volunteer faculty classroom observers, and "peer partners," faculty working reciprocally to promote teaching).

Creating Case Studies

The two original case studies, "The Case of the Disgruntled Philosophy Professor" (Appendix A) and "The Case of the Crammed Chemistry Course" (Appendix C) grew out of a desire to offer meaningful, relevant training workshops for faculty chairs and faculty development consultants at a large research institution committed to teaching enhancement. Recognizing the value of designing the workshops in collaboration with the instructional consultants on campus, I asked for background information on two professors who might seek one-on-one consultation. As quickly as one could say "FAX," I had the facts, bulleted phrases that stimulated me to create fic-

tional characters based on actual people who would not be—because of the leaps of imagination, including dialogue—compromised. Subsequently, I have modified the original case studies to fit other training situations, based on input from the host institutions. The disgruntled philosophy professor, for example, underwent radical revisions before he could fume in a community college setting. The rigid, elitist professor interested only in upper-level students was replaced by an instructor named Robert with many of the same attitudinal problems but with a focus on students' perceived writing failures (Appendix B).

Tailoring case studies to the unique demands of each training situation makes sense because instructional consultants must speak to their audiences, whether they are working one-on-one or training others to do so.

Conducting Case Studies

As instructional consultants realize, having positive curriculum/content is not sufficient in and of itself. The recent publication of Astin's (1993) definitive study of undergraduate learning reinforces for all of us the fact that how faculty deliver the curriculum is as important as the curriculum itself. Thus, how a case is presented can potentially affect the participants' learning. The format must lead to honest, productive exchanges with full participation.

The most commonly used format is the whole-group case method developed by the Harvard Business School (Christensen & Hansen, 1987). This method has several drawbacks, however, for faculty developers seeking to train consultants: (1) with this approach, the participants should receive the case ahead of time, a process not always possible at voluntarily attended workshops seeking to include as many participants as possible; (2) the facilitators must be unusually skilled at thinking on their feet while probing, parrying, challenging, summarizing, and sometimes curtailing the group's comments; (3) the large-group format promotes interactions where only one individual at a time is "center stage" (actively and openly engaged); (4) whole-group formats—particularly if the exchanges are dynamic and thought-provoking—provide risky arenas where less vocal members, sometimes women and minorities, may not speak up; and finally, (5) such exchanges, while intellectually stimulating, may not lead to the skill enhancement that is the whole point of the session.

Many facilitators have successfully used cooperative learning strategies to train observers, an approach somewhat similar to the problem-centered format described by Wilkerson and Feletti (1989). I have used these case studies with task-oriented groups of four (quads) who work together to formulate responses to the focus questions. Group roles—recorder, spokesperson, and leader—can be preassigned or the group members can simply number off ("one-two-three-four"), with the understanding that one of them will be designated by their number to report the group's findings, a technique called "Numbered Heads Together" in the cooperative learning literature. In addition to experiencing the power of case studies and acquiring insights into providing effective feedback, through this approach participants become familiar with an innovative cooperative learning structure that results in attentiveness, mutual coaching and support, respect for multiple viewpoints, and increased critical thinking.

Cooperative faculty pairs is another effective format. Such pairs approximate more exactly the client-faculty relationship that occurs during a typical consultation process. With pairs, too, virtually everyone is actively engaged—talking and listening reciprocally—in the learning process. The discussion setting provides stimulation but few risks for either the participants or the facilitator, who moves congenially among the pairs.

Because the case studies are brief (less than a page), faculty do not have to receive them in advance, although advance distribution is desirable whenever feasible. Each group or pair reads both case studies, but they jointly prepare their responses to only one. In thirty minutes most participants can work through all three focus questions, whether working in pairs or in quads. If less time is available, the facilitator can simply eliminate beforehand the third question, which is more complex, although certainly valuable. Groups working more rapidly than others who finish their assigned or selected case study in the allotted time can begin an in-depth examination of the second case study, one of the advantages, among many, of using paired case studies.

Not unexpectedly, a great deal of learning and sharing goes on as the participants discuss the case studies in their quads or pairs. Learning also occurs during the report-outs, which can be handled a number of ways. It is important to leave sufficient time for them because faculty, just as students do, like a sense of closure. Some workshop participants have suggested even further closure through a summation by the facilitator. If the quads or pairs have been given acetate sheets, then the group spokesperson, however identified, can make a fairly formal presentation. However, since most workshop time is limited, probably the best report-outs for the first two questions, taken one-at-a-time, are simply oral presentations.

Depending on the time available, cross-case analysis of the teaching issues identified in the first focus question can be very useful. Neither of the teachers, for example, endorses a teaching role where students and faculty members are mutual partners in the learning experience. Neither acknowledges or recognizes the importance of relating material to students' prior learning or academic needs. A workshop participant once noted that the disgruntled philosophy professor was like Lawrence Welk meeting MTV.

The second focus question, eliciting questions to help the teachers described in the cases rethink their basic premises and future options, produces creative, thoughtful responses. When these case studies are used in conjunction with workshops on providing effective feedback following a classroom observation, I emphasize beforehand the nature and value of feedback which respects the recipient, elicits creative, action-oriented responses, avoids judgments, and so forth. Thus, the questions framed by the workshop participants tend to be insightful, effective, and sensitively phrased: "What do you see as relevant issues of philosophy which might touch the average citizen sitting in your class?"; "What techniques might you use in your chemistry course to find out what students actually know?"

The third focus question results in particularly rich learning experiences for new instructional consultants wanting to learn how to provide constructive feedback. The word "roleplay" scares faculty about as much as it frightens students. Thus, the third question, which builds on the second one by asking for what amounts to an interactive dialogue, does not mention the term. Nonetheless, it results in creative role plays—which participants always volunteer to enact—driving home the range of responses which are appropriate, given the nature of the teaching problems and the presumed reactions of the teachers themselves. This section of the workshop invariably results in applause and mutual congratulations, as well as positive learning.

Conclusion

Using case studies in workshops to train instructional consultants is clearly a powerful way to develop or strengthen interpersonal and diagnostic skills. The case studies should be tailored to the participants' needs, goals, and experience levels and to the specific institution. Sufficient time must be available to allow them to unfold in all their complexity. The facilitator must select an organizational format which optimizes the time available and the expertise and needs of the participants. Focus questions need to frame a carefully guided, interactive discussion. These cases, and others like them, give life to an oft-quoted Teton Lakota Indian saying: "Tell me and I'll listen. Show me and I'll understand. Involve me and I'll learn."

References

Astin, A. W. (1993). *What matters in college: Four critical years revisited.* San Francisco: Jossey-Bass.

Christensen , C. R., & Hansen, A. J. (1987). *Teaching and the case method: Text, cases, and readings.* Boston: Harvard Business School.

Wilkerson, L., & Boehrer, J. (1992). Using cases about teaching for faculty development. *To Improve the Academy, 11,* 253-262.

Wilkerson, L. & Feletti, G. (1989). Problem-based learning: One approach to increasing student participation. *New Directions for Teaching and Learning, no. 37,* 51-60. San Francisco: Jossey-Bass.

Appendix A

The Case of the Disgruntled Philosophy Professor

Barbara Millis

"I really don't think I have a problem," professor X announced as he dropped heavily into the solid office chair. "I think my students have a problem. In fact I know they do. I don't usually bother with this faculty development rigermarole, but I happened to thumb through a new book, *Teaching College Freshman*, I spied in a colleague's office. The first chapter confirmed my long-held suspicions: research indicates that current college freshman are not as well-prepared as previous generations. Furthermore, they don't seem as willing to work hard. They want to establish a 'personal relationship' with their professors, quite a challenge I must say in the large introductory course I am now forced to teach."

"Of course today's students resent the hard work I make them do. Of course they give me low ratings because I don't pretend to be their 'buddy.' I don't intend to coddle them. Students are totally off-target to suggest that I am out-of-touch with them and can't relate the course material to real world topics and concerns. What do they want me to do: translate Plato's parable of the cave into lyrics for some mindless 'rock' or 'rap' or whatever modern music is called now? I can't even understand half the questions they ask."

The professor shifted uneasily in his chair. "Certainly, I want to teach well. Who doesn't? I ask students for their comments about this lecture material and the course in general, but all I get are unfocused or inane complaints, such as 'Be clearer and better organized' or 'Be there for us.' As a full professor, I resent having to slide backwards to teach this introductory course open to every Tom, Dick and Harry —oops! I guess I could be accused now of sexism; please add a 'Jane' to that—who can beg, borrow or steal the tuition money. I can't take the time to write lectures for non-majors who have no genuine interest in the discipline. If they get confused—and I guess I'm hearing that they do—it's not my fault. It's the department's fault for assigning me a course like this. This new 'hold-me-touch-me-feel-me' idea of putting freshmen in touch with senior professors is misguided. I really excel when I am working with the superior students I have earned the right to teach. I feel—um—'uncomfortable,' to say the least, teaching ill-prepared, disrespectful students who seem to consider me an 'old fogy' at best."

"What do you suggest I do?"

Questions to Accompany
"The Case of the Disgruntled Philosophy Professor"

1. What teaching issues can you extract/derive from this monologue?

2. What questions (three to five) would you want to ask professor X to help him rethink his basic premises and his future options?

3. Based on the responses you hypothesize professor X would provide, what suggestions would you want to give him? Please identify both the responses you think he would give and your advice.

Appendix B

The Case of the Disgruntled Philosophy Professor
(Community College Version)

Barbara Millis

"I don't really think I have a problem," Robert announced as he dropped heavily into the solid office chair. "I think my students have a problem. Current college freshman are not as well-prepared as previous generations. Furthermore, they aren't willing to work as hard."

"In my introductory philosophy class, for example, I had students select research topics weeks ago. The midterm draft was due today, and only half the students turned in anything at all. What I got was pathetic: paper rife with grammatical errors and disjointed topic sentences. The students are clamoring for extra time and a reduction in the paper's length. Twenty pages is certainly not unreasonable when 70 percent of their final grade depends on it."

Robert shifted uneasily in his chair. "Of course I want to teach well. Who doesn't? I've been at this community college for seventeen years. I respect its open door policy, but students need to assume some responsibility for their learning. I appreciate the fact that many of them work and have families, but they can't expect to be 'coddled' or their degree will be worthless. They need to know how to write and to write clearly and cogently. I'm not going to reduce this assignment. The students will simply have to figure out how to complete this paper on time."

"What do you suggest I do?"

Questions to Accompany
"The Case of the Disgruntled Philosophy Professor"

1. What teaching issues can you extract/derive from this monologue?

2. What questions (three to five) would you want to ask Robert to help him rethink his basic premises and his future options?

3. Based on the responses you hypothesize Robert would provide, what suggestions would you want to give him? Please identify both the responses you think he would give and your advice.

Appendix C

The Case of the Crammed Chemistry Course

Barabara J. Millis

"Wow, wasn't today's lecture lower than a pit," said Ann scowling as she strapped on her book bag. "I wore out two pencils—I'd just stopped to sharpen them before class—and still couldn't keep up with what the professor was saying."

"Saying doesn't cut it," snapped Manuel. "I'm a serious student, even though I don't plan to major in chemistry. I thought I'd learn things that would help me in my future life sciences courses. Man, you have to be a Nobel Prize winner to follow what that lady wants to pour into our heads. Those diagrams flowed over all the board, and she'd erase them before I even realized they were important. Of course—idiot!—I guess I ought to know everything is important to her, everything except our learning."

The professor's perception:

"Hi, Mary," sighed Sarah, the chemistry teacher. "I've felt it was my turn in the barrel again today. Have you ever stood on your feet for fifty minutes, lecturing as rapidly as you can, but knowing you'll never make it through the material? My students seem to be avid learners, taking notes all the time, so I feel bad when I can't finish everything."

Mary scrutinized her friend carefully, knowing that students frequently complained about the pace and content of her lectures. "Have you ever thought that you may be concentrating too much on content? You might think about reducing the amount of time you lecture, perhaps working that material into homework assignments, and spending more class time on active learning activities," she ventured.

"Are you kidding?" responded Sarah. "Some of these kids seem to know zilcho about cemistry even though they have presumably taken the prerequisite. I have to maintain department standards and be certain that I cover all the appropriate material. I can't waste time on ill-prepared students with frivolous in-class activities that detract from my lectures."

"Sarah," Mary said. "I don't want you to misinterpret this suggestion, but because of your own uneasiness about student learning, I think it might be a good idea to consult the department chair. I would be glad to offer suggestions also, of course. In fact, you might enjoy visiting my afternoon class to observe a cooperative learning technique—jigsaw—that I use to help my students nail down the structural analysis of proteins."

Questions to Accompany
"The Case of the Disgruntled Philosophy Professor"

1. What teaching issues can you extract/derive from this monologue?

2. What questions (three to five) would you want to ask Sarah to help her rethink her basic premises and her future options?

3. Based on the responses you hypothesize Sarah would provide, what suggestions would you want to give her? Please identify both the responses you think she would give and your advice.

Professional Organizations Concerned with Instructional Consultation

Kathleen T. Brinko

United States — National

American Association for Higher Education (AAHE)
Gene Rice or Pat Hutchings
One Dupont Circle, Suite 360
Washington, DC 20036-1110
(202) 293-6440

Historically Black Colleges and Universities (HBCU)
    Faculty Development Network
Stephen L. Rozman
Tougaloo College
Tougaloo, MS 39174
(601) 977-7861

National Council for Staff, Program & Organization
    Development (NCSPOD)
Natalie Margolis
4 Computer Drive West
Albany, NY 12205
(518) 446-0367

National Institute for Staff
    and Organizational Development (NISOD)
Suanne D. Roueche
The University of Texas at Austin
SZB 348
Austin, TX 78712
(512) 471-7545

Professional & Organizational Development
    Network in Higher Education (POD)
David Graf
Iowa State University
158 Exhibit Hall South
Ames, IA 50011
(515) 294-3808

Special Interest Group on Faculty Evaluation
    and Development (SIGFED) of the American
    Educational Research Association (AERA)
Ken Jerich
Curriculum and Instruction
232 DeGarmo Hall
Illinois State University
Normal, IL 61761
(309) 438-5456

United States — Regional

Bush Regional Collaboration in Faculty Development
Lesley K. Cafarelli
Minnesota Private College Research Foundation
401 Galtier Plaza, Box 40
175 Fifth Street East
St. Paul, MN 55101
(612) 228-9061

Great Lakes Colleges Association (GLCA)
Marcia Hancock
535 W. William, Suite 301
Ann Arbor, MI 48103
(313) 761-4833

Great Plains Faculty Development Consortium
James E. Groccia
Program for Excellence in Teaching
University of Missouri-Columbia
Columbia, MO 65211
(573) 822-6260

Illinois Staff and Curriculum Development Association
Multicultural Resource Development and
     Advising Center
HH 80
Western Illinois University
1 University Circle
Macomb, IL 61455
(309) 298-3387

Institute for College and University Teaching (ICUT)
Beth Bowser
Hunter Library
Western Carolina University
Cullowhee, NC 28723
(704) 227-7278

Massachusetts Faculty Development
     Consortium (MFDC)
Susan Pasquale
Office of Educational Development
Room 384
Harvard Medical School
260 Longwood Avenue
Boston, MA 02115
(617) 432-0391

Southern Regional Faculty & Instructional Development
     Consortium (SRFIDC)
Linda Nilson
Center for Teaching
Vanderbilt University
Box 1537-B
Nashville, TN 37235
(615) 322-7290

Utah Consortium of Faculty Developers
Lynn Sorenson
Faculty Center
Brigham Young University
Box 22710, 167 HGB
Provo, UT 84602
(801) 378-7420

Virginia Tidewater Consortium
Lawrence Dotolo
5215 Hampton Blvd.
129 William Spong Hall
Norfolk, VA 23529-0293
(757) 683-3183

Washington Center for Improving the Quality
     of Undergraduate Education
Jeanine Elliott
The Evergreen State College
Olympia, WA 98505
(360) 866-6000, ext. 6609

International

International Consortium for Educational Development
     in Higher Education
Graham Gibbs
Centre for Higher Education Practice
Open University
Walton Hall
Milton Keynes MK7 6AA
UNITED KINGDOM
01908 858439
01908 858438

The Consulting Committee on Faculty Development of
     the Association of Atlantic Universities (AAU)
Sheila Brown
Mt. St. Vincent University
166 Bedford Highway
Halifax Nova Scotia B3M 2J6
CANADA
(902) 457-6116

Higher Education Research & Development Society of
    Australasia (HERDSA)
P O Box 516 Jamison
ACT AUSTRALIA 2614
06 253 4242

Oxford Centre for Staff Development (OCSD)
Oxford Brookes University
Gipsy Lane Campus
Headington Oxford 0X3 0BP
ENGLAND
0865 750918

Society for Teaching and Learning in Higher
    Education (STLHE)
Pat Rogers
Department of Education and Mathematics
York University
4700 Keele Street
North York Ontario M3J lP3
CANADA
(416) 736-5009

South African Association of Academic
    Development (SAAD)
Kibbie Naidoo
Faculty Educational Development Programme
University of Natal
King George V Avenue
Durban 4001
SOUTH AFRICA
031 2601243

Staff and Educational Development Association (SEDA)
David Baume
Educational Development and Support Service
London Guildhall University
Old Castle Street
London El 7NT
ENGLAND
071 320 1095

Contributors and Chapter Reviewers

Gabriele Bauer
Center for Teaching Effectiveness
University of Delaware
111 Pearson Hall
Newark, DE 19716-1106
gabriele@udel.edu

Beverly Black
The Center for Research on Learning and Teaching
The University of Michigan
3300 SEB
Ann Arbor, MI 48109-1259
(313) 763-2396
bevblack@umich.edu

Laura L. B. Border
University of Colorado at Boulder
Graduate Teacher Program
Norlin S461, C.B. 362
Boulder, CO 80309
(303) 492-4902
border@spot.colorado.edu

Kathleen T. Brinko
Appalachian State University
Hubbard Center for Faculty and Staff Support
155 Whitener Hall
Boone, NC 28608
(704) 262-6152
brinkokt@appstate.edu

Charles Claxton
Appalachian State University
Leadership and Educational Studies
Edwin Duncan Hall
Boone, NC 28608
(704) 262-2875
claxtoncs@appstate.edu

Patricia A. Cook
Manchester Community-Technical College
60 Bidwell Street
Manchester, CT 06040

Bette LaSere Erickson
University of Rhode Island
Instructional Development Program
201 Chafee
Kingston, RI 02881
(401) 874-4293
betteidp@uriac.uri.edu

Glenn R. Erickson
University of Rhode Island
Instructional Development Program
IDP 201 Chafee
Kingston, RI 02881
(401) 874-5078
erickson@uriacc.uri.edu

L. Dee Fink
University of Oklahoma
Instructional Development Program
116 Carnegie Bldg.
Norman, OK 73019
(405) 325-3521
dfink@ou.edu

Jennifer Franklin
University of Arizona
University Teaching Center
1017 N. Mountain Ave.
Tuscon, AZ 85721
(602) 621-9585
franklin@ccit.arizona.edu

Joanne Gainen*
2201 Monroe #1403
Santa Clara, CA 95050
(408) 244-8267
jgainen@aol.com

Barbara Hofer
University of Michigan
Center for Research on Learning and Teaching
3300 SEB
Ann Arbor, MI 48109-1259
(313) 936-2596
bhofer@umich.edu

Michael Kerwin
University of Kentucky
Community College System
302 Breckinridge Hall
Lexington, KY 40506-0056
(606) 257-1539
ccsmk@pop.uky.edu

Ghislaine Kozuh
University of Texas at Austin
Center for Teaching Effectiveness
Main Bldg. 2200
Austin, TX 78712-1111
(512) 232-1772
kozuh@mail.utexas.edu

Eric Kristensen
Faculty and Instructional Development
Berklee College of Music
1140 Boylston St.
Boston, MA 02215-3693
(617) 747-2229
ekristensen@berklee.edu

Lisa Firing Lenze
University of Rochester
Warner Graduate School of Education and Human
    Development
Dewey Hall
Rochester, NY 14627
(716) 388-9125
DLL@frontiernet.net

Karron Lewis
University of Texas at Austin
Center for Teaching Effectiveness
2200 Main Bldg. Austin, TX 78712-1111
(512) 232-1776
kglewis@mail.utexas.edu

Michele Marincovich
Stanford University
Center for Teaching and Learning
114 Sweet Hall
Stanford, CA 94305-3087
(415) 723-2208
michele.marincovich@forsythe.stanford.edu

Robert J. Menges
Northwestern University
2115 N. Campus Drive
Evanston. IL 60208-2610
(847) 467-1746
r_menges@nwu.edu

Barbara J. Millis
United States Air Force Academy
HQ USAFA/DFE
2354 Fairchild Dr., Suite 4K25
USAF Academy, CO
80840-6200
(719) 333-3976
millisbj.dfe@usafa.af.mil

Diane E. Morrison
Centre for Curriculum and Professional Development
5th Floor, 1483 Douglas St.
Victoria, BC V8W 3K4
CANADA
(604) 387-6378
dmorrison@camosun.bc.ca

Jody D. Nyquist
Center for Instructional Development and Research
University of Washington
Box 353050
Seattle, WA 98195-3050
(206) 543-6588
nyquist@cidr.washington.edu

Erin Porter
University of Texas at Austin
Center for Teaching Effectiveness
Main Bldg. 2200
Austin, TX 78712-1111
(512) 232-1775
eporter@mail.utexas.edu

WIlliam C. Rando
Academy for the Art of Teaching
Florida International University
PC 106-107
University Park, FL 33199
(305) 348-4214
randow@solix.fiu.edu

Bill Searle
Connecticut Center for Teaching
Asnuntuck Community-Technical College
170 Elm St.
Enfield, CT 06082
(860) 253-3149
as-bills@commmnet.edu

Mary Ann Shea
University of Colorado at Boulder
Faculty Teaching Excellence Program and President's
    Teaching Scholars Program
Norin Library, C. B. 360
Boulder, CO 80309
(303) 492-4985
maryann.shea@colorado.edu

Myrna Smith
Raritan Community College
Department of English
Box 3300
Somerville, NJ 08876
(908) 526-1200 ext. 8309
msmith@rvcc.raritanval.edu

Ronald Smith
Concordia University
Centre for Teaching and Learning Services
7141 Sherbrooke St.
Montreal, Quebec H4B lR6
CANADA
(514) 848-2498
rasmith@vax2.concordia.ca

Mary Deane Sorcinelli
University of Massachusetts
Center for Teaching
239 Whitmore
Amherst, MA 01003
(413) 545-1255
msorcinelli@acad.umass.edu

Milton G. Spann, Jr.
Appalachian State University
National Center for Developmental Education
302D Edwin Duncan Hall
Boone, NC 28608
(704) 262-6103
spannmg@appstate.edu

Charles M. Spuches*
Instructional Development, Evaluation and Services
SUNY College of Environmental Science and Forestry
Room 8 Moon LRC
Syracuse, NY 13210
(315) 470-6810
cspuches@mailbox.syr.edu

Michael Theall
Center for Teaching and Learning
University of Illinois at Springfield
460 Brookens
Springfield, IL 62794-9243
(217) 786-7157
theall@uis.edu

Richard Tiberius
University of Toronto
Clark Institute of Psychiatry
250 College Street, 8th Floor, Rm 826
Toronto, Ontario M5T 1R8
CANADA
(416) 979-4985
r.tiberius@utoronto.ca

Lee Warren*
Harvard University
Bok Center
Science Center 318
Cambridge, MA 02138
(617) 495-4869
lawarren@fas.harvard.edu

David Way
Cornell University
Instructional Support
14 East Avenue
Ithaca, NY 14853-2801
(607) 255-2663
dgw2@cornell.edu

Judy Wilbee
University College of the Cariboo
Professional Development
Box 3010 McGill Rd.
Kamloops, British Columbia V2C 5N3
CANADA
(604) 828-5196
wilbee@cariboo.bc.ca

Dina Wills*
Lehigh University
29 Trembley Drive
Bethlehem, PA 18015
(610) 758-3638
dw03@lehigh.edu

Donald H. Wulff
Center for Instructional Development and Research
University of Washington
Box 353050
Seattle, WA 98195-3050
(206) 543-6588
wulff@cidr.washington.edu

*These persons reviewed early drafts of the chapters.